The
First
Gospel

PUBLISHED VOLUMES

Robert W. Funk, *New Gospel Parallels. Vol. 2: John and the Other Gospels*

John Dominic Crossan, ed., *Sayings Parallels: A Workbook for the Jesus Tradition*

John S. Kloppenborg, *Q Parallels: Synopsis, Critical Notes, and Concordance*

Vernon K. Robbins, *Ancient Quotes & Anecdotes: From Crib to Crypt*

Robert W. Funk, *New Gospel Parallels, Vol. I,2: Mark*

Arland D. Jacobson, *The First Gospel: An Introduction to Q*

The
First
Gospel

An
introduction
to Q

Arland D. Jacobson

1992

Polebridge Press   *Sonoma, CA*

Library of Congress Cataloging-in-Publication Data

Jacobson, Arland Dean
    The first Gospel : an introduction to Q / Arland D. Jacobson.
      p. cm. — (Foundations & facets. Reference series)
    Includes bibliographical references and index.
    ISBN 0-944344-27-5 (alk. paper) : $29.95. — ISBN 0-944344-28-3
(pbk. : alk. paper) : $19.95
    1. Q hypothesis (Synoptics criticism) I. Title. II. Series.
BS2555.2.J335 1991 226'.066–dc20.   91-35783
                                                    CIP

Contents

Preface

The present work has its roots in a doctoral dissertation under James M. Robinson at the Claremont Graduate School, accepted in 1978 and entitled "Wisdom Christology in Q." The dissertation has been incorporated, in revised fashion, in chapters 5, 6, and 7, and to a lesser degree in other locations. Portions of articles on "The Literary Unity of Q" and "The History of the Composition of the Synoptic Sayings Source, Q" have also been incorporated. Almost everything else is new. To the extent possible, dissertation material has been brought into conversation with more recent research. At times, I have also changed my mind about certain matters.

The completion of this book was made possible by a sabbatical granted me by Concordia College in Moorhead, Minnesota. I enjoyed the hospitality and wonderful facilities of the Institute for Ecumenical and Cultural Research at St. John's University in Collegeville, Minnesota, and made generous use of the Alcuin Library. During my absence as director of the CHARIS Ecumenical Center, my assistants, Phyllis Paulson and Ann Zavoral, took on added responsibilities and performed them with their usual efficiency and good humor. I want to thank them publicly for that, and I want to thank Concordia College for making the sabbatical possible. My wife and family suffered, as I supposed, my absence on countless evenings and weekends, not to mention the sabbatical, because "Dad is working on the book." Erik and Karin were good-humored about the matter. But the bulk of added responsibilities, especially during the sabbatical, fell upon my wife, Willy, to whom I dedicate this book with love and gratitude.

Special thanks also to Robert W. Funk for asking me to revise and expand my dissertation for publication, and for seeing the project through to completion. Thanks to Julian Hills of Marquette University for his careful editing of the manuscript, and to the Polebridge Press staff for their invaluable help: David Carter for words of encouragement and Char Matejovsky for turning the manuscript into a book.

Introduction

The earliest gospel about Jesus did not survive intact. Both Matthew and Luke undertook, independently, to improve upon this gospel by attaching chunks of it to a narrative framework. What we are left with, therefore, are fragments of a document scattered throughout Matthew and Luke. This gospel, a collection of sayings, did not survive independently so it has no name, only the non-descript designation "Q," abbreviated from the German *Quelle*, or "source."

An introduction to the Sayings Source, Q, is less like a tour of an old and stately building than it is like a guided expedition into an untamed wilderness. Therefore much that is said about Q will be tentative and open-ended, a proposal more than a definitive statement. But it is hoped that this will prove useful both to specialists in gospel research and to novices and students.

Why enter this wilderness called Q? Because many of us suspect that deep in its heart may lie the secret of that fateful time when Judaism gave painful birth to Christianity. Q was, as far as we can tell, the earliest gospel, if by "gospel" we mean a theologically-shaped presentation of Jesus tradition. And then there is Jesus of Nazareth. To the believer he is, as exalted Lord, close at hand; but as a historical figure he remains as mysterious and puzzling as ever. Rightly or wrongly, Western civilization has long believed that the nature of a thing can best be understood from its origins. Therefore, if Q is the first gospel, then it may hold clues both about the origins of Christianity and about Christianity's central figure, Jesus.

"Q," as noted, is an abbreviation for the German word, *Quelle*, meaning "source," "spring" or "fountainhead." Specifically, Q is the name given to a hypothetical document widely held to have been used as a source by Matthew and Luke who, in writing their gospels, also used Mark and some other materials. This is a theory of gospel origins which not everyone accepts, but it has been and continues to be accepted by most scholars. So understood, Q is a source both in a literary sense and in the historical sense: a source of information about the origins of Christianity. It is, many scholars believe, the oldest gospel document to which we have access, compiled by some of the earliest members of the movement that Jesus ignited.

An expedition into this wilderness needs to be distinguished from a raid.

1

Archaeologists often lament the fact that ancient sites are plundered by amateurs who want only to pick up an artifact here, an artifact there. Q has often been raided for artifacts too—for relics of the early Jesus movement. In the case of a literary source, the difference between a serious expedition and a raid is that a raid is interested only in individual texts or sayings while an expedition tries to reconstruct the document, much as an archaeologist might try to reconstruct both the plan of a site and its history. This is very painstaking work; it cannot offer the instant gratification that amateur plunderers experience. But it is a more responsible procedure, and in the end a more rewarding one. Yet even today, after nearly three decades of steadily mounting interest in Q, far too little attention is paid to the systematic reconstruction of this lost but precious document.

What characterizes this new study is above all the attempt to, so to speak, map the literary terrain of Q so that individual sayings and groups of sayings can be understood within a larger context—the kind of reconstructive work that is demanded by any document from antiquity that has survived only in multiple but divergent copies.

In the case of Q, such reconstruction is necessary not only because the document is not as such extant, but also because its contents are so very familiar—in their Matthean and Lukan contexts! A major goal of this book is therefore to encourage the reader to imagine what this material looked like in a different context, namely in the context of Q. *My contention is that this recontextualizing of the Q material requires a fundamental reappraisal of its interpretation.*

A couple of examples will show what I mean. Q is, in my judgment, not a Christian document at all, at least it was not "Christian" for most of its history as a document. To be sure, it became part of the tradition of the church, but only as recontextualized by Matthew and Luke. The study of Q therefore requires of us some exegetical imagination to interpret it as a "Jewish" rather than as a "Christian" document, granted, of course, that "Jewish" has no single definition. In Q, we are confronted with a Jesus who is not a Christian but a Jew, and must be so interpreted. Likewise, a commentary on Q—which this book does not claim to be—might offer a quite different interpretation of the same texts treated in a commentary on Matthew or Luke. But recontextualizing is possible only by means of reconstruction.

Two reconstructive procedures are necessary: (a) reconstruction of the original *wording* of each saying or group of sayings, and (b) reconstruction of the original *sequence* of the material. It is not possible to do either in isolation from the other, but, as in many large tasks, some division of labor is inevitable.

The task of reconstructing the wording of Q has been attempted a few times by individual scholars.[1] At present, the "Q Seminar" of the Society of Biblical

---

1. The most accessible are Harnack, *Sayings of Jesus*; Polag, *Fragmenta Q* (English translation of the Greek text, without the textual apparatus, in Havener, *Q*); and Schenk,

Literature, under the leadership of James M. Robinson, is attempting a complete, collaborative reconstruction. From time to time, the work of this group will be published in the *Journal of Biblical Literature*. This text will form the basis for a commentary on Q that Robinson is preparing for the Hermeneia Series of biblical commentaries.

The task of reconstructing the sequence for the whole of Q has yet to be attempted. My doctoral dissertation sought to establish the sequence for the first half to two- thirds of Q.[2] Other attempts have been made by John Dominic Crossan[3] and John S. Kloppenborg,[4] but for neither was establishing the sequence of Q a central focus. The fact that no thoroughgoing effort to establish the sequence of Q has been made is proof that even after three decades of research—since the modern period of Q research began in the early 1960s—the study of Q is still in its infancy. This book makes no claim of having definitively established the sequence of Q, but it does seek to make progress toward that end.

In recent decades, the study of the canonical gospels has increasingly focused on the composition of each gospel, in terms both of how the author worked with available traditions (redaction criticism) and of how the gospel as a whole works as a literary composition (literary criticism). These approaches represent a shift, from the atomistic mining of the gospel text for theological riches to a more holistic approach, one that takes seriously the nature of the document in which the various traditions are found. The concept of "literary unity" is one way of grasping Q in a more holistic manner, in which its genre and the genres or forms it contains are coordinated with themes and perspectives that recur in the source.[5] It remains my conviction that the parts of Q must be understood in relation to the whole, even though it is true that we can know the whole of Q only from its parts. It is a back and forth process—parts to whole, whole to parts.

Another shift that has occurred in the study of Q is the shift from regarding Q as a "source" to regarding it as a "gospel." The intent in using the term "gospel" is to treat Q not as raw material for the "real" gospels or as a mere collection of Jesus' sayings which, one typically assumes, presupposed knowledge of Jesus' death and resurrection. The word "gospel" is used provocatively to suggest that Q by itself represents a view of Jesus, a view which did not necessarily have its principal focus on Jesus' death and resurrection. The use

Synopse zur Redenquelle. Reconstructive groundwork, without a print-out of the resulting reconstruction, was done by Schulz, *Q*. A print-out of the Greek text of Q containing only the words where Matthew and Luke agree, with the uncertain words indicated by parentheses, as though Q were a tattered papyrus, was published in 1985 by The Institute for Antiquity and Christianity at Claremont and entitled *Pap. Q*. The most important tool for the study of Q is Kloppenborg's *Q Parallels*.

2. Jacobson, "Wisdom Christology."
3. Crossan, *In Fragments*.
4. Kloppenborg, *Formation of Q*.
5. See Jacobson, "Literary Unity of Q."

of the word "gospel" suggests that Q and the canonical gospels are comparable entities. Simply calling Q a source does not make this point.

A word also needs to be said about the translations of Q that are in this book. Usually the translations are rather stiffly literal so as to call attention to the similarities and differences between Matthew and Luke. More idiomatic translation is offered when appropriate. This book has been written with the assumption that the reader has open on her or his desk a copy of the gospels, preferably a Greek and/or English synopsis.

Finally, I hope that this book will make clear to the reader how much work remains to be done. This is not an introduction to a subject which is thoroughly understood by the experts, so that the novice has only to listen attentively. Quite the contrary! Only a few paths into this wilderness have been struck. If this book lures some readers into this wilderness and encourages them to take up the task of exploration and even, perhaps, provides a few glimpses of what may be discovered, then it will have accomplished its goal.

1
Source
Reexamining some # Criticism
basic assumptions

For 150 years, scholars in increasing numbers have contended that the earliest canonical gospel was Mark, that Matthew and Luke used this gospel in writing their own gospels, and that Matthew and Luke also used another source, one that must have existed even thought it is a hypothetical entity. They called this source "Q," probably for the German word *Quelle*, which means "source" or "fountain."[1] The view that Mark and Q were the primary sources for the synoptic gospels is called the Two Document hypothesis.[2]

The edifice of synoptic studies for several generations has rested almost entirely upon the Two Document hypothesis. To the extent that a hypothesis may be judged by its fruitfulness, the Two Document hypothesis has certainly made a good case for itself. Indeed, so widespread is its acceptance that most scholars simply presuppose it. And though an extensive campaign against it has been mounted in recent years, the Two Document hypothesis has survived largely unscathed. But it has not gone unchallenged.

The Griesbach hypothesis, set forth in 1789–90 by Johann Jakob Griesbach, has been resurrected in the twentieth century by William R. Farmer.[3] According to this hypothesis, Matthew was the first gospel, Luke then used Matthew, and Mark still later offered a kind of epitome of both. The Griesbach

---

1. The symbol Q seems to have been used first by Weiss in an article published in 1890 ("Die Verteidigung Jesu gegen den Vorwurf des Bündnisses mit Beelzebul" [Jesus' defense against the charge of being allied with Beelzebul]). See Neirynck, "The Symbol Q" and "Once More: The Symbol Q." The use of Q apparently became widespread in the English-speaking world during the first decade of the twentieth century. Hawkins (*Horae Synopticae*, 107) acknowledges that between the first edition of his book (1899) and the second (1909), the symbol Q caught on. Similarly, in 1908 Bacon ("A Turning Point," 55) wrote, "We must substitute the strictly algebraic symbol Q (*Quelle*) of Wellhausen and Harnack for the question-begging Λ (Λόγια) of Holtzmann's *Die synoptischen Evangelien* and the old school."

2. See Wiesse, *Die evangelische Geschichte kritisch und philosophisch bearbeitet* (A Critical and Philosophical Study of the Gospel History).

3. Griesbach, *Commentatio qua Marci evangelium totum e Matthaei et Lucae commentariis decerptum esse monstratur* (Demonstration in which the entire Gospel of Mark is shown to be excepted from the Memoirs of Matthew and Luke), 1789–90. The Latin text with English translation is available in Orchard and Longstaff, *J. J. Griesbach*. In 1961, Farmer announced he had found "A 'Skeleton in the Closet' of Gospel Research"; his book on *The Synoptic Problem* was published in 1964. It was this book which resurrected the Griesbach hypothesis.

hypothesis has succeeded in establishing itself as the only real alternative to the Two Document hypothesis, although its followers remain a fairly small group. But the Griesbach hypothesis is not the only challenge to the Two Document hypothesis and, more generally, to source-critical analysis.

These challenges to the basic assumptions of synoptic research cannot be simply ignored. The situation at present is that the defenders of the Griesbach hypothesis attack classical formulations of the Two Document hypothesis but ignore recent Q research, while defenders of the Two Document hypothesis rarely bother to respond to the work of the Griesbach scholars. Other challenges to source criticism in general and to the Two Document hypothesis in particular are routinely ignored. Even if such challenges are finally judged to be of little merit, consideration of them may lead to greater methodological clarity. That is precisely what is claimed in this chapter. We shall first examine some of the basic assumptions of source criticism, and then turn to the synoptic problem in particular.

Source Criticism

Source criticism is surely the least glamorous of the various tools employed by biblical criticism. Its heyday was in the nineteenth and the early twentieth centuries. However, in recent years the use of source-critical methodology has experienced a revival, although reflection on the methodology is virtually absent. Nevertheless, it turns out that source criticism is a useful tool for several kinds of investigation that are of current interest. Thus source criticism can be used to identify and describe sources used by an author so as to bring into sharper profile the literary and theological characteristics of that author (redaction criticism). Further, the many ancient documents which are being published or republished require source-critical analysis to describe their compositional history and their relationship to other documents. Finally, recent efforts to map out the history of early Christianity have been aided by the identification of sources used by extant documents; in effect, new sources for the study of early Christianity are thereby "created."

Although source criticism is a literary tool, its function for our purposes, and for synoptic studies in general, is primarily historical and theological. Its method may be said to have two moments: (1) examination of a document for signs of literary disunity which may be construed as evidence of the use of sources, and (2) the establishment the literary unity of the putative source(s). The first task is analytic, the second synthetic.

The first or analytic task involves basically three types of evidence.[4] (a) *redundancy:* repetition of the same textual material either within a single document or in more than one document (e.g., Matt 13:12; 25:29; Luke 8:18; 19:26; Mark 4:25); (b) *anomalies (aporias):* evidence of literary "seams," in-

---

4. Cf. the list of four "criteria" in Collins, *Introduction*, 123–26.

cluding hard connections (e.g., Luke 11:33 in relation to Luke 11:29–32 as well as to 11:34–36); types of anomalies include shifts in form (e.g., Luke 6:22–23 in relation to Luke 6:20–21), shifts in vocabulary or style (e.g., Luke 10:21–22 in relation to 10:13–15 or 10:17–20), and shifts in theology or point of view (e.g., Luke 11:19 in relation to 11:20; 10:3 in relation to 10:2; 12:8 in relation to 12:7); (c) *broken connections:* evidence of an insertion which, when removed, restores the broken connection (e.g., Luke 3:9 and 3:17).

The second moment, which is synthetic or reconstructive, must adopt different methods depending on the nature of the material. In the case of a single insertion, of course, there is nothing to reconstruct since all we have is the fragment inserted into the text. So the principle distinction is between putative sources which are singly attested and those which are multiply attested.[5]

Hypothetical sources which are singly attested cannot be reconstructed as to their original wording, though some conjectures may be made on the basis of familiarity with the redactional traits of the author of the text in which the source is found. Neither can the original order of the material be reconstructed except when restorable connections can be demonstrated. Thus, in the case of singly-attested putative sources, the only reconstructive activity that is possible is to link the various textual elements supposed to have derived from another source and now incorporated into a text. To do this, there are only two types of evidence. The first is literary unity, that is, evidence of a coherent text, such as peculiarities of vocabulary and style, consistency in form, consistency in theology or point of view, and structural or compositional integrity. The second type of evidence is restorable connections between the disparate fragments. The task, in other words, is to show that the disparate bits and pieces of text supposed to have derived from sources actually belonged together in a source. Of course, the sources themselves may be composite.

The reconstruction of a hypothetical source which is multiply attested is, of course, more certain but no less difficult. One must have the kinds of evidence, mentioned above, for sources that are singly attested. But, in addition, it is now possible to attempt a reconstruction of the wording and the sequence of the source material. In cases where deviations exist in wording or sequence, an effort must be made to account for their deviations on the basis of a knowledge of the redactional tendencies of the authors of the texts in which the putative sources are located. It is especially important to show that the various source components really add up to a document; that is, the demonstration of the putative source's literary unity is absolutely essential. This has not been sufficiently recognized in the past.

A corollary of this emphasis on evidence for literary unity is that source criticism cannot be regarded as a first step which is left behind when we move

---

5. This discussion focuses on hypothetical sources rather than extant sources. Therefore, methodology for dealing with a situation such as the use of Mark by Matthew and Luke is not considered here.

on to study the theology of the source, its genre, and so on. Rather, these latter approaches must also be regarded as part of the source-critical task even though they employ methodologies which go beyond source criticism. To insist that all these other methodologies belong under the umbrella of source criticism means that they need to be seen as contributing part of the answer to the question of the source's existence. In practice, this means that rather than simply presupposing the Two Document hypothesis, synoptic scholars need to call attention to the import of all their conclusions for the solution of the synoptic problem.

The Assumptions Underlying Source Criticism

Source criticism rests upon certain assumptions, rarely if ever enunciated, about how the gospels came into existence. In the case of synoptic source criticism, the basis assumption is that the gospels came into being through scribal activity involving sources, usually conceived of as literary. Further, source criticism assumes that knowing how the gospels came into being is somehow important. Both of these assumptions have been called into question in recent years, and so it is necessary to examine these points to see if the source-critical foundations of the Two Document hypothesis, and of the Q hypothesis in particular, still hold.

1. Literary authorship vs. oral composition

The most basic assumption is that synoptic relationships are literary ones, and thus that the gospels are the products of scribal activity. This literary understanding of gospel origins was not essentially challenged by form criticism, even though the latter assumed an important role for oral tradition. This was not seen as a theoretical problem so long as there was assumed to exist a basic continuity between oral and written stages of the gospel tradition. However, precisely that can no longer be assumed. Indeed, some now argue that the gospels are essentially products of oral traditional composition. To understand why these must be seen as sharply opposed alternatives it is necessary to discuss briefly the differences beween orality and textuality.[6]

Those who distinguish orality (and aurality) from textuality sometimes see this distinction as so fundamental that we must say that oral cultures think and act differently from literate cultures. Walter J. Ong, for example, asserts that "more than any other single invention, writing has transformed human consciousness."[7] Ong specifies this difference by describing the "psychodynamics

---

6. For the larger context of this discussion see Ong, *Orality and Literacy*. For the gospel tradition see esp. Güttgemanns, *Candid Questions;* Lord, "The Gospels as Oral Traditional Literature"; and Kelber, *The Oral and the Written Gospel*.

7. Ong, *Orality and Literacy*, 78.

of orality."[8] Of critical important is the fundamentally different relationship between speaker, oral "text," and audience in the oral context, and the relationship of author, text, and readership in the literate context. In an oral context, the speaker is in direct contact with the audience, which helps shape his or her "text." This direct connection between text and speaker is lost when the text is committed to writing. Once this happens, the author no longer presides over the text: the oral performer has control over the performance by means of emphasis, gesture, and so on, to an extent impossible for an author.

For our purposes, it is sufficient merely to point to this gulf between orality and textuality. More specifically to the point are differences in the ways texts are composed and transmitted in oral and literate contexts. Oral texts do not exist autonomously. There must be speakers. When speakers cease to relate a story, hymn or poem, it vanishes. Thus oral texts endure only so long as they play some useful role in a society.

The originator of the text is usually unknown. Even if known, there is no way to judge whether later retellings are exactly like the original performance since in an oral culture there is, as Ong stresses, no way to look up anything. Indeed, the very idea of doing so would be foreign to an oral culture. In such a culture, the concern is not to preserve the text exactly but to perform it persuasively. This means that there is no "original text" and that the tendency is toward creative adaptation of the text to the situation and the audience rather than toward exact replication of the text. Often the wording will be the same from one oral performance to the next, whether by the same or by a different performer, but this sameness tends to be limited to sterotyped phrases, epithets, and brief sayings such as proverbs. The sequence of the parts of an oral text may also vary, with some being added or omitted as seems proper to the occasion. These same dynamics are still at work even in literate contexts for some types of oral behavior, such as the telling of jokes. Jokes are generally of unkown origin, and the concern is not to relate the joke exactly as written, even if it is written, but to tell it in a way that produces the best effect. These observations are not, however, valid for all oral speech. Ordinary conversation may share the same psychodynamics, but here it is not a case of a text being performed and thus transmitted.

These introductory comments about orality and literacy are sufficient to indicate that they pose fundamental questions for source criticism. The very idea of a "source" is alien to orality. Indeed, Albert B. Lord, a pioneer in the study of oral traditional composition, has argued that the synoptic gospels are to be viewed as oral traditional literature.[9] If this is true there can be no synoptic "problem," for each gospel is only a performance, a creative rendition of the same oral tradition.

8. Ong, *Orality and Literacy,* chap. 3: "Some Psychodynamics of Orality," 31–77.
9. Lord, "The Gospels as Oral Traditional Literature."

The reactions of Charles H. Talbert and Leander E. Keck to Lord's proposal[10] are certainly representative of the larger community of biblical scholars. Despite appreciation for Lord's insights, Talbert and Keck firmly reject his proposal. One would be hard pressed, in fact, to find any biblical scholar today who would say that the canonical gospels are products of oral composition, or, more precisely, transcriptions of oral performance.

There are a number of reasons for this opposition to Lord's proposal. They are discussed here primarily because these reasons touch on important aspects of the question of how the gospels were composed. This too is a neglected question in synoptic research, even though every scholar makes a number of assumptions about how in fact the gospels were composed.

(a) *Palestine in Jesus' day was not an oral culture.* It was, in fact, a remarkably literate society with a strong orientation to texts, especially in its religious life. Speaking of the hellenistic Mediterranean in general, George A. Kennedy comments that "the New Testament could not have been written at a time of greater literacy, education, or understanding."[11] Even if it was not typical, the Qumran community shows the remarkable literary productivity possible at the time. And clearly Qumran was not alone in this, for many other writings have been preserved among what are now known as apocryphal and pseudepigraphical writings. Of course, oral traditions also must have flourished. But whether in Jesus' day there was a controlled process of transmitting oral tradition through memorization, as Birger Gerhardsson argues, is doubted by most scholars, who find little evidence for it in first-century sources.[12]

(b) *While the gospels contain evidence of oral habits, they are to be thought of as literary, not oral, compositions.* Matthew, whose gospel manifests more oral traits than the other gospels, is a literary, not an oral, composition.[13] The main proposals for a non-literary origin of the gospels (the gospel as expanded kerygma and the liturgical genre hypothesis) have both been discredited in favor of various literary models, predominantly Greco-Roman in origin.[14] Others have noted the various ways in which the gospels evince familiarity

10. Talbert, "Oral and Independent or Literary and Interdependent?"; Keck, "Oral Traditional Literature."

11. Kennedy, "Classical and Christian Source Criticism," 127.

12. Gerhardsson, *Memory and Manuscript* (1961) and *The Gospel Tradition* (1966). Gerhardsson is well aware that Galilean society "—even the small towns in the Galilean countryside—was no pre-literary society" (*The Gospel Tradition*, 32). In the same book he notes the complex interrelationships that existed between oral and written tradition (33–35). For a critique of Gerhardsson's thesis see M. Smith, "Comparison," and Kloppenborg, *Formation of Q*, 44–46.

13. See the article by Lohr on "Oral Techniques in the Gospel of Matthew." Lohr makes clear that the oral techniques he discusses are not evidence of oral composition but of the survival of such techniques among authors. The comments of Pierre Hadot are worthy of note; he observes that philosophic works in Greco-Roman antiquity were closely tied to oral conduct and thus cautions against a sharp distinction between orality and writing ("Forms of Life and Forms of Discourse," 496–500).

14. These proposals and models are discussed in Aune, *The New Testament and Its Literary Environment*, 23–27 and chaps. 1–2.

with the rules of rhetoric in the ancient world,[15] especially the use of chreiai and elaborated chreiai.[16] This points to specialized forms of oral discourse if not—especially in the case of elaborated chreiai—to literary composition.

(c) *Much of the evidence supposedly indicating oral composition can also be found in literary composition.* Oral composition is characterized by flexibility (i.e., variation in wording and in the sequence of the components or themes in a text), as well as by the use of formulaic expressions. But, as Talbert notes,[17] the same tendencies can be found among authors of written texts. Lohr provides many examples of the use of formulaic expressions in Matthew, but these are used to give a traditional cast to the material used.

(d) *The remarkable agreements among the synoptic gospels in order as well as wording point toward literary activity.* Since the oral mode is focused on creative performance, the expected tendency is toward variability. To be sure, the components of a unit of oral tradition may well retain their general sequence, yet within the general outline of the tradition, variability is normal. But the synoptic gospels manifest such strong agreement that oral composition is unlikely.

Compared with other instances of apparent literary dependence in early Christianity, the level of agreement in the synoptics is unusually high. For example, one may compare the use of Jude by 2 Peter, of Colossians by Ephesians, and of the Nag Hammadi tractate Eugnostos by the Sophia of Jesus Christ. More ambiguous, because we do not have the text being copied, are the cases of mutual dependence by the Didache and Barnabas upon a common "Two Ways" document, and by the Pseudo-Clementine Homilies and Recognitions upon a common Kerygmata Petrou.[18] In these five instances, the salient feature is agreement in order, not in wording. Evidence for the latter varies, from agreements on certain words, phrases and themes (Jude/2 Peter) to extensive, exact copying (Eugnostos/ Sophia).

It is clear that the assumption of oral composition for the synoptics is unjustified. Therefore, two of the basic assumptions of synoptic source criticism—that the relationship among the synoptics is a literary one and hence that these gospels were products of scribal activity—are vindicated. However, this does not mean that the relationships among the synoptics are exclusively literary. Oral tradition may have played and probably did play a

15. See, e.g., Kennedy, *New Testament Interpretation through Rhetorical Criticism;* Vernon Robbins, *Jesus the Teacher;* Mack and Robbins, *Patterns of Persuasion;* and now Mack, *Rhetoric and the New Testament.*

16. A chreia "is a saying or action that is expressed concisely, attributed to a character, and regarded as useful for living" (Hock and O'Neil, *The Chreia in Ancient Rhetoric I: The Progymnasmata,* 26). On the elaboration of the chreia, see Mack and Robbins, *Patterns of Persuasion.*

17. Talbert, "Oral and Independent or Written and Dependent?" 93–102.

18. Parallel versions of some of these texts are available in translation. For Jude/2 Peter, see Frankemölle, *1. Petrusbrief, 2. Petrusbrief, Judasbrief,* 89–91; for Eugnostos/Sophia of Jesus Christ, see Robinson, *The Nag Hammadi Library,* 220–43; for Didache/Barnabas, see Kraft, *Barnabas and the Didache,* 81–177.

role, not only in the transmission and shaping of the material but also in informing the compositional techniques of the evangelists. Such observations have important consequences for source critical methodology, as Keck has pointed out:

> The greater the role of oral tradition in early Christianity, the less viable the Griesbach hypothesis becomes, because this hypothesis forces the whole discussion into strictly literary terms. Streeter's hypothesis . . . can be adapted far more easily to take account of oral tradition than can any hypothesis insisting that the solution lies in a genealogical relation among three documents.[19]

It should also be noted that the compositional processes assumed by source criticism and, in particular, by the Two Document hypothesis, seem to accord well with what is known of compositional techniques used in analogous Greco-Roman literature. F. Gerald Downing, who has stressed this point, argues that, by contrast, the compositional techniques assumed by the Griesbach hypothesis simply do not accord with that we know of Greco-Roman literature.[20] A similar point has been made by Migaku Sato with respect both to compositional techniques and to types of writing material available in Palestine.[21] A recent investigation of ancient Near Eastern literatures makes a similar claim with respect to the source critical analysis of the Hebrew Bible, which is methodologically comparable to gospel source criticism, namely that the compositional habits assumed by source critics correspond well with the compositional habits discernible in analogous literatures.[22]

2. Source criticism and historical study

The value of source-critical analysis has been put into question in recent years by a variety of new critical approaches to texts. Literary criticism and structuralism both stress the final form of the text, and their practitioners tend, to varying degrees, to devalue diachronic analysis.[23] And yet even these approaches have not demonstrated any methodological weakness in source criticism as such. Rather, they have called diachronic analysis into question as the principal prerequisite for any further study of the text. Thus the value of source-critical analysis may be affirmed, but in a qualified way.

This does not mean, however, that it is simply a matter of taste whether one approaches the text synchronically or diachronically. These approaches are not necessarily complementary, as the literary critics and structuralists have shown. The legitimacy of a source-critical approach to any particular text thus

19. Keck, "Oral Traditional Literature," 120–21.
20. Downing, "Compositional Conventions and the Synoptic Problem." Cf. also Hadot, "Forms of Life and Forms of Discourse," 496–500.
21. See Sato, *Q und Prophetie*, 62–65, 390–93. Sato's proposal will be discussed at greater length in chap. 3.
22. Tigay, *Empirical Modes for Biblical Criticism*.
23. The literature is now extensive. See, e.g., Peterson, *Literary Criticism*.

can no longer be taken for granted. If a text can be shown to possess such internal coherence as to render dubious the various aporias which source critics claim as evidence of sources, then of course the very basis for source-critical analysis is eroded. This means that source-critical analysis cannot ignore arguments for the literary unity of texts. At the same time, few would deny that the gospels are composite works, however skillfully their authors may have edited their material.

Since the attempt to write the compositional history of Q requires the source-critical analysis of a hypothetical entity, the implication of the above remarks is that one must also attend to the question of the literary unity of Q. Indeed, that is one of the central concerns of this book. This also has implications for the way one approaches the compositional analysis of Q. That is, it is methodologically preferable to work backward from the "final form" of Q, i.e., from the order of Q as it can be reconstructed from Matthew and Luke, and to establish whatever literary unity this reconstruction may have, and only then to analyze aporias to determine whether these point to later additions or are simply evidence of the composite nature of Q.

The value of source criticism has also been questioned by those who insist that the critic's central task is to understand the final form of the canonical text.[24] However, a preference for the final form of the text rests upon theological rather than literary grounds, and the question is not one of literary unity but of intertextuality—the way one document relates to others in the canon. Brevard S. Childs, for example, has no objection in principle to source criticism, and he assumes the Two Document hypothesis,[25] but for him this is merely interesting background.

It may be admitted, then, that source criticism need not be the initial stage of exegesis, and that literary-critical approaches need not presuppose such analysis. It may further be recognized that source criticism has a limited role, primarily as a tool for the historical study of a text. But for the historian, it is precisely this role which is absolutely indispensable.

The Nature of the Synoptic Problem

We turn now to consideration of some fundamental questions about the nature of the synoptic problem, in particular about the ways in which the synoptic problem is conceived and its solution sought.

The synoptic problem contains a hidden assumption, which is really a hypothesis. The hypothesis is that there is some sort of relationship, perhaps literary, among the first three canonical gospels. This hypothesis is intended to explain the abundant agreements among the gospels. The relationship clearly

---

24. See, e.g., Sanders, *Canon and Community*, and Childs, *The New Testament as Canon*.
25. Childs, *The New Testament as Canon*, 61–62.

is no simple one, however, because there are numerous and puzzling disagreements as well. That a relationship, probably literary, exists among the gospels is assumed by virtually all scholars today; the problem (hence, the "synoptic problem") is to describe that relationship.

A source hypothesis can explain only some kinds of agreements and disagreements among the gospels. This is necessarily so because of at least three random factors: first, uncertainty about the condition of the text; second, the alleged presence of oral tradition; and third, the probable creative freedom of the evangelists. For the sake of clarity, therefore, the synoptic problem should be described as the problem of describing the general relation (if any) among the gospels. At best, a source hypothesis can be only a "macro-hypothesis."

Clearly no source hypothesis will be able to explain everything. Likewise, a source hypothesis is not falsified by its inability to explain certain data, so long as the data can be plausibly explained as due to one or more of the random factors. The limited explanatory power of any hypothesis renders it non-falsifiable in the strict sense.[26]

It is not clear what would constitute corroboration of a source hypothesis. We should dismiss any hope of ever "proving" a source hypothesis, because we cannot know all the factors in the genesis of the gospels. In the case of a direct literary relationship between two or more extant documents, however, we would, as noted, expect evidence of redundancy, anomalies or aporias, and broken connections; we would seek evidence of the literary unity of the suspected source material; and we would strive to show the restorable connections between the "fragments." Such corroboration of a source hypothesis would be cumulative.

But the quest for such corroboration involves more than simply showing that a hypothesis is possible; it must be shown to be more satisfactory than rival hypotheses. And there are other problems, to be noted later, that render appeal to some of the usual arguments unconvincing. Perhaps a more useful way to corroborate a hypothesis would be to see what it implies, and then to test the resulting deductions. Such devising of new tests would be more lively and illuminating than the repeated reassembling of the "data" in order to claim that one's hypothesis "explains" them.

There are two other matters which bear on the problem of corroboration. The first has to do with what constitutes data. It would appear that the data to be explained by a source hypothesis (i.e., the agreements and disagreements of various kinds) are generated by the hypothesis itself, including the basic hypothesis that there is a relationship among the gospels (i.e., the synoptic

26. A source hypothesis seeks to explain a unique event, the genesis of the gospels; it does not seek to explain what is typical. Therefore a source hypothesis has no predictive power. Since it cannot predict anything, it cannot be tested and falsified in the way scientific hypotheses can be tested and falsified. For an effort to falsify from a different perspective see Talbert and McKnight, "Has the Griesbach Hypothesis Been Falsified?" and the response of Buchanan, "Has the Griesbach Hypothesis Been Falsified?"

problem). The problem of circularity of argument inherent in this situation is, I think, psychological. The situation is this. The basic data to be "explained" by a source hypothesis are simply *general patterns* in the agreements and disagreements among the gospels. We see these general patterns by means of our hypothesis.[27] It is very difficult, therefore, to see the general patterns without also "seeing" the hypothesis. However, if one cannot see the alledged general pattern, or if a general pattern seems apparent in the abstract but is not convincing in detail, then to the extent that the hypothesis depends on that general pattern it is discredited.[28]

The fact that the data and the hypothesis are so closely related may explain why debates among source critics have often produced more heat than light. But what appears to be a problem can be converted into an asset; i.e., the very fruitfulness of a hypothesis in generating data can be used as a measure of its validity. What I have in mind is not the sheer accumulation of data but the gaining of insight. In this sense, the criterion of usefulness mentioned by Joseph A. Fitzmyer may have real probative value.[29]

Another matter which bears on the problem of corroboration is the ambiguity of the data. Some data at least can be explained in more than one way. A good example of this is the so-called phenomenon of order. The same facts can be stated in ways prejudicial to the Two Document hypothesis (Matthew and Luke generally support the order of Mark; when one fails to do so, the other does) or to the Griesbach hypothesis (when Mark does not follow the order of Matthew, he follows the order of Luke). E. P. Sanders is certainly correct in stating that "of all the synoptic phenomena, the phenomenon of order is perhaps the most difficult to state in general terms which can claim accuracy."[30] Joseph B. Tyson attempted a "neutral statement" of the phenomenon of order and reached the conclusion that his data neither gave a clear preference for, nor disallowed, any of three major hypotheses (Griesbach, Augustinian, and Two Document).[31] If the data are so ambiguous as to admit

---

27. Popper (*The Logic of Scientific Discovery*, 280) has argued that this is true for science in general: "We do not stumble upon our experiences . . . we have to 'make' our experiences." We do so by asking questions and constructing hypotheses. Good hypotheses are those which survive deliberate attempts at falsifying them, and which are fruitful.

28. Fitzmyer ("The Priority of Mark," 134, 137, 139, 145–46) claims that Farmer's argument is plausible in the abstract but unconvincing in detail, a view that I share.

29. See Fitzmyer, "The Priority of Mark," 133–34. Farmer rightly objects that in the hands of redaction critics (who typically presuppose the Two Document hypothesis) the argument from usefulness can be circular ("The Two Document Hypothesis," 391–93). However, circularity cannot be avoided, though it does need to be recognized. And while majority opinion in such matters certainly can err, it cannot be ignored that the preponderance of scholars for about a century have found that the Two Document hypothesis has proven reliable and productive in detailed exegesis of synoptic texts.

30. Sanders, "The Argument from Order," 246. Sanders argues that the evidence supporting the *independent* use by Matthew and Luke of two other sources (i.e., Mark and Q) is not unambiguous.

31. Tyson, "Sequential Parallelism," 276–308. Tyson defines "sequential parallelism" as "those cases where two or more parallel pericopes follow one another without interruption in

several possible explanations, then the fact that any one hypothesis can explain the data is no proof of its validity. Probably the phenomenon of order can be understood only through detailed redaction-critical observations.[32]

There is an irony about the argument from order, in that the more successful it is (i.e., the more strictly an evangelist is claimed to have adhered to a general pattern) the more anachronistic it seems in view of the renewed appreciation of the literary and theological creativity of the evangelists. It seems to me that this problem is especially apparent with the Griesbach hypothesis, according to which Mark's composition was governed by harmonistic principles which seem quite trivial.[33]

These reflections upon the synoptic problem suggest the need to exercise caution in our claim to have proved or disproved a hypothesis. They suggest a more fundamental need to be clear about what we are doing. Arguments for source hypotheses are typically set forth as though the hypothesis were the logical and necessary conclusion to which the researcher was forced after objectively gathering and studying the data. We gather data, however, only if we have a hypothesis to begin with. No doubt it is because we begin with hypotheses, and thus have much invested in them, that we are anxious to prove them right. Perhaps our energies have been misdirected. We should spend less time trying to prove our hypotheses and more time trying them out to see whether they lead to genuine historical and literary understanding.

Still, it would not be wise to waste time trying out hypotheses which are purely *ad hoc* inventions. So there is a need to have a hypothesis set forth in a way which will commend it to other researchers. An *ad hoc* hypothesis is one with an idiosyncratic view of the problem, or one which takes for granted what most regard as highly unlikely. Thus one way to test a hypothesis is to explore its assumptions.

I will briefly examine Farmer's argument for the Griesbach hypothesis,[34] not because I regard it as an *ad hoc* invention but because it is convincing only if certain conditions are assumed. Farmer begins (Step I) with the thesis that "the similarity between Matthew, Mark, and Luke is such as to justify the assertion that they stand in some kind of literary relationship to one another."[35] This "assertion" (or hypothesis) finds general assent today. Farmer adds that this literary relationship "could be one involving direct copying."[36]

two or three gospels" (278). The Augustinian hypothesis holds that, while Luke and Mark both knew Matthew, Mark was essentially the epitomizer of Matthew.

32. See the appendix, "The Argument from Order," in Neirynck, *The Minor Agreements*.

33. For example, the Griesbach hypothesis would appear to deny theological intentionality to the structure of Mark. Farmer's suggestion, that the Markan structure was governed by Petrine speeches in Acts ("Modern Developments," 291–92), seems to conflict with the principle that Mark's conflation maintained strictly the order witnessed concurrently (and thus accidentally) by Matthew and Luke. That Mark had access to Acts as well as to Luke is vaguely hinted in *The Synoptic Problem* (30–31, 236–37) and is now assumed by Farmer ("Modern Developments," 288–91).

34. See chap. 6 of *The Synoptic Problem*.

35. Farmer, *The Synoptic Problem*, 202.

36. Farmer, *The Synoptic Problem*, 203.

This possibility too may be readily granted, although Farmer offers little evidence for it. Direct copying, however, becomes embedded as a postulate in Step II. And this dubious hypothesis of direct copying governs the rest of Farmer's argument.

What Farmer does in Steps II and thereafter is to propose one hypothesis (Griesbach) to explain another (direct copying).[37] His argument thus rests upon the fallacy of *petitio principii*. As a matter of fact, Farmer's definition of the synoptic problem as the task of discovering the chronological order in which the gospels were written itself presupposes direct copying. The Two Document hypothesis, of course, does not share this view of the synoptic problem; that Mark is the first gospel is essential, but it is a matter of relative indifference which is second and third. When this is noticed, it becomes clear immediately that Farmer's definition of the problem presupposes his way of solving it. When direct copying is presupposed, there are only six ways that one can account for agreements among the gospels (Step IV). Of these six, only one has any considerable scholarly support today, namely the Griesbach hypothesis. Thus Farmer's argument is really this: if you assume that direct copying by the evangelists of each other's gospels is the only way to explain the agreements among them, then the Griesbach hypothesis is more satisfactory than the other five, which have little scholarly support.

Farmer's initial rejection of any appeal to hypothetical documents (Step III) is a red herring. Everyone would grant that appeal to a hypothetical source should not be one's first tactic in explaining synoptic relationships. However, it is precisely the fact that most scholars have judged direct copying of Matthew by Luke or vice versa to be unlikely that has led to the modern preference for the Q hypothesis. To be sure, Farmer is not opposed in principle to positing a hypothetical source[38]; in fact, he assumes a number of them, including one that resembles Q, as will be noted later.

The main argument for a direct literary relationship between Matthew and Luke seems to be the so-called minor agreements of Matthew and Luke against Mark. This evidence, however, is ambiguous in that there are many ways to explain each agreement. The "phenomenon" is more impressive if one holds, with Farmer and Dungan,[39] that all minor agreements arose from a

---

37. The Griesbach hypothesis as proposed by Farmer requires three instances of direct copying: of Matthew by Luke; of Matthew by Mark; and of Luke by Mark. Although Mark's use of Matthew and Luke is problematic in itself, our main concern here is with Luke's use of Matthew. The Two Document hypothesis presupposes that Matthew and Luke are independent. On the problem of claiming that Luke used Matthew see Kümmel, *Introduction*, 63–64, and esp. Fitzmyer, "The Priority of Mark," 147–50. Farmer seems to admit that Luke's direct copying of Matthew is dubious, but he believes that Orchard (*Matthew, Luke and Mark*) has solved this problem ("Modern Developments," 282–83).

To assume direct copying would be permissible in Step II if the eighteen fundamental ways that the gospels may be related to each other had been tested. Farmer, however, assumes that one of these eighteen must be the correct one, and for him the only question is, which one?

38. "There is nothing wrong with hypothecating the existence of an otherwise unknown source or sources if there exists evidence that is best explained thereby" ("A Fresh Approach to Q," 46 n. 4).

39. See Farmer, *The Synoptic Problem*, chap. 4, and Dungan, "Mark—the Abridgement,"

single cause, and that the agreements must all be taken together as representing a "web" of evidence. But one cannot assume that all instances in a class of phenomena are the result of a common cause; if such a web is felt to exist, its existence needs to be argued. In fact, however, it would appear that there are a number of reasons for these minor agreements.[40]

Among the problems with assuming that Luke used Matthew is the fact that Luke, with very rare exceptions, never places the sayings material of the "double tradition" in the same context as Matthew. Even more serious is the problem of explaining why Luke so often seems to preserve a form of a saying which is more primitive than that preserved in Matthew.[41] Indeed, it is precisely this problem which led Farmer to concede "the necessity of positing the existence of collections of 'sayings material' behind Matthew and Luke. . . ."[42] Farmer does not wish to identify this source or sources with Q. On the other hand, it is hard to see why, in practice, there would be much difference between them, for Farmer would exclude from his sayings collection(s) material Luke could have found in Matthew. Since in any unit of sayings material Luke can usually be found preserving something that seems earlier than Matthew, the possibility of assigning that material to Q would have to remain open; this is true for the bulk of the "double tradition." Thus even on the Griesbach hypothesis it appears necessary to posit the existence of something resembling Q.

To summarize: To speak of the "synoptic problem" and of its "solutions" is to use obfuscating language. The "synoptic problem" conceals a hypothesis, and the "solutions" to this problem are themselves hypotheses. Therefore, one needs to consider what it means to create, use, and test hypotheses, especially literary ones. Upon examination one such hypothesis, the Griesbach hypothesis as presented by Farmer, has been found to be built on faulty logic.

But while the Two Document hypothesis remains a viable hypothesis, it cannot simply be taken for granted. In particular, it must be shown that the disparate units of text where Matthew and Luke agree against Mark really belong together as parts of a single document whose structure and coherence can be demonstrated. If this can be shown at least for significant portions of the double tradition, then the Two Document hypothesis, and the Q hypothesis in particular, will have gained powerful support. It is precisely to this task that we shall turn in chapter four and, in greater detail, in succeeding chapters. But first it is necessary to review the history of scholarship on Q.

55–60. Farmer and Dungan argue that Streeter "atomized" the phenomenon by dividing the minor agreements into various types based on several hypotheses concerning their origin.

40. See Neirynck, *The Minor Agreements*.

41. See, e.g., Luke 6:20–23//Matt 5:3–12; Luke 7:35//Matt 11:19; Luke 11:2–4//Matt 6:9–13; Luke 11:20//Matt 12:28; Luke 11:30//Matt 12:40; Luke 11:49//Matt 23:34; Luke 16:18//Matt 5:32.

42. Farmer, "A Fresh Approach to Q," 46 n. 4.

2

From Source
to Gospel

*A Short History
of Early Q Research*

1988 saw the sesquicentennial of the Two Document hypothesis and thus also of the "discovery" of the synoptic sayings source, Q. By common consent, Christian Hermann Weisse is credited with formulating for the first time, in 1838, the Two Document hypothesis.

At the time it emerged, the Two Document hypothesis was revolutionary. The notion that the authors of the synoptic gospels had used sources was in the air, having been introduced in the latter part of the eighteenth century.[1] But both claims made by the Two Document hypothesis were novel: that Mark was the first gospel, and that Matthew and Luke had both used a primitive collection of Jesus' sayings. The most notable advocates of the priority of Mark were Karl Lachmann, who presented this view in an 1835 essay,[2] and Christian Gottlob Wilke, who published a more complete study in 1838.[3] Weisse's study, which appeared the same year, independently developed an argument for the priority of Mark.

Q and Markan Priority

The argument for the priority of Mark is of critical importance to the "discovery" of Q. It is true that one might conjecture the existence of a sayings source used by Matthew or Luke, or by both of them, without acknowledging the priority of Mark. In fact, as we shall see, this was done by Friedrich D. E.

1. A brief account of the various hypotheses is given in Kümmel, *Introduction*, 38–80. Individual contributors are described in Kümmel, *The New Testament*, esp. 74–88, 144–55. On Weisse, see also Schweitzer, *The Quest of the Historical Jesus*, 121–36. Other detailed accounts, critical of the Two Document hypothesis, are found in Farmer, *The Synoptic Problem*, esp. 1–47; and in Stoldt, *History and Criticism of the Marcan Hypothesis*, 1–131. Accounts favorable to the Two Document hypothesis may be found in Tuckett, "The Griesbach Hypothesis in the 19th Century," and idem, *The Revival of the Griesbach Hypothesis*.
2. Lachmann, "De ordine narrationum in evangeliis synopticis" (The Order of the Narratives in the Synoptic Gospels). A partial translation is available in Palmer, "Lachmann's Argument."
3. Wilke, *Der Urevangelist; oder exegetisch-kritische Untersuchung über das Verwandtschaftverhältnis der drei ersten Evangelien* (The Primal Evangelist or an Exegetical-Critical Investigation of the Family Relationship of the First Three Gospels).

19

Schleiermacher. But without the assumption of the priority of Mark, the Q hypothesis would have foundered.

Weisse's claim that Matthew and Luke had used, in addition to Mark, a collection of Jesus' sayings was also a novel claim, although it too had a certain pre-history. Johann Gottfried Eichhorn, in his elaboration of Gotthold Ephraim Lessing's hypothesis that all the gospels were dependent upon a lost Hebrew Primal Gospel, had suggested in 1794 that the material common only to Matthew and Luke required a special literary source, though he himself was not able to demonstrate its existence or character.[4] Another pre-Two Document hypothesis advocate of a special source for the double tradition material was Schleiermacher, in an 1832 essay "Concerning the Testimonies of Papias about our First Two Gospels."[5] Schleiermacher interpreted Papias' all-too-brief comments to mean that Matthew had composed a collection of Jesus' sayings, but this was not to be identified with the canonical Gospel according to Matthew. Rather, the cannonical gospel was called Matthew precisely because its unknown author used Matthew's collection of sayings. Schleiermacher, however, did not assume that Luke used this collection, nor, in fact, did he assume Markan priority.

Holtzmann, Wernle, and Wellhausen

As noted earlier, arguments for the priority of Mark and the existence of a sayings source used by Matthew and Luke were first combined in a Two Document hypothesis by Weisse. A more comprehensive and persuasive presentation of the Two Document hypothesis was published in 1863 by Heinrich Julius Holtzmann,[6] and it was this version of the Two Document hypothesis which would so dominate synoptic research that most scholars would come to regard it as the indispensable foundation for their study of the gospels.

From the outset the synoptic Sayings Source was regarded as a very primitive document. Commonly it was thought to have been written by Matthew, as Schleiermacher had earlier argued. And since Mark was not an apostle, Q might naturally have assumed pride of place as the first document known from the early Chrstian movement, if not as the first gospel. But while Q was valued

---

4. See Kümmel, *The New Testament*, 78. Kümmel notes that Lessing was the "first to attempt to trace the development of the gospel tradition by a purely literary examination of it" (77). The reference is to an essay published in 1778 entitled, "Neue Hypothese über die Evangelisten als bloss menschliche Geschichtsschreiber betrachtet" (New Hypothesis Concerning the Evangelists Regarded as Merely Human Historians). An English translation of this essay is available in Chadwick, *Lessing's Theological Writings*, 65–81. Eichhorn's study, published in 1794, was entitled "Über die drey ersten Evangelien" (Concerning the First Three Gospels).

5. Schleiermacher, "Über die Zeugnisse des Papias von unsern beide erste Evangelien" (Concerning the Testimonies of Papias about our First Two Gospels).

6. Holtzmann, *Die synoptischen Evangelien: Ihr Ursprung und geschichtlicher Charakter* (The Synoptic Gospels: Their Origin and Historical Character). See Kümmel, *The New Testament*, 151–55.

highly, it lacked enough narrative to make it a significant source for the life of Jesus, a matter of great interest at this time. And so the high esteem for Q was more theoretical than real in the early stages of the Two Document hypothesis. Few important works on Q appeared, attention instead being given to Mark as the earliest gospel.[7] Indeed, significant work on Q would not emerge until near the turn of the century. This was in part because the Two Document hypothesis itself was only now gaining its ascendancy, in part also because Q was not yet seen as representing an independent tradition.

After Holtzmann, the next significant contribution to the study of Q was Paul Wernle's slim but influential volume entitled *Die synoptische Frage* (The Synoptic Problem), published in 1899. Wernle broke with the typical view, inherited from Schleiermacher, that Q is to be identified with the document ascribed by Papias to Matthew.[8] Neither is Q a translation of an Aramaic doument, for "the speeches in Matthew and Luke go back to a common Greek source."[9] Wernle astutely notes tensions within the document, and concludes that it grew by stages;[10] indeed, he speaks of "the history of the collection."[11] However, his theory concerning "Judaistic" additions to an earlier "free, almost revolutionary Gospel of Jesus"[12] cannot be accepted, as Siegfried Schulz has also noted.[13] Nevertheless, the idea that Q underwent a process of growth is an important insight which was not exploited until recently.

According to Wernle, Matthew usually preserves the Q text better than Luke.[14] Neither Matthew nor Luke has preserved the original order of Q,[15] but Luke is a better witness to it than Matthew.[16]

Significantly, Wernle divides Q into three groups of discourses and related materials: (a) the discourses on righteousness (the Sermon on the Mount/ Plain); a miracle story about the centurion in Capernaum; the mission discourse; Jesus' thanksgiving to the Father; and the blessing of the disciples; (b) the discourse about John; the Beelzebul controversy; the discourse about seeking signs; and the woes against the Pharisees; and (c) a discourse on prayer; a discourse on treasure and care; the parables of the mustard seed and leaven; possibly the parables of the lost sheep and lost coin; exhortation to the disciples; the apocalyptic sayings; and the parables of the banquet and the pounds.[17] He notes that the second group is polemical, and that the third is not

7. See Harnack, *The Sayings of Jesus*, xi: "It is strange how much more attention has been devoted to St. Mark. . . ."
8. Wernle, *Die synoptische Frage*, 228–29.
9. Wernle, *Die synoptische Frage*, 229.
10. Wernle, *Die synoptische Frage*, 231.
11. Wernle, *Die synoptische Frage*, 228–33.
12. Wernle, *Die synoptische Frage*, 230.
13. Schulz, *Q*, 15.
14. Wernle, *Die synoptische Frage*, 185.
15. Wernle, *Die synoptische Frage*, 90–91.
16. Wernle, *Die synoptische Frage*, 226.
17. Wernle, *Die synoptische Frage*, 226–27. For a summary of the proposed contents of Q see also Wernle, *Die Quellen des Lebens Jesu*, 48.

polemical but consists of warnings directed to Christians. The opening speech by John the Baptist and the temptation account are later additions, intended as "an historical introduction."[18] Thus, Wernle supposed that Q had a logical structure. The principle by which it was organized was not chronological but catechetical,[19] that is, it was not written to provide an accurate record of Jesus' ministry but to provide instruction for new members of the community who had not known Jesus personally.

Finally, Wernle noted that Q provides a glimpse into "the oldest theology of the primitive community."[20] But this theology turns out to be no different from that of Mark, since Wernle held that Q simply presupposed the theology expressed in Mark; indeed, Q was written for people who were already Christians.[21] Its christology appears, for example, in the discourses on confession and the parousia. Its purpose was to instruct the believer in what it means to follow the path of the kingdom of God.

The view that the sayings source had already been Christianized was set forth by Julius Wellhausen in a series of commentaries on the synoptics.[22] Then, in 1905, he drew these observations together in his *Einleitung in die drei ersten Evangelien* (Introduction to the First Three Gospels). Wellhausen contended that Jesus was no Christian but a Jew, although he held at the same time that Jesus' views were well in advance of those of his Jewish contemporaries. The gospels, and Q as well, already evidence the process of Christianizing Jesus, including the creation of an eschatology with Jesus as its center. Jesus, in Wellhausen's view, was unmessianic and non-apocalyptic.

It was in Luke, Wellhausen thought, that one could find the most faithful reproduction of the Q text, although Luke himself created the framework for the material.[23] For the most part, Matthew and Luke used the same Greek translation of an original Aramaic Q, but occasional evidence of Aramaic translation variants suggested to Wellhausen that they both also had access to the Aramaic original.[24]

Wellhausen's most controversial position, however, emerges in his comparison of Mark and Q.[25] Both documents have been Christianized, but the process has proceeded farther in Q than in Mark. Therefore, as far as historical accuracy is concerned, Mark has priority. This does not mean that Q is dependent on Mark. Rather, the situation is more complicated, since the two sources have influenced each other. Mark and Q both begin the same way, with John the Baptist, and there are other points of agreement. But there are also signs that sometimes Q, more often Mark, has preserved the oldest form of

18. Wernle, *Die synoptische Frage*, 226.
19. Wernle, *Die synoptische Frage*, 227–28.
20. Wernle, *Die synoptische Frage*, 228.
21. Wernle, *Die synoptische Frage*, 228.
22. Wellhausen published commentaries on Mark (1903), Matthew (1904), and Luke (1904).
23. Wellhausen, *Einleitung*, 67.
24. Wellhausen, *Einleitung*, 68.
25. Wellhausen, *Einleitung*, 73–89.

the tradition. For example, in the speech of John in Q there is still evidence of the old tradition that John spoke of a "nonhistorical Messiah of the future,"[26] namely the judge who comes with fire (Q 3:17).[27] But in other places Q is secondary. For example, the temptation story in Mark is "not messianic,"[28] whereas it is in Q. Even clearer evidence of Mark's priority over Q is found in the comparison of Mark 3:28–29 with Luke 12:10. Here Wellhausen argues that Mark's christology is low: the spirit active in the prophets is also active in Jesus, and to reject this spirit is to blaspheme God, since the spirit is God at work. But in Q the spirit is the spirit of the Christian community. Indeed, we can see, says Wellhausen, that "the sons of men" in Mark 3:28 has become "the son of man" in Luke 12:10//Matt 12:32. Such evidence suggests that Q has proceeded farther along the path toward Christianization than has Mark; so Mark has priority in terms of both narrative and discourse material.[29] Wellhausen thinks that Mark and Q are both to be located in Jerusalem, and that Q must have been composed a considerable time after 67 or 68 C.E.

Harnack: Q's Literary Unity

One of the most comprehensive and important studies of Q was that of Harnack, published in 1907.[30] The motivation for writing the book, as Harnack notes in the preface, was precisely to oppose Wellhausen's conclusions about Q. His study includes one of the first attempts to reconstruct the Greek text of Q, though he does not try to establish its original sequence. However, Harnack has been widely criticized for too consistently giving preference to the Matthean text, and for allowing his judgment of Q in general to be clouded by his liberal theological assumptions.

One of Harnack's most important contributions, however, has not received the attention it deserves. His chief aim was to demonstrate the literary unity of Q. He recognized that a careful investigation "from the point of view of grammar, style, and literary criticism" is essential.[31] The consequences of such an investigation must be taken seriously.

> If such an investigation fails of its aim—that is, if it is shown that nothing connected or distinctive is evolved from the study of the passages in question— than it follows that Q vanishes as a tangible entity, indeed disappears altogether. . . .[32]

26. Wellhausen, *Einleitung*, 74.

27. Passages in Q are cited throughout this book according to their Lukan location, following the precedent of the Society of Biblical Literature's Q Seminar. Thus Q 3:17 refers to the Q text underlying Luke 3:17//Matt 3:12.

28. Wellhausen, *Einleitung*, 74.

29. Wellhausen, *Einleitung*, 87.

30. Harnack, *Sprüche und Reden Jesu* (Sayings and Discourses of Jesus). The 1908 English translation, *The Sayings of Jesus*, is cited below.

31. Harnack, *The Sayings of Jesus*, xi.

32. Harnack, *The Sayings of Jesus*, xi.

Here Harnack seized upon a point which is absolutely crucial, though virtually ignored in most of the literature: there can be no basis for assuming that the numerous fragments of "double tradition" text belong to a single document unless those fragments display features that suggest they originally belonged together.

Harnack confesses that evidence for the literary unity of Q falls short of being a convincing demonstration. Nevertheless, he adduces a number of interesting features:

- there is a preponderance of simple verbs
- adjectives are frequently used as substantives
- certain adjectives are relatively frequent: "worthy" (ἄξιος), "blessed" (μακάριος), "whole" (ὅλος), "much" or "many" (πολύς), "evil" (πονηρός)
- the absence of "from (the side of)" (παρά) is striking
- sentences are usually connected with "and" (καί); δέ is comparatively infrequent
- for "if," ἐάν is twice as frequent as εἰ
- the particle τε never occurs
- temporal clauses with "as" (ὡς) are entirely absent
- the genitive absolute occurs only once
- participial constructions are extraordinarily frequent
- the construction of "to be" (εἶναι) with the participle is very rare
- the various constructions with "become" (γίνεσθαι) are entirely absent (though common in Luke and present in Matthew)
- there is copious use of interrogative sentences.[33]

In addition, some other curious features are noted: no disciples are mentioned by name in Q, and the word "disciples" (οἱ μαθηταί) is absent; christological titles are missing, including "christ" (ὁ χριστός) and "lord" (κύριος)[34]; sayings are common and narrative rare; only two miracle stories occur; strong emphasis is placed on the significance of John the Baptist, and he is given a sermon of his own; and "the Passion and all references to the Passion are absent from Q." Further, "the geographical horizon of Q is bounded by Galilee, and indeed much more strictly than that of the synoptists." With regard to content, "Q appears to be undoubtedly more homogeneous than any of the three [synoptists]."[35]

Harnack's conclusion, which diverges sharply from Wellhausen's, has been widely cited:

> Q is a compilation of discourses and sayings of our Lord, the arrangement of which has no reference to the Passion, with a horizon which is as good as absolutely bounded by Galilee, without any clearly discernible bias, whether apologetic, didactic, ecclesiastical, national, or anti-national.[36]

33. Harnack, The Sayings of Jesus, 147–63.
34. Harnack, The Sayings of Jesus, 153.
35. Harnack, The Sayings of Jesus, 163–72.
36. Harnack, The Sayings of Jesus, 171 (Harnack's emphasis).

Harnack is also able to show that the order of Q is preserved surprisingly well by Matthew and Luke, once their agreements are carefully studied. The resulting structure appears meaningful to Harnack:

> Q was no gospel like St. Matthew, St. Mark, and St. Luke, and yet it was not a merely formless compilation of sayings and discourses without any thread of connection. Rather we learn from the beginning and the conclusion (eschatological discourses) that it possessed a certain definite arrangement of subject matter and the outlines of a chronological order. It was, however, in no sense a biographical narrative, but essentially a collection of discourses.[37]

Later, Harnack observes that "Q in character occupies the mean position between an amorphous collection of sayings of our Lord and the definite literary form of the written gospels, and so prepared the way for the latter."[38]

Wellhausen had claimed that Mark is earlier than Q in terms of its stage of development. This conclusion is examined at length by Harnack and found wanting.[39] He can find no instance in which Mark is primary. Indeed, he emphatically reverses the opinion of Wellhausen: Q is primary to Mark.[40] Harnack also contends that Q was originally written in Aramaic;[41] that it was not yet under the influence of "Paulinism";[42] and that its horizon is Jewish and Palestinian.[43] He is unwilling, however, to assume an apostolic origin for Q.[44] The fate of Q was also considered by Harnack. His oft-quoted conclusion was that "it found its grave in the gospels of St. Matthew and St. Luke, and probably elsewhere in some apocryphal gospels."[45]

Bacon: Q and Wisdom Tradition

Several other significant works on Q prior to the modern period may be mentioned. These are the essays edited by William Sanday and published as *Oxford Studies in the Synoptic Problem* (1911); Burnett Hillman Streeter's *The Four Gospels* (1924); and T. W. Manson's *The Sayings of Jesus* (1949). While all of these are important, none represents a fundamental advance in the study of Q. Manson's book is very useful as a commentary, and Streeter's book contains many astute observations. However, the work of another scholar, Benjamin Wisner Bacon, held the potential for a significant advance.[46]

Bacon represents an advance in several respects. Perhaps most importantly,

37. Harnack, *The Sayings of Jesus*, 181.
38. Harnack, *The Sayings of Jesus*, 228.
39. Harnack, *The Sayings of Jesus*, 193–246.
40. Harnack, *The Sayings of Jesus*, 250–51.
41. Harnack, *The Sayings of Jesus*, 247.
42. Harnack, *The Sayings of Jesus*, 248.
43. Harnack, *The Sayings of Jesus*, 248.
44. Harnack, *The Sayings of Jesus*, 248–49.
45. Harnack, *The Sayings of Jesus*, 251.
46. In addition to the articles cited below, see Bacon, "The 'Son' as Organ of Revelation" (1916); "Wisdom" (1921); "Baptist" (1926); "The Redaction of Matthew 12" (1927).

he recognized that Q belongs to the wisdom tradition not only formally but conceptually, in that it presents Jesus as a messenger of personified Wisdom. However, the implications of this insight were obscured by the fact that Bacon assimilated the wisdom elements in Q to an Isaian/Pauline theology of suffering and humiliation,[47] thus assimilating Q to the Pauline kerygma. This is perhaps most clearly expressed in the following quotation.

> Q is concerned primarily with the *nature of Jesus' ministry as a whole*, its "mighty work," its effect upon the "publicans and sinners," its "glad tidings to the poor," its rejection by the great. The whole career of Jesus is depicted as meeting a clearly conceived messianic ideal. Moreover that ideal is the Isaian Suffering Servant, as in the great Pauline summary of "the mind of Christ" (Phil ii.5–11). *A priori* it would be impossible that an evangelist with such a purpose should write without reference to the Passion. . . .
>
> It is true that the Isaian ideal appears in Q in the later adaptation of the Wisdom writers. Jesus' career is accordingly depicted as that of the Revealing Son in whom Redemptive Wisdom has taken up her abode (that She may reveal to her "babes" and "children" the unknown Father [Matt. xi.25–27=Luke x.21–22]), and this involves a presentation very largely under the form of great didactic discourses.[48]

This understanding of the theology of Q enabled Bacon to be among the first to declare flatly that Q was indeed a gospel:

> It [Q] will not have been a mere agglutination of sayings, but a presentation of the *kind of ministry* represented by Jesus' career, a true *Gospel* (*pace* Harnack), in which Jesus was set forth as the redeeming "Wisdom" of God, the Suffering Servant of Isaian prophecy, humbled in obedience unto rejection and death, and, therefore, also "highly exalted." It will have been a gospel more akin to Paul and John than many [sic] of our extant synoptics.[49]

Precisely this assimilation of the wisdom elements in Q to the standard kerygma of the death and resurrection of Jesus resulted in Bacon's failure to bring clearly to expression the distinctive nature of Q. Had he developed the implications of these elements as the expression of a theology quite different from that of the other gospels, he would have been able to move toward recognition of Q as an independent theological development. Q had gained the distinction of being a gospel at the price of losing its distinctiveness over against the synoptics and Paul. Nevertheless, he did call attention to these wisdom elements, and to the fact that Q is no "mere agglutination of sayings."

Bacon also deserves credit for taking note of the significance of the Oxyrhynchus papyri containing what we now know to be fragments of the Gospel of Thomas in Greek:

---

47. This assimilation is based upon the unsupportable argument that Matt 12:(17)18–21 (=Isa 42:1–4) came from Q; see Bacon, "The Nature and Design of Q," 674–88, esp. 680–88.

48. Bacon, "The Plaint of Wisdom," 506.

49. Bacon, "The Nature and Design of Q," 688; cf. Bacon, "The Q Section on John the Baptist," 54–55.

The discovery by Grenfell and Hunt of papyri of the 2nd and 3rd century, in which sayings attributed to Jesus are agglutinated with no more of narrative framework than the bare words, "Jesus saith" (λέγει 'Ἰησοῦς), proves that such compilations actually circulated, fulfilling a function similar to the *Pirke Aboth*, or "Sayings of the Fathers" in the contemporary and earlier synagogue.[50]

Likewise, Bacon was correct in insisting that Luke rather than Matthew best preserves the "order, arrangement, and spirit" of Q,[51] and in rejecting, like Wernle, the identification of Q with the logia mentioned by Papias.[52]

Tödt: Q's Independent Kerygma

The decisive step in the study of Q, separating present-day research from all previous research, had not yet been taken. This step is the recognition that Q represents an independent tradition, one different from that found in Mark, John or Paul. Bacon had come close to finding this key in his emphasis on the wisdom elements in Q. Harnack had come close as well because he emphasized that Q made no reference to the passion of Christ.[53] But further progress in Q research would have to await the realization that Q is, in some sense, a gospel in its own right and is not merely ethical instruction which presupposes the belief structures of other early Christian communities.

Q is certainly no narrative of the life of Jesus. Indeed, it contains almost no stories of Jesus at all (exceptions: Q 4:1–13; 7:2–10). It lacks, like Mark, both infancy and resurrection stories. And unlike any of the four canonical gospels, it contains no account of Jesus' death, not even a passing reference to it. That Jesus performed miracles is mentioned (Q 7:2–10; 11:14, 20; 7:22; cf. Q 10:9, 13). Clearly, Jesus did preach. In Q, Jesus utters warnings, instructions, blessings, woes, and a few short parables, and perhaps a couple of longer parables. But this hardly adds up to what scholars were accustomed to thinking of as a gospel. Moreover, since Q contains mainly teachings of the kind held to have been used in the early church to instruct converts to Christianity, it was widely assumed that Q must have been a very early catechetical document. Once relegated to the status of a catechetical supplement to the gospel, Q did not even come under consideration as itself a gospel.

The deficiency from which Q suffers is particularly grievous when one begins with the assumption that the gospel is, by definition, the good news that Jesus died for humankind's sins and rose again; a document lacking even the slightest reference to these things could scarcely be a gospel. True, there are some passages which imply knowledge of Jesus' death (see Q 11:45–51; 13:34–35; cf. Q 14:27), but these give no evidence whatever that Jesus' death

---

50. Bacon, "Logia," 45.
51. Bacon, "A Turning Point in Synoptic Criticism," 58–59.
52. Bacon, "Logia," 45–49.
53. Harnack's distancing of Q from the passion kerygma produced reactions, of course. See, e.g., Robertson, *The Christ of the Logia* (1924).

was understood to be redemptive. Thus on account of its theological deficiencies as well Q was deemed unqualified for gospel status.

In 1959, the dissertation of a student of Günther Bornkamm, Heinz Eduard Tödt, was published.[54] In it, Tödt argued that Q contains much more than instruction. It has a message of its own—a kerygma, to use a term popular in the Neo-Orthodox and Bultmannian schools. The kerygma of Q centered, said Tödt, in the identification of Jesus with the "son of man" announced by Jesus as yet to come. The dawning of the realization that the expected son of man of the future is none other than the Jesus who had been on earth was called by Tödt "Christological cognition."[55] Once the community came to see Jesus as this coming son of man, they took up his sayings once again, and the result is what we know as Q. Jesus' teachings would be used to prepare people for the decisive return of this son of man; it would disclose the criteria by which the son of man would judge the world. Correspondingly, "the fellowship bestowed on earth by Jesus will be confirmed by the Son of Man."[56]

Tödt faulted the Bultmannian school for its monolithic conception of the kerygma—a kerygma centered exclusively in the death and resurrection of Jesus. This kerygma coincides perhaps only too well with Protestant, especially Lutheran, theology; but it was not, argued Tödt, the earliest kerygma. We must reckon with the possibility of more than one kerygma. Indeed, Tödt spoke of "two spheres of tradition," one centered on the passion, the other on the sayings of Jesus.[57] It was in this second but earlier tradition that christology as such arose, according to Tödt.[58]

In arguing that Q represented a quite different tradition, with its own internal logic, Tödt's work marks a turning point in Q research. And yet his own account of the theology of Q cannot be accepted. Not only does it concentrate on a son of man christology to the exclusion of other elements in Q, such as wisdom, but a central assumption concerning the emergence of the Son of man christology must be rejected.

Tödt criticizes his contemporaries for their monolithic conception of the kerygma as focused exclusively on the passion and resurrection of Jesus. Since Q lacks reference to either, scholars had neglected it in favor of Mark. But Tödt brings passion and resurrection in through the back door. For he cannot conceive of any tradition which failed to take account of Jesus' death and resurrection. Arguing that the central point of the resurrection stories is the "renewed bestowal of that fellowship which Jesus bestowed on earth and which the Son of Man at his parousia will confirm,"[59] Tödt argued that Q must presuppose that renewed fellowship since the Q community "resumed" the

54. Tödt, *Der Menschensohn in der synoptischen Überlieferung;* English translation: *The Son of Man in the Synoptic Tradition* (1965).

55. Tödt, *Son of Man,* 254.

56. Tödt, *Son of Man,* 263.

57. Tödt, *Son of Man,* 268–69; cf. 232–35, 237–38.

58. Tödt, *Son of Man,* 231.

59. Tödt, *Son of Man,* 251.

preaching of Jesus. That is, Q clearly regarded it as still valid to preach Jesus' message despite his death. How can we account for this except by saying that they too had experienced this renewed fellowship by means of the resurrection? Thus, "as understood by this community, the passion and resurrection were not what had to be preached but what enabled them to preach."[60] Tödt further notes that the resurrection story appears relatively late in the history of the synoptic tradition.[61] We can now see why: there was a form of the tradition which presupposed but did not preach Jesus' resurrection.

Upon investigation, however, there is not a shred of solid evidence to support this hypothesis.[62] What evidence there is is all circumstantial: how are we to account for Q having been written at all if Jesus' movement ended abruptly with his death? But, as we shall see, there are other ways to account for this. Moreover, Tödt operates with a straight-line evolution of early Christian theology which is problematic both in its assumption of a straight-line evolution and in its focus upon intellectual development. The latter, in fact, detracts from one of the signal contributions of Tödt's book, namely his emphasis on the community of Q. And the assumption of a straight-line evolution has become dubious; it has become increasingly clear that we have to reckon with a multiplicity of independent movements in the emergence of both Judaism and Christianity.

Another problem with Tödt's study is his lack of attention to the character and structure of Q as a whole. We are early alerted to this when Tödt notes his agreement with Harnack that Matthew has best preserved the order of Q.[63] Tödt displays relatively little interest in the structure of Q, except for a few clusters of sayings.[64] The reason for this lack of interest in Q as a document is probably that, like Martin Dibelius, Tödt assumes that Q was not really a written document but rather a stratum of tradition,[65] arranged thematically,[66] but having no real author or redactor.[67] Had Tödt paid greater attention to the structure of Q, he would have noted that the son of man sayings, which occur almost entirely in the latter half of Q, simply do not provide any clue as to the theological basis for the organization of the first half of Q. Thus, for this reason as well, focusing on son of man christology in Q cannot get at the logic by which Q is organized and thus at the theological assumptions that undergird it.

We shall see later that there are additional problems with Tödt's sketch of the emergence of son of man christology; for example, Tödt assumes that at

60. Tödt, *Son of Man*, 250.

61. Tödt, *Son of Man*, 251.

62. Tödt, however, appeals to the "continuity of the fellowship with Jesus on earth with the fellowship in heaven which bestows salvation," which he detects in Q 12:8 (*Son of Man*, 57).

63. Tödt, *Son of Man*, 41 n. 1.

64. Tödt, *Son of Man*, 48–49; 270–71.

65. Tödt, *Son of Man*, 237; cf. Dibelius, *From Tradition to Gospel*, 235.

66. Tödt, *Son of Man*, 269.

67. Tödt, *Son of Man*, 237.

least the sayings about the son of man as a future figure distinct from Jesus are authentic sayings of Jesus. It was first in Q that a "Christological cognition" occurred which identified Jesus with this future son of man. However, if the authenticity of any of the future son of man sayings is called into question, as it is by a number of scholars, then Tödt's interpretation as a whole is undermined in a fundamental way.

Even if Tödt's account of the theology of Q cannot be accepted, however, he does deserve credit for introducing the crucial notion that Q may represent an independent kerygma. Once this point was made, it became much more difficult to marginalize Q. For if Q represents an independent kerygma, it probably represents a distinct community. And given the peculiar nature of Q, this must have been, by more familiar standards, a very peculiar community.

Despite Tödt's contributions, Q did not come to be regarded as a gospel. Two obstacles to this remained: the lack of a passion and resurrection kerygma in Q, and the fact that it is a sayings collection.

Q: A Gospel

It is true that it seems *a priori* unlikely that any gospel could have emerged which did not deal in some way with Jesus' death. One would expect some kind of ideological explanation of his death. Lacking any, the only alternative would seem to be that chosen by Tödt, that is, to argue that the passion and resurrection kerygma was presupposed by Q. As it turns out, however, one of the most remarkable features of Q is an ideological explanation of a different sort, deriving from the deuteronomistic tradition. The importance of this tradition was demonstrated by Odil Hannes Steck in his 1967 monograph, *Israel und das gewaltsame Geschick der Propheten* (Israel and the Violent Fate of the Prophets).[68] According to this tradition, Israel's impenitence is evidence of her stubborn refusal to hear the prophets who were sent to her, and especially of her alleged violent treatment of these prophets. Here, argues Steck, is a way of explaining the death of Jesus, although the tradition does not have its roots in an apologetic tradition relating to the death of Jesus but rather in a call to repentance issued to Israel. Thus a primary objection to seeing Q as a gospel is now removed, since Q does in fact have its own ideological solution to the problem of Jesus' death. To be sure, it would now be somewhat paradoxical to speak of Q as a "gospel," since there is nothing specifically Christian about this view of Jesus' death. Nevertheless, if by "gospel" we mean a document dealing with Jesus, representing a coherent theological perspective and thus capable of standing alone, then Q could with some justice be pronounced a gospel.

From a quite different point of view, W. D. Davies came to a similar conclusion in a monograph published the same year as Steck's (1963), entitled *The Setting of the Sermon on the Mount*. Davies showed that Q cannot be

---

68. This book will be discussed at greater length later.

understood simply as a catechetical supplement to the gospel, thus rejecting the views of Dibelius, Manson, and Vincent Taylor.[69] The "distinctiveness of Q" resides in its "'crisis' significance," argued Davies.[70] Indeed, Davies' study of Q pushed him toward a recognition that it is a gospel:

> The words of Jesus in Q point not as much to the normalities of catechetical instruction as to the moral enthusiasm of the earliest Christians, the 'first fine careless rapture' of a community which confronted and dared the impossible. . . . The Church had preserved a tradition of the ethical teaching of Jesus which it regarded as in itself part of the crisis wrought in his coming. To put it yet more forcefully, this teaching itself helped to constitute the crisis. Q sets the ethical teaching of Jesus in its utterly radical and critical context as part of the drawing near of the Kingdom, that is, that teaching is not primarily a catechetical necessity or an addendum to the Gospel but itself part of the Gospel.[71]

A second obstacle to the recognition of Q as a gospel was its lack of narrative. Werner Georg Kümmel, for example, insisted that a mere collection of sayings cannot be regarded as a gospel.[72] But the discovery in 1945 of a small library of ancient Coptic manuscripts near Nag Hammadi, Egypt, revealed that such an assumption as to what constitutes a gospel is without basis. Five of the documents in this library are called gospels, yet they bear little resemblance to the quasi-biographical canonical gospels. A number of other gospels from the early and later church are known either by description or from (often fragmentary) texts, and they show a similar variety.[73] Thus the term gospel seems not to have had any fixed meaning in the early church. Certainly the most impressive example of a non-narrative gospel is the Gospel according to Thomas, one of the documents found at Nag Hammadi. It is a gospel of the sayings collection type. The claim, therefore, that Q cannot be regarded as a gospel because it is a sayings collection would also seem to be without merit. Moreover, Q has in more recent years been shown to be a member of a sayings collection genre designated *logoi sophon*.[74] Subsequent studies by Max Küchler[75] and Kloppenborg[76] have provided additional evidence concerning the genre of Q.

There is now no longer any reason to deny to Q the status of gospel. To be sure, the task of defining in what sense Q might be called a gospel remains; but the impediments to such a claim have been removed. It is also true that defining Q as a gospel does not in and of itself represent an advance in our understanding of Q. Its importance is primarily to prevent the marginalization

---

69. Davies, *Setting*, 380.
70. Davies, *Setting*, 381.
71. Davies, *Setting*, 386.
72. Kümmel, *Introduction*, 71–74.
73. See, e.g., Cameron, *The Other Gospels*, for translations of a number of these gospels.
74. See, e.g., Robinson, "LOGOI SOPHON."
75. Küchler, *Frühjüdische Weisheitstraditionen* (Early Jewish Wisdom Traditions).
76. Kloppenborg, *Formation of Q*.

of Q as simply one more piece of early Christian ethical teaching, and to allow consideration of Q as representing a quite distinct point of view, a point of view not necessarily the same as that found elsewhere in the New Testament. Also at stake in the designation of Q as a gospel is its use for reconstructing the early history of Christianity. For if Q were only one of many different resources stashed away in the library of some sectarian group, then little could be inferred from the document about the group which used it. But if Q presents to us the distinctive beliefs of a specific group of people, then it becomes a window into that particular group, and thus becomes even more historically significant.

To call Q a gospel, even if only provisionally, is not, however, to imply that it is Christian. The point of view found in Q seems fairly clear: despite very sharp tension with other Jewish groups, the community reflected in Q could not conceive of itself as anything but Jewish. And yet it is equally clear that most Jews were unable to recognize what they saw in this community as an expression of fidelity to Jewish tradition. Quite the opposite! It is far less clear what issues divided these groups. This problem cannot be solved here. But it is important to note that in calling Q a gospel, we have not decided its relation to the "Judaisms"—to use Jacob Neusner's term[77] —of the first century or to the emerging Christian movement.

Thus, although Q has been known for 150 years, it is only recently that it is coming to be seen as a gospel or at least as an independent tradition. With this realization, a turning point has been reached. At the same time, the very divergent assessments of the nature and theology of Q suggest the need to discover a method of studying Q which is more appropriate to the nature of the document, and which can inspire more confidence than was possible with the older methodologies.

77. See, e.g., Neusner, "Comparing Judaisms."

3
Recent
Q Research

*Recovering the
Compositional History*

In 1973, Ulrich Luz was able to report on "The Rediscovered Sayings Source."[1] Neglected for several decades, Q, Luz noted, had become an important object of investigation in the late 1960s and the early 1970s. Three substantial monographs had been produced (Lührmann, Paul Hoffmann, and Schulz) and a dissertation was awaiting publication (Polag).[2] In fact, there was even more activity than Luz recognized, because American dissertations by Paul D. Meyer and Richard A. Edwards were written at about the same time.[3]

Although it may seem too grand to speak of a paradigm shift, it is nevertheless the case that a fundamental change had occurred within this area of synoptic studies. Tödt's book had been a watershed document because it showed that Q could no longer be considered simply a paranetic supplement to the early church's kerygma; Tödt argued strenuouly that Q represents a theologically independent tradition. His argument was a direct assault on the dominant paradigm of a single, monolithic kerygma in the early church.

However, it was not solely Tödt's work that effected this paradigm shift; others were moving in a similar direction, most notably Robinson. Moreover, Tödt's work must itself be seen within its proper context, because the rediscovery of Q coincided with the emergence of redaction criticism. The first example of this at that time unnamed method was Bornkamm's 1948 essay on "The Stilling of the Storm in the Gospel of Matthew."[4] The name "redaction criticism"—or more precisely, "history of redaction" (*Redaktionsgeschichte*)—was coined by Willi Marxsen in 1954,[5] just one year after the publication of

---

1. Luz, "Die wiederentdeckte Logienquelle."
2. Luz, "Die wiederentdeckte Logienquelle," 527. The reference is to Lührmann, *Die Redaktion der Logienquelle* (1969); Hoffmann, *Studien zur Theologie der Logienquelle,* submitted as a *Habilitationsschrift* in 1968 and published in 1972; Schulz, *Q* (1972); and Polag, *Die Christologie der Logienquelle,* a 1968 dissertation published in 1977. Cf. Neirynck's comment about "the remarkably productive quinquennium from 1968 to 1972" ("Study of Q," 32).
3. Meyer's University of Iowa dissertation, "The Community of Q," was accepted in 1967; Edwards' University of Chicago dissertation, "The Sign of Jonah," was written in 1967 and published in 1971.
4. Bornkamm, "Die Sturmstillung im Matthäusevangelium"; ET in Bornkamm, Barth, and Held, *Tradition and Interpretation in Matthew.*
5. See Rohde, *Rediscovering,* 10.

another landmark work, Hans Conzelmann's redaction-critical study of Luke.[6] Marxsen's study of Mark followed in 1956.[7]

It was the intention of redaction criticism to explore how the theological convictions of the author of the document shaped the editing of the material; correspondingly, from the way an editor (or redactor) shaped the material one might discern the theological assumptions at work in the redaction. Here was a method ideally suited to focus attention on the theological assumptions embedded in Q, and thus to call attention to the distinctive character of Q. And the study which first did this was indeed a redaction-critical analysis, namely Tödt's 1956 dissertation under Bornkamm.[8] Other dissertations under Bornkamm also attended to the unique perspective of Q, namely Ahira Satake's 1962 study, "Church Organization in the Apocalypse of John,"[9] and Steck's 1965 study, "Israel and the Violent Fate of the Prophets."[10] The latter, however, was methodologically more closely related to Steck's other Heidelberg advisor, Gerhard von Rad. Most important of the dissertations, however, was the 1968 Heidelberg *Habilitationsschrift* by Lührmann entitled "The Redaction of the Sayings Source."[11]

Methodology in Recent Studies of Q

The paradigm shift in the study of Q was not occasioned only by the emergence of redaction criticism. The discovery of the Nag Hammadi codices brought a call for a reassessment of the way early Christianity developed, since it appeared that the picture was far more complicated than had previously been assumed. This reassessment coincided with a renewed appreciation of Walter Bauer's *Orthodoxy and Heresy in Earliest Christianity* (1934). Bauer had emphasized that heresy was not to be seen as the later decay of originally orthodox Christian teachings, but rather as the survival of variant forms of Christianity which could claim an antiquity equal to, or greater than, that of orthodoxy. They became "heresy" only when that species which became "orthodoxy" gained enough strength to pronounce them such.

---

6. Conzelmann, *Die Mitte der Zeit* (The Center of Time), 1953. ET: *The Theology of St. Luke*, 1960.

7. Marxsen, *Der Evangelist Markus–Studien zur Redaktionsgeschichte des Evangeliums*, 1956; ET: *Mark the Evangelist: Studies on the Redaction History of the Gospel*, 1969.

8. It should be noted that Tödt, like Dibelius, prefers to treat Q as a "stratum of tradition" (*Son of Man*, 237, 244); accordingly, he speaks of the "community" rather than of an author or redactor. Nevertheless, Tödt explicitly rejects Dibelius' assumption that Q lacked any meaningful arrangement and agrees with Manson's claim that Q was arranged according to a plan (*Son of Man*, 242–43). Tödt's work, therefore, can be called redaction-critical only in the broadest sense, although Tödt does distinguish between tradition (Jesus' teachings) and its transformation in Q. It is perhaps better to describe Tödt's method as composition criticism; see his comments in *Son of Man*, 246–69.

9. Satake, *Die Gemeindeordnung in der Johannesapokalypse*, 1966; see pp. 171–88.

10. Steck, *Israel und das gewaltsame Geschick der Propheten*, 1967.

11. Lührmann, *Redaktion*.

If one sought evidence of diversity in the earliest stages of Christianity, one could hardly do better than turn to Q. Here is a document which is at once extremely early and yet different from Pauline and other types of early Christianity. Indeed, certain features of Q, such as its genre as a sayings collection and the role it gives to Wisdom or Sophia, suggested some sort of relationship to the Nag Hammadi documents, where these features are also important. Thus, the study of Q held promise of making comprehensible some aspects of the diversity of early Chrstianity. This is the context in which to understand the interest in Q displayed early on by Robinson and Helmut Koester.[12] Here the focus was not the redaction-critical analysis of Q but rather the genre of Q and the wisdom theology that comes to expression in Q and which would seem to fit hand in glove with its genre as a collection of sayings.

In at least one important respect, the studies of Tödt and of Robinson and Koester converged. Both represented Q as a distinct tradition quite separate from other streams of early Christian tradition. Both approaches thus seemed to be part of a paradigm shift in the study of Q. The pictures of Q's theology that emerged in the work of Tödt on the one hand and Robinson and Koester on the other, however, were very different. For Tödt, the theology of Q is centered in its christology, and its christology is to be located in the way in which the title "son of man" is used. Accordingly, the eschatological character of Q was emphasized, although Tödt recognized that specifically apocalyptic features of the son of man figure do not appear in Q.[13] But Robinson and Koester seized upon the wisdom components in Q. Accordingly, the eschatological character of Q was de-emphasized.

However much one may protest that wisdom and eschatology are not mutually exclusive, the fact remains that there are important differences between them, especially when eschatology is cast in apocalyptic terms. This, in fact, happened in the discussion of the theology of Q as the focus upon a son of man christology in Q tended to shift to a general characterization of Q as "apocalyptic."[14] Correspondingly, scholars tended to come down on either one side or the other of the widening chasm between wisdom and apocalyptic.

If there is disagreement over the basic nature of Q, however, there does seem to be growing agreement over how to adjudicate the issue. The solution must be found by reconstructing the history of the composition of Q. The most logical assumption is that if wisdom and apocalyptic are indeed distinct and opposed traditions, then their appearance in Q is probably due to the insertion of wisdom materials into a basically apocalyptic document, or vice versa. In any case, the relationship between these components of Q can best be discovered by seeing how they relate to each other in the composition of Q. Therefore the question of methodology is absolutely crucial.

12. See the essays collected in Robinson and Koester, *Trajectories.*
13. See Tödt, *Son of Man,* 224, 227, 262–63.
14. See, e.g., Kee, *Jesus in History,* 81–82, and Perrin and Duling, *The New Testament: An Introduction,* 103–6.

Determining the history of the composition of Q is important in other respects as well. If indeed Q does have a compositional history, if it grew by stages, then one can speak of the theology of Q or the genre of Q or the community of Q only for specific moments in the compositional evolution of Q. Reconstructing the compositional history of Q, however, is a formidable, some would say impossible, task. Indeed, before proceeding further, we must pause to take notice of some scholars who reject the project from the very outset.

Edwards distinguishes two types of redactional analysis: "emendation analysis" (the study of changes made in individual units of traditional material) and "compositional analysis" (the study of the way units of traditional material are arranged).[15] Neither of these, says Edwards, is applicable to Q. The first type of analysis presupposes "a precise analysis of the [text of the] sources,"[16] while the second presupposes a knowledge of the order of Q,[17] and we have neither. Indeed, Edwards is skeptical of any effort to reconstruct the text of Q.[18] Nevertheless, Edwards earlier wrote a book on Q based on redaction-critical methodology,[19] and he seems to regard his method in *A Theology of Q* as a form of redaction criticism, albeit concerned only with the final redaction of the document.

For somewhat different reasons Hoffmann, who earlier seemed to be moving toward a redaction-critical analysis of Q,[20] has concluded that there is no significant difference between tradition and redaction in Q. He does not deny that both exist in Q; his argument is that where redaction is discernible, its tendency is toward "identification" with tradition rather than "distancing," or with continuity rather than discontinuity.[21] Hoffmann's unwillingness to distinguish tradition and redaction in Q has been widely criticized.[22]

Despite the skepticism of Edwards and Hoffmann, it will be argued here that the conclusion is often inescapable that redaction must be distinguished from tradition in Q. To cite but one example, Q 6:20b–22 is composed of four beatitudes. The first three are formally and materially similar, but the fourth is different both formally and materially. Here it would seem that we are faced with a clear instance of a later addition. Whether this addition is part of a layer or stage in the history of the composition of Q, however, must still be demonstrated. That is, it must be shown that there are good reasons for linking Q 6:22

15. Edwards, *A Theology of Q*, 15.
16. Edwards, *A Theology of Q*, 22–23.
17. Edwards, *A Theology of Q*, 18, 22–23.
18. Personal conversation at a meeting of the Catholic Biblical Association, St. Paul, Minnesota, August, 1983.
19. Edwards, *Sign of Jonah*.
20. Hoffmann, "Die Anfänge" and "Jesusverkündigung."
21. Hoffmann, *Studien*, 2–3.
22. E.g., by Devisch, "Le document Q," 92; Luz, "Die wiederentdeckte Logienquelle," 532; Lührmann, *Redaktion*, 8 [Hinweise]; Polag, *Christologie*, 9; Neirynck, "The Study of Q," 54–55; and Uro, *Sheep Among the Wolves*, 5–6. See too Schulz's criticisms of Lührmann's method (*Q*, 37–39).

to other bits of Q which together comprise a layer of material. However difficult this task may prove to be, it needs to be attempted; even failed attempts may add to our knowledge of the document.

There are basically three methods of distinguishing strata in Q and thus of writing a history of the composition of Q. They are form criticism, redaction criticism, and history of traditions analysis. Here redaction criticism includes composition analysis and, indeed, other methods of literary criticism; in other words, redaction criticism here includes those analytical tools needed to understand the "redaction" (editing) process.

Reconstructing the History of Q: Early Attempts

1. Redaction Criticism[23]

Several scholars exemplify this approach, the earliest being Lührmann and Polag. For our purposes, Polag's analysis must be set aside because he offers no criteria for distinguishing early and later strata.[24] We shall concentrate, therefore, on the pathbreaking work of Lührmann.[25]

Lührmann's method was to study the longer sayings compositions in Q, identifying by form-critical analysis originally isolated sayings and studying how these have been combined in the longer compositions. In this case, the analysis of the editing process (i.e., redaction criticism) presupposes both form-critical analysis and history of traditions analysis, the latter being incorporated into the former.

Lührmann's achievement was to demonstrate that originally isolated sayings had been edited in a tendentious way that is discernible when the same tendencies can be observed in a number of sayings compositions in Q. This meant that it was no longer possible to speak of Q simply as a collection; one had now to speak of a redactor.[26] Lührmann was the first to show this clearly. His work therefore represents a fundamental advance in the study of Q.

It will be useful to study a couple of examples to see how his method works. In Luke 12:2–9//Matt 10:26–33, we have four sayings or clusters of sayings: Luke 12:2//Matt 10:26; Luke 12:3//Matt 10:27; Luke 12:4–7//Matt 10:28–31; and Luke 12:8–9//Matt 10:32–33.[27]

---

23. For surveys of redaction-critical studies of Q see Devisch, "Le document Q," 86–89; Worden, "Redaction Criticism of Q"; Neirynck, "The Study of Q"; Kloppenborg, "Tradition and Redaction"; Schmithals, "Evangelien," 620–23, and *Einleitung, passim*; and A. Lindemann, "Literaturbericht," 257–63.

24. Note, however, that Polag (*Christologie*, 6–17) says that redactional activity can be detected in (1) the framework material—introductory and concluding statements; (2) linguistic peculiarities; (3) the sequence and grouping of the sayings; and (4) the selection of the material.

25. In addition to Lührmann, *Redaktion*, see idem, "Liebet eure Feinde."

26. Note that Lührmann follows Bultmann in understanding "collection" (*Sammlung*) as essentially devoid of redactional intent and, on that basis, distinguishes "collection" from "redaction" (*Redaktion*, 14–16, 19–20, 84–85).

27. For the full analysis, see Lührmann, *Redaktion*, 49–52.

Luke 12:2
Nothing is covered up
that will not be revealed,
or hidden
that will not be known.

Matt 10:26
. . .nothing is covered
that will not be revealed,
or hidden
that will not be known.

Luke 12:3
Therefore whatever you have said
in the dark shall be heard in the light,
and what you have whispered
in private rooms
shall be proclaimed upon the housetops.

Matt 10:27
What I tell you
in the dark, utter in the light;
and what you hear whispered

proclaim upon the housetops.

Luke 12:4–7
I tell you, my friends,
do not fear those
who kill the body
and after that have no more
that they can do.
But I will warn you whom to fear:
fear him who, after he has killed,
has power to cast into hell;
yes, I tell you, fear him!
Are not five sparrows sold for
two pennies?
And not one of them
is forgotten before God.

Why, even the hairs on your head
are all numbered.
Fear not;
you are of more value
than many sparrows.

Matt 10:28–31

And do not fear those
who kill the body
but cannot kill the soul;

rather
fear him who can destroy
both soul and body in hell.

Are not two sparrows sold for
a penny?
And not one of them
will fall to the ground
without your father's will.
But even the hairs on your head
are all numbered.
Fear not, therefore;
you are of more value
than many sparrows.

Luke 12:8–9
And I tell you, every one who
acknowledges me before men,
the son of man also will acknowledge
before the angels of God;
but he who denies me before men
will be denied before
the angels of God.

Matt 10:32–33
So every one who
acknowledges me before men,
I also will acknowledge
before my father who is in heaven;
but whoever denies me before men
I also will deny before
my father who is in heaven

The first and last sayings were originally independent, as the parallels in
Mark show (with Q 12:2, cf. Mark 4:22 and GosThom 5, 6; with Q 12:8–9, cf.
Mark 8:38). The addition of Q 12:3 establishes for the initial saying (Q 12:2) a
different context than that saying has in Mark. In Q, what cannot be covered
up is the proclamation by Jesus' followers. And Q 12:8–9 also shows itself to be
an addition by the fact that it deals with confessing rather than proclaiming.

The middle unit (Q 12:4–7) is self-contained, framed by statements about not fearing. It has no intrinsic connection with the other sayings, and thus is also an independent unit.

Two observations may now be made. First, the originally independent saying in Q 12:8–9, which deals with confession, is a later addition to an already existing unit. This unit (Q 12:2–7) had already been brought together in a primitive "collection" which, according to Lührmann, predates the redaction of Q. The redactional activity, then, consisted in attaching Q 12:8–9 to this older unit. A second observation is that sayings can be given a new meaning simply by this method of combining originally independent sayings and thus creating a new context. So we can discern here at least three layers: (a) originally independent sayings; (b) a primitive collection; and (c) the redaction of Q.

Similarly, in Q 7:18–35, Lührmann finds three originally independent units: (a) Q 7:18–23, (b) Q 7:24–30 (and 16:16), and Q 7:31–35.[28] These units were assembled in the collection that underlies the redaction of Q. They were assembled on the basis of theme: all deal with John the Baptist. Already in this collection a certain amount of compositional activity can be observed. For example, an introduction has been provided (Q 7:24). Similarly, Q 7:28 was added, along with Matt 11:12 and its parallel. The introduction and the other additions have in common the subordination of John to Jesus—something which cannot be traced back to Jesus himself. The concluding parable and its interpretation (Q 7:31–35) introduce, however, a new emphasis. Here, John and Jesus are juxtaposed to "this generation." This theme of "Jesus and 'this generation'" turns out to be a recurring theme in Q. Lührmann finds it not only in Q 12:8–9, discussed above, but also in Q 11:14–23, 24–26, 29–32 and in Q 11:39–52. It is precisely the recurrence of this and other themes which Lührmann points to as evidence of theologically tendentious editing of a "collection" of sayings.

The picture of the history of Q that emerges from Lührmann's analysis is sketchy because he offers no constructive treatment of the "collection" which underlies the later redaction; nor does he account for the transition from collection to redaction. From his scattered comments, however, it is clear that for him the collection was basically a loose anthology of sayings containing Jesus' proclamation of the kingdom,[29] and emphasizing the coming son of man[30] and an opposition between John's disciples and Jesus.[31] The later redaction was probably produced by a hellenistic Jewish-Christian community, possibly in Syria, around 50 or 60 C.E.[32] The later redaction was char-

28. See Lührmann, *Redaktion*, 24–31.
29. Lührmann, *Redaktion*, 94.
30. Lührmann, *Redaktion*, 40–41 n. 6; 85–86.
31. Lührmann, *Redaktion*, 86.
32. Lührmann, *Redaktion*, 88.

acterized by a "re-apocalypticizing" of Jesus' message,[33] with strong emphasis on judgment, especially against "this generation."[34] The redaction reflects wisdom influence,[35] the delay of the parousia,[36] and a mission to the gentiles.[37]

Lührmann's method is as satisfactory as any devised to distinguish earlier and later stages of Q. However, the distinction between "collection" and "redaction" is problematic because it implies that only during the redactional stage did theological motives play a role in shaping the material. Even by Lührmann's own analysis, however, theologically tendentious shaping of the material is evident already at the collection stage. In this respect, Polag's practice of speaking of this extensive, underlying collection (*Hauptsammlung*) as the first redaction of Q is preferable. Moreover, Lührmann rather arbitrarily assumes a single redaction of Q. But one must ask instead if it is not probable that Q grew gradually, undergoing a series of redactional alterations and/or additions.

2. History of Traditions

A second way to write a history of Q is to examine the material from a history of traditions point of view. Schulz uses this method to distinguish earlier from later materials on the basis of a variety of criteria, both formal and material. Another scholar who uses this method, Steck, is more concerned to plot the evolution of "traditions" in the sense of specific clusters of themes. For the present, we shall confine our attention to Schulz's method.

Schulz began by isolating Q material identified by Bultmann and Dibelius as late, i.e., as hellenistic Jewish-Christian. From this material, Schulz derived a number of features which are indicators of a more developed form of the tradition. These criteria enabled Schulz to identify other late material beyond that identified by Bultmann and Dibelius, and from these pericopes he derived still more indicators of lateness.[38] Some of these are: the use of expanded apophthegms; "I say to you" as a literary device rather than as an introduction to prophetic utterance; and the use of allegory and narrative.

Besides these formal criteria there are material criteria. These include the use of christological titles to refer to the earthly Jesus; the use of the Septuagint; polemic against a "divine man" christology; polemic against all Israel (not just the leaders); deuteronomistic statements about the prophets; allusions

33. Lührmann, *Redaktion*, 94.

34. Lührmann, *Redaktion*, 24–48, 93–94.

35. Lührmann, *Redaktion*, 29–31, 38–39, 45–48, 65–68, 75–83, 91–92, 97–100.

36. Lührmann, *Redaktion*, 69–72, 86, 94.

37. Lührmann, *Redaktion*, 58, 60, 86–88. As Lührmann sees it, the Q community no longer had in view a conversion of Israel. Rather, "for Israel there remains only the judgment" (93, cf. 47).

38. Schulz discusses these criteria in *Q*, 47–53. Kloppenborg ("Tradition and Redaction," 40) has assembled a complete list of Schulz's indicators of lateness. The early material consists of Q 6:20b-21, 27, 38, 41–42; 11:1–4, 9–13, 39, 42–44, 46–48, 52; 12:4–8, 22–31, 33–34; 16:17–18.

to Wisdom as pre-existent; and statements which presuppose the delay of the parousia.[39] All the material bearing these traits is, so to speak, peeled off; what remains is the early material.

Schulz not only divides the material into what is early and what is late, he also assigns the two groups of material to two phases in the history of a single community. The early material is assigned to a Palestinian community in the Transjordanian border area.[40] It was led by prophets, and thus is to be distinguished from the Aramaic-speaking community of the "Hebrews" in Jerusalem which was led by the "pillars," as well as from the Greek-speaking Jerusalem community called the "Hellenists" in the Acts of the Apostles.[41] The former Jerusalem community was Torah-observant but was also characterized by the apocalyptic expectation of an imminent parousia. The early Q community shared this latter trait, but combined it with prophetic enthusiasm. Unlike the "Hellenists" in Jerusalem, who adopted a critical stance toward the Torah, the Q community intensified the demands of the Torah, much as the Essenes at Qumran did. For example, Jewish law was generally understood to permit divorce, but the Q community prohibited it (Q 16:18).

The earlier stratum of Q, according to Schulz, consisted exclusively of sayings material—individual sayings and brief sayings compositions.[42] Its chief characteristic was its prophetic enthusiasm. It had no interest yet in the earthly Jesus,[43] though it presupposed Jesus' resurrection/exaltation.[44] It was, in fact, the living Lord who spoke through the prophets in this community; that is what distinguishes them from the Old Testament prophets.[45] This primacy of the Lord who is present in the community did not, however, diminish the longing for his return; on the contrary, it strengthened that hope.[46] In spite of all this, the Q community remained a part of the Jewish community; it had, for example, no sacraments, and it bound itself to the Law.[47]

The later Q material is assigned by Schulz to a Syrian hellenistic Jewish-Christian community, probably in the Transjordan-Decapolis area.[48] The material contains a number of new genres: narrative; apophthegms; "I" sayings, parables; and an apocalypse.[49] But the decisive change is that now the earthly Jesus has become part of the community's kerygma.[50] His public

---

39. Schulz, *Q*, 166.
40. Schulz, *Q*, 166.
41. Schulz, *Q*, 166–67.
42. Schulz, *Q*, 52–53, 57, 165.
43. Schulz, *Q*, 61 and *passim*.
44. Schulz, *Q*, 63–64 and *passim*.
45. Schulz, *Q*, 60, 64.
46. Schulz, *Q*, 65.
47. Schulz, *Q*, 169.
48. Schulz, *Q*, 481.
49. Schulz, *Q*, 481.
50. Schulz, *Q*, 481–82.

ministry is interpreted, in part, by means of the symbol of the divine Sophia, in part by the use of the titles "son of God" or "son." His death, never mentioned explicitly, is interpreted by means of the deuteronomistic view of history, according to which God repeatedly sent prophets to call Israel to repentance, but Israel consistently rejected and even killed them. Jesus is the last of these prophets, and his death, therefore, attests to Israel's hardness of heart; allusions to his death are made in warnings to Israel to repent.[51]

The later material reflects other changes too. We now hear of the delay of the parousia,[52] and it is clear that there has been a break with other Jewish groups.[53] Indeed, the Q community now suffers persecution. Still, there are important elements of continuity as well; thus, the community is still apocalyptic and faithful to the Torah.[54]

Schulz's history of traditions approach to Q has been criticized by many scholars because of the criteria he uses to distinguish earlier from later material.[55] These criteria are questionable partly because they presuppose a scholarly distinction between Jewish and hellenistic cultures which has broken down in recent years. Moreover, these criteria seem to contain within themselves the conclusions Schulz draws about the two phases of the Q community. Thus, if only genuinely prophetic material is early, then it will be obvious that the early material will turn out to be "prophetic." More serious is the fact that Schultz makes no effort to understand the internal structure of Q as a document, nor does he investigate the relationship among the pericopes in Q.

However, the problems with Schulz's assumptions may have caused his results to be dismissed too quickly. Schulz's analysis shows that Q is not, as a whole, a literary unity, and it sets before us the task of trying to account for the diversity, even the contradictions, in the material. His proposal that the Q community itself evolved is a plausible but not a necessary conclusion. The document could, for example, have passed from one community to another, and its internal disunity could simply be the product of that history. But however the problem is tackled, Schulz's analysis requires us at least to seek to make sense of each layer in Q. This means showing how the formal and material content of Q are of a piece.

3. Assessment

Form criticism and history of traditions analysis are the primary means of sorting out older and more recent layers of material, and both Lührmann and

---

51. Schulz, *Q*, 483.
52. Schulz, *Q*, 484–85.
53. Schulz, *Q*, 485–86.
54. Schulz, *Q*, 484.
55. See, e.g., Luz, "Die wiederentdeckte Logienquelle," 528, 530–31; Hoffmann, review of Schulz, in *BZ* 19 (1975), 104–15; Edwards, *A Theology of Q*, 147; Kloppenborg, "Tradition and Redaction," 38–45.

Schulz used these methods. But it is quite possible for a document to be composed of both early and late materials, as all our gospels in fact are, and yet to have been composed only at a late stage. Matthew, for example, was written later than Mark, yet it contains much material that is at least as old or older than the Markan material. Thus the presence of early materials tells us little if anything about the history of the document itself. Only if we can reconstruct the whole compositional history of Q shall we be in a position to draw inferences about the community in which it was used. This means that the purely analytical tools—form criticism and history of traditions analysis—are inadequate by themselves. They must be supplemented by the demonstration of *how the early and late materials were combined*. We must strive to gain access to the literary evolution of the Q materials. Failure to do this vitiated Schulz's analysis. Even Lührmann did not go far enough, since he confined his attention to individual sayings compositions and did not try to make sense of Q as a whole.

The Methodology of the Present Study

The method used in this study of Q may be be characterized as a type of composition criticism. The terms "composition analysis" or "composition criticism" are used here in preference to "redaction criticism." Norman Perrin and his pupils tended to distinguish between "redaction," in the sense of alteration in the wording of a text, and "composition," in the sense of the arrangement of traditional material into a larger whole.[56] When it is possible to study a document whose written source is extant, as in the case of Matthew and Luke in their use of Mark, it is proper to speak of the study of the various alterations of the Markan material by Matthew and Luke as "redaction criticism." But when no written *Vorlage* exists, access to the theological tendencies of the compiler/author is available chiefly through analysis of the structure of the document and the interior dynamics of its parts. Such analysis can be called "composition criticism." Technically, composition criticism includes not only observations of how materials have been brought together and arranged but also the discovery of the compositional tendencies typical of other literature of the day. This is because material was usually assembled according to patterns which can be detected by comparison with other literature. However, this study is largely limited to two aspects of the composition of Q: the sequence of the material and the thematic relationships among the various pericopes.

Sayings collections appear to be particularly poor candidates for compositional analysis because they are generally rather haphazardly arranged. But

---

56. Perrin, *What is Redaction Criticism?* esp. 65–67. See also Edwards, *A Theology of Q,* 14–18, and Donahue, *Are You the Christ?* 41–45.

this apparent lack of organization, this use of simple organizational techniques such as association by catchword, theme, or formal analogy, is not really evidence of compositional primitiveness. As Max Küchler observes, "Wisdom sayings have a tendency to lead as contextless an existence as possible, so as to prove useful in ever new contexts."[57] This observation implies that trivial means of stringing sayings together are adopted for a very specific purpose: to preserve the multivalency of the sayings. The use of catchwords, for example, to link seemingly unrelated sayings makes clear that the sayings are not meant to interpret one another. Instead, the focus is upon the sayings themselves. The stereotyped formula, "Jesus said," used in the Gospel of Thomas, together with the usual lack of apparent connection between the sayings, is a way of keeping the sayings hermeneutically open, and focuses attention on the individual sayings themselves. Thus the way Thomas is put together corresponds with the hermeneutic implied in its opening saying: "Whoever finds the interpretation of these sayings will not experience death." The pondering of the individual sayings leads to life.

In Q we are dealing with a very different situation. In Q, sayings are not, for the most part, intended to be pondered individually. They are made into building blocks for larger literary schemes. Clearly, we have at least "speeches" or sayings compositions; but we probably have even larger structures. If the genius of a sayings collection is its ability to preserve the hermeneutical openness of discrete sayings, then Q has transcended the category of "sayings collection." To be sure, it is still comparable to other sayings collections, but its purpose is different. Likewise, a certain "orthodoxy" is evident, in that now an interpretation is imposed on the sayings. But the extent to which such an orthodoxy is evident is far less than when a mythic world is created through narrative, and sayings become fixed in their meaning. The juxtaposition of sayings, in fact, not only limits (or makes more "orthodox") but can also release new possibilities of interpretation. Thus the beatitudes serve to provide a context of interpretation for the whole inaugural sermon, but linking them together—allowing them to become a solemn-sounding "liturgical" chant—also allows each beatitude to interpret the others and thus to augment their meaning. Reverberations of meaning are created by the seemingly primitive organizational technique of association by formal analogy. If, then, Q has moved beyond the usual function of the sayings collection, attention to its structure is critical.

Particular attention in this study will be given to the relationship of the so-called wisdom pericopes in Q (Q 7:31–35; 10:21–22; 11:29–32; 11:49–51; and 13:34–35) to their original contexts in Q. The hypothesis to be tested is that this remarkable series of texts, unique to Q in the synoptic tradition, was introduced as part of a larger redactional effort. In particular, we shall be

---

57. Küchler, *Frühjüdische Weisheitstraditionen*, 167.

concerned to observe the relationship between these texts and the contexts in which they now occur. If it can be shown that these wisdom pericopes were inserted as part of a more extensive revision of Q, then we will have gained insight into the theological motives that shaped that revision. In the pursuit of this goal, the method used in this study involves three steps.

1. Reconstruction of the Sequence of Q

The sequence of Luke according to the generally accepted view, is nearer to the Q sequence than Matthew's order. However, whenever Matthew and Luke disagree on the sequence of their materials, an effort is made to account for the disagreement. It is assumed that when Matthew and Luke can be shown to have a common sequence of material, we have discovered the original order of Q.

2. Analysis of the Reconstructed Q Material

Once the original sequence (but not necessarily the original wording) of a series of Q pericopes has been reconstructed, that material is analyzed. Attention is directed particularly to themes that emerge in the material and to evidence of literary disunity. Literary disunity is detected using the typical criteria: "hard connections" such as grammatical shifts; breaks in the train of thought; shifts in audience; shifts in tradition or theology; and so on. Note is also taken of what happens when pericopes are juxtaposed, for example when "reverberations" can be heard that result from the association of pericopes. For example, annexing the story of the Centurion's servant (Q 7:1–10) to the Q "sermon" by Jesus has the effect of fixing on certain elements in the "sermon," and of thus bringing them into prominence: the relation between hearing and doing (cf. Q 7:7–8 and 6:47–49); emphasis on Jesus' word (cf. Q 7:7 and 6:47); the lack of faith in Israel (cf. Q 7:9 and 6:39, 41–42). Moreover, the miracle story serves to illustrate the power of Jesus' word, and thus to bring home the point of the concluding parable in the "sermon."[58]

3. Determining the Stages in the Composition of Q

The next step is to collect evidence of the reworking of earlier material and the insertion of new material. If, for example, one discovers two verses in different pericopes, both sharing a common point of view and both identifiable as later additions, then the emerging pattern allows one to conjecture "stages" in the composition of Q. If other redactional activity is found which conforms to this same pattern, then a "stage" in the composition in Q may be postulated. It is particularly satisfying when one is able to recover a text which, when the later additions are removed, is a coherent whole, with connections (e.g., catchwords) linking material which has been interrupted by later insertions.

---

58. See Robinson, "Kerygma and History," 56–57.

When this evidence has been collected and evaluated, an attempt will be made to interpret theologically the development brought to light through literary-critical analysis.

In contrast to Lührmann, I try to work backward: starting with the larger literary units, analyzing them to detect evidence of their literary unity, and noting any material which appears to disrupt this larger literary unity. That is, I do not begin by form-critically "decomposing" sayings compositions and asking how they were assembled, but rather by trying to catch sight of larger literary structures in Q. These two approaches, which one may characterize as proceeding *backward* from the present text or *forward* from the originally separate units that comprise sayings compositions, are quite different methodologically. However, they are not mutually exclusive; in fact, I use the latter while giving priority to the former. But there is an inherent limitation in the method of proceeding backward from the reconstructed text of Q, and that is that this method is able to penetrate only to that layer which was most extensively subjected to redaction; it does not necessarily provide entry into the oldest stages in the composition of Q.

Reconstructing the History of Q: Recent Attempts

In recent years several significant attempts have been made to reconstruct the compositional history of Q. We shall examine several of these. We begin with Dieter Zeller's methodological comments. These do not constitute a proposed reconstruction, but they are useful aids to reflection on the nature of the reconstructive process.

1. Dieter Zeller

Zeller maintains that, given the ambiguities that often surround the term "redaction," it is necessary to identify what constitutes redaction. He believes that redaction in Q manifests itself in two kinds of activity: the *interpretive expansion* of pre-existing units of material, and the *assembling* of these units.[59] The latter kind of redactional activity is evident in several compositional features.

(a) *Semantic connections.* These are achieved either by recurring lexemes (usually catchwords) or by some underlying semantic structure. Examples of recurring lexemes are "spirit" ($\pi\nu\epsilon\hat{\upsilon}\mu\alpha$) in Q 3:16 and and Q 4:1, and "lamp" ($\lambda\acute{\upsilon}\chi\nu\sigma s$) in Q 11:33 and 11:34. An example of underlying semantic structures is the duality of human action, or action before a human forum and the action of God or before God, which pervades Q 12:2–12.

(b) *Syntactical-grammatical connections.* Of particular importance here are anaphoric and kataphoric elements, that is, features which establish a link with what precedes (kataphoric) or what follows (anaphoric). Examples of

59. Zeller, "Redaktionsprozesse," 395–409.

anaphoric elements are "therefore" (ἄρα) in Q 12:42 and "therefore" (διὰ τοῦτο) in Q 12:22. The use of the imperative in Q 12:39 is kataphoric.

(c) *Formal connections.* Sometimes materials have been joined together simply because they are formally similar. Examples of this are to be found in Q 9:57-60 and 13:18-21.

(d) *Pragmatic connections.* Minor narrative elements have sometimes been added, e.g., the brief introduction to John's preaching in Q 3:7, whose content is derived from the sayings themselves (Q 3:16).

But to speak of a *stage* in the redaction of Q, one must note more than occasional, random activity. It is necessary to observe recurring activity which brings about internal coherence within fairly extensive chunks of material. Accordingly, Zeller classifies several types of redactional activity in increasing order of magnitude in terms of the amount of material being considered.

(a) *The addition of "commentary sayings."*[60] Occasionally, existing sayings are attached to units of material by way of commentary. Such commentary is especially noticeable when it is in tension with the sayings(s) to which it is attached. For example, in Q 12:8-10 the added "commentary saying" (Q 12:10) reflects a new *Sitz im Leben*.

(b) *The formation of thematic complexes.* Redactional activity is observable not only within a sayings composition (e.g., Q 12:22-24) but also between one sayings composition and another. Thus, Q 12:8-12 is linked to Q 12:22-24 by the anaphoric "therefore" (διὰ τοῦτο) in Q 12:22 as well as by the phrase "do not be anxious" in Q 12:11 and Q 12:22. But here we have not merely a catchword connection but a theme, since "anxiety" is really the theme of Q 12:22-24.

(c) *The compilation of macro-texts.* Extensive tracts of material can be brought together by rather minor redactional activity. Thus Q 12:2-12 is linked by catchword to Q 12:22-31 and probably to Q 12:33-34 as well. In the sermon on the mount/plain, the last beatitude (Q 6:22-23) provides a setting for all the sayings which follow, by speaking of behavior with respect to opponents. The final prophetic rebuke in Q 6:46 brings to clear expression the relation of the hearer to the speaking Lord which was at issue in Q 6:37-38, 41-45, and the concluding parable (Q 6:47-49) continues this theme.

(d) *The arrangment of the macro-texts into a sequence.* Redactional activity is to be seen where a meaningful sequence of larger units occurs. An example of this is Q 7:1-10 in relation to the sermon on the mount/plain. The miracle story betrays internal redactional activity that gives special emphasis to the theme of the authority of Jesus' word—a fitting addendum to the sermon.

On the basis of the examination of a few selected texts, Zeller offers a few conclusions concerning the shifting *Sitz im Leben* of the Q material. First, the oldest complexes (e.g., Q 12:22-31; 10:3-16; 12:2-9) were brought together by itinerant, miracle-working missionaries. But some of the material in Q is

---

60. See also Wanke, *"Bezugs- und Kommentarworte"* and "'Kommentarworte.'"

clearly addressed to a different group. For example, admonitions about the danger of possessions are clearly related to well-to-do Christians, not to poor missionaries. We may, with some justice, conclude that the traditions of these itinerant preachers found a new *Sitz im Leben* in sectarian communities founded by these same missionaries. Still other material in Q suggests that the original mission to Israel has been abandoned, and that a certain openness, at least, to gentiles has begun to be evident. The final redactors were no longer active as prophets, says Zeller; probably, they were early Christian teachers.

Of course, Zeller's conclusions are debatable. The presence of material addressed both to poor (or voluntarily poor) itinerant missionaries and to the more well-to-do does not of itself require the conclusion that there has been a change in *Sitz im Leben*. Q could have been a manual used by the itinerant preachers which contained both material directed to the preachers themselves and material used by the preachers but not directed to them. A decision between these two alternatives requires the kind of literary control for which I argued earlier; that is, what is needed is a systematic analysis of all the material, with a procedure for distinguishing stages of redaction. Nevertheless, Zeller has provided a very useful programmatic essay.

2. John S. Kloppenborg

We turn next to the work of John S. Kloppenborg, whose 1984 Toronto dissertation, "The Literary Genre of the Synoptic Sayings Source," was published in 1987, in revised form, as *The Formation of Q: Trajectories in Ancient Wisdom Collections*. Two of his articles are also relevant to understanding his methodology.[61]

The method adopted by Kloppenborg is, as Kloppenborg himself notes, very similar to that of Lührmann, Zeller and the present writer.[62] In practice, it is perhaps closest to Lührmann in that it begins with the form-critical decomposition of sayings compositions. Kloppenborg, however, goes beyond other analyses to date in investigating ancient wisdom collections and in coordinating this investigation with the results of his redaction-critical investigation of Q.

Kloppenborg makes a move at the very outset of his investigation which is of fundamental importance. He begins with the observation made by Lührmann, Steck and myself that an announcement of judgment pervades much of Q. He then observes that several blocks of material cluster around "the motifs of the coming judgment, the urgency of repentance, the impenitence of 'this generation' and the ramifications of Gentile faith."[63] But, notes Kloppenborg, there

---

61. See Kloppenborg, "Tradition and Redaction" and "The Formation of Q."
62. Kloppenborg, *Formation*, 98. For Zeller see (in addition to "Redaktionsprozesse") "Die Bildlogik"; "Prophetisches Wissen"; "Weisheitliche Überlieferung"; *Die weisheitlichen Mahnsprüche*; "Der Zusammenhang"; and *Kommentar zur Logienquelle*.
63. Kloppenborg, *Formation*, 101. Kloppenborg identifies five such complexes: (1) Q 3:7-9,

are several other clusters of Q sayings "which appear to be organized along entirely different lines, and which in general lack the motif of judgment and the call to repentance."[64] The first five clusters of sayings exhibit "several common features which invite the conclusion that these four [sic] blocks belong to the same redactional stratum,"[65] namely, the same projected audience (the impenitent and the opponents of the Q group), forms (especially "chriic forms"), and motifs clustering around the theme of judgment.[66] Correspondingly, the second group of clusters of sayings also have common features: the same implied audience (members of the community), similar forms (sapiential sayings), similar motifs (poverty, discipleship, the kingdom of God) and structural similarities.[67] Kloppenborg's redactional analysis yields evidence which confirms his judgment that the second, or sapiential, block of material is the "formative" stratum, namely instances such as Q 6:23c and Q 10:13–15 where sayings containing the themes of judgment familiar from the first five clusters have been secondarily inserted into sapiential material. What we have, therefore, are two basic recensions of Q, followed by a third stage during which only the temptation account (Q 4:1–13) was added.

The first recension contained Q 6:20b–23b, 27–49; 9:57–62; 10:2–11, 16; 11:2–4, 9–13; 12:2–7, 11–12, 22b–31, 33–34; 13:24; 17:33; 14:34–35.[68] He describes this recension as "sapiential," and asserts that many of the sayings in these texts which are often described as prophetic need not be so understood. This recension of Q is a book of "instruction," a genre characterized by the predominance of imperatives or admonitions, usually ascribed to a named sage.[69] Further, the sayings in this recension are "community-directed."

Kloppenborg's second recension consists of a series of interpolated sayings (Q 6:23c; 10:12–15, 21–24; 12:8–10; 13:26–30, 34–35; 14:16–24) together with blocks of new material (3:7–9, 16–17; 7:1–10, 18–26, 31–35; 11:14–26, 29–36, 39–52; 12:39–40, 42–46, 49, 51–53, [54–56], 57–59; 17:23, 24, 26–30, 34–35, 37b). This second recension more than doubles the size of the original Q, adding, by my count, 115 verses to the original 73. The theme pervading this material is the announcement of judgment, often expressed in the deuter-

16–17; (2) Q 7:1–10, 18–52; (3) Q 11:14–52; (4) Q 12:39–59; (5) 17:23–37. Cf. Kloppenborg, "The Formation of Q," 450.

64. Kloppenborg, *Formation*, 101. He lists (1) Q 6:20b–49; (2) Q 9:57–62; 10:2–16, 21–24; (3) 11:2–4, 9–13; (4) Q 12:2–12; (5) Q 12:22–24; and (6) Q 13:24–14:35.

65. Kloppenborg, *Formation*, 166. The reference to "four" blocks is no doubt an error; five was intended.

66. See Kloppenborg, *Formation*, 167–70.

67. See Kloppenborg, *Formation*, 238–43.

68. Comparison of the tables of contents in the dissertation and in its revised, published version might appear to suggest that Kloppenborg shifted some material earlier assigned to the first recension to the second recension, and vice versa. But that is not the case, as closer examination reveals. The only important change is that in the book the speech beginning with Q 12:39 is more clearly identified as a "speech" or sayings composition.

69. For the genre "instruction," see Kloppenborg, *Formation*, 264–89; for the earliest recension of Q as member of that genre, see *Formation*, 371–72.

onomistic language of reproach for unfaithfulness to God's covenant. Sapiential sayings now give way to prophetic sayings, and these are no longer exclusively community-directed. The genre of Q also shifts, to chreia collection.[70]

Although Kloppenborg does not indicate how this proposed history of the composition of Q might translate into a history of the Q community, there are some implications for such a history. The earliest or "formative" layer of Q itself involved the redaction of earlier sayings which had been largely intended for wandering missionaries. The redaction at this formative stage consisted of various additions which had the effect of broadening the significance of these sayings so that they would be relevant to a larger community. It was this missionary-sending community which produced the first recension of Q. Kloppenborg does not adopt the increasingly common phrase "wandering charismatics," presumably because, according to his view, the oldest material was sapiential, not prophetic. Thus we have as predecessors of Q, and presumably as the earliest bearers of its tradition, wandering (sapiential) missionaries. They were succeeded by a community which was perhaps established by these missionaries but was itself a sedentary, Greek-speaking Jewish-Christian community.

What prompted the second recension seems to have been the failure of the mission to Israel. This is reflected in the often bitter announcements of judgment against those fellow Jews who refused to receive the missionaries and their message. For reasons not immediately apparent, the prophetic mode now comes to dominate, though the tendency at work in the redaction is "historicizing" rather than "contemporizing." This is evident in the "chriic" forms into which the sayings are cast. Several other features of this second recension are noteworthy: the sudden appearance of a large batch of material related to John the Baptist; the appearance of the idea of Sophia; the deuteronomistic perspective; an infusion of apocalyptic material; and the generally "polemical" nature of the material.

This is an attractive reconstruction in that it traces a trajectory from the earliest followers of Jesus, the wandering missionaries, on to the earliest Palestinian (?) communities. It sees already in Q itself, in its second recension, the polemic that would eventually lead the sect to separate from Judaism. It also agrees with Koester's view that the earliest tradition in Q was sapiential, not apocalyptic.[71]

Nevertheless, some questions must be asked concerning Kloppenborg's reconstruction. Kloppenborg makes a rather sharp distinction between the sapiential nature of his first recension and the qualities of his second recension (prophetic and apocalyptic announcement of judgment; "chriic" forms; po-

---

70. For the chreia form and genre see Kloppenborg, *Formation*, 264–89; for Q as member of that genre see *Formation*, 322–25.

71. See Koester, "One Jesus and Four Primitive Gospels," 185–87; "Apocryphal and Canonical Gospels," 112–19; "Überlieferung und Geschichte der frühchristlichen Evangelienliteratur," 1512–24; and "Q—At the Conclusion of Five Years of the Seminar," esp. p. 7.

lemic as opposed to community instruction). On the one hand, it is curious that although the first recension is "sapiential," it is only in the second recension that we get the figure of Wisdom. Further, there are a number of sayings in Kloppenborg's first recension which are commonly identified as prophetic. This is especially true of Q 10:2–16 and Q 12:2–12. M. Eugene Boring, for example, identifies as prophetic (i.e., either created or shaped by Christian prophets) the following sayings assigned by Kloppenborg to the first recension: Q 10:2, 3, 4, 5–11, 16; 12:2–3, 4–7, 11–12, 22–34.[72] Thus the distinction between the first two recensions as a distinction between sapiential and prophetic material seems in need of further examination. Of course, even if Kloppenborg is wrong in finding no prophetic material in his first recension, that would not of itself argue against the correctness of his division of the material into two main recensions. But it would call into question his view of the genre of the first recension.

Another distinction between the first and second recensions is that the latter "is characterized by chriic forms."[73] Yet Q 9:57–62, assigned by Kloppenborg to the first recension, contains formally the best examples of chreiai in Q. The phrase "chriic forms" is rather ambiguous. For example, Q 7:1–10 is described as "chriic." Q 3:7–9 seems to have been provided with a brief setting (with no direct relation to the saying), but the saying itself is a prophetic utterance. And the number of chriic forms adduced seems rather small: Q 3:7–9; 7:1–10, 18–23; 10:21–22; 11:14–15.

According to Kloppenborg, large chunks of new material make their appearance in the second recension. This includes all the sayings related to John the Baptist, the Beelzebul controversy, and the Q apocalypse. Apparently, this material circulated neither as isolated sayings nor as a single collection of material but as "speeches," i.e., sayings compositions.

This need to postulate an influx of new materials which had been "edited" at the (presumably) oral stage raises additional questions. Where did these materials come from? How can we account for the sudden appearance of a large block of Baptist materials? The peculiarities of the theology of Q suggest that the community was relatively isolated; but the influx of materials suggests that, at the second recension stage at least, the community was not so isolated. In short, the problems with Kloppenborg's division of the material into two recensions are considerable. Though he has contributed a sophisticated analysis of Q, his proposed compositional history of Q is not without its problems.[74]

72. Boring, *Sayings of the Risen Jesus.* See esp. chap. 11, "Christian Prophecy in Q," 137–82.

73. Kloppenborg, *Formation*, 322. A list of chreiai in this recension is given by Kloppenborg on p. 168.

74. Kloppenborg's proposal has already generated much discussion, and has found an appreciative response. Suggestions for testing his proposal have been offered by Crossan ("Tradition in the Formation of Q") and Koester ("Q—At the Conclusion of Five Years of the [SBL Q] Seminar"). Crossan provides a tentative examination at the "gross level" of the antiquity of the traditions in Kloppenborg's two main recensions, concluding that his test

3. Walter Schmithals

For purposes of comparison, it may be useful to consider a radically different proposal. Schmithals' proposal is just that. In fact, a proposal more radically different from Kloppenborg's is hard to imagine.[75]

Walter Schmithals has proposed a new sketch of the history of Q, though it builds upon the work of the German redaction critics.[76] His point of departure is the claim that unchristologized sayings had a different circle of tradents than christological sayings. Thus, he posits an early "sayings tradition" called Q^1 which includes material in Mark, most notably the Q/Markan doublets. This was not a document so much as a "growing layer."[77] It is prophetic-apocalyptic material devoid of christology, characterized by fervent expectation of the Kingdom or the son of man (not yet identified with Jesus) and an "interim ethic"; this material was Palestinian and Aramaic. Although Schmithals does not assign this material to a specific group, he does speak of a "community" which persisted in its "pre-Easter status"[78] at least until 70 c.e. But some apparently persisted even longer; Schmithals identifies these individuals or groups with the Judaizing sectarians condemned by early Christian writers.[79] He hints that the Apollos of Acts 18:25–26 may have belonged to this community, and may have been responsible for carrying this tradition to Corinth, where Paul encountered it.[80]

Mark, claims Schmithals, sought, among other things, to convert this group to the church or the kerygma around the year 75 c.e.[81] Mark used parts of Q. In fact, Schmithals thinks it not impossible that the "author" of Q and the author of Mark were one and the same![82] The christological, universalistic redaction of Q was composed as an *"expansion"* of Mark,[83] and Q and Mark were disseminated together. This accounts for Matthew and Luke indepen-

appears to confirm Kloppenborg's results. Koester examines the relationship between Kloppenborg's two recensions and the Gospel of Thomas, and concludes that this test also lends credence to Kloppenborg's proposal. More precisely, these tests suggest that a number of the sayings assigned to Q^1 (i.e., the first stage of Q) are older than many of the sayings in Q^2. Affirmative too is Mack's examination of the social history of Q in relation to Kloppenborg's two basic layers ("The Kingdom That Didn't Come"). Critical of Kloppenborg's analysis is Horsley ("Questions"). Kloppenborg has responded in *"The Formation of Q* Revisited." In "Formative and Redactional Layers in Q" Kloppenborg compares several major stratigraphic proposals (Kloppenborg, Polag, Jacobson, Sato, Schenk, Schmithals).

75. Kloppenborg has responded to Schmithals' proposal, characterizing it as methodologically unsound; see "Formative and Redactional Layers in Q."

76. Schmithals, *Einleitung,* esp. 384–404; a much briefer version is found in "Evangelien," 620–23.

77. Schmithals, *Einleitung,* 401, quoting the Jülicher-Fascher *Einleitung.*

78. Schmithals, *Einleitung,* 404.

79. Schmithals, *Einleitung,* 403.

80. Schmithals, *Einleitung,* 404.

81. Schmithals, *Einleitung,* 403.

82. Schmithals, *Einleitung,* 403.

83. Schmithals, *Einleitung,* 403.

dently incorporating Q into the Markan framework. The redaction created a new beginning for Q, with John the Baptist now as precursor of the messiah (Q 3:1–22), followed by the temptation (4:1–13); the redacted Q ended with a specially composed parable in 19:11–27.[84] Schmithals has no list of newly added materials, but they include, besides those already mentioned, Q 7:18–23 and 14:15–24, plus smaller additions (Q 6:22; 7:34; 10:21–22; 12:8–9, 10; 11:30; 12:40; 13:25–26, 29–30, 35b; 17:24, 26, 30; 22:28–30 and, apparently, 9:57–62).[85] Schmithals is unclear about wisdom sayings in Q, indicating his uncertainty whether they were even in Q^1.[86] This material is problematic for Schmithals' scheme since he holds that Q^1 was entirely apocalyptic.

The major weakness of Schmithals' proposal is that it is not based on a careful redaction-critical analysis of the text; or if it is, that analysis is not provided. Rather, it seems to be spun out of theories and assumptions, many beholden to conventional theological assumptions in Germany about the evolution of early Christianity. Its procedure is similar to, but less sophisticated than, that of Schulz in that it simply separates Q into two piles, christological and non-christological, without regard to the task of showing how specific sayings compositions or larger units within Q might have evolved.

Schmithals' proposal, moreover, is weak at certain specific points. For example, it is unable to deal with the wisdom material in Q—a fundamental weakness. In this connection, Schmithals' failure to take seriously the genre of Q should also be noted. Further, Schmithals makes much of the Q/Mark doublets, claiming that, with the exception (!) of the Baptist and temptation accounts, all the doublets in Q are (a) sayings and (b) non-christological. This is hardly surprising since most of Q consists of non-christological sayings. In any case, the doublets do not provide the weighty evidence Schmithals assumes; he has not noticed the fundamental differences between the uses made of this material by Mark and by Q. Likewise, the judgment that Mark used Q is at best debatable. How little Schmithals attends to the differences between Mark and Q is shown by his suggestion that their authors might be one and the same!

4. Migaku Sato

Sato's *Q und Prophetie* (Q and Prophecy), originally a doctoral dissertation under Luz (accepted in 1984–85), is one of the most significant contributions to the study of Q. It represents easily the most elaborately argued alternative to the view of Robinson, Koester and Kloppenborg that Q is a sapiential collection. Because of its importance, but also because it is not as readily accessible to the non-specialist, Sato's book needs to be treated more fully.

84. Schmithals, *Einleitung*, 397–98.
85. Schmithals, *Einleitung*, 398, 399.
86. Schmithals, *Einleitung*, 402.

His basic argument is that Q belongs to the *"Makro-gattung"* (major genre) of "prophetic book." The "major genre" of "prophetic book" has not, as Sato notes, been the subject of scholarly examination, which has focused instead on the "minor genres" (*Mikro-gattungen*) of prophetic speech. A study of the superscriptions to the prophetic books shows that there was a clear consciousness of the identity of the prophetic book at least by the time of the post-exilic deuteronomistic movement.[87] Prophetic books have four basic characteristics: (a) a claim of direct divine origin for the prophetic oracles they contain; (b) identification of the divine oracles with a specific human figure; (c) use of specifically prophetic minor genres; and (d) evidence of original oral proclamation.[88]

Q, Sato argues, shares most of the characteristics of a prophetic book. By contrast, he gives a number of reasons why Q is more adequately seen as a prophetic than as a wisdom book: its exclusive focus on a charismatic figure who is decisive for salvation (something without parallel in wisdom literature); the sayings are not general as in wisdom literature but directed to specific situations, as in prophetic books; like prophetic books, but unlike wisdom, Q has an eschatological cast; and Q contains many typically prophetic minor genres.[89] It should be noted that these arguments are less appropriate with respect to Kloppenborg's proposal than to Robinson's, because Kloppenborg's genre analysis is based more on non-Jewish hellenistic and Egyptian works rather than on Israelite wisdom. Sato argues that Q, at least in its more developed stage, was *consciously* modeled after the prophetic book[90]; therefore, the ways in which Q deviates from prophetic books become all the more problematic: Q has more wisdom sayings than is typical of prophetic books, it contains no superscription or quotation formulas, and Sato's hesitant claim that Luke 3:21–22//Matt 3:16–17 provides the analogue to a prophetic call story fails because the text was not in Q. These problems do not fundamentally call Sato's thesis into question, however.

Sato's careful examination of minor genres in prophetic books is a valuable contribution.[91] He notes first that prophetic books lack certain minor genres: similitudes or parables; miracle stories; legends and accounts of the death of the prophet.[92] This too is similar to Q which, to be sure, has a few similitudes (mostly in prophetic contexts) and perhaps a parable or two, but little interest in miracles or legends.[93] He acknowledges that Q differs from prophetic books

---

87. Sato, *Q und Prophetie*, 70–74.
88. Sato, *Q und Prophetie*, 76–83.
89. Sato, *Q und Prophetie*, 4–5.
90. Sato, *Q und Prophetie*, 95, 383.
91. Sato, *Q und Prophetie*, 80–81.
92. Sato, *Q und Prophetie*, chap. 4 (pp. 108–313), "Comparison of the Minor Genres in the Old Testament Prophetic Books and in the Q Source."
93. Sato, *Q und Prophetie*, 81–82.

in two respects: it has more wisdom sayings than is typical of prophetic books, and it has a sending narrative, which has no parallel in the prophetic books.[94]

The most basic of the minor prophetic genres is the "announcement" (*Ankündigung*), which is amply attested in Q (e.g., Q 3:16; 10:9b, 15; 11:20; 12:10; 13:28-29; 17:34-35; 7:22).[95] It is to Sato's credit that he also investigates the subsequent history of these genres in intertestamental literature; in this case, he shows that the "announcement" is very rare in apocalyptic literature.

Another basic minor genre is the "doom saying" (*Unheilswort*) found, for example, in Amos 3:9-11. This form is also rare in apocalyptic literature (Sato frequently calls attention to the differences between prophecy and apocalyptic literature). It is found in Q in 11:31-32; 11:49-51 and 13:34-35. Sato notes how unusual it is that the "doom saying" against the nation as a whole, which was so common among the pre-exilic prophets and then almost disappears, reappears in Q.[96] He assumes that some of the prophetic oracles in Q are the products of prophets in the Q circle (who are not to be lumped together with other early Christian prophets), and that here we encounter something novel and remarkable—like the Hebrew prophets, they are the mouthpieces for prophetic revelation, but the source of this revelation is the exalted Jesus rather than God.[97] In Q as well as in the prophetic books, the doom saying reflects the prophet's confrontation with the present situation and the motif of the reversal of all relationships. In a brief excursus in this context, Sato considers the possibility of a Sophia christology in Q,[98] and concludes that Sophia and Jesus are not identified, but that some "functional elements" of the divine Sophia idea have influenced the understanding in Q of the exalted Jesus/son of man.

Sato's results in the cases of other minor genres contain some surprises. The "salvation saying" (*Heilswort*)[99] is only faintly echoed in a few Q passages (6:20b-21; 6:22-23; 12:11-12). The "salvation oracle" (*Heilsorakel*), on the other hand, is of priestly origin and is attested in Q only in 12:32, though echoed in 12:4-7.[100] The "reproach" (*Scheltwort*) is another minor genre that is not specifically prophetic though it was "prophetized" and used either alone or as part of a doom saying.[101] Independent reproaches are found only in Q 6:46 and 7:33-34, and in combination with other genres in Q 3:7 and 13:34.

94. Sato, *Q und Prophetie*, 82.
95. Sato, *Q und Prophetie*, 116-46.
96. Sato, *Q und Prophetie*, 160; for the whole discussion of this minor genre, see pp. 146-60.
97. Sato, *Q und Prophetie*, 160; cf. 393-96.
98. Sato, *Q und Prophetie*, 160-61.
99. Sato, *Q und Prophetie*, 161-66.
100. Sato, *Q und Prophetie*, 166-75.
101. Sato, *Q und Prophetie*, 175-83. Sato coins the word "prophetizing" to designate the adaption of non-prophetic literary forms to the prophetic tradition, whose main features are described on pp. 96-106; see esp. p. 99.

The similitude in 7:31–32 has a function similar to the reproach. In the case of the "woe" (*Weheruf*), Sato follows Gunther Wanke in distinguishing between woes that begin with הוי and those that begin with the more uniquely prophetic אוי; the latter tend to be used in groups.[102] This distinction gradually disappeared, especially in the Septuagint. In Q, woes are found in 11:39–52; 10:13–14 and 6:24–26 (which Sato assigns to the Lukan recension of Q). Most of these are the characteristically prophetic אוי-woes.[103]

Another minor genre, the "admonition" (*Mahnwort*), has its origins in the wisdom tradition, although it too was "prophetized" by the prophets (e.g., by giving it an eschatological motivation). The wisdom admonitions in Q are not prophetic admonitions but they do show considerable evidence of being "prophetized."[104]

The "messenger formula" (*Botenformel*) is not really a minor genre but only a formula. It is common in the prophets but rare in apocalyptic literature and in Q, occurring in the latter only once (11:49). Sato attributes this to the dissolution of the formula over time. It should be noted, however, that in other cases Sato claims that Q reintroduced minor prophetic forms, so his suggestion is not entirely convincing. Sato argues that a direct relationship of the "I say to you" (λέγω ὑμῖν) formula to the messenger formula cannot be confirmed; its origins may lie as much in the wisdom tradition as in prophecy. The odd non-responsorial "amen" (always linked to "I say to you") has its origin, according to Sato, in Jesus. Even though this formula is completely lacking in Q, Sato thinks it probable that the "I say to you" formula implies more than the mere strengthening of personal authority which is typical of the "I say to you" formula, i.e., that implicit is some of the eschatological character of the "amen [truly], I say to you."[105]

Some minor genres which are often taken to be "prophetic" are, according to Sato, not truly so. The "sentences of holy law" are not really a genre; "eschatological correlatives" really belong to the genre, "comparison"; the "macarism" or beatitude has its origin in wisdom, though Jesus again "prophetized" this form.[106] And the "I have come" (ἦλθον) sayings are a type introduced by Jesus.[107]

If Q is like a prophetic book in the ways already described, it is also like them, according to Sato, in its compositional history. Many of the same compositional techniques used in prophetic books (thematic association;

---

102. Sato, *Q und Prophetie*, 183–85.

103. Sato, *Q und Prophetie*, 194–201.

104. Sato, *Q und Prophetie*, 202–25.

105. For the whole discussion, see Sato, *Q und Prophetie*, 226–47.

106. The macarism was "prophetized" by use of direct address; focus on the "poor"; and the use of the eschatological "for" (ὅτι); also the first beatitude, unlike the next two, is not simply compensatory—it does not declare that the "poor" will become rich (Sato, *Q und Prophetie*, 254–56).

107. On sentences of holy law, eschatological correlatives, and ἦλθον sayings, see Sato, *Q und Prophetie*, 264–99.

catchword connection; framing; chronological order) are found in Q.[108] Unlike other prophetic books, however, Q does not use a hymnic ending for the document as a whole or for collections within it, nor does Q conclude with a promissory word (or saying of doom). However, the latter technique was used to conclude units within Q.

One of the most interesting parts of Sato's book is his sketch of the compositional history of Q,[109] though this analysis is strangely disconnected from the rest of the discussion. First, he distinguishes among the "individual saying" (*Einzelspruch*), the "sayings group" (*Spruchgruppe*) containing only a few sayings, the "sayings collection" (*Spruchsammlung*)—a larger group of sayings, and "redaction," which is an independent, written entity. It is not possible to review his examination of the structure and composition of Q. However, the basic results may be sketched. He identifies the Q material in Luke 3:2 to 7:28 as "Redaction A." Its theme is John the Baptist. Numerous links exist between the first and the later parts of this unit, e.g., the focus on John in chapters 3 and 7, the title "coming one" (3:16; 7:19), and the wilderness context (3:3; 7:24). Jesus' first and last sayings deal with the "kingdom" (6:20b; 7:28b) and with the "poor" (6:20b; 7:22b). Jesus' "programmatic speech" (Q 6:20b-49) may be seen as an elaboration of the Baptist's call for bearing fruit. Sato regards 7:27 and the temptation account as later additions. Within Redaction A are various individual sayings and sayings groups (e.g., 3:7-9, 16-17) and a sayings collection (6:20b-49).

Sato identifies the next block of Q material as Q 9:57-10:24. This is "Redaction B." It has a brief narrative (or apophthegmatic) introduction (9:57-60) and focuses on the theme of the sending of disciples. The judgment that this is a self-enclosed unit, incidentally, leads him to interpret the troublesome "these things" (ταῦτα) in 10:21b as the presently accessible salvation mentioned in 10:5-6 ("peace") and 10:9 ("kingdom"). But here too are later additions: Q 10:22 and 10:(12), 13-15. Sato regards Redactions A and B as independent units with different *Sitze im Leben*.

Redactions A and B were brought together in another stage, Redaction C, during which other material was also added: 7:31-34, 35 as the bridge between Redactions A and B; 11:14-32, 39-52 and 13:23-35, and perhaps also 12:2-34 and 17:23-27. During this stage, 10:12, 13-15 were added to Redaction B. Two themes, now combined, predominate in Redaction C: the announcement of judgment to "this generation" and the Sophia motif. At various undeterminable times, other smaller insertions were made as well, such as the temptation account (4:2b-13), as well as 7:27; 10:22 and perhaps 6:43-45; 6:39, 40 and 17:23-37. Sato's division of the material in the first part of Q is almost identical with that proposed in this book, even though the two analyses were based on independent research.

108. Sato, *Q und Prophetie*, 83-90.
109. Sato, *Q und Prophetie*, 28-68.

The basic conclusion by Sato is that Q grew by stages. This growth, he argues, continued after the three discernible stages he describes, i.e., in the different recensions of Q to which Matthew and Luke had access. This leads Sato into the adventurous, if risky, effort to identify the material peculiar to Matthew and Luke which probably belonged to each recension.[110]

Interesting too is Sato's effort to specify upon what materials Q would have been written, and, more importantly, to determine whether the compositional process he describes makes sense in terms of the known methods of assembling written materials.[111] The evidence available, says Sato, indicates that Q would probably have been written on a loose-leaf parchment notebook, with holes punched in the pages so that the leaves could be bound with (probably) leather thongs. It is doubtful that the codex (book) yet existed. The loose-leaf notebook, however, would have facilitated just such literary growth as Sato describes. This same process, Sato believes, lies behind the compositional history of the prophetic books. They, to be sure, were written on scrolls, but there is evidence that earlier stages of composition utilized wooden tablets (see Isa 8:1; 30:8; Ezek 37:16-17; Hab 2:2), ostraca or papyrus for preliminary sketches and notes.[112] Hans Walter Wolff postulated such sketches behind, e.g., Hos 4:1-9:9; 10:9-15; 12:1-15; 13:1-14; 14:2-9 and Mic 1:6-3:2.[113] Separate portions of prophetic books may, in fact, have been used for preaching and instruction even after the composition of the whole book.[114]

Sato also draws a number of parallels between the presumed bearers of the Q tradition, whom he sometimes calls the "Q circle," and groups of the disciples of prophets. He follows the description of the earliest Jesus community in Gerd Theissen's *The Sociology of Early Palestinian Christianity*, according to which there were two groups: the wandering charismatics and the settled sympathizers.[115] These had a complicated complementary relationship. Sato, however, goes beyond Theissen in arguing that the wandering charismatics functioned both as bearers of the Jesus tradition and as prophets. This allows him to account both for the preservation of the Jesus tradition and for the creation of new sayings of the exalted Lord. It also suggests a more complicated *Sitz im Leben* for Q—in fact, *Sitze im Leben* for various parts of Q—as already noted for Redactions A, B, and C.[116] The two roles of the wandering charismatics corresponds to their two functions: to provide instruction for the narrower circle of wandering charismatic followers and to proclaim the master's (=Jesus') message to the people as a whole. Sato finds parallels for these

110. Sato, *Q und Prophetie*, 47-62.
111. Sato, *Q und Prophetie*, 62-68, 390, 392-93.
112. Sato, *Q und Prophetie*, 391-93; see also 74-46, 320-22.
113. Sato (*Q und Prophetie*, 320) here makes reference to Wolff's commentaries on the Minor Prophets, but does not give exact references.
114. See Sato, *Q und Prophetie*, 320-22.
115. Sato, *Q und Prophetie*, 379-81.
116. Sato, *Q und Prophetie*, 388-90, 393-99.

roles and functions in the prophetic tradition, where disciples gathered who also left their homes, wandered from place to place, and preserved their master's words.[117] In many respects, John seems to have been a precursor in these matters. Interesting is Sato's claim that John is a "prophetic 'mutation' within the apocalyptic tradition," and that he and Jesus both represent the "re-prophetizing of apocalyptic."[118] Both are throwbacks to the earlier prophetic period, especially to Elijah and Elisha. A similar claim is made of Q as a whole: it represents "an atavism in terms of the history of the genre" of the prophetic book.[119]

The strength of Sato's book lies in its careful examination of the minor and major genres of prophetic speech, and in showing numerous parallels between Q and prophecy as a phenomenon in Israel's history.[120] He believes that Jesus was a prophet,[121] but also that there was a prophetizing of the Jesus tradition, especially in Redaction C where a conscious effort was made to conform the Jesus tradition to the genre of prophetic book. Precisely here, however, Sato becomes vulnerable to criticism, because if the Jesus tradition was "prophetized," then it could be argued that prophecy is a secondary accretion, as, in fact, Mack has argued.[122] On the other hand, Sato's argument is carefully nuanced; he does not simply force everything into a prophetic Procrustean bed.

Even though Sato's book presents a comprehensive theory about Q, however, its examination of the Q materials is not comprehensive. Especially problematic is his decision to make compositional history the first step rather than the goal of the analysis. This is all the more troubling when one notes how isolated this compositional history is from the exegetical portion of his study.

Questions also need to be raised about specific points, such as his heavy emphasis on discipleship even though the word "disciple," and disciples' names, are absent from Q; his claim that the absence of a passion narrative can be attributed to the desire to imitate the genre of prophetic book[123]; his judgment that in Q John the Baptist is clearly subordinated to Jesus; his assumption that Q presupposes Jesus' exaltation/resurrection[124]; and his estimate of the role of eschatology in Q. Nevertheless, Sato's book represents a significant and viable alternative to the sapiential understanding of Q.

117. See Sato, *Q und Prophetie*, 391–92, 395–96, 398–99, 400–403 and the more extensive investigation of the phenomenon of prophetic disciples, 314–42.

118. Sato, *Q und Prophetie*, 373.

119. Sato, *Q und Prophetie*, 301; see also 407.

120. So large a role does the study of Hebrew prophecy play in the book that one reviewer noted that it could have been entitled, "Prophecy and Q" (review by Suhl, 671).

121. See esp. Sato, *Q und Prophetie*, 373–75.

122. Mack, *A Myth of Innocence*, 85–87.

123. Sato, *Q und Prophetie*, 382–83.

124. Sato, *Q und Prophetie*, 378.

Methodology: Toward a New Consensus

There is growing agreement on a methodology for the study of Q which is appropriate to the document and which can yield answers to the questions that are most fundamental. What is needed is a history of the composition of Q. Redaction and composition criticism are the primary tools for such a history, though form-critical analysis of the sayings compositions is also indispensable. It may be that a rhetorical analysis will also prove useful in moving us beyond the present impasse. But if there is significant agreement about which scholarly tools to use, there is less agreement about the particulars of the compositional history of Q. This is perhaps to be expected at this relatively early stage in the history of the study of Q. Differences are apparent in the weight that is given to the sapiential and prophetic components in Q and, perhaps more fundamentally, to sapiential and prophetic models for the genre of Q. These differences suggest that the basic character of Q remains unclear. Progress toward answering this question may, perhaps, be made by examining the question of the literary unity of Q, which is the question to which we turn in the next chapter.

4
The Literary Unity of Q

Form Critical and Thematic Coherence

The issue addressed in this chapter is whether there is evidence that the various passages where Matthew and Luke are in agreement over against Mark really belong together as part of a single document. This point has been stressed several times already. An effort to discover evidence of literary unity must take first place methodologically, since only if such evidence can be found is it possible to hold that Q was a single document, and thus to proceed with the compositional analysis of Q.

Literary unity may be defined as "the concept that a literary work shall have in it some organizing principle in relation to which all its parts are related so that, viewed in the light of this principle, the work is an organic whole."[1] Since in Q we are dealing with traditional sayings material rather than free composition by an author, we might expect to find the kind of miscellaneous assortment of sayings that one often finds in sayings collections rather than a high degree of literary unity. Nevertheless, the idea of literary unity is useful because it directs attention to a unity of conception which may stand behind quite varied aspects of a document, including its genre, its vocabulary and word usage, its themes, its smaller forms, and its redactional traits.

In the following, I shall first call attention to certain features of Q which are distinctive, especially over against Mark, in terms of form as well as content. Then we shall see if some "organizing principle" can render comprehensible the characteristics that are noted.

Before doing that, however, we may note one small but very striking example of the distinctive usage of Q over against that of Mark. In Q, the quotation formula, "I say to you" ($\lambda\acute{\epsilon}\gamma\omega$ $\dot{\upsilon}\mu\hat{\iota}\nu$) *never* occurs with the word "truly" ($\dot{\alpha}\mu\acute{\eta}\nu$ or $\dot{\alpha}\lambda\eta\theta\hat{\omega}\varsigma$), although there is one instance of "yes, I tell you" ($\nu\alpha\acute{\iota}$, $\lambda\acute{\epsilon}\gamma\omega$ $\dot{\upsilon}\mu\hat{\iota}\nu$, Q 7:26). In fact, the word "truly" does not occur anywhere in Q; at least, there is no double attestation of it. But Mark has fourteen instances of the "I say to you" formula, and in all but two, he has "truly" ($\dot{\alpha}\mu\acute{\eta}\nu$); see Mark 3:28; 8:12; 9:1, 13, 41; 10:15, 29; 11:23, 24; 13:30; 14:9, 18, 25, 30). In at least one case the absence of "truly" is easily explainable: it is used in the previous

---

1. Thrall and Hibbard, *A Handbook to Literature*, 500.

verse (11:23, 24). The consistency of Markan usage is as dramatic as the fact that "truly" (ἀμήν) is never found in Q, even though it occurs often in Matthew and six times in Luke. Not only does this illustrate the difference in usage between Mark and Q, but it is also a potent argument for the Two Document hypothesis.

A Form-Critical Survey of Q

We shall be looking here for forms distinctive of Q and/or for distinctive qualities in these forms, especially those attributable to redactional activity. What is distinctive of Q can often be seen by comparing the Q material with Mark.[2]

1. Forms Common in Q but Rare in Mark

(a) Macarisms. There are at least seven macarisms scattered throughout the Q material.[3] By contrast, Mark has only two (Mark 11:9–10); one of these is from the Old Testament, the other is a formulation based upon it. Also, Q consistently uses μακάριος (except Q 13:35=Ps 117:26 LXX); Mark uses forms of εὐλογεῖν (to bless). What is striking, then, is the relative abundance of macarisms in Q and their scarcity in Mark.

At least one macarism in Q is identifiable as a later creation, namely Q 6:22–23, but here we can observe two stages of composition.[4] The first concerns the suffering of the righteous on behalf of the son of man; the second stage (Q 6:23c) interprets the persecution encountered as merely one more instance of Israel's persistent opposition to the prophets. In the first stage (Q 6:22–23b), a traditional macarism (cf. GThom 68; 1 Pet 4:14) is taken up and interpreted in light of the son of man. The second stage puts those blessed not in the tradition of martyrs but of prophets, and introduces the deuteronomistic tra-

---

2. I assume the literary independence of Mark and Q, as well as their use of some shared traditions. For the study of the theology of Q, it is advisable to include only those possibly shared traditions where there is significant evidence of Q, and where there is sufficient recoverable Q material to support the argument that this material presents a point of view different from Mark's. I include among these esp. Mark 1:1–8; 4:30–32; 6:6b–13; 8:11–13 and their Q parallels.

There has been a good deal of recent research on the problem of the relation between Mark and Q. See Laufen, *Die Doppelüberlieferungen*; Luz, "Das Jesusbild"; Devisch, "La relation"; Schenk, "Der Einfluss"; Vassiliadis, "Prolegomena." For Lührmann's use of Mark in studying the redaction of Q, see *Redaktion*, 20–21; recently, Lührmann has written more extensively on this subject (see "The Gospel of Mark and the Sayings Collection Q"). Schillebeeckx depends upon the distinction between Mark and Q in his attempt to examine the emergence of christology; see *Jesus: An Experiment*, 100–102, 146–54, 183–94, 219–29, 233–43, 264–69, 274–76, 282–91, 403–23, 429–32, 472–80; 486–99, 533–44. Schillebeeckx is heavily indebted to Schulz, but his work represents the first effort by a systematic theologian to make extensive use of recent Q research.

3. Q 6:20, 21 (twice), 22–23; 7:23; 10:23; 12:43; possibly also Luke 11:28 (Q?).

4. So Steck, *Israel*, 20–26.

dition of the violent fate of the prophets.[5] Thus, where redaction can be most easily observed, namely in relation to an old collection of macarisms, the tendency at work at the latest stage derives from the deuteronomistic tradition and emphasizes that the addressees, the Q community, stand in direct continuity with the prophets of old who also experienced Israel's impenitence in the form of hostility to them and their message.

(b) Woes. There seem to have been at least nine woes in Q, seven of which had already been gathered into a sayings composition.[6] By contrast, Mark has no woes at all.

Again, redactional activity is observable in Q, namely at the end of the collection of woes. The old woes accuse Jewish leaders of hypocrisy and reflect inner-Jewish debate.[7] To them have been added an expanded woe (Q 11:47–48) and a threat (Q 11:49–51) which accuse Israel of always persecuting the prophets. The threat says that "this generation" will now experience God's wrath. Thus, where redactional activity is observable we again encounter the deuteronomistic tradition. Here, however, it is linked with the idea of Wisdom as sender of the prophets. This association of a particular form of wisdom tradition with the deuteronomistic tradition is, as we shall see, found elsewhere in Q and is unique in the gospel tradition.

(c) The Eschatological Correlative. The eschatological correlative, a form identified by Edwards,[8] occurs four times in Q,[9] but never in Mark. As with the macarisms and woes, the eschatological correlatives tend to be clustered together (three of the four occur in Q 17:22–37). The eschatological correlative is a prophetic form of speech.[10] It belongs to the tradition rather than to the redaction of Q.[11]

---

5. Steck, *Israel*, 257–60.

6. The woes are in Q 10:13 (twice); 11:39 (Matthean version only), 42, 43, 44, 46 (Lukan version only), 47, 52; and possibly Q 17:1 (on this last, see Bultmann, *History of the Synoptic Tradition*, 144–45). On the collection of woes, see Bultmann, *History of the Synoptic Tradition*, 113–14; Lührmann, *Redaktion*, 43–48; Boring, *Sayings of the Risen Jesus*, 153–57; and Kloppenborg, *Formation*, 139–47. Later we will examine the original sequence of the Q woe collection.

7. This will be discussed in chap. 7.

8. See Edwards, "The Eschatological Correlative."

9. Q 11:30; 17:24, 26, 28.

10. See Schmidt, "The LXX *Gattung* 'Prophetic Correlative,'" 517–22. Schmidt claims to have found the LXX prophetic form which stands behind the "sentences of holy law" (Käsemann) and the eschatological correlative. His evidence calls into question Edwards's view that the eschatological correlative was created by the Q community. However, his evidence is drawn only from the Old Testament, excluding the apocrypha (but see, e.g., Bar 4:24, 33). His assumption of direct use of the LXX ignores the underlying correlatives in the Hebrew text (e.g., . . . כֵּן . . . כַּאֲשֶׁר in Isa 20:3–4; 55:10–11; Jer 5:19; 31:28; 32:42; 42:18; Ezek 12:11) and the possible continuation of such prophetic usage in later Jewish writings. But if Schmidt's view is correct, then the apocalyptic son of man sayings in Q 17:24, 26, 28, 30 presuppose a prophetic tradition which used the LXX. See further Aune, *Prophecy*, 168–69, and Kloppenborg, *Formation*, 129–30. Aune notes that the correlative form is not peculiar to prophetic speech; however, the eschatological correlative is prophetic.

11. In the small sayings composition in Q 11:29–32, the latest stage is, as we shall see later,

(d) Prophetic Threats (*Drohworte*). Q has a number of prophetic threats. Bultmann discusses fifteen such sayings or clusters of sayings.[12] Of the fifteen, twelve (or thirteen, if Luke 6:24–26 is assigned to Q) occur in Q. Mark has two such sayings, both also known to Q. But the prophetic threats in Mark (8:38; 12:38–40) are really only warnings, while in Q most of the sayings announce judgment in view of impenitence or failure to respond to a divine appeal.[13] Especially revealing is a comparison of Mark 12:38–40 with Q 11:39–52. Mark has mere warnings, but in Q we have prophetic woes. Common in the prophetic threats in Q is the use of invidious comparison[14] and of explicit reference to a call and its rejection.[15] Rhetorical questions are also common.[16]

It is relevant at this point to note that a comparison of word usage related to the prophetic announcement of judgment reveals a sharp contrast between Mark and Q. Words related to judgment are common in Q but completely missing from Mark.[17] Even more striking are the frequent references to the "day" ($\dot{\eta}\mu\dot{\epsilon}\rho\alpha$) of judgment.[18] Mark has the "days" of tribulation and the "day" of the parousia, but he speaks of the "day" of judgment only once (Mark 13:32). It may be noted that in Q the "day" is often associated with the son of man; that is not characteristic of Mark's use of the son of man title. Further, the pejorative epithet, "this generation," while found in Mark (8:12, 38; 9:19; 13:30), is used with greater uniformity in Q.[19]

(e) *Doppelbildworte* (Paired Figurative Sayings). This phenomenon, noted by Joachim Jeremias,[20] has recently been investigated by Michael G. Steinhauser.[21] Of the nineteen instances cited by Steinhauser, eleven are from Q[22] and only three from Mark.[23]

to be found in Q 11:31–32, which reflects wisdom and deuteronomistic traditions. The eschatological correlative in Q 11:30 belongs to an earlier stage in the redaction of Q.

12. Bultmann, *History of the Synoptic Tradition*, 111–18.

13. Q 3:7–9; 6:46; 10:13–15; 11:31–32, (39), 42–44, 46–47, 52, 49–51; 12:8–9, 54–56; 13:26–27, 28–29, 34–35; 17:26–27, 34–35. Q 11:47–51 takes the form of a prophecy of disaster; see Steck, *Israel*, 51–53, and March, "Prophecy," 159–62.

14. Q 10:13–15; 11:31–32; 12:54–56; 13:28–29.

15. Q 10:13–15; 11:31–32, 49–51; 12:8–9; 13:34–35.

16. Q 3:7–9; 6:46; 10:13–15; 12:54–56.

17. κρίνειν: Q, 3 times; Mark, 0 (Q 6:37–38 [twice]; 22:30); κρίσις: Q, 4/6; Mark, 0 (Q 10:14; 11:31, 32, 42; cf. Matt 10:15; 11:24 [cf. Lk 10:12]); κριτής: Q, 3; Mark, 0 (Q 11:19; 12:58 [twice]).

18. Matt 7:22 (cf. Luke 6:46; 13:26–27); Luke 17:24 (cf. Matt 24:27); Q 17:26, 27, 30; Matt 11:22 (cf. Luke 10:14); Q 12:40; Matt 10:15 (cf. Luke 10:12); Q 12:46; 6:22–23.

19. The genitive τῆς γενεᾶς ταύτης occurs in Q 7:31; 11:31, 32, 51. As we shall see later, this phrase reflects deuteronomistic usage.

20. Jeremias, *Parables*, 90–92.

21. Steinhauser, *Doppelbildworte*.

22. Q 6:43–44a, 45 (trees and treasure); 6:44b (grapes and figs); 7:32 (boys and girls); 9:58 (foxes and birds); 11:9–13 (stone and serpent); 11:17–18 (divided kingdom and divided family); 12:24–28 (birds and lilies); 12:33 (thief and moth); 13:24 (gate and path); 17:34–35 (two in bed and two grinding).

23. Mark 2:21–22 (patch and new wine); 3:24–26 (divided kingdom and divided family [cf. Q 11:17–18]); 4:21–25 (lamp on a stand and under a bushel).

2. Forms Common in Mark but Rare in Q

(a) Conflict stories. There are eleven conflict stories in Mark but only one in Q, namely the Beelzeboul controversy (Q 11:14–23). This one story is traditional, since Mark has a variant of it (3:22–30). Neither the Q version nor its Markan variant is typical of the conflict stories. For example, it does not involve a disputed point in Jewish law.[24] We shall examine this story in greater detail later. However, we may note here that characteristically the other conflict stories are put to the service of christology, both in Mark and in the pre-Markan tradition.[25]

(b) Miracle stories. The rarity of miracle stories in Q has often been noted.[26] There are two such stories: Q 7:1–10 and Q 11:14. The latter serves as a setting for the Beelzeboul controversy and thus is used in a way similar to a use of miracles in the Fourth Gospel, namely to introduce discourses.

The healing of the centurion's servant or child (Q 7:1–10) is not a typical miracle story. Indeed, Bultmann discusses it in an addendum to his section on apophthegms.[27] The earliest form of this story is probably to be seen in the pre-Johannine tradition behind John 4:46–54. Comparing this earlier form to the version in Q brings to light two important features of the Q redaction. First, the stress in Q shifts from the miracle itself to Jesus' word.[28] Second, the Q version has been edited to reflect a theme found elsewhere in Q, namely the positive response of gentiles which puts Israel to shame (Q 7:9).[29]

It should be noted that throughout Q, miracles are associated with the kingdom of God (Q 11:20; 10:8–9; cf. Q 10:23–24); and in Q the proper response to miracle is repentance (Q 10:13–15; cf. Q 10:5–11, especially Q 10:8–9). By contrast, in Mark and in the pre-Markan tradition this eschatological context gives way to christological motifs.[30]

(c) Parables, similitudes, comparisons. The use of metaphor and comparison is certainly not rare in Q, but certain qualities seem to be distinctive of

24. See further Hultgren, *Jesus and His Adversaries*, 100–106.

25. See esp. Luz, "Das Jesusbild," 368–70. Hultgren, who stresses apologetic as the motive for the pre-Markan collection of conflict stories in Mark 2: 1–3:6, also notes that they "would have provided . . . an answer to the question . . . of why Jesus was put to death" (*Jesus and His Adversaries*, 177). For a comparison of Q and Markan traditions concerning Jesus and the Law, see E. Schillebeeckx, *Jesus: An Experiment*, 233–43.

26. Mark has eighteen miracle stories in addition to summaries, and, toward the end of the gospel, a series of instances of miraculous foreknowledge.

27. Bultmann, *History of the Synoptic Tradition*, 38–39.

28. See Blank, "Zur Christologie ausgewählter Wunderberichte," 112–17, and Robinson, "Kerygma and History," 56–58.

29. Note Q 7:9; cf. Q 10:13–15; 11:29–32; and see Lührmann, *Redaktion*, 37, 63. "Israel" here is a religious self-designation; see Kuhn, "Ἰσραήλ," 359–65.

30. See Luz, "Das Jesusbild," 355, 360–67. Bultmann attributed the relative scarcity of miracle stories in Q not to the general lack of narrative in Q but to the view of Jesus in Q as "eschatological preacher of repentance and salvation, the teacher of wisdom and the law" (*History of the Synoptic Tradition*, 241).

parabolic language in Q over against that in Mark. The element of comparison is more common in Q than in Mark.[31] Unlike the Markan parables, the Q parables often contain comparisons of two (or more) situations or people. Also, the introductory formulas in Mark differ from those in Q.[32]

The difference between the Markan and Q parables may also be seen in the fact that the parables in Q are often clearly eschatological.[33] Many of the Q parables are really part of a prophetic call for a response in view of an imminent decisive moment.[34] Striking too is a group of parabolic sayings which begin with $\tau\iota\varsigma\ \dot{\epsilon}\xi\ \dot{\upsilon}\mu\hat{\omega}\nu;$ ("who among you?") and appeal to everyday experience.[35] Such sayings are absent from Mark, though present in material unique to Luke.[36] "Who among you . . . ?" is not a typical introduction to a parable; it may reflect prophetic usage.[37]

Thus if a general tendency can be observed in the Q parabolic material, it is that in Q this material is used in the context of prophetic preaching. Where redactional activity is observable, a tendency may be noted to allegorize, though not for christological purposes.[38] Two parables have been attached to longer sayings compositions (Q 7:31–35 and 11:24–26); they serve the purpose of announcing judgment upon "this generation."

(d) Apocalyptic predictions. Bultmann lists a number of examples of these, most of which are Markan.[39] Only one apocalyptic prediction is found in Q (Q 17:23–24). The single instance in Q is a prophetic warning against purveyors of apocalyptic speculation.

31. See Edwards, *A Theology of Q*, 71–79. Several expressions are common in Q but are absent from Mark: $\pi\lambda\epsilon\iota\omega\nu$ (Q 11:31, 32; 12:23; cf. Q 7:26); $\pi\acute{o}\sigma\omega\ \mu\hat{\alpha}\lambda\lambda o\nu$ (Q 11:13; 12:24, 28); $\dot{\alpha}\nu\epsilon\kappa\tau\acute{o}\varsigma$ (Q 10:12, 14). The word $\pi\alpha\rho\alpha\beta o\lambda\acute{\eta}$ does not seem to have occurred in Q.

32. The Q parables are often introduced with the verb $\dot{o}\mu o\iota o\hat{\upsilon}\nu$ (to compare) or with $\dot{o}\mu o\iota\acute{o}\varsigma$ $\dot{\epsilon}\sigma\tau\iota\nu$; see Q 7:32; 13:18–19, 21; 6:48; cf. also Luke 6:47; 13:20; Q 7:31. Such an introduction occurs only once in Mark—in the one parable it has in common with Q (Mark 4:30–32); more commonly, $\dot{o}\varsigma$ is used by Mark (4:26–29, 31; 13:34).

33. Luz calls attention to the lack of eschatological context in the parables in Mark ("Das Jesusbild," 357).

34. See Q 3:9, 17; 6:47–49; 12:39–40, 42–46, 57–59; 13:25–29; 14:16–23; 19:12–13, 25–26. On the use of parables by the prophets, see Westermann, *Basic Forms of Prophetic Speech*, 201–2.

35. Q 12:25; 11:11; Matt 12:11 (contrast Luke 14:5); Luke 15:4 (contrast Matt 18:12); cf. Q 11:33.

36. Luke 11:5; 14:28; 17:7–10 (this last is occasionally assigned to Q: see Polag, *Fragmenta Q*, 86, and Weiser, *Knechtsgleichnisse*, 106–12).

37. Kloppenborg (*Formation*, 219) follows Berger ("Materialien," 31–33) in seeing this formula as not peculiar to prophetic speech. The only verbally identical usages, however, are in the prophets (Isa 42:53; 50:10; Hag 2:3; the phrase does not introduce parables in these cases). The sapiential examples cited by Berger and Kloppenborg are similar only in being rhetorical questions expecting the answer, "No one." See further Aune, *Prophecy*, 165–66. Aune thinks the evidence of prophetic usage is too slight to regard the phrase as prophetic speech.

38. See Q 7:31–35; 19:12–27; 14:16–24; 13:18–19. In 13:18–19 note the explicit reference to a "tree" in v. 19 (and see Crossan, *In Parables*, 98–99).

39. Bultmann (*History of the Synoptic Tradition*, 120–25) lists Mark 9:1, 12–13; 13:2, 5–27, 28–29, 30, 31, 32; 14:58; Matt 7:15; 25:31–46; 26:61; Luke 17:20–21; 19:42–44.

(e) Chreiai. This form has received considerable attention recently. James Butts has identified twenty-two chreiai in Mark[40] and nine chreiai in the Lukan special material.[41] However, there are only two chreiai in Q (Q 9:57–58, 59–60), although there are also three instances in which only one gospel casts Q material in chreia form,[42] and other instances where sayings are arguably cast in the form of chreiai.[43]

3. Results of the Form-Critical Survey

This form-critical survey of Q has not covered all the types of material in Q, but several things seem clear. First, the fact that forms common in Mark (miracle stories; conflict stories; apocalyptic predictions; chreiai) are rare in Q and that other forms which are common in Q (macarisms; woes; eschatological correlatives; prophetic threats; *Doppelbildworte*) are rare in Mark suggests that Mark and Q represent independent traditions. Second, the prophetic character of much of the Q material is evident not only in the use of prophetic forms but also in those characteristics which distinguish the parables in Q from those in Mark. Third, the survey suggests a considerable measure of literary unity in Q simply in terms of form and general content.

Finally, in those places where redactional activity can be observed most clearly, the latest levels show the influence of the deuteronomistic and/or wisdom traditions; these redactional additions condemn Israel for her impenitence and resistance to God's messengers.

Traditions Shared by Mark and Q

There are several instances where traditions are shared by Mark and Q. By comparing them, we can often sense more clearly what is distinctive of Q. We are not concerned here with short sayings but with longer sayings compositions, where redactional tendencies are more easily observable.

1. The Mission Discourse
(Mark 6:6b–13; Q 10:2–16; see also Luke 9:1–6).

The Markan version is brief, and tells only of the sending out two-by-two of the twelve, of the restricted provisions (no bread, no bag, etc.), and of their authorization to cast out demons. Later, the disciples report back to Jesus

---

40. Butts ("The Chreia in the Synoptic Gospels," 133–37) lists Mark 1:16–20; 2:16–17a, 18–19, 23–27; 3:22–26, 31–35; 4:10–11; 7:5–8, 24b–30; 8:11–12; 9:38–39; 10:13–14, 17–22, 35–40; 11:15–17, 27–33; 12:13–17, 28–31, 41–46; 13:1–2; 14:3–9; 15:39. Discussions of the chreia form may be found in Robbins, "The Chreia"; Hock and O'Neil, *The Chreia in Ancient Rhetoric*, 3–60; Robbins and Mack, *Patterns of Persuasion*, 1–29; and Berger, "Hellenistische Gattungen," 1092–110.

41. Butts ("The Chreia in the Synoptic Gospels," 133–37) lists Luke 9:39–40, 61–62; 11:27–28; 12:13–14; 13:1–5, 31–33; 16:14–15; 17:20–21; 19:41–44.

42. Matt 11:2–5 (contrast Luke 7:18–19, 22); Luke 13:22–24 (contrast Matt 7:13); and Luke 17:5–6 (contrast Matt 17:20).

43. See, e.g., Kloppenborg, *Formation*, 168–69.

(Mark 6:30). The Q version differs from Mark's at many points. Present in Q but absent from Mark are the following:

- an introductory saying about the abundant harvest;
- a commissioning ("I send you . . .");
- the warning that the "laborers" will be like lambs in the midst of wolves;
- the peace greeting;
- the saying about the laborer worthy of his wages/food;
- the proclamation that the kingdom is near;
- the proclamation of judgment against those rejecting the "laborers";
- the woes against Galilean cities; and
- the concluding messenger-saying (Q 10:16).

In contrast to Mark, who omits any reference to the kingdom, Q makes it clear that in the person of the "laborers" the kingdom draws near to Israel, and that this means judgment, so that those in Israel who reject the "laborers" reject God and bring wrath upon themselves.[44] What we have in Q, therefore, is not really a mission at all but rather an errand of judgment. The results seem predetermined, for the discourse opens with a saying describing the laborers as lambs in the midst of wolves. Here the image of God's lamb, Israel, in the midst of hostile gentile wolves has been sarcastically inverted.[45] The appended prophetic threat (Q 10:13–15),[46] which says that gentiles would have responded better than Israel, assumes the failure of the call for Israel to return to Yahweh.[47]

The traditions shared by Mark and Q must have related an account of a sending of messengers to call Israel to repentance and, should that fail, to announce judgment upon Israel.[48] The Markan redaction adds some christianizing details.[49] More importantly, the Markan redaction uses the account to

44. The image of the harvest in Q 10:2 establishes the context for understanding the function of the "laborers." Harvest is a common metaphor for judgment (see, e.g., Isa 27:12; Hos 6:11; Joel 3:13; Mark 4:26–29; John 4:35; Rev 14:14–20). The laborers are harvest-workers sent out by the "lord of the harvest," who is probably the same figure that appears in Q 3:17 (i.e., Yahweh). Cf. Luke 11:23 and see Hoffmann, *Studien*, 289–92. The remarkable feature here is that the laborers are not angels (as in Matt 13:41; cf. Rev 14:19) but humans, and that the eschatological judgment takes place already in the "mission" of the laborers.

45. See Hoffmann, *Studien*, 294–95.

46. The double saying in Q 10:13–15 is clearly not a continuation of the instruction in Q 10:3–12; it has been added to serve as a comment on the sending discourse.

47. For a more detailed discussion of the whole discourse, see below, chap. 6, and now also Sellew, "Early Collections of Jesus' Words," 59–162; Uro, *Sheep Among the Wolves*; and Meyer, "The Gentile Mission in Q" and "The Community of Q," 7, 28, 75–78, 86.

48. For an analysis of the tradition see Hahn, *Mission in the New Testament*, 41–46. The original character of the account can be glimpsed in Mark 6:11 (cf. Q 10:10–11), an announcement of judgment, which fits poorly into the picture the redaction seeks to create. Mark can interpret this only as the usual call to repent; indeed, he seems to think that the Twelve preached Jesus (cf. 6:14). The two-by-two sending may also be primitive: if judgment is to be announced (Mark 6:11), two witnesses are required (Deut 17:6; 19:15).

49. In Mark, the "laborers" become the Twelve. Reflection on early Christian missionary practice may be seen in the more realistic, if austere, requirements in Mark 6:8–9, in the reference to staying at a house (Mark 6:10) and anointing the sick with oil (6:13). The

illustrate the fact that the disciples, whose activity parallels that of Jesus, will be rejected just as Jesus was (see Mark 6:1–6a).[50] This same motif is pursued in Mark 6:14–29, where the Baptist becomes the "forerunner of Jesus' passion."[51] Thus the Markan redaction has adapted the mission account to the passion kerygma, while the Q redaction was concerned to speak of Israel's impenitence and of the fateful consequences of her refusal to heed those sent to her.

2. John the Baptist
(Mark 1:1–11; 6:17–29; 9:9–13; Q 3:7–9, 16–17; 7:24–28 and 16:16; 7:31–35; see also Q 3:1–6).

The are fundamental differences between Q and Mark. The most important one is that in Q John appears as a prophet in his own right, whereas in Mark he is subordinated to Jesus.[52]

In the first common material, Q speaks of two baptisms: John's baptism of water in preparation for the coming judgment, and the baptism of wind ($\pi\nu\epsilon\hat{\upsilon}\mu\alpha$) and fire by Yahweh, i.e., the judgment itself.[53] Likewise, Q and Mark both cite Mal 3:1 with reference to John. But in Q the context is different, and the meaning is that John is the forerunner of Yahweh's judgment; Mark uses the passage to declare John the forerunner of Jesus. The subordination of John to Jesus may go back to pre-Markan tradition.[54]

Thus neither in Mark nor in the pre-Markan tradition is John a prophet in his own right. But in Q John is independent, a preacher of repentance before the imminent judgment of Yahweh.[55] Especially in Q 7:31–35, Q places both John and Jesus in a common front against "this generation" which rejected both.

3. The Beelzebul Controversy
(Mark 3:19b–27; Q 11:14–20).

In the Markan redaction, a charge that Jesus is possessed by Beelzebul, the $\mathring{\alpha}\rho\chi\omega\nu$ ("ruler") of the demons, is shifted to a new context: the accusation by Jesus' family and others that he is a demoniac. In this way, Mark prepares the way for the identification of Jesus as bearer of the spirit (3:30).[56]

The Q version differs at a number of points. The setting is different: a brief miracle story, instead of the accusations by Jesus' relatives and the scribes. The Q version lacks the parable of the divided house, as well as the parable of the

---

missionaries' authority over demons may also be redactional (6:7; cf. 3:14). Hoffmann (*Studien*, 237–43) shows that Mark's version has been adapted to the early hellenistic Christian mission.

50. See Grässer, "Jesus in Nazareth," 11, 21–22.

51. Knigge, "The Meaning of Mark," 68–69. See also Marxsen, *Mark the Evangelist*, 38–40, and Wink, *John the Baptist*, 1–17.

52. See Marxsen, *Mark the Evangelist*, 33.

53. This is discussed at greater length in chap. 5.

54. See Luz, "Das Jesusbild," 353–54, 360.

55. It will be argued in chap. 5 that Q 7:28 is a late addition to Q which subordinates John to Jesus.

56. See Luz, "Das Jesusbild," 360.

strong man bound and the concluding saying about blaspheming the holy spirit. On the other hand, there are several new elements in the Q version: a rhetorical question about other Jewish exorcists; the saying linking exorcism with the kingdom; and a concluding parable about the seven unclean spirits which return to reside where only one had lived before.

The basic difference is that in Q attention is focused on the kingdom rather than on Jesus. Exorcism is linked directly to the kingdom (Q 11:20). But the context does not permit this saying to refer exclusively to Jesus' exorcisms. Rather, the coming of the kingdom is the presupposition for all exorcisms.[57] That alone makes comprehensible why the other Jewish exorcists (the "sons" of Jesus' opponents, Q 11:19) will stand in judgment over their fathers, the Jewish leaders.

In Mark, Jesus overcomes the opposition by showing that their accusations are foolish; indeed, he is not possessed by an unclean spirit but by the holy spirit. In Q, however, the issue is the kingdom, not Jesus himself.[58] The parable appended to the Q version (Q 11:24-26) implies that "this generation" has provided a hospitable dwelling place for unclean spirits. Thus the Q version concludes with a harsh condemnation of the Jewish leaders.

4. The Sign to This Generation
(Mark 8:12b; Q 11:29-32).

An originally isolated saying (Q 11:29) has been developed in Q into a brief sayings composition. In the pre-Markan tradition, the saying was probably already attached to the feeding miracle.[59]

The Markan redaction serves a christological purpose. Jesus shows his superiority over the Pharisees (who, for Mark, are "this generation") by overcoming their attempt to test him and by refusing to demonstrate his divine origin.[60]

In Q the saying has undergone at least two stages of expansion. The original saying (Q 11:29) contains an exceptive clause: no sign except the "sign of Jonah." This enigmatic saying has prompted an explanation in Q 11:30: "For as Jonah became a sign to the men of Nineveh, so will the son of man be to this generation."[61] Here "sign" is not understood as a prodigious miracle but, in

---

57. See Noack, *SATANÁS und SOTERÍA*, 70-72. Though Noack denies that the connection between Q 11:19 and 11:20 is original, Bultmann observes that if it is, then the logical implication is that the exorcisms of the Jewish exorcists also demonstrate the coming of the kingdom (*History of the Synoptic Tradition*, 14).

58. Q 11:23 does not introduce a more exclusive view of Jesus, but rather repeats what is said elsewhere in Q, that to reject Jesus (or John or the "laborers") is to reject God.

59. Cf. Mark 8:1-10, 11-13 with John 6:1-3, 30. On this, see Haenchen, *Der Weg Jesu*, 285-87, and Schulz, *Q*, 254 n. 537, 255-56.

60. For this interpretation, see Luz, "Das Jesusbild," 353 n. 1. Edwards notes that Mark's πειράζοντες ("testing") is redactional, and that it serves a christological purpose; see Mark 8:11 and Edwards, *Sign of Jonah*, 76.

61. Lührmann, however, sees Q 11:30 as the last addition to the composition—as a saying

the prophetic sense, as a warning concerning the future. And "son of man" is not the apocalyptic figure but simply Jesus.[62]

The second stage in the development of the composition is the addition in Q 11:31-32 of a double saying.[63] This addition expands on the judgment of "this generation." Indeed the Ninevites repented, but "this generation" rejected Jesus. Therefore these gentiles—the men of Nineveh who repented at the kerygma of Jonah, and the Queen of Sheba who responded to the *sophia* of Solomon–will arise in the judgment to condemn Israel. One should note here a phenomenon attested elsewhere in the redaction of Q, namely the close association of wisdom and prophetic preaching (e.g., Q 11:49) and, with that, the condemnation of Israel for her impenitence.

5. Results of Comparing Material Common to Mark and Q

In comparing the use by Mark and Q of shared traditions, certain themes and interests keep recurring. Mark adapts the tradition to his christology and to the passion kerygma. In Q, the recurring themes are the impenitence of Israel or "this generation," judgment, and the fateful consequences of rejecting God's messengers. These themes are evident within the sayings compositions as well as in additions at the end of the compositions (Q 10:13-15 added to 10:2-12; Q 7:31-35 added to 7:24-28 + 16:16; Q 11:24-26 added to 11:14-20, 23; Q 11:31-32 added to 11:29-30). Particularly striking are certain traits peculiar to Q: the eschatological significance of rejecting not only Jesus but others as well (John the Baptist, Q 7:31-35; "laborers," Q 10:2-16; other Jewish exorcists, Q 11:19) and the use of various examples to shame Israel (Q 10:13-15; 11:31-32; 11:19).[64]

---

created to link Q 11:29 to 11:31-32, both of which he takes to be originally independent sayings (*Redaktion*, 40-42).

62. The use of the future in Q 11:30 does not require that the son of man there be an apocalyptic figure; see Vielhauer, "Jesus und der Menschensohn," 151-52, and Schulz, *Q*, 256.

63. The double saying is a product of the Q community. The structure of the saying and the use of gentile examples to shame Israel both reflect a scheme of "primitive Christian polemic" (Fridrichsen, *The Problem of Miracle*, 75, and Bultmann, *History of the Synoptic Tradition*, 13); see Q 10:13-15. Q 11:31-32 and 10:13-15 both stand close to the deuteronomistic call to repentance (see Steck, *Israel*, 286). The influence of the wisdom tradition is evident both in the unexpected inclusion of the example of the *sophia* of Solomon and in the peculiar type of Old Testament interpretation found here and elsewhere in Q; on this see Lührmann, *Redaktion*, 75-83, 98-99.

64. Similar themes dominate other sayings compositions in Q which have no parallels in Mark: (a) *The Sermon on the Mount/Plain*. We will argue later that the Sermon, which had attained its basic shape prior to the redaction of Q, was edited so as to introduce, from Q 6:39 on, a polemic against the Jewish leaders. This editing of the Sermon in Q was buttressed by Q 7:1-10, which was attached to the end of the Sermon; there a gentile's readiness to believe puts Israel to shame. (b) *The Woes* (Q 11:39-52). Here the concern to denounce the Jewish leaders and to announce judgment is obvious, and is strengthened through the attached threat in Q 11: 49-51. (c) *The Q Apocalypse* (Q 17:23-27). Here too the concern about the impending judgment is obvious, but this material is addressed to the community, not to Israel, and there is no reproach of Jewish leaders.

The Theological Basis for the Literary Unity of Q

The study thus far strongly suggests that Q stands within a prophetic tradition. Indeed, it is clear from the redactional addition in Q 6:23c that the community saw themselves as successors to the persecuted prophets of the past. They understood themselves as prophetic messengers[65] sent to call Israel to repentance in view of the imminent kingdom of God, but experiencing rejection (Q 10:10–12, 13–15). Particularly important to note are two passages (Q 11:49–51 and 13:34–35) which seem to give programmatic expression to the tendencies we have seen to be at work in much of the Q material. Both passages are frequently recognized as additions to Q,[66] primarily because both present Wisdom as sender of the prophets.[67] Steck has shown that both passages stand in direct continuity with the deuteronomistic tradition,[68] whose influence was noted earlier in other passages as well (Q 6:23c; 10:13–15; 11:31–32). The suggestion is at hand that it is the deuteronomistic tradition which provides the theological framework for the redaction of Q, and thus is the theological basis for its literary unity. Because of the importance of that tradition to the question of the literary unity of Q, we must now examine it in some detail. We shall be particularly concerned with one aspect of the deuteronomistic tradition, namely the statements about the prophets which occur in reviews of Israel's history and thus are part of what Steck calls the "deuteronomistic sketch of history."[69]

In the deuteronomistic tradition, Israel's history is pictured as a history of disobedience. God's forbearance was shown in sending prophets to warn the people, but they rejected and even killed them. Therefore God's wrath was— or will be—experienced. References to the prophets are a recurring but not a constant element in the deuteronomistic tradition; the rejection of the prophets is cited as simply one indication of the intractability of the people. Certain

65. Note, e.g., the prophetic sending formula in Q 10:3; also Q 7:27; 11:49; 13:34.

66. See, e.g., Lührmann, *Redaktion*, 97.

67. The speaker in Q 13:34–35 is not Jesus but Wisdom; see Bultmann, *History of the Synoptic Tradition*, 114–15; Steck, *Israel*, 230–32; Meyer, "The Community of Q," 22–28; Schulz, *Q*, 349–50 n. 194; Meyer, *Der Prophet aus Galiläa*, 50–51. Jesus cannot be the speaker because the speaker is the one who sent the Old Testament prophets. Since Wisdom is explicitly named as sender of the Old Testament prophets in Q 11:49, one must assume the same for Q 13:34–35.

68. Steck, *Israel*, 26–58, 222–39.

69. The deuteronomistic sketch of history can be seen especially in penitential prayers such as Ezra 9:6–15; Neh 1:5–11; 9:5–37; Tob 3:1–6; Dan 9:4b–19; Bar 1:15–3:8; and in confessions of sin (Lam 3:42–47; Ps 106:6–46). See Steck, *Israel*, 110–37. However, Steck indicates that the deuteronomistic view of history is also to be found in a tradition of preaching, including Deut 4:25–31; 28:45–68 + 30:1–10; 1 Kgs 8:46–53; 2 Chr 15:1–7; 29:5–11; 30:6–9; Jer 7:25–34; 25:4–14; 29:17–20; 35:15–17; 44:2–14; Zech 1:2–6; 7:4–14; Tob 13:3–6; Bar 3:9–4:4; 4:5–5:9; TestLevi 10:2–5; 14; 15:1–4; 16:1–5; TestJud 23:1–5; TestIss 6:1–4; TestZeb 9:5–9; TestDan 5:4–9; TestNaph 4:1–5; TestAsh 7:2–7; 1 Enoch 91:12–17 + 93:1–10 (Apocalypse of Weeks); 85–90 (Animal Apocalypse); and 91–104 (parenesis); Jub 1:7–26; PssSol 8; 9; 17; 4 Ezra 3:4–25, 27; 7:129–30; 14:27–35; 2 ApocBar 1:1–5; 4:1–6; 31:1–32:7; 44:1–46:7; 77:1–17; 78–87; Ps.-Philo, *Biblical Antiquities*; CD 20:28–30; 1:3–13a; 4QLuminaries 1:8–7:2.

distortions of history are conventional: the prophets appear almost exclusively in the role of preachers of repentance; far more prophets are said to be killed than can be accounted for in Jewish literature; there is a tendency to expand the list of prophets (see, e.g., Q 11:49–51 which begins with Abel!). It is noteworthy that the guilt of the ancestors is said to remain even up to the present (Ezra 9:7; Neh 1:6; Ps 79:8; cf. Q 11:49–51) The primary concern of the tradition is the call for Israel to return to Yahweh.[70]

Steck identifies seven elements characteristic of the deuteronomistic tradition in its later, expanded form:

(a) The whole history of Israel is pictured as one of persistent disobedience. See Q 6:23c; 11:47–51; 13:34–35; 14:16–24.

(b) Therefore Yahweh again and again sent prophets to call Israel to return, to repent. See Q 11:47–51; 13:34–35; 14:16–24.

(c) Israel always rejected these prophets, often even killing them. See Q 6:23c; 11:47–51; 13:34–35; 14:16–24. In Q, Israel's impenitence is expressed not only by accusations of complicity in the death of the prophets (e.g., Q 11:47–51) and by continued opposition to the prophets (Q 6:23c; 14:16–24; cf. 7:31–35; 10:2–16; 9:58) but also by other accusations (see Q 11:39–52; 3:7–9; 6:39–46; 7:24–27, 31–35; 11:24–26; 12:54–56). The use of gentile (or other) examples to shame Israel also exposes her impenitence (Q 7:9; 10:13–15; 11:31–32; 11:19). The epithet "this generation" is used to characterize Israel as impenitent.

(d) Therefore Yahweh punished, or will punish, Israel. In the earliest deuteronomistic tradition, the catastrophes of 722 and 587 B.C.E. are cited. In the later form of the tradition, Israel's sentence of condemnation (*Unheilsstatus*) is said to continue (see, e.g., Jub 1:7–26; cf. Q 11:47–51; 13:34–35).

(e) But now a new call for repentance is issued. See Q 3:7–9, 16–17; 6:20–49; 10:2–12; 7:31–35; 11:29–32; 11:39–52. In Q, even miracles are understood in the context of repentance (see Q 10: 13; 11:14–20; 10:5–12; and cf. Q 11:20 with 10:9).

(f1) If Israel repents, Yahweh will restore her, gathering those scattered among the nations.

(f2) And Yahweh will bring judgment upon Israel's enemies. In Q, the many statements about the kingdom of God and the son of man take the place of element (f1).[71] In place of promises to Israel (but see Q 13:35) Q offers a redefinition of Israel (Q 3:7–9; 13:28–29; cf. 7:35; 10:13–15; 11:19, 31–32; 13:19; 14:16–24; 16:16; 22:28–30). The threat of rejection of those who reject the call to return is attested often in Q (e.g., Q 10:1–16; 12:10) and is also attested as part of the (f1) element in pre-Christian deuteronomistic preach-

---

70. For the role of repentance in the deuteronomic history, see Wolff, "The Kerygma of the Deuteronomic Historical Work," 83–100, and Brueggemann, "The Kerygma of the Deuteronomistic Historian," 387–402.

71. So Steck, *Israel*, 286 n. 6.

ing.[72] An additional aspect of element (f) is the eschatological separation of the righteous from the sinners, which is found in Q as well.[73]

In its oldest form, the deuteronomistic tradition was at home in levitical circles. Later, the tradition was borne by the hasidic movement which, in the first half of the second century B.C.E., united several groups to form a common front against hellenization and deteriorating religious conditions, especially in the priesthood and the urban population. As Steck notes, *"the levitical tradition of the deuteronomistic sketch of history was that conception which made possible a theological grasp of contemporary events in the context of the concern for the conversion of Israel."*[74] In the formation of this renewal movement we can see the mingling of several traditions: levitical-deuteronomistic, eschatological, and wisdom (see, e.g., Bar 1:15–5:9; the Testaments of the Twelve Patriarchs).[75] During the period from 150 to 100 B.C.E., the hasidic movement broke up into several groups. From this point on, Steck contends, the deuteronomistic tradition became the common property of a number of groups and it is difficult to isolate any one as the primary bearer of that tradition.[76]

That Q stands within the deuteronomistic tradition seems evident. The elements constitutive of the deuteronomistic view of history are widely attested in Q. The basic concern— to call Israel to repent—underlies both Q and the earlier deuteronomistic tradition. One may conclude, therefore, that the deuteronomistic view of history which comes to clear expression in Q 11:47–51 and 13:34–35 represents the theological framework undergirding a large part of the Q material.

Once it is understood that the deuteronomistic tradition provides the theological framework for Q, several peculiar features of Q become explicable. First, the absence of a passion narrative in Q becomes understandable because, in the deuteronomistic tradition, Jesus' death would be understood not as a salvific act but as evidence of Israel's continuing impenitence. Second, Q is peculiar in giving independent status to John the Baptist. Rather than being the forerunner of Jesus, John is presented in Q as a prophet (Q 7:26) who functions as forerunner of Yahweh by issuing a call to repentance (Q 3:7–9,

72. Steck, *Israel*, 217–18.

73. Steck, *Israel*, 187, 286 n. 5. Steck cites Q 17:34–35, to which may be added Q 3:7–9, 17; 13:23–24, 25, 27, 28–29; 10:13–15.

74. Steck, *Israel*, 206; Steck's emphasis.

75. See Steck, *Israel*, 205–8. The terms "prophet" and "wise" could both be used to designate people who called for obedience to the Law; see Steck, *Israel*, 208 nn. 4, 5. It is important to note that the mingling of traditions (wisdom and deuteronomistic) occurred, according to Steck, within a specific context, namely in the hasidic movement. However, Steck argues that this movement had broken up into a number of parties by the time of Jesus, so tracing a line from Q to a specific part of the hasidic movement becomes difficult.

76. See Steck, *Israel*, 209–12. Steck assumes that in addition to the Q community there was a complex renewal movement, evidenced in texts such as the Psalms of Solomon; the Assumption of Moses; Ps.-Philo, *Biblical Antiquities*; 4 Ezra; and the Second Apocalypse of Baruch. The movement had scribal leaders designated the "wise" (p. 212 n. 5) and perhaps— though this is not directly attested—"prophets" (p. 212 n. 6); the term "messenger" (or "apostle," cf. 3 Kgdms 14:6 LXX) may have been used (pp. 214–15; see Luke 11:49).

16–17).[77] Remarkably, John and Jesus are even placed in tandem (Q 7:31–35).[78] This treatment of John is possible because, in the context of the deuteronomistic tradition, John and Jesus are both seen as sent to call Israel to repentance.[79] Third, Wisdom plays an important role in Q. Jesus is implicitly a messenger of Wisdom (Q 7:31–35; 11:47–51; 13:34–35; 11:29–32), but he functions more as prophet than as wise person. Q is formally a collection of sayings, but it includes a large amount of prophetic material. These features are comprehensible in terms of the deuteronomistic tradition, where a wisdom component was long at home, especially within the hasidic movement where the deuteronomistic and wisdom traditions had merged.[80] However, the notion of Wisdom as sender of prophets as part of the deuteronomistic tradition is not attested in pre-Christian tradition or elsewhere in early Christian tradition, even though the deuteronomistic tradition was adapted by Christians very early.[81] The peculiarity of the role of Wisdom in Q—its association with prophets and prophetic material—derives from the identification of Wisdom and Torah (see Sirach 24; Bar 3:9–4:4; 1 Enoch 42). When Torah is Wisdom and the prophets are seen primarily as calling people to return to Wisdom and hence to Torah, then the prophets can be regarded as the "wise" and Wisdom as the sender of prophets.[82]

Thus the organizing principle which gives literary unity to Q and provides coherence to its various characteristics is to be found in an understanding of

77. The reference to "sandals" in Q 3:16 does not require a human figure instead of Yahweh; the sandals are to be understood as belonging to John himself, not to the figure to come. See Bretscher, "'Whose Sandals'?" 81–87. The meaning is that John is not worthy to wear his sandals in the presence of the coming one (cf. Exod 3:5). However, since the whole fragment, "but he who is mightier . . . untie," interrupts the contrast between the two baptisms, it may be a later addition.

78. See Robinson, "Jesus as Sophos and Sophia," 5–6.

79. Schillebeeckx (*Jesus: An Experiment*, 126–36) correctly emphasizes that John stood within the deuteronomistic and Hasidic traditions, and that he represented not the apocalyptic tradition but a renascence of ancient Israelite prophecy.

80. Steck (*Israel*, 147) notes that the deuteronomistic view of history is not linked to Wisdom in Sirach but they are joined shortly thereafter in Tobit (pp. 147–49) and then in Testament of the Twelve Patriarchs (pp. 150 n. 1; 151 n. 5); the Apocalypse of Weeks (1 Enoch 93:1–10 + 91:12–17; see p. 154 n. 4); 4 Ezra (pp. 177–80); Ps.-Philo, *Biblical Antiquities* (p. 176) and esp. Bar. 3:9–4:4 (pp. 164–65 n. 5). See Prov 1:20–33 (Steck, *Israel*, 205 n. 2; 222; 225 nn. 1, 3; 232).

81. It is attested in the pre-Markan tradition (Mark 12:1b–9; see Steck, *Israel*, 269–73) and the pre-Pauline tradition (1 Thess 2:15–16; Steck, *Israel*, 274–79); also see Acts 7:52 (Steck, *Israel*, 265–69).

82. The role of Wisdom in Q is not directly related to the role of Wisdom in such christological hymns as Col 1:15–20. The setting of the latter is liturgical and focuses upon the cosmic role of Wisdom. In Q, Wisdom is not co-creatrix nor (aside from Q 10:21–22) revealer. Q does not identify Jesus with Wisdom (against Christ, *Jesus Sophia*). Aside from Q 10:21–22, Wisdom in Q is not hidden but public; she speaks through prophets in the places people gather (cf. Prov 1:20–21). However, one may see a connection between Q and those traditions which have seen Jesus as the last of a chain of divine envoys; see Robinson, "Jesus as Sophos and Sophia," "Basic Shifts in German Theology" (pp. 82–86), and "Very Goddess and Very Man." Jesus appears as a member of the chain of envoys in the Koran where, furthermore, deuteronomistic themes can be detected (Sura 2:87; 5:70–71; 6:34; see Steck, *Israel*, 91–99).

Israel and the mission to her of John and Jesus, an understanding shaped by the deuteronomistic and wisdom traditions as they were mediated by the hasidic movement. Indeed, one may perhaps say that in Q we see the soil of the hasidic movement still clinging to the roots of earliest Christianity.

Some Qualifications

The claim advanced here concerning the literary unity of Q must be qualified in several respects. First, the nature of the claim must be clarified. It is not that in identifying the source of literary unity in Q we have explicated the theology of Q. Put otherwise, the deuteronomistic and wisdom perspective is not the *content* of the Q proclamation; it is simply the vehicle for its expression. The deuteronomistic tradition seems to have provided a framework within which a community could reflect theologically upon the disappointments of the Jesus movement among their fellow Jews. The integration of the figure of Wisdom into the deuteronomistic sketch of history served to draw John and Jesus into Israel's *Heilsgeschichte* as the last in a series of Wisdom's envoys.

Second, the comprehensiveness of the claim must be qualified. The deuteronomistic-wisdom perspective has shaped the composition of most of Q, but not all of it. As we shall see, it is most clearly evident in roughly the first half of Q, where the most explicit formulation of this perspective is found (Q 11:47–51), and where clear echoes of it are often present (Q 6:23b; 7:31–35; 10:13–16; 11:29–32). But, as I shall argue later, large chunks of the rest of Q were also shaped by this perspective (Q 12:49–53, 54–56; 13:18–19, 21–22, 34–35; 14:16–24, 26–27; 17:33; 14:34–35), with one other explicit formulation of the perspective, in Q 13:34–35. But not everything in Q can be understood in relation to the deuteronomistic-wisdom tradition. My argument is only that at the basic, compositional stage, this was the dominant theological perspective.

5
John
and Jesus

*The First
Section of Q*

For reasons that will become apparent, Q has been divided by the present writer into "sections" which represent compositional units in Q. The first such section extends from Q 3:1–6 (or 3:7–9) to Q 7:31–35. The sequence of the first section of Q can be reconstructed without much difficulty. To be sure, establishing the exact wording of the text is more difficult, especially for the beginning of the section. However, the goal here is not the reconstruction of the wording of the Q but the reconstruction of its sequence, and thus of its basic structure.

The Sequence of the First Section

The initial Lukan and Matthean pericopes containing Q material are listed here, according to the present Lukan sequence.

John the Baptist	Luke 3:1–6	Matt 3:1–6
John's Preaching	3:7–9, 16–17	3:7–12
Temptations	4:1–13	4:1–11
Jesus' Preaching	6:20–49	5:1–7:27
Centurion's Servant	7:1–10	8:5–13
John and Jesus	7:18–35	11:2–19
On Following Jesus	9:57–60	8:19–22
"Mission Charge"	10:2–16	9:35–10:16

This list shows clearly that Matthew and Luke give their Q material in the same sequence, except for the pericope concerning John and Jesus. It is striking that with the pericope on following Jesus (Luke 9:57–60//Matt 8:19–22) Matthew and Luke resume their agreement on the order of Q. The simplest explanation of this state of affairs is that Matthew has dislocated the pericope concerning John and Jesus. The evidence, as we shall see, leads to just this conclusion.

1. Matthew's Dislocation of a Pericope

It has been suspected for a long time that Matthew's location for the Q pericope in 11:2–19, which differs from the Lukan sequence for the Q materials, is secondary.[1] Editorial activity by both Luke and Matthew is evident in connection with the miracles of Jesus mentioned in Q 7:18–23. Matthew has emphasized Jesus' deeds (Matt 11:2, 19), but none of the miracles cited in Matt 11:5 (=Q 7:22) occurred in Q. This problem—miracles cited to attest Jesus which were not given in Q—was also sensed by Luke, who solved it by having Jesus perform miracles on the spot for John's disciple to see (Luke 7:20–21).[2] The reason why Matthew delayed the Q section on John and Jesus is therefore apparent; at the same time, Luke did not have to dislocate the pericope on John and Jesus, because he inserted the missing miracles into the pericope itself. But why Matthew would save this section until after he had given the "Mission Charge" is not immediately obvious.

It is well known that Matthew collected similar materials into larger complexes, including Matthew 5–7 (teachings) and Matthew 8–9 (miracles). As a result of those collections, a portrait of Jesus emerged which Julius Schniewind spoke of as the "Messiah of the word" and the "Messiah of the deed."[3] These two large complexes are followed in Matthew 10 by material on discipleship, including the "Mission Charge." The significance of this arrangement was noted by Heinz Joachim Held:

> Jesus is not only the Messiah in word and deed whose authority was given by God but he is also the Lord who makes his disciples share in his authority.[4]

Thus Jesus' teaching and miracles, and the activity of the disciples, belong together in Matthew's view, and he has arranged his material accordingly.

It would also appear that Matthew used the Q pericope on John and Jesus as a critical point in his total arrangement. As Held noted concerning this text:

> The evangelist's presentation has. . .reached a kind of conclusion. After he has shown the Christ in his word and deed he now allows the Baptist to put the decisive Christological question (Matt 11:3 σὺ εἶ ὁ ἐρχόμενος, ἢ ἕτερον προσδοκῶμεν; [Are you the coming one or shall we look for another?]).[5]

Further,

> The question of the Baptist has a double function: on the one hand it clearly expresses the decisive question which comes out of what has gone before and so forms the conclusion which once again illuminates the Christological theme of the preceding chapters. On the other hand, the chapters which follow must be

---

1. Matthew's dislocation of this pericope was noticed already by Streeter, *The Four Gospels*, 273. So likewise Marxsen, *Introduction to the New Testament*, 148; Bultmann, *History of the Synoptic Tradition*, 356; Schweizer, *Matthew*, 69–70; and Lührmann, *Redaktion*, 61. Harnack (*Sayings of Jesus*, 175) prefers, as usual, the Matthean sequence.

2. So Bultmann, *History of the Synoptic Tradition*, 23, 129, 336; Manson, *The Sayings of Jesus*, 67; Hoffmann, *Studien*, 192–93; Schulz, *Q*, 191–92. However, Lührmann (*Redaktion*, 26) thinks only Luke 7:21 is redactional.

3. Schniewind, *Matthäus*, 8, 37–38, 106–7.

4. Held, "Matthew as Interpreter," 252.

5. Held, "Matthew as Interpreter," 251.

understood even more in the light of this question and the negative or positive answers to it.[6]

Thus redaction criticism is able to reveal a plan in Matthew's composition which could account for the displacement of the pericope on John and Jesus. The alternative, that Matthew preserved the order of Q and Luke has altered it, is more difficult by far. Luke's arrangement is hard to account for as the result of his own compositional activity, and the fact that he obviated the need to move the section on John and Jesus by having Jesus perform the requisite miracles on the spot further encourages the conclusion that Luke's order represents Q.

2. Luke 7:18–23//Matt 11:2–19: Conclusion to the First Section of Q

The first section of Q begins and ends with material dealing with John the Baptist; more precisely, we first have material dealing with John, then material dealing with Jesus, and then a section dealing with John and Jesus. Was this arrangement deliberate? There are indications that it was. The introductory and concluding pericopes dealing with John both cite an Old Testament passage referring to a "way" being prepared (Isa 40:3 LXX in Q 3:4, and Exod 23:20; Mal 3:1 in Q 7:27). Moreover, the quotation formulas used are very similar (see Matt 3:3 [cf. Luke 3:4] and Q 7:27), but are not found elsewhere in Q. As we shall see, the view of John in both sections is consistent, but it differs from Mark and the gospels in which Q is embedded by allowing John to appear as a prophet in his own right. Finally, at the very end of the section on John and Jesus (i.e., in Q 7:31–35), John and Jesus appear together forming a single front to which is opposed "this generation." Thus at the beginning of Q we have significant indications of deliberate compositional activity. Initial and closing pericopes dealing with John the Baptist form compositional "clamps" enclosing a quite large body of material. This phenomenon was also noted by Manson[7] and M. Jack Suggs.[8] The first section of Q thus includes:

John	Q(?) 3:1–6
John's Preaching	Q 3:7–9, 16–17
Temptations	4:1–13
Jesus' Preaching	6:20–49
Centurion's Servant	7:1–10
John and Jesus	7:18–35

It is only at the end of this section that the relationship between John and Jesus becomes clear: both are messengers of Wisdom and stand opposed to "this generation" (Q 7:31–35). The understanding of John and Jesus that surfaces in the final pericope of the first section of Q reveals the theological understanding which governed the composition of the whole section.

6. Held, "Matthew as Interpreter," 251.
7. Manson, *The Sayings of Jesus*, 66.
8. Suggs, *Wisdom*, 37–38.

Analysis of the First Section of Q

1. John the Baptist (Luke 3:1-6//Matt 3:1-6)

There is scant verbal evidence of Q in this pericope, but there are some striking agreements in the order of the material, as can be seen below.

Luke	Matthew	Mark
a.		Introduction (1:1)
b. *Time indication (3:1-2a)	Time indication (3:1a)	
c.		Malachi/Isaiah quotation (1:2-3)
d. Coming of the Word of God and of John (3:2b)	Coming of John (3:1b)	Coming of John (1:4a)
e. Location (3:3a)	Location (3:1b, 5)	Location (1:4a)
f. Characterization of John's preaching (3:3b)	Summary of John's preaching (3:2)	Characterization of John's preaching (1:4b)
g. *Isaiah quotation (3:4-6)	Isaiah quotation (3:3)	(see "c" above)
h.	John's clothing & food (3:4)	Response to John (1:5)
i.	Response to John (3:5-6)	John's clothing & food (1:6)

*Parts marked with an * contain minor verbal agreements between Matthew and Luke.

The main argument for the existence of Q in this pericope rests on the order of the Q material. The Q account presumably contained (a) a general indication of time, possibly a reference to Herod[9]; (b) a reference to the location of John's activity, perhaps "all the region about the Jordan" (Luke 3:3; Matt 3:5)[10]; and (c) the quotation of Isa 40:3 LXX with a citation formula. Thus Q contained at most only a brief introduction to John, such as, "In those days, John came preaching in all the region of the Jordan, as it is written in the book of the words of Isaiah the prophet, 'A voice crying in the wilderness, prepare the way of the Lord, make his paths straight.'"

This simple picture of John as a preacher and prophet is maintained consistently in Q, except for a few later additions. By contrast, Mark has made John part of "the gospel of Jesus Christ" (1:1). In Mark, John prepares the way for Jesus by bringing about a national repentance:[11] "all" go out to him, confessing their sins.[12] In Q, however, John prepares the way of the Lord (=Yahweh) who is soon to come in judgment. In Mark, John bears witness to Jesus not just as an important contemporary but clearly as a *successor* who eclipses John in importance. In Q, John and Jesus are allowed to stand along-

---

9. That a gospel might begin in this way is shown by the Gospel of the Ebionites, whose beginning is reported in Epiphanius, *Panarion* 30.13, 6: ἐγένετο ἐν ταῖς ἡμέραις ʽΗρώδου βασιλέως τῆς ʼΙουδαίας . . . ἦλθεν (τις) ʼΙωάννης . . . ("It happened in the days of Herod, king of Judea, that there came [a certain] John. . .). Matthew has "in those days. . ." as his introduction, which in his context refers to the days of Archelaus (Matt 2:22).

10. Though used in quite different contexts (Luke 3:3; Matt 3:5) this phrase occurs in both Luke and Matthew. Hoffmann thinks this may be a remnant of the Q introduction to 3:7-9 (*Studien*, 17); so also Easton, *St. Luke*, 36-37, and Schweizer, *Matthew*, 48.

11. Robinson, *Problem of History*, 25.

12. In Q, by contrast, John is rejected (Q 7:33).

side one another; they are observably different (Q 7:33–34), but they form a common front against "this generation."

The different views of the relation of John to Jesus in Mark and Q can also be observed in the use of the quotations from Mal 3:1.[13] In Mark, the two Old Testament references to the preparation of a way (Isa 40:3; Mal 3:1) are joined together at the beginning, and it is clear that John's work of preparing a way is something done *before* Jesus arrives and is intended to prepare the way for Jesus. However, in Q the quotation from Mal 3:1 occurs later (Q 7:27), so that even *during* Jesus' ministry John's work of preparing a way continues to have validity; that is, John prepares the way for the coming of Yahweh in judgment.[14]

2. *John's Preaching (Q 3:7–9)*

Except for a possible brief introduction, discussed above, Q 3:7–9 is the beginning of Q. It announces a fundamental theme: who are the true people of God? This is a theme which reverberates throughout Q, coming to especially clear expression in Q 13:28–29. The note of judgment sounded here also echoes throughout Q. If Luke 22:28–30//Matt 19:28 was in Q, and if it concluded Q, both of which are uncertain, then Q began and ended with the same theme. Further, John's gruff opening, "Offspring of vipers!" (γεννήματα ἐχιδνῶν, which the King James Version translated as "generation of vipers") introduces a reproachful term which will be echoed later: "this generation" (Q 7:31; 11:29, 31, 32, 51; cf. Matt 12:34; 23:33). His call for a turning to God which is evidenced by "fruit" (i.e., practical action) will be elaborated in Jesus' longer sermon in Q 6:20b–49.[15]

If John's brief address was introduced by the citation of Isa 40:3, that would imply that John prepared the way of the Lord (=Yahweh) by preaching repentance, not by baptizing or by speaking of Jesus. It is unclear whom John addressed. Both Matthew and Luke use the word "baptism" or "baptize" in their introductions to the speech. Schulz's reconstruction seems perhaps the best: "John said to those coming for baptism. . . ."[16]

Mark characterizes John's proclamation as "a baptism of repentance for the forgiveness of sins." (1:4), which probably reflects a christianized view of John's baptism; in Q, John's baptism was not sacramental.[17] Indeed, if Q

13. The comparison is valid even if Mark 1:2–3 (or at least the citation from Mal 3:1) is a later gloss.

14. In Q, John's role would have been understood in a way similar to that of the Qumran community; cf. 1 QS 8:13–14.

15. Rightly noted by Sato, *Q und Prophetie*, 33–34; cf. Hoffmann, *Studien*, 27.

16. Schulz, *Q*, 367; Matthew's "Pharisees and Sadducees" are almost certainly redactional; cf. Schulz, *Q*, 366–67; Trilling, "Die Täufertradition," 383.

17. Against Thyen, "ΒΑΠΤΙΣΜΑ ΜΕΤΑΝΟΙΑΣ," and with Schulz, *Q*, 372 n. 325. It should be noted first that Mark and Q both locate John "in the wilderness" (Mark 1:4//Matt 3:1//Luke 3:2), and both cite Isa 40:3 LXX. Thus, underlying both Mark and Q must be a tradition identifying John's activity as preparing the "way" and locating John in the desert, an interpretation of Isa 40:3 similar to that at Qumran (1 QS 8:14; 9:19), though it may be noted

contained the brief introduction conjectured by Schulz, then, according to Q at least, John found it necessary to warn that baptism is no substitute for good works as evidence of repentance.[18] John's baptismal activity, though mentioned in Q 3:16, plays no significant role in Q, despite its relatively lengthy treatment of John. It corresponds to this that Q does not use the epithet, "the Baptist."[19]

Formally, John's brief speech resembles prophetic speech, especially the announcement of disaster,[20] though, unlike the announcement of disaster, this speech contains an explicit admonition, thus implying that judgment is not inevitable. The use of prophetic speech, as well as prophetic themes such as "the coming wrath" (=the day of the Lord), corresponds well to the portrayal of John by Q as a prophet, indeed, as "more than a prophet" (Q 7:26).

It is doubtful whether the speech is a unity. If Q 3:8 were omitted, the flow of thought would be much better, and the speech would then conform to the prophetic announcement of disaster. Q 3:8 is probably a redactional addition,[21] integrated into its context by picking up the theme of bearing fruit from Q 3:9. Further, the addition picks up the theme of paternity (by vipers!) in 3:7, and expands upon that idea. This would mean that what is really new in Q 3:8 is the admonition about not presuming upon one's status as a child of Abraham, followed by the basis for this admonition ("for I tell you. . ."), i.e., Q

that the LXX also located the "voice" rather than the "way" in the wilderness (in contrast to the Masoretic text of Isa 40:3). The use of a non-LXX translation of Mal 3:1 also antedated Mark and Q (Mark 1:2//Matt 11:10//Luke 7:27); it may have been added in part because it too speaks of "preparing the way." Both of these pre-Markan and pre-Q traditions relate to John as a wilderness preacher, not as a baptist. Other traditions in Q (3:7-9; 7:24-27, 33) as well as in Mark (1:5, 6; 6:14-16) relate to John primarily as a wilderness preacher. That John was preparing a way is probably implicit in Mark 1:5. By contrast, there are few passages in the synoptics which describe John's baptizing activity aside from the use of the title "baptist" or "baptizer," and all of these relate John's baptizing to the appearance of Jesus. Therefore, these passages come under greater suspicion of having been christianized. Thyen's arguments to the contrary are not convincing: (1) "A baptism of repentance" for the forgiveness of sins is attested only by Mark 1:4; a similar view may be implicit in Mark 11:30-33. This tradition would seem to be inferior to the traditions noted above which underlie both Mark and Q since it is attested only by Mark, and by him only in or or two places. (2) Thyen's "clearest evidence" (p. 132 n. 6) that John' baptism was sacramental is the correspondence between John's baptism and the eschatological baptism with fire. This evidence depends on the Q reading of the tradition in Mark 1:8//Matt 3:11//Luke 3:16, but John's baptism is not treated as sacramental in another Q passage, 3:7-9. (3) Thyen finds "indirect evidence" (p. 132 n. 4) for his view in Josephus' denial that John's baptism granted forgiveness of sins (*Ant.* 18.117), but here Josephus only says what we also find, e.g., in 1 QS 3:4-6, with no reference to John's baptism.

18. This was also the view at Qumran, as we have seen.

19. Creed (*St. Luke*, 51) thinks that the reading in Luke 3:7, βαπτισθῆναι ἐνώπιον αὐτοῦ (Codex D, Itala; Creed mistakenly has ἔμπροσθεν in the text), may be original. If so—and if Luke represents the Q wording—then John did not actually baptize; the people merely came out to baptize themselves before him. Against such a view of John's baptism as a self-baptism, see Thyen, "ΒΑΠΤΙΣΜΑ ΜΕΤΑΝΟΙΑΣ," 132 n. 3.

20. Sato (*Q und Prophetie*, 209-11) treats it as a "mixed form," i.e., a mixture of reproach (*Scheltwort*) and admonition (*Mahnwort*). John's rhetorical question ("Who warned you. . .?") probably reflects the prophetic summons to flee; on this see Aune, *Prophecy*, 131, 311-12.

21. Cf. Hoffmann, *Studien*, 27. Kloppenborg (*Formation*, 104) is hesitant, but concedes that 3:8bc appears to be an insertion, though of indeterminate redactional level.

3:8bc. This new material provides a new assessment of what is wrong with John's addressees: not failure to produce fruits, but presumption upon their ancestry. The redactional expansion of John's speech reflects a desire to heap new accusations upon the present generation. The addition also makes clear that it is Israel as a whole ("children of Abraham") who is now addressed, not only those coming for baptism.

But the addition also introduces an entirely novel idea: being a child of Abraham is, to be sure, still the basis for one's expectation of God's salvation, but God can create of "these stones" entirely new children for Abraham![22] Thus, God's election of Israel is not denied, and yet at the same time it is suggested that others might be created as children of Abraham. Who these new children would be is not said. But, in the context of Q, we are bound to think of instances in which non-Israelites are used to put Israel to shame. That is also what seems to be implied here. So the identity of these others is unimportant; it is their function which is important, that is, their repentance represents a challenge to those who have assumed they constituted Israel. Consequently, it is best to regard Q 3:8 as a redactional creation reflecting the same interests that we will find elsewhere in the deuteronomistic redaction of Q.[23]

3. John's Preaching Continued (Q 3:16–17)

Q is clearly in evidence here, at least in Q 3:17, where the agreement between Luke and Matthew is very extensive. However, there is evidence of Q also in Luke 3:16//Matt 3:11. Here, as in Luke 3:1–6//Matt 3:1–6, the evidence for Q is largely structural:

Luke 3:16	Matthew 3:11	Mark 1:7–8
a. I baptize . . .	I baptize . . .	
b. the stronger one	the stronger one	the stronger one
a.		I baptize . . .
c. he will baptize . . .	he will baptize. . .	he will baptize . . .

Matthew and Luke agree in placing the saying about the stronger one between the contrast saying (I baptize/he will baptize), while Mark has the saying about the stronger one first. In addition, there are a few minor verbal agreements in the "a" strand: . . . $\mu\acute{\epsilon}\nu$ . . . $\beta\alpha\pi\tau\acute{\iota}\zeta\omega$ . . . $\delta\acute{\epsilon}$ . . . (. . .[particle]. . .I baptize. . . but. . .). There are no verbal agreements in the second strand ("b")

---

22. This may be based upon Isa 51:1–2; cf. Klostermann, *Matthäusevangelium*, 23. Whether "stones" is a metaphor for people of no account is unclear.

23. The combination of arrogance and refusal to repent also occurs in Q 10:13–15. The arrogance and presumption of the Jewish leaders are attacked in Q 6:41–42; 11:43 (cf. Rom 2:17–24). By contrast, see the centurion's lack of presumption (Q 7:7). For these motifs, see besides Q 10:13–15 also Gen 11:4–8; Job 15:7–13; Isa 2:11, 17; 10:12–19; 14:12–15; Ezek 28:1–10; Luke 14:11. Likewise, those who arrogantly refuse to heed the message being preached will suffer humiliation (cf. Q 3:8b; 10:13–15). "Children" are mentioned here (Q 3:8b) and in Q 7:35.

except δέ (but). In the "c" strand, Matthew and Luke are in close verbal agreement; the most striking instance comes at the end: "he will baptize with the holy spirit *and fire*."

There are serious difficulties here, however, as will soon become apparent. The words "and fire" clearly show that the baptism to which John's baptism with water is contrasted is not a Christian baptism but a baptism of judgment.[24] Correspondingly, in Q the πνεῦμα (spirit or wind) will not have been the "holy πνεῦμα (spirit)" but simply "wind."[25] As Olof Linton showed, this interpretation is certainly the preferable one, not only because it makes sense of the words "and fire" (wind and fire both being agents of judgment), but also because it fits the context (i.e., Q 3:17).[26] Moreover, in Q, 3:16–17 would have followed directly after John's preaching in Q 3:7–9, as it in fact does in Matthew.[27] Thus the context fore and aft of the contrast saying deals exclusively with judgment. This confirms the view that the baptisms which are contrasted must be those of water and of wind/fire.

It is clear that the saying about the "stronger one" is an intrusion into this context.[28] There are two alternatives for dealing with it: (1) not including it in Q at all, or (2) regarding it as a later addition to Q. These alternatives need to be considered.

First, as noted earlier, Q 3:16 is a three-stranded saying: a two-stranded contrast saying ("I baptize"/"he will baptize") separated by the saying about the "stronger one." Matthew and Luke have a common wording for the second part of the contrast saying ("he will baptize. . ."); to a lesser degree, this is also true of the first part ("I baptize. . ."). But there is no agreement (except δέ) on the "stronger one" saying. Therefore, the saying about the "stronger one" could have been taken from Mark and inserted independently by Matthew and Luke. However, because Matthew and Luke insert the saying about the "stronger one" at the same point, breaking up the contrast saying to do so, one is driven to the conclusion that some form of the saying about the "stronger one" existed in Q. Since Luke's wording for the "stronger one" saying seems to derive from Mark, we must look to Matthew, whose version of this saying differs from both Mark and Luke. That Matthew's version of the saying, which speaks of the "coming one," is to be attributed to Matthean redaction is improbable, however, because a strikingly similar saying occurs in John 1:27,[29] also linked to a saying by the Baptist that "I baptize. . ." (John 1:26). We

24. Dibelius, *Täufer*, 50; Bultmann, *History of the Synoptic Tradition*, 246, 424; Schweizer, et al., "πνεῦμα," 398–99; Grundmann, *Lukas*, 105; Hoffmann, *Studien*, 24, 28–31; and Schulz, *Q*, 376–77.
25. So Schweizer, "πμεῦμα," 399, with references.
26. Linton, "Q-Problem," 47.
27. There is a catchword connection: "fire" (Q 3:9 and 3:16).
28. So Dibelius, *Täufer*, 54.
29. Cf. Acts 19:4, where Paul uses a similar tradition to set right some disciples of John in Ephesus. This tradition is curious in its context, for it alleges that John's disciples had never heard of the baptism with the holy spirit. Yet when Paul corrects them, he says nothing about the expected "I baptize. . .but he will baptize." Instead, we have "John baptized with the

are thus led to the conclusion that Matthew has preserved an independent tradition in Matt 3:11b, and that, because Matthew and Luke agree on the location of this saying (between the halves of the contrast saying), this independent tradition is to be assigned to Q.[30] However, the phrase "one stronger than me" ($\dot{\iota}\sigma\chi\upsilon\rho\acute{o}\tau\epsilon\rho\acute{o}s$ $\mu o\upsilon$) was probably inserted by Matthew from the Markan version.

What is gained by this lengthy argument concerning the "coming one" stronger than John? Clearly, we cannot rely much on Matthew's wording of the saying, except in a general way. What is gained is this: a saying which broke up the saying contrasting two baptisms had already been added in Q. The reason for inserting the saying must have been to alter the meaning of the contrast saying. That is, the original contrast between a baptism of water (repentance) and a baptism of fire (judgment) was transformed by the inserted saying into a contrast between John's old baptism with water and Jesus' baptism with the spirit. Thus we have here a later addition to Q which stresses John's inferiority to Jesus (cf. Q 7:28, which is also a later addition with the same emphasis).

The saying about the "coming one" stronger than John not only breaks up and reinterprets the contrast saying in Q 3:16, but it breaks up the linkage of Q 3:7–9 to 3:16–17. This material belonged together before the redactional insertion of the "coming one" saying, as can be seen from the context as well as from the catchword connection ("fire"). When this material is examined, without the inserted "coming one" saying, it can be seen that John's preaching is entirely preoccupied with the coming judgment.

4. The Baptism of Jesus (Luke 3:21–22//Matt 3:13, 16–17//Mark 1:9–11)

One might presume that Q would have had an account of Jesus' being baptized by John because the temptation account would seem to presuppose an identification of Jesus as "son" such as we have in the baptism account, but if it did there are few traces of it left. Yet one may suspect faint traces of it beneath the text of Matthew and Luke.[31] There are few verbal agreements: the

baptism of repentance, telling the people to believe in the one who was to come after him. . . ." This suggests that Luke has preserved here another instance of the tradition attested in the Fourth Gospel. Cf. Acts 13:24–25.

Justin *Dial.* 49.3 probably does not represent an independent tradition; it agrees at virtually every point with Matthew. Yet if Justin used Matthew, he must have understood "coming one" as a title, for he has (with Luke) omitted $\dot{o}\pi\acute{\iota}\sigma\omega$ $\mu o\upsilon$ (behind me) and gives simply $\mathring{\eta}\xi\epsilon\iota$ $\delta\grave{\epsilon}$ $\acute{o}$ $\dot{\iota}\sigma\chi\upsilon\rho\acute{o}\tau\epsilon\rho\acute{o}s$ $\mu o\upsilon$ (and one stronger than I will come) (without $\acute{o}$ $\dot{\epsilon}\rho\chi\acute{o}\mu\epsilon\nu os$).

30. Similarly Hoffmann, *Studien*, 16, 18; Schulz, *Q*, 368.

31. See, e.g., Grundmann, *Matthäus*, 95–96. Bultmann (*History of the Synoptic Tradition*, 251) thinks Q had no account of the baptism of Jesus, or at most only the baptism itself; he is not persuaded (p. 251 n. 5) by the common argument that the temptation account presupposes the baptism account. Similarly, Knox, *Sources*, 2. 4; Vögtle, "Taufperikope," 108–11. Vögtle thinks that if Q did have a baptism account, which he doubts, it would not have differed significantly from Mark's. Strecker (*Der Weg*, 150, 178) thinks Matthew depends on oral tradition. Arguing for a Q version of the baptism account: Creed, *St. Luke*, 55–58; Schürmann, *Lukasevangelium*, 197, 218.

use (in not quite the same form or location) of an aorist passive participle form of βαπτίζειν (to baptize); the use of the verb ἀνοίγειν (to open); the placement of καταβαίνειν (to come down) before ὡς περιστεράν ("as a dove"); the coming of the spirit ἐπ᾽ αὐτοῦ ("upon him")[32]; and possibly Matthew's πνεῦμα θεοῦ ("spirit of God"). Yet all this does not add up to very much material. If Q did contain an account of Jesus' baptism, it probably said no more than that Jesus was baptized, the heavens opened, and the spirit descended upon Jesus.[33]

There is no evidence that the heavenly audition of Q 3:22 ("You are my son. . .") existed in Q, except for the circumstantial evidence, often adduced, that the reference to "son of God" in the immediately succeeding temptation account presupposes the audition in the baptism account. A very brief account featuring Jesus as the culmination of a line of prophets sent by Wisdom—and resembling the account in the Gospel of the Hebrews[34]—might have been appropriate in Q, because of the similar idea found in Q 11:49. But the evidence for Q in 3:21–22 is too uncertain to permit its use as evidence for the theological character of Q.

5. The Temptations (Q 4:1–13)

The temptation story has produced a colorful history of interpretation.[35] However, with some exceptions, more recent interpretations tend to turn away from the overly subtle interpretations of the past, largely by concentrating on details internal to the story.[36]

Although Lührmann does not think the temptation pericope comes from Q,[37] he is in a minority among commentators. On the normal criterion for Q of

32. The attestation for the preposition in Mark 1:10 is divided: εἰς is attested by B D f[13] and a few others, ἐπί by ℵ A L W Θ f[1] the "Majority text" (Nestle-Aland[26]) and the Syriac MSS. While εἰς with καταβαίνειν is actually more common in the New Testament than ἐπί, it is not usually used when καταβαίνειν means "come down from above, descend" (as opposed to "come down" from one geographical location to another). The εἰς in Mark 1:10 is generally accepted, probably because it is attested in B and D, and because it is the *lectio difficilior*. In Mark 1:10, εἰς must mean "to," not "into."

33. If Q contained this and nothing more, it might represent a tradition like that presupposed in the Fourth Gospel. That is, John does not know who Jesus is until after the baptism, when the spirit descends and identifies him. In contrast to Mark, who seems to have Jesus coming alone to be baptized, Q would, if anything, seem to have had Jesus as one of many being baptized. Matthew has gone beyond Mark in stressing Jesus' *intention* to be baptized (see Barth, "Matthew's Understanding of the Law," 137).

34. See Jerome *Commentary on Isaiah 4* (on Isa 11:2), where the Spirit (=Wisdom) descends upon Jesus and says to him, "My son, in all the prophets I was waiting for you, that you might come, and I might find rest in you. . . ." The Latin text is given in Aland, *Synopsis*, 27: *Fili mi, in omnibus Prophetis exspectabam te, ut venires, et requiescerem in te.* On the phrase "in all the prophets I was waiting for you," see Bacon, "'Son' as Organ," 411–13, and Vielhauer, "Jewish-Christian Gospels," 161, 163–64.

35. See the survey of interpretations in Schnackenburg, "Der Sinn der Versuchung Jesu," 101–4, 126–28. For more recent bibliography, see Fitzmyer, *Luke I-IX*, 519–20.

36. More recent interpretations include Schottroff and Stegemann, *Jesus von Nazareth*, 72–77 (ET: *Jesus*, 53–57); Zeller, *Kommentar*, 21–25; Kloppenborg, *Formation*, 246–62. Smith provides an example of an interpretation not based on details internal to the story (*Jesus the Magician*, 104–6).

37. Lührmann, *Redaktion*, 56. Likewise, Argyle, "The Accounts of the Temptations," 382.

agreement between Matthew and Luke against Mark, there can hardly be found any reason to deny the story to Q. Lührmann's objection to it, however, is based on another consideration—the fact that it is so different from the rest of the Q material. There is validity to this objection but it cannot, without further ado, be used to exclude the account from Q.

The fact that the Q introduction to the pericope has been blurred by the redactional activity of Matthew and Luke makes it difficult to study the context of the temptation account in Q. However, if Q contained a baptismal account, there is a catchword connection between it and the temptation account: $\pi\nu\epsilon\hat{\upsilon}\mu\alpha$ ("spirit" or "wind"). The temptation scene is located, as was John's activity, in the wilderness ($\check{\epsilon}\rho\eta\mu\sigma$).

It is perhaps only accidental that the final temptation (in Matthew) leaves Jesus on a mountain, and that the sermon, which in Q would have followed immediately, has (in Matthew) Jesus preaching from "the mountain," the devil having fled, and the crowds/disciples having drawn near. The three temptations are matched formally by the three (plus one) beatitudes which introduce Jesus' preaching; however, I see no material relationship between the two threesomes.

Determining the meaning of the temptation account is no easy matter; it has provided grist for the mill of many an imaginative interpreter. One will do well to begin with certain obvious features of the pericope.

First, Jesus and the devil ($\delta\iota\acute{\alpha}\beta\sigma\lambda\sigma$) are put face to face; the devil here makes a rare personal appearance. The devil tempts Jesus three times and, having failed, departs (so the Q account seems to end). The devil has not been "bound"[38] or defeated, only repulsed. No angels come to minister to Jesus in Q (cf. Mark 1:13). And though a "son of God" has shown himself impervious to the assaults of the devil, we are not left with the impression that the devil simply gave up and went home. He will, no doubt, continue his ways. This inconclusiveness of the confrontation corresponds to the absence in the Q account of a Mark-like eschatological setting.[39] It also corresponds to the fact that we are not dealing with a confrontation between the son of God and the devil (note that $\upsilon\iota\acute{\sigma}$ [son] is anarthrous). No final victory over the devil, thus, was in view; in fact, the devil remains ruler over the "kingdoms of the world" (Q 4:5).

The second obvious feature of the Q temptation account is the use of biblical quotations. These are remarkable for several reasons. They come from the LXX[40] and so presumably from a primarily Greek-speaking community. One might assume that such quotations would be late relative to most of the other Q material, yet the use of the LXX is typical for Q.[41] Further, all of Jesus'

Argyle holds that Q is of Aramaic origin, and excludes the temptation account from Q because of the use of the LXX.

38. So Kümmel, *Promise and Fulfilment*, 109 n. 13.
39. On Mark's setting, see Robinson, *The Problem of History*, 28–32.
40. See Stendahl, *The School of St. Matthew*, 88–89.
41. Johnson, "The Biblical Quotations in Matthew," 139 n. 14; 152–53.

quotations in the Q temptation account come from one place: Deuteronomy 6–8. This suggests that Q might have intended to present Jesus as the faithful son who stands in contrast to the faithless generation addressed by Moses in Deuteronomy 6–8.

There are other possible allusions to deuteronomic and Exodus traditions: the wilderness setting; testing; 40 days (cf. 40 years); a bread miracle; a view of the kingdoms of the world (cf. Moses' view from Mount Nebo); hunger; Jesus' obedience. Yet few of the possible allusions in the temptation account point unerringly to Deuteronomy. Deuteronomy mentions manna but not bread from stones. The mountain-top view of the world is only vaguely similar to Moses' view; among other things, one view is of the Promised Land, the other of "this world." Moreover, though Mark (and, following him, Luke) has Jesus being tempted *during* the forty days in the wilderness, Matthew (apparently representing Q) has Jesus tempted *after* the forty-day fast.[42] If Q had had in mind the identification Jesus=son of God=Israel tested in the wilderness,[43] it would seem that the details would have been arranged to fit better, at least if such an identification was the main point of the account. Nevertheless, the Q temptation account has a certain deuteronomic character, and the use by Jesus of three quotations from Deuteronomy 6–8 was probably not accidental. We will notice elsewhere that the deuteronomistic tradition is important in Q. In this respect, the Q temptation account is comprehensible as a product of the Q community, perhaps the product of later Q scribes. That the temptation account was, in fact, the product of scribes, or that scribal debates stand in the background, has often been affirmed.[44] This would mean that the pericope was probably produced in a wisdom milieu.[45] We shall return to these suggestions shortly.

A third obvious feature of the Q temptation account which is often em-

---

42. Or does Matthew only wish to intensify Jesus' hunger to provide a basis for the temptation? Schulz (*Q*, 178) argues that Matthew here preserves the Q version.

43. So, e.g., Polag, *Christologie*, 147.

44. Bultmann (*History of the Synoptic Tradition*, 254) regards the temptation story as "scribal Haggadah"; see also Haenchen, *Der Weg Jesu* [The Pathway of Jesus], 64–72, and Schulz, *Q*, 184. Schulz (pp. 184–85) also notes that the motif typical of the Markan controversy dialogues—the discussion about the validity of the Torah—is altogether absent from Q; quite the contrary, here "the Torah alone legitimates and grounds the divine sonship of the earthly Jesus" (p. 189). Haenchen (*Der Weg Jesu*, 68) prefers to call the pericope a didactic poem (on p. 72 he defends the use of "poem"); he considers the Q temptation to have been produced by "Christian scribes" (pp. 67, 69, 72). Gerhardsson calls the pericope "haggadic midrash," and has devoted a monograph to the subject: *The Testing of God's Son*. Also attributing the story to scribes: Fridrichsen, *The Problem of Miracle*, 125–26; Thomas, "Torah Citations," 95–96; Polag, *Christologie*, 146–47; Percy, *Die Botschaft Jesu*, 17.

45. Whatever may be the relation of scribe to Pharisee, it seems clear that scribes and sages are the same. This is evident in Sir 38:24–39:11 (cf. Ahiqar 1:1 and the collocation of "scribe" and "sage" in Matt 23:34; 1 Cor 1:20). The successors to Ezra the scribe were the sages (*m. 'Abot*). See also Moore, *Judaism* 1. 37–47; Black, "Scribe," 246–48; Jeremias, *Jerusalem*, 112–16, 233–45; Urbach, "Sages," 636–55 and *The Sages*; and Horsley, *Jesus and the Spiral of Violence*, 62–77. Saldarini regards scribes and sages as distinct, though these roles could merge, as in Sirach (*Pharisee, Scribes and Sadducees*, 256).

phasized is that it has to do with miracles. More precisely, it deals with two attempts by the devil to get Jesus to act with the expectation of a miraculous divine intervention, prefaced each time with the devil's, "If you are a son of God. . . ." The last temptation in Matthew, whose order is generally regarded as representing Q,[46] does not use the title "son of God" and does not involve a miraculous intervention. Rather it involves the devil's effort to get Jesus to worship him in exchange for control over the kingdoms of the world.

The significance of the miraculous interventions is not clear. Samson Eitrem, for example, argued that the first two temptations involved the performance of typically magical feats.[47] This corresponds, so it is usually held, to the hellenistic notion of the $\theta\epsilon\hat{\iota}os$ $\grave{a}\nu\acute{\eta}\rho$ (divine man).[48] But neither of these interpretations is tenable. There is no one in the wilderness to watch such magical feats. And the assumption that "son of God" is a title conceptually equivalent to other instances of this title in the New Testament (and elsewhere) is not justified by the text, which speaks of "a son of God." Moreover, the emphasis in the story is on Jesus' answers, and they have nothing to do with rejecting the use of magic.[49] Unconvincing also is Hoffmann's view that the story implies a rebuttal of the messianic views of radical Jewish freedom movements.[50] Schulz rightly objects that Hoffmann fails to notice the difference between the first two non-messianic temptations and the third messianic one.[51]

The first two temptations may contain polemic against a view of Jesus as miracle worker.[52] However, the assumption behind them is not that a son of

46. See, e.g., Schulz, *Q*, 177. For a different view see Percy, *Die Botschaft Jesu*, 17–18.

47. Eitrem, *Die Versuchung Christi*. For the creation of bread as a magical act, cf. Schulz, *Q*, 186 n. 88. For the "flight" from the pinnacle of the Temple, see Wetter, "*Der Sohn Gottes*," 87–89, 139–40; Betz, *Lukian von Samosata*, 168; Smith, *Jesus the Magician*, 105, 194. Percy correctly objected (*Die Botschaft Jesu*, 15–16) that this magical interpretation flies in face of the text itself; the emphasis in the story lies rather on Jesus' answers.

48. On the $\theta\epsilon\hat{\iota}os$ $\grave{a}\nu\acute{\eta}\rho$ christology, see Betz, "Jesus as Divine Man," and Tiede, *The Charismatic Figure as Miracle Worker*, esp. 241–92.

49. Wetter ("*Der Sohn Gottes*," 139–40) argues that "son of God" is associated with the first two temptations, which concern miracles, and this confirms the link between "son of God" and miracle-working; further confirmation of this is found in the last temptation, where there is no miracle and no "son of God" title. This, he says, is "hardly accidental."

This distinction between the first two and the last temptation is very common. See, e.g., Hahn, *The Titles of Jesus*, 158, 295; Schweizer, *Matthew*, 58. But the distinction is convincing only when one judges that the first two temptations are really calls to Jesus to perform miracles, and that lying behind these calls is the idea of a miracle-working "son of God." But the "miracles" are not messianic, both because they really do not represent eschatological repetitions of *heilsgeschichtlich* times and because, as Percy (*Die Botschaft Jesu*, 14) and Haenchen (*Der Weg Jesu*, 67) point out, no one is there to watch the miracles.

50. Hoffmann, "Die Versuchungsgeschichte," 207–23; Blank, "Zur Christologie," 117–21; cf. Jeremias, *New Testament Theology*, 71–72. Against the idea of messianic overtones are Braun, "Qumran," 107–8; Bultmann, *History of the Synoptic Tradition*, 254–55; Percy, *Die Botschaft Jesu*, 13–18; Kloppenborg, *Formation*, 254–56.

51. Schulz, *Q*, 187 n. 100.

52. See Betz, "Jesus as Divine Man," 119; Schulz, *Q*, 187–90. Support for this view seems to be dwindling; see, e.g., Schottroff and Stegemann, *Jesus and the Hope of the Poor*, 56–57; Kloppenborg, *Formation*, 253–54.

God has power to perform miracles. Rather, it is that a son of God has a right to expect that Yahweh will intervene miraculously to rescue one of the elect endangered by hunger or by falling (Q 4:3, 9–11). Indeed, the devil even proposes to put this expectation of divine deliverance to the test. This becomes especially clear in the second temptation, where testing God is explicitly rejected (Q 4:12). But even the first proposal (Q 4:3–4) is rejected not because it would involve the exercise of miracle-working powers but rather because it focuses on the divine provision of food, and hence implies that God's own can expect such deliverance from vulnerability.[53] This is, no doubt, intended to be paradigmatic for the members of the community. Jesus ironically proves himself a son of God by not accepting the very challenges designed to prove him a son of God. From this we are to learn that a true son of God accepts vulnerability, does not expect divine resolution of all human problems, but rather lives in obedience to Yahweh.

When the emphasis is placed on the rejection of the expectation of divine deliverance in the first two temptations, then their connection to the third temptation becomes more evident. A true son of God does not live in the expectation that Yahweh will hand control of the kingdoms of the world over to the elect. This is hard to read as anything but anti-apocalyptic, although it does seem to presuppose the apocalyptic view that the devil is in control of the kingdoms of the world.

The question that must be asked, of course, is why the Q community found it necessary to warn against a piety that focuses on the expectation of divine deliverance. This could be a corrective to the piety to be found in certain contemporary Jewish groups. But since, as I shall argue, the temptation story both presupposes (and thus stands in continuity with) other Q materials, and at the same time is so different from the rest of Q, we must judge that it was a later addition from within the Q community. If that is the case, then it must be directed either against other Jewish groups well-known to the Q community, or against tendencies at work in the Q community itself. What was the piety opposed by this story? It must have been a piety whose views are expressed by the devil. That is, the temptation story was intended to counter an enthusiastic, apocalyptic expectation of divine intervention.

There are several signs of lateness in the temptation pericope: the use of the title, "son of God"[54]; the use of the LXX and, indeed, of the only explicit

53. Nevertheless, the contrast with the traditions of Jesus' miraculous feedings (Mark 6:30–44; 8:1–10; John 6:1–13) is striking.

54. The title "son" occurs elsewhere in Q (10:22), but this is the only instance of "son of God." And yet it is doubtful that in the temptation story "son of God" is to be understood as a christological title; one would do so only because it is used elsewhere in Christian tradition as a title, not because the context of the story calls for such an interpretation. In any case, it is difficult to see a relationship between the revealer "son" in Q 10:22 and the obedient "son of God" in the temptation story.

quotations in the whole of Q[55]; the apparently late literary form[56]; and the use of the name διάβολος for the Evil One, which is attested nowhere else in Q.[57] All of this gives warning of the possibility that the temptation account was added to Q after the other material had already been assembled, or that at least it might have undergone expansion and development at a very late stage in the history of Q.

Another factor which suggests that the temptation account was a late addition is the fact that it seems to presuppose the rest of the Q material. It was this which led Petr Pokorný to call the pericope "a summary created by its learned collector."[58] Among these possible allusions we may list these:

• Jesus being "led" to be tempted (cf. Q 11:4: "lead us not into temptation");
• his changing stones to bread (Q 4:3; cf. Matt 7:9, which is probably original over against Luke 11:11-12,[59] "What person among you, if his son asks for bread, will give him a stone?");
• Jesus' consistent refusal to perform miracles seen as violations of true obedience (cf. Jesus' saying about signs in Q 11:29);
• the emphasis on the word (Q 4:4: "A human being does not live by bread alone but by every word. . ."; cf. the story of the centurion's servant in Q 7:1-10[60] and the parable of the builders or houses in Q 6:47-49);
• the reference to the devil's kingdom (only in Q 4:5-6 and 11:18).

One might also speculate that a community which knew of promises such as Q 12:7 ("Why, even the hairs on your head are all numbered") might be led to reflect on deliberate exposure to danger as a test of the Father's gracious care, and come to such a conclusion as Jesus does in Q 4:12.[61] One could notice other apparent allusions. But this evidence falls short of proof since it rests on mere allusions. Yet as part of a larger argument for the lateness of the pericope, it does carry some weight. Of course, it was not the purpose of the pericope to be a summary; the point is only that much of Q seems to be presupposed by the pericope.

55. Stendahl, *School of St. Matthew*, 149; Schulz, *Q*, 185.
56. The fact that the temptation account is narrative sets it apart from the rest of Q (except Q 7:1-10), and therefore its tradition history is likely to be different from that of the sayings material. It is further likely that narrative antedated sayings rather than the other way around—a point confirmed by the content of the narrative material.
57. The notion of the devil (or Satan) as a tempter is certainly to be found in pre-Christian Judaism (1 Chr 21:1 LXX), but not the idea of Satan as ruler of the world (Foerster and von Rad, "διάβολος," 77; Hammer, "Devil," 838). To some extent, a distinction may be made between Palestinian usage (which prefers "Satan") and hellenistic usage (where devil, "or διάβολος) predominates. Hammer notes that the authentic letters of Paul use σατανᾶς whereas the inauthentic ones use διάβολος ("Devil," 838).
58. Pokorný, "The Temptation Stories," 126.
59. So Schulz, *Q*, 162.
60. Robinson, "Kerygma and History," 56-58.
61. We seem to have in Q 4:9-12 polemic against an enthusiasm which supposes itself to be totally under God's care and immune to danger. If so, we have further evidence of the lateness of the pericope, since it will have arisen, in part at least, to combat tendencies not yet evident in Q but which could have been fostered by some of the material in Q.

Whether or not the temptation account was later added to Q, it is still possible to ask what sort of introduction to Jesus it would have provided the reader/hearer of Q. As noted earlier, the story has paradigmatic significance for the community. But beyond that, it also implies that Jesus is to be seen as the exemplary Jew, able to muster scripture quotations which repulse the devil. At the same time, he is the model of unwavering obedience to God—he is a true son of God. Moreover, as Schniewind has pointed out, Jesus' quotation from Deuteronomy 6 has a direct relationship to the Shema.[62] Thus Jesus takes his stand on the central Jewish confession. This quotation comes as the climax to the whole account.[63]

It has been noted that the temptation account may have been the product of scribes. This may provide the most important clue to the nature of the pericope. For it is quite clear that the bones upon which the flesh of the story is hung are the quotations from Deuteronomy.[64] These quotations may also be chronologically primary. That is, the scenes may have been invented to fit the quotations.[65] It is, on the face of it, improbable that the scenes or temptations existed independently and then were assembled by a Q compiler, who inserted quotations from Deuteronomy to fit the scenes.

Despite Bultmann's association of the Q temptation account with "historical stories and legends," he is certainly aware of the similarity of the Q account to rabbinic disputations.[66] The classification by Bultmann is actually based on the narrative framework, and was occasioned no doubt by the treatment of Mark's temptation account in the same category. But it is a characteristic of controversy dialogues that the scenes are all "imaginary."[67] So it would be quite in character for the Q temptation account, considered as a controversy dialogue, to contain imaginary scenes created to match the quotations at hand.[68] Further, the fact that we have to do with three quotations, all from Deuteronomy 6–8, suggests that the pericope was a unified composition and was not built up from individual scenes.[69]

It is possible that one or more of the scenes in the Q temptation account circulated as independent traditions, at least according to some scholars. For

62. Schniewind, *Matthäus*, 29; see also Polag, *Christologie*, 148.
63. So also Schulz, *Q*, 187. Cf. John 14:30–31, where Jesus tells the disciples that "the ruler of this world is coming" but "He has no power over me; but I do as the Father has commanded me. . . ."
64. This is often noted; see, e.g., Dupont, "L'origine du récit des tentations."
65. The same phenomenon occurs in the passion narrative. Conzelmann, for example, notes that "entire motifs, indeed entire scenes (e.g., Jesus before Herod, Luke 23:6–16) are created out of Old Testament texts" (*Jesus*, 83–84).
66. Bultmann, *History of the Synoptic Tradition*, 254. Bultmann even cites controversies carried out with scripture quotations, including one in which a rabbi disputes with the Lord of the demons (p. 254 n. 5).
67. Bultmann, *History of the Synoptic Tradition*, 40; see also 46–47.
68. Percy (*Die Botschaft Jesu*, 17–18) has a similar view; cf. also Lohmeyer, "Die Versuchung Christi," though Lohmeyer reckons with three versions, and not with a Q version of the temptation.
69. So too Schulz, *Q*, 185; Thomas, "Torah Citations," 95.

example, Ernst Lohmeyer held that the third temptation—the one where Jesus is offered the kingdoms of this world—existed as a separate tradition.[70] Lohmeyer has in mind a saying of Jesus attributed to the Gospel of the Hebrews and attested in Origen and Jerome, most fully in Origen *Commentary on John* 2.12.87 (on John 1:3).[71] There Jesus is quoted as saying, "Even so did my mother, the holy spirit, take me by one of my hairs and carry me away on to the great mountain Tabor." Whether this strange saying refers to the temptation or to the transfiguration or, for that matter, to something else not recorded in the canonical gospels, is a matter of dispute.[72]

If the third temptation, where the devil takes Jesus up to a high mountain, does preserve a recollection of the tradition contained in the Gospel of the Hebrews, where the holy spirit takes Jesus to Tabor, then radical changes have occurred. The spirit/mother has become the devil; the specific mountain, Tabor near Nazareth, has become merely a "very high mountain"; the account has become a temptation; and the quotation of Jesus has become a vignette about him. Even if Q did draw upon such a tradition, there is no evidence that it circulated as a *temptation*. Therefore there is no reason to challenge the view that the Q temptation account was a unified composition.

The setting for the first temptation, moveover, appears to have been no more extensive than necessary to introduce the dialogue in Q 4:3–4. The words Matthew and Luke have in common permit only a conjectural reconstruction, perhaps: "Jesus was led (by the spirit [?]) into the wilderness. And he was hungry."[73]

The second temptation (Q 4:9–12) has a striking parallel in Wis 2:17–20.[74] There the foolish enemies of the "righteous man" (who is also a wise man) complain that he "boasts that God is his father" (Wis 2:16). And they then begin plotting:

> Let us see if his words are true,
> and let us test what will happen at the end of his life;
> for if the righteous man is God's son, he will help him,
> and will deliver him from the hand of his adversaries. . . .
> Let us condemn him to a shameful death,
> for, according to what he says, he will be protected. (Wis 2:17–18, 20)

---

70. Lohmeyer and Schmauch, *Das Evangelium des Matthäus*, 53. Lohmeyer appeals to "a tradition of πειρασμοί" on the basis of Heb 4:15, and mentions especially the third temptation as attested independently by the Gospel of the Ebionites. See also Lohmeyer, "Die Versuchung Christi."

71. The Greek text of the fragment is printed in K. Aland, *Synopsis*, 34. See also Vielhauer, "Jewish-Christian Gospels," 164, and his introduction to "The Gospel of the Hebrews," 158–63 (see also p. 120).

72. Vielhauer ("Jewish Christian Gospels," 120) says it has to do with the temptation, not the transfiguration. Concerning Jesus being transported by the spirit who holds one of the hairs of his head, cf. Ezek 8:3; Bel 36.

73. Similarly, Schulz, *Q*, 179.

74. So Lohmeyer, "Die Versuchung Christi," 103–4.

Here is to be found the phrase, "if he is God's son. . ." (cf. Q 4:3, 9), and with it the idea that God will protect him.[75] Of course, it was not the view that one should set up a test of God's gracious care, as the devil proposes.[76] But temptation, in fact, is a regular *topos* in the wisdom literature.[77] For example, one finds the view that the Lord disciplines a person as a father does his son (Prov 3:11–12; cf. Sir 2:1, 5); this view is applied to the "righteous man" of the Wisdom of Solomon (see Wis 3:5–6). In Sir 4:17–18 this same view appears in the form of a testing by Wisdom herself to find those worthy of her (cf. Wis 1:1–5).

It would seem therefore that the influence of the wisdom tradition was fundamental to the formation of the Q temptation account. And since there is little evidence that the temptation scenes existed as independent traditions,[78] we may conclude that the Q temptation account is a unified whole, the product of scribal activity.

Since the temptation account seems to have been added at a later stage in the growth of Q, it probably reflects currents at work in this later stage. One such current seems to have been scribal wisdom.[79] Matthew may represent the true continuator of this tradition. It has been argued that he represents a scribal wisdom (cf. Matt 13:52) which identified Jesus with Wisdom, but with Wisdom understood as Torah.[80] The fact that in Matthew Q appears broken up and rearranged into discourses, and subjected as well to expansion and revision, can be understood as an indication that Q had been more thoroughly assimilated and more constantly used in the Matthean group than in the Lukan group. Correspondingly, Luke's less free use of Q can be understood as reflecting a lesser degree of assimilation and adaptation of the document.

We may conclude that Q did contain an account of the temptations of Jesus, but that the account was added at a late stage in the history of Q. We noted the scribal, midrashic character of the account, built up out of three quotations from Deuteronomy 6–8 LXX. Jesus emerged as a model scribe whose role as "son" may reflect the wisdom tradition, especially Wisdom of Solomon 2. As such, however, he becomes a paradigm for the community: here is what a true "son of God" is (cf. Q 6:35). The central thrust of the temptation story is a call for obedience to Yahweh, a call issued in the context of expectations that

---

75. Matthew, in his passion narrative, picks up the phrase, "If he is God's son. . ." (Matt 27:40; cf. 27:43). On this, see Lohmeyer, "Die Versuchung Christi," 104, and Schweizer, *Matthew*, 513.

76. Cf. Sir 3:26b: "Whoever loves danger will perish by it."

77. See Andrews, "*Peirasmos*," 229–44; Lohmeyer, "Die Versuchung Christi," 114; Dibelius and Greeven, *James*, 69–74, and the excursus, "The Abraham Example," 168–74; Bultmann, *History of the Synoptic Tradition*, 254–57; Kloppenborg, *Formation*, 260–61.

78. So Schulz, *Q*, 185 n. 81.

79. See also Lührmann's appendix, "Zur weiteren Überlieferung der Logienquelle," in *Redaktion*, 105–21.

80. See Suggs, *Wisdom*, 99–127; Bornkamm, "The Risen Lord," 203–29, and Stendahl, *School of St. Matthew*, *passim*.

Yahweh will intervene dramatically to deliver the elect from their troubles and hand them the kingdoms of the world.

The community which produced the temptation account must have maintained the central Jewish confession of one God, and so regarded itself as standing firmly within Jewish tradition. At the same time, it regarded Jesus as a model of obedience, a true "son" in contrast to Israel which had proven disobedient in the wilderness (cf. Exod 4:22; Hos 11:1). This would suggest that Q, at the latest stage that we can discern prior to its use by Matthew and Luke, was not moving toward separation from its Jewish identity or from observance of the Torah; rather, it seems to have been resisting apocalyptic and enthusiastic tendencies which would have pulled it in that direction.

6. Jesus' Preaching (Q 6:20–49)

Traditionally called a "sermon," the preaching ascribed to Jesus by Matthew and Luke is really a pastiche. This is evident from an analysis of the content as well as from superficial features, such as grammatical shifts from the second person singular to the plural, and back to the singular (e.g., Q 6: 27–28, 29–30, 31). The "sermon," therefore, needs to be thought of as a small collection of sayings. We cannot here provide an analysis of the structure of the sermon, but there is no reason to think that it is without structure, despite the evidence, already noted, of breaks and unevenness.

The Wisdom Background of the Sermon

The sermon is really, as noted, a collection of sayings. Thus, formally it stands within the wisdom tradition. The form of the individual sayings is also typical of the wisdom tradition. If one follows Bultmann's classification, all of the sayings in the Q (Lukan) sermon are wisdom sayings of various kinds, except for the beatitudes (and woes), a prophetic saying in Q 6:46, and the similitude in Q 6:47–49.[81] Even the sayings which Bultmann did not class form-critically as wisdom sayings are closely related to the wisdom tradition. The beatitudes, for example, have their roots in the wisdom tradition,[82] though they seem to have received their present form through apocalyptic influence.[83] And it is by no means clear that Q 6:46, which Bultmann classifies

---

81. Bultmann, *History of the Synoptic Tradition*. For Q 6:27–28, see p. 79; Q 6:29–30, pp. 79, 105; Q 6:31, pp. 77, 81, 103; Q 6:32–36, p. 79; Q 6:37–38b, p. 79; Q 6:39, pp. 81, 99, 102; Q 6:40, pp. 76, 99, 103; Q 6:41–42, pp. 79–80; Q 6:43–44, p. 74; Q 6:45, p. 75 (for v. 45a) and p. 73 (for v. 45b); Q 6:46, pp. 116–17 (prophetic); Q 6:47–49, pp. 173, 193 (similitude). The beatitudes (pp. 111–12) and woes (pp. 109–10) are listed in the category of prophetic and apocalyptic sayings, the latter as minatory sayings.

82. See, e.g., Koch, *The Growth of the Biblical Tradition*, 6–8, 16–18. See also Kieffer, "Wisdom and Blessing," 291–95; Bertram and Hauck, "μακάριος," 365–66; George, "La 'forme' des Béatitudes," 398–403; Gerstenberger, "The Woe-Oracles," 249–63.

83. Koch, *The Growth of the Biblical Tradition*, 7. Cf. Robinson, "Formal Structure," 98 and 278 n. 25; Schweizer, "Formgeschichtliches zu den Seligpreisungen Jesu," 121–26.

as a "prophetic saying," is really prophetic. Certainly, the Matthean form of the saying should be regarded as a prophetic saying. However, Bultmann himself regarded the Lukan form as the original and said that "in Luke the address ['lord, lord'] is only to the teacher."[84] Finally, the similitude of the two builders/houses has its closest parallels in the wisdom parables of the rabbinic tradition, e.g., *m. 'Abot* 3:22; *'Abot R. Nat.* 24.[85] Thus the predominantly sapiential character of the material in Jesus' "sermon" is clear.

Material parallels from the wisdom tradition to sayings in Q 6:20–49 are too numerous to collect here. However, it is worth calling attention to a few of them:

84. Bultmann, *History of the Synoptic Tradition*, 116 and n. 2; cf. 126. See also Fuller, *Foundations of New Testament Christology*, 119 and 137 n. 66; Barth, "Matthew's Understanding of the Law," 74.

85. The eschatological character of the parable, emphasized by Jeremias (*Parables of Jesus*, 194), is flatly denied by Linnemann, ("Zeitansage und Zeitvorstellung," 239). Cf. Jeske, "Wisdom and the Future," 113–14; Edwards, *A Theology of Q*, 92–93. Both Jeske and Edwards stress the wisdom character of the parable. Windisch (*Meaning of the Sermon on the Mount*, 42), who stresses the wisdom background of Jesus' sermon, notes that in this parable we again have traditional wisdom material, though united in the "most intimate association" with eschatology.

The most important observation to be made in this context, however, concerns the use of a house parable as the conclusion to a collection of sayings. Sawyer ("The Ruined House," 519–31) has noted that the figure of the ruined house occurs at the end of a number of collections, including Proverbs 1–9; Job 3–27 (at the end of three cycles of speeches), Ecclesiastes and the sermon in Q 6:20–49. To these may be added the reference to a ruined house in Prov 15:25, 27 at the end of a minor collection (Proverbs 10–15) and the more general reference to ruin in Prov 24:21–22 (at the end of another minor collection in Prov 22:17–24:22). Perhaps to be included here are Q 13:34–35 (the last of the wisdom pericopes in Q, though its original context in Q is uncertain), and Q 11: 24–26 in relation to the Beelzebul pericope (Q 11:14–23).

The observations above should be understood in the context of the general tendency to close a collection of sayings, teachings, or admonitions with warnings about the fateful consequences of obeying or disobeying the preceding material and/or reference to the reward awaiting those who follow these teachings. A reference to a house in ruin seems to have been a stereotyped way of conforming to the general pattern for concluding collections. Finkelstein ("Introductory Study," 16 n. 6) noted that "apparently the redactor of the Mishna made an effort to conclude each chapter of *Abot* with some statement referring to the reward of merit." Promises of reward are also used to conclude small collections within Q (Q 6:20b-23, 27–35, 36–38; 12:22–34; cf. 17:22–33 and perhaps 22:28–30 as the conclusion to Q as a whole). The fateful consequences of the content of the collection are emphasized at the end of Q 10:1–16; 11:14–23; 12:2–9 (cf. Prov 1:32–33 as the conclusion to the poem in 1:20–32). When Matthew adds the adjectives "wise" and "foolish" to the parable of the houses/builders at the end of the sermon, he is again following a precedent for concluding a collection; cf., e.g., the end of the collections in Proverbs 1–9 and 10:1–22:16. Matthew also follows a typical pattern when he introduces the invitation of Jesus/Wisdom in 11:28–30. Such invitations seem to conclude wisdom poems in which Wisdom is identified with Torah and issues an appeal; see Sir 6:18–37 (as the conclusion to Sirach 1–6); Sir 24:19–22; 51:23–30; Prov 3:21–26 (as the conclusion to the poem in 3:13–26); Proverbs 9; Bar 4:1 (as conclusion to Bar 3:9–4:4); and Prov 24:13–14 (near the end of the small collection in 22:17–24:22).

The phenomenon of the conclusion to collections of wisdom material or wisdom poems will require further study, but it is evident that the Q sermon conforms to patterns typical of the wisdom tradition. Much of the rest of Q consists of small collections of material which offer similar conclusions. Observations such as these increase our confidence in the integrity of the collections of sayings in Q, and make clear how powerfully tendencies of the wisdom tradition continued to operate in Q.

If your enemy is hungry, give him bread to eat;
and if he is thirsty, give him water to drink;
for you will heap coals of fire on his head,
and the Lord will reward you.
    (Prov 25:21–22; cf. Q 6:27; Rom 12:20)

Do not say, "I will do to him as he has done to me;
I will pay the man back for what he has done."
    (Prov 24:29; cf. Q 6:29,31; Prov 20:22; 19:11)

Do no evil, and evil will never befall you.
Stay away from wrong, and it will turn away from you.
    (Sir 7:1–2; cf. the warning metaphor about falling into the pit
    you dig for others: Ps 7:15; 9:15; Prov 26:27; Eccl 10:8; Sir 27:26)

Such parallels could easily be multiplied. They are especially numerous for the central section of the sermon (Q 6:27–38). But parallels are not limited to the Jewish wisdom tradition.[86] The "Golden Rule" (Q 6:31) arose, apparently, among the Sophists of the end of the 5th century B.C.E.[87] It found its way into Judaism via the wisdom tradition, as can be seen from the places where it is attested: Sir 31:15 LXX; Tob 4:15; Aristeas 207; b. Šabb. 31a (Hillel); Syriac Menander, lines 250–51. The Golden Rule is also reflected in *m. 'Abot* 2:15 (Eliezer)[88]; see also *m. 'Abot* 2:17 (Jose) and 4:15 (Eleazar).

Although one can find views contrary to these in the wisdom writings (e.g., Sir 12:4–7), it is surprising that non-revenge and love of the enemy are taught primarily in the wisdom writings. Moreover, we have seen that the conclusion to the sermon in Q 6:47–49 (the parables of the builders/houses) conforms to the practice typical of the wisdom tradition for ending collections of material.[89]

D   The Q Version of the Sermon

It is proper to regard the section on Jesus' Preaching (Q 6:20–49) as a compositional unit, although we continue to call it a "sermon" only in deference to traditional usage. The Q form of this sermon, if not the exact wording, is recoverable with a considerable degree of certainty. The agreement between Luke and Matthew is very impressive, especially when one thinks in terms of groups of sayings. The following table, compiled by Lührmann,[90] shows this clearly.

---

86. See, e.g., the Egyptian "Instruction of Amen-Em-Opet" iv.12-v.6 (*ANET*, 422), xxii.1–8 (*ANET*, 424); the Akkadian "Counsels of Wisdom" 1.35–40 (*ANET*, 426). See also Schottroff, "Non-Violence and the Love of One's Enemies," 15–22.

87. So Dihle, *Die Goldene Regel*; see the review by Robinson in *JHP* 4 (1966): 84–87.

88. Numbered 2:10 in the Marti-Beer edition of 'Abot (Marti and Beer, "Abot"). In *m. 'Abot* the "Golden Rule" is attributed to R. Eliezer.

89. See above, n. 85.

90. Lührmann, *Redaktion*, 53.

Beatitudes	Luke 6:20–23	Matt 5:3–12
Woes	Luke 6:24–26	
Sayings	Luke 6:27–36	Matt 5:38–48
Sayings	Luke 6:37–42	Matt 7:1–5
Sayings	Luke 6:43–45	Matt 7:15–20
Parable	Luke 6:46–49	Matt 7:21–27

Some differences between Matthew and Luke in the sequence of individual sayings are not indicated in this table, but it is accurate in reflecting small collections of sayings and in giving these collections in their proper sequence. The basic structure of the sermon thus is the same in Luke and Matthew. Matthew's collection has been expanded; yet the basic expansion has occurred in one place—Matthew 6. Minor additions are found in Matt 5:13–17, largely dealing with the law, and including the "antitheses,"[91] and in Matt 7:6–14, most of which comes from Q but occurs in different contexts in Luke. The major addition, Matthew 6, contains much Q material (Matt 6:19–34) which occurs in a different context in Luke, plus a large chunk not from Q which deals with cultic matters.[92] As is generally recognized, Luke's sermon probably represents the Q version of the preaching of Jesus; but the expansions in Matthew's sermon have in no instance broken the basic sequence of the material as given by Luke. Moreover, with very minor exceptions (Luke 6:24–26, 39–40), everything in Luke's sermon may be found in Matthew's sermon. Finally, the expansions in Matthew have not altered the beginning or end of the sermon.[93] As to the location of the sermon within Q, there are no problems. In both Luke and Matthew the sermon follows the temptations and is followed by the story of the centurion's servant.

The Q introduction to the sermon has been but poorly preserved. There is a certain illusory similarity in the introductions by Luke and Matthew to their respective sermons. This illusion is enhanced by Aland's *Synopsis,* which has major sections entitled "The Sermon on the Mount" and "The Sermon on the Plain," each of which has an "Introduction" containing identical texts: Matt 4:24–5:2; Mark 3:7–13a; Luke 6:17–20a. One thus gains the impression that Luke and Matthew have placed their respective sermons at identical points in the Markan framework. But more careful examination reveals that Matthew has inserted the sermon between Mark 1:39 and 1:40,[94] whereas Luke has inserted his sermon between Mark 3:7–19 and 4:1–9. (Mark 3:20–35, the Beelzebul controversy, was largely omitted by Luke, who used the Q version

91. See Suggs, "The Antitheses," 433–44. Suggs regards the antitheses as redactional creations of Matthew. That is also the view of Hasler, "Der Herzstück der Bergpredigt," 90–106.

92. See Betz, "Jewish-Christian Cultic *Didache*," 55–69.

93. Bornkamm ("Bergpredigt," 1047) also holds that "Matthew thus has clearly taken over the framework of the speech from Q. . . ." Likewise Conzelmann and Lindemann, *Arbeitsbuch,* 61–62.

94. Or between Mark 1:20 and 1:22, as Neirynck contends ("The Sermon on the Mount," 350–57).

instead.) The illusion is created by the fact that in Matt 4:23–25 the summary from Mark 1:39 has been taken over and expanded with statements resembling but not identical to the Markan summary statements in 3:7–13. Matthean dependence on Mark is clear only in Matt 4:25//Luke 3:7–8, and is confined to phrases. Still, the fact that Matthew looked past Mark 1:3a to Mark 3:7–13, and that this latter passage in Mark was also the introductory pericope for the Lukan sermon, may be of some significance.

Although Luke and Matthew thus seem to place their "sermons" at different points in the Markan framework, there is one curious feature which they have in common. Both introduce their sermons by having Jesus address the disciples (Luke 6:20a; Matt 5:1). This coincidence is all the more curious because both evangelists conclude the sermon by referring to a different audience—the "people" in Luke 7:1 and the "crowds" in Matt 7:28. If this presupposes a shift in audience during the sermon, there is no hint of it in the text. Matthew gives no indication of such a shift; Luke has two quotation formulas in the middle of the sermon (Luke 6:27, 39), but neither refers to a shift in audience. Because of their redactional activity at the beginning and end of their respective sermons, Luke and Matthew provide no sure indication of the Q opening and closing of the sermon. Nevertheless, it is surely remarkable that both Matthew and Luke seem to preserve a recollection of this shift in audience during the Q sermon. Such a shift seems, in fact, to correspond to the structure of the sermon.

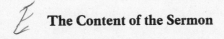 **The Content of the Sermon**

1. The Beatitudes (Q 6:20b–23)

The problems raised by the beatitudes cannot be fully explored here. There is general agreement, however, that the Lukan beatitudes more closely represent Q than do those in Matthew, though Luke may be responsible for the direct address in the second person (singular in Luke 6:20b; plural in 6:21a and 21b).[95] Also generally accepted is the view that Luke 6:22–23//Matt 5:11–12 are later additions to the original beatitudes because they differ in form and content.[96]

The small collection of beatitudes, whatever their origin, had therefore

---

95. This does not mean that the wording in Luke must be Q's wording, or even that the number of beatitudes in Luke equals the number in Q. The problem here is that Luke's woes (6:24–26) echo language occurring only in the beatitudes peculiar to Matthew. For a list of these coincidences, see Steck, *Israel*, 22. Dupont held that Luke probably did not turn Matthew's extra beatitudes into woes, nor did the converse occur (*Les Béatitudes*, 1. 342). However, with Lührmann ("Liebet eure Feinde," 414 n. 8) and Steck (*Israel*, 22) I think that this evidence is probably to be understood to mean that Luke has omitted or altered part of the Q text of the beatitudes.

96. An exception to this general agreement is provided by David Daube ("The Last Beatitude").

already been supplemented in Q by the addition of one more. This added beatitude (Q 6:22) and the call to rejoice attached to it (Q 6:23) are clearly the results of later editorial activity in Q.[97] The beatitude and saying in Q 6:22–23 are given in direct address; Matthew shifts from the third person in 5:3–10 to the second person at this point, i.e., at 5:11. Moreover, in contrast to the beatitudes in Q 6:20b–21, which deal with general human afflictions, the beatitude in Q 6:22 deals with persecution for the sake of the son of man (Matthew has "on account of me").[98] The discussion of abuse by enemies and others in the next section (Q 6:27–36) can hardly be unrelated to the mention of persecution in Q 6:22. This means that it is probable that the beatitude in Q 6:22 presupposed the existence of at least a connection between the beatitudes and the following section on loving enemies. That is, the addition of Q 6:22–23 probably occurred after the sermon was already assembled.

It is clear, even before Q 6:22–23 is examined more closely, that it was addressed to the members of the Q community. But this means that all of the beatitudes are now understood as directed specifically to the community. The community probably adopted as self-designations the words in the beatitudes, "poor," "hungering," and "weeping." The addition of Q 6:22–23 caused a shift from the idea of the eschatological reversal of fortunes (Q 6:20b–21) to the idea of the persecution of the righteous and of the prophets. There is no announcement now of the kingdom; rather, we hear of a promised "reward" in heaven.

But another shift is noticeable within Q 6:22–23 itself. Steck has shown that in Q 6:22–23 we are dealing with materials identifiable conceptually and linguistically as the product of the tradition of the suffering of the righteous.[99] But in Q 6:23c (οὕτως γὰρ ἐποίουν τοῖς προφήταις ["for so they did to the prophets"]) we encounter material which is not logically a part of Q 6:22–23,[100] and which comes from a different tradition. It reflects the role of the prophets in the deuteronomistic view of history. This fragment in Q 6:23c seems to be directed, further, to the leaders of the community, the abused, rejected preachers who stand in the succession of the prophets.[101] It is noteworthy that, though there are parallels to Q 6:22 in the Gospel of Thomas (saying 68) and 1 Pet 4:14, neither mentions the persecution of prophets. If, as is probable, GThom 68 and 1 Pet 4:14 independently attest the saying in Q 6:22,[102] then Steck's analysis is confirmed and the most distinctive editorial

---

97. There is no trace of the added beatitude in the little collections of beatitudes in Acts of Thomas 94 or the Acts of Paul and Thecla 5–6. However, see GThom 68 (cf. Q 6:22); 69a (cf. Matt 5:10). Also 1 Pet 3:14 (cf. Matt 5:10); 4:14 (cf. Q 6:22).

98. See Tödt, *Son of Man*, 255; Steck, *Israel*, 259.

99. Steck, *Israel*, 257–60; also see pp. 20–26. Hare (*The Theme of Jewish Persecution*, 116–17) also regards Q 6:23c as a later addition.

100. Steck, *Israel*, 258–59; so too Schulz (*Q*, 456–57 n. 404).

101. Steck, *Israel*, 259–60.

102. Cf. also Clement of Alexandria *Stromateis* IV.6.41.2 (Stählin). Steck (*Israel*, 26 n. 4) does not think GThom 68 is relevant here because he does not think it represents an

activity in Q 6:22–23 is the addition of the deuteronomistic idea of the persecution of the prophets.

It should be noted, however, that along with the addition of the idea of the persecution of the prophets we also have the title, "son of man." It is curious that this title is here embedded in the context of material which is clearly rooted in the tradition of the suffering of the righteous.[103] The association of "son of man" with the suffering of the righteous may indicate that the Q community did not understand the title "son of man" as a reference to an apocalyptic figure of judgment.[104] Even if one assumes that the phrase "for the sake of the son of man" was a later addition, one cannot assume that apocalyptic interests were at work, because the idea of suffering "for the sake of" occurs not in apocalyptic literature but, for example, in 4 Maccabees, where it is associated with martyrdom.[105]

If a shift in the understanding of the beatitudes was noticeable with the addition of Q 6:22–23b, another shift thus becomes apparent with the addition of Q 6:23c. The persecution mentioned in Q 6:22–23b is now no longer related simply to the situation of confession; it is put in the context of the persecution of the prophets. Indeed, there is a line of prophets, extending back into the history of Israel, who suffered the same fate. This idea of the violent fate of the prophets is part of the deuteronomistic view of history, as we have seen. Steck identifies these prophets as wandering preaching of repentance in the deuteronomistic tradition.[106]

Elsewhere in Q when we meet the deuteronomistic view of history, we find it closely linked to ideas about Jesus that are drawn from the wisdom tradition. The fact that we have located a fragment in Q 6:23c which stands out from its context as a later addition will have to be borne in mind later when we consider the stages in the evolution of Q, particularly because it would appear to represent the same stage as the wisdom texts.

---

independent tradition, a judgment based on the investigation of Schrage (*Das Verhältnis des Thomas-Evangeliums zur synoptischen Tradition*); but see Sieber, "A Redactional Analysis," esp. 32–34. For 1 Pet 4:14 (and 3:14) as independent of the Q sayings, see Dupont, *Les Béatitudes*, 1. 226–27; also Steck, *Israel*, 26 n. 4.

103. See Steck, *Israel*, 257–60. Because Steck leaves undecided the question whether Luke or Matthew is to be followed (i.e., ἕνεκεν ἐμοῦ or ἕνεκα τοῦ υἱοῦ τοῦ ἀνθρώπου in Matthew and Luke respectively), he also does not deal with the use of "son of man" in this context.

104. Tödt's view (*Son of Man*, 123, 255–56) that the term son of man in Q 6:22 designates Jesus' activity on earth with full authority (by reason of his identification with the coming son of man) is of doubtful validity. See Perrin, "The Son of Man in the Synoptic Tradition," 13–14. Perrin shows that Tödt's judgment that the present son of man sayings use the title to designate Jesus as acting with full authority is based on Mark's use of the title, not that of Q.

105. See, e.g., 2 Macc 7:9, 11, 23; 8:21; 13:14; 4 Macc 6:27, 30; 13:9; 16:19, 25. Satake ("Das Leiden der Jünger") attributes the soteriological structure of the saying about suffering "for the sake of" (ἕνεκεν) to Jewish apocalyptic tradition (pp. 5–7), but he notes that parallels are not to be found in Jewish apocalyptic writings but rather in 2 and 4 Maccabees (pp. 11–13).

106. See Steck, *Israel*, 257–60. The continued persecution of the prophets would be understood as evidence of Israel's continued hard-heartedness. See also pp. 283–89.

2. The Woes (Luke 6:24–26)

Because Matthew lacks the woes, I do not attribute them to Q. The juxtaposition of blessings and woes, however, would correspond nicely to the structure of the Q sermon as it is analyzed below; therefore, the inclusion of the woes in Q would by no means be an obstacle to my general argument concerning the sermon.

3. Loving Enemies (Q 6:27–35)

The quotation formula in Luke 6:27a//Matt 5:44 introduces this part of the sermon; it is not a fragment of an antithesis which only Matthew has fully preserved.[107] Luke's "to those hearing" may be his own transition from the woes[108] or perhaps it was already linked to the similar expression in Q 6:47, 49.[109] It is the only quotation formula found in the Q sermon except for Q 6:39, concerning which more will be said later. The important point here is only that the quotation formula in Q 6:27a was in Q, and it introduced the sermon as a whole (excluding the beatitudes).

What occurs in Luke 6:27–35 as one section, occurs in Matthew as two antitheses: Matt 5:38–42 (with material parallel to Luke 6:29–30) and Matt 5:43–48 (with material parallel to Luke 6:27–28, 32–36). Although the antitheses are probably products of Matthean redaction, it is true that Q 6:29–30 is separable from its context and so provides some justification for Matthew's treatment of it as a separate antithesis.[110] Nevertheless, Luke represents the original Q version more closely than does Matthew. This has been shown by Lührmann.[111] The view that Luke's repetition of the love command (Luke 6:27, 35) is evidence of the secondary nature of his version is shown by Lührmann to be false. Thus the Q collection of sayings in Q 6:27–35 was clamped together by the repeated command to love the enemy; it was already the *inclusio* to a compositional unit in Q.

4. On Reciprocity (Q 6:36–38)

It is probable, though not certain, that Q 6:36 should be taken with Q 6:37–38, despite Matt 5:48 (which is parallel to Luke 6:36 but attached by Matthew to the unit analyzed above [Q 6:27–35]).

At first glance, Luke would seem to have broken up what forms a unit in

107. So rightly, Suggs, "The Antitheses," 439–40. Surprisingly, the formula crops up again in a parallel passage in Justin 1 *Apol.* 15.9.

108. Schulz, *Q*, 127.

109. Lührmann, "Liebet eure Feinde," 147.

110. Luke 6:27–28, 31 have the second person plural, Luke 6:29–30 (and Matt 5:39b–42) the second person singular. A similar separation seems evident in the parallels in Did 1:3 (cf. Justin 1 *Apol.*. 15.9; Ps.-Clem. Hom. 3.19.3; 12.32.1; 2 Clem 13:4) and Did 1:4 (cf. Justin 1 *Apol.* 16:1–2; Ps.-Clem. Hom. 15.5.5).

111. Lührmann, "Liebet eure Feinde," esp. 415–22. Lührmann is also able to show that the section in Q was attached (as in Luke, except for the woes) directly to the beatitudes.

Matthew (i.e., Matt 7:1–5). However, as Taylor noted,[112] Luke 6:39, 40 are in their correct Q location, for the Matthean locations are clearly redactional.[113] Moreover, Luke 6:41–42//Matt 7:3–5 are only artificially linked with Luke 6:37–38//Matt 7:1–2 (as in Matt 7:1–5). The only connection is the general theme of judging (which is not explicitly mentioned in Q 6:41–42). And Q 6:41–42 is clearly a self-enclosed unit which only seems, in Matt 7:1–5, to be part of a formal structure parallel to Matt 7:7–11. If, however, the structure which is found in Matt 7:7–11 (and Luke 11:9–13) did have a real parallel in Matt 7:1–5, then one would expect that Matt 7:5 would bring a conclusion to the whole piece, which is clearly not the case. Thus the apparent structural parallelism between Matt 7:1–5 and 7:7–11 is illusory, and the Lukan arrangement is to be preferred.

5. Teachers and Disciples (Q 6:39–40)

The location of these sayings has already been discussed above. It may be added that Luke introduced a quotation formula in 6:39a. Possibly Q had a similar formula here too, in order to mark a break between Q 6:38 and 6:39. According to Barth, ὁδηγοὶ τυφλῶν ("guides of the blind") "takes up one of the titles of honour (Rom 2.19) claimed by the Rabbis."[114] It is at this point in the Q sermon that polemic begins; it continues through the rest of the sermon, especially Q 6:39–46. This turning point in the sermon may have been the point at which a shift in audiences occurred, from the disciples to the crowds.

6. The Speck and the Log (Q 6:41–42)

Here we have a quite remarkable set of circumstances. The Q version is a three-part saying: two rhetorical questions followed by a conclusion in the form of a rejoinder. Several points are to be noted.

First, a parallel to these sayings exists in GThom 26,[115] whose form is almost certainly more primitive than the Q version. GThom 26 has no polemic, and only a general application. The first part of the saying (cf. Q 6:41) is given in the form of a statement rather than in the form of an accusing rhetorical question. And the version in Thomas is shorter (the second part of the Q version, 6:42a, is not present). Finally, no gnostic coloration is visible. Thus, GThom 26 preserves an independent, probably more original, version of the saying in Q 6:41–42.[116]

Second, the part of the Q saying which is missing in GThom 26 (i.e., Q 6:42a) has a remarkably close parallel in a saying attributed to R. Tarphon (*b.*

112. Taylor, "The Original Order of Q," 104–5.
113. For Q 6:39 see also Strecker, *Der Weg*, 139.
114. Barth, "Matthew's Understanding of the Law," 88 n. 2. Barth is here following Haenchen, "Matthäus 23," 47.
115. GThom 26: "Jesus said: You see the mote in your brother's eye, but you do not see the beam in your own eye. When you cast the beam out of your own eye, then you will see clearly to cast the mote from your brother's eye."
116. Similarly, Grobel, "How Gnostic is the Gospel of Thomas?" 371.

'Arak. 16b): "R. Tarphon said, 'If one said to another, "cast the mote out of your eye," he would answer, "cast the beam out of your eye!"'" The context is R. Tarphon's lament that no one would now accept reproof and correction. Implicit, therefore, is the offer to give instruction, described as taking out the speck from another's eye; to this, the uncooperative fellow retorts, "Cast out the beam that is in your eye!" This saying, which appears in similar form elsewhere,[117] must have provided the basis for Q 6:41-42, especially for the portion in Q 6:42a which has no parallel in GThom 26.

From this the conclusion must be drawn that Q 6:41-42 was given a polemical character by Q. Ironically, Q takes precisely the stance of the defiant fellows who refused rabbinic instruction. Put otherwise, the accusation hurled defiantly by a stubborn generation is here taken seriously: the leaders cannot instruct because they themselves need instruction. They are "blind" (Q 6:39). The connection between Q 6:39 and 6:41-42 now becomes obvious. The polemic which is encountered here is given in fuller form in the woes in Luke 11 and Matthew 23.

7. Good and Bad Trees/Good and Evil Persons (Q 6:43-45)

Although some Lukan redaction may be suspected here, the presence of Matthean redaction in both 7:16-20 and 12:33-35 seems clear.[118] Thus it seems safe to assume that Matthew developed two sayings groups out of the material from Q 6:43-45.[119]

The similarity of the material in Q 6:43-45 to John's Preaching in Q 3:7-9 (especially 3:8-9) is striking. In fact, Matthew has enhanced that relationship by giving Matt 3:10b almost verbatim in 7:19 (which has no parallel here in Luke); the same situation obtains in Matt 12:33-35 where, in v. 34, Matthew inserted John's invective, "brood of vipers!" Matthew only enhanced a relationship that already existed in Q. But a new feature may be noted in that Q 6:43-45 lacks any connection to judgment and, in contrast to John's use of this imagery, is part of a general reflection on the human condition. There is in Q 6:43-45 (excepting Matthew's redacted version in 12:33-35) no call to "bear fruit!"; rather, the imagery is turned toward distinguishing between the "good tree" and the "bad tree." This accounts for the addition of Q 6:44b and for the addition likewise of Q 6:45.

Q 6:43-45 has a parallel in GThom 45 (and 43). This parallel provides evidence that the linkage of Q 6:43-44 to 6:45 may have been traditional. GThom 45 has its parallel in Q 6:43-44; GThom 43 is probably a secondary development.[120] But logion 43 does provide significant evidence of a different

---

117. See Strack-Billerbeck, *Kommentar*, 1. 446.

118. Bultmann, *History of the Synoptic Tradition*, 52 (for Matt 12:33-35), 95 (for Matt 7:16-20).

119. Likewise Grundmann, *Matthäus*, 331 n. 14.

120. It could be argued that the seemingly clumsy explanatory addition in GThom 45 ("for they give no fruit") may not be merely an explanation of why grapes cannot be gotten from thorns; its function may rather be to forge a link to logion 43.

kind: it is linked not only to logion 45 (by imagery if not also by editorial addition) but also to logion 44, which deals with blasphemy against the father, the son and the holy spirit (only blasphemy against the last is unforgivable). Curiously, one of Matthew's parallels to Luke 6:43–45, namely Matt 12:33–35, comes directly after his version of the saying about blasphemy against the spirit (Matt 12:31–32); this linkage is attested only in Matthew, not in Mark or Luke. This situation calls for an explanation. It is by no means clear that GThom 43–44 depend upon Matthew for their connection, nor is the reverse likely. The explanation must be sought in a different direction.

It was noted above that although John's Preaching (Q 3:7–9) used the imagery of the tree and its fruits as part of a call for repentance, the same imagery is used in Q 6:43–45 to speak of the distinction between the "good tree" and the "bad tree." Luke's version implies no more than a distinction between true and false believers. However, in Matthew the imagery of the tree and its fruits is used to distinguish between true and false prophets (Matt 7:15–20); this usage accounts for the greater distortion of the Q saying which occurs in Matt 7:16–20 as compared with Matt 12:33–35. What is encountered in Matthew, however, is probably only an expression of a widespread view that prophets can be tested and known on the basis of their deeds (cf. Didache 11 and Herm Man 6.2:4). Closely related to this is the distinction between true and false confession, where the image of the tree and its fruits (or the idea of being known by works) proved useful (as in Matt 12:33–35; see also IgnEph 14:2; John 15:2, 6 [and cf. Q 3:9!]; Jas 3:12). In view of this widespread tradition, it may be that Matthew and the Gospel of Thomas independently linked the saying about blasphemy against the spirit to the image of the tree and its fruits. What is visible then in both Matthew and the Gospel of Thomas is the use of the material in Q 6:43–45 for what may be called polemical purposes; in Luke 6:43–45 this is not yet true. But we can see a tendency to use the imagery of the tree and its fruits not only for inner-community exhortation but to go beyond this and use the imagery for polemical purposes. It will be argued later that this development can be traced already to Q itself.

8. Acclamation without Obedience (Q 6:46)

It was noted above that the Lukan form of this saying is to be regarded as more closely representing Q. The location of the saying within the sermon is attested by both Matthew and Luke; it immediately precedes the parable of the two builders/houses.

9. Builders/Houses (Q 6:47–49)

The location of this parable at the end of the sermon is attested by Luke and Matthew. Its location at the end of the sermon conforms, as noted earlier, to a pattern typical of collections of wisdom material. The introduction to the parable, which refers to those who hear and do Jesus' λόγοι ("words") comes from Q. The term λόγοι apparently designates the collection (i.e., the sermon) as a whole.[121] Though the parable may contain an implicit claim concerning the authority of Jesus' words,[122] it cannot be overlooked that the parable emphasizes the *doing* of Jesus' words; there is no reference here to confessing Jesus before people or to any christological assertion. However, the fateful consequences of hearing and doing imply that the preceding sayings are "wisdom" and hold the key to life; Jesus thus is a spokesperson for this wisdom. It is probable therefore that the parable (or double parable) along with its introduction does not contain late redactional work; there is no reason to assume the unit did not belong to the sermon from the point it was first assembled.

F   The Structure of the Sermon

The observations on the various parts of the Q sermon may now be drawn together in an analysis of the structure of the sermon. First, it is to be noted that the sermon is not a collection of isolated sayings but a collection of small groups of sayings. The only exceptions to this are Q 6:39, 40, 46. Second, Q 6:39 represents a break in the continuity of thought in the sermon. From Q 6:27 to 6:38 the line of thought is relatively smooth; this suddenly changes in Q 6:39. However, I have contended that Q 6:39 is not out of place; Q had it at this point. The quotation formula, which is probably to be attributed to Luke, may have occurred in a different form in Q in order to mark the break in thought.[123]

Next, one must note that everything before Q 6:39 is best understood as addressed to disciples or the faithful. But Q 6:39 seems to be addressed to others (this is clearer later, especially in Q 6:42, 46) and it contains polemic, as do all the following verses at least through Q 6:45. Thus, with Q 6:39 the whole sermon snaps in two. This is in accord with the observation made earlier, that both Luke and Matthew seem to presuppose a shift of audience in the sermon, for both begin the sermon as addressed to disciples and end it with the people in general as the audience. Moreover, it was noted that the sayings in Q 6:41-42 contain an addition over against what seems to have been the traditional form of the sayings; this addition brings out the polemical nature of the sayings: they now carry forward the point that the opponents (presumably Jewish leaders) are "blind" leaders (Q 6:39).

If Q 6:39-45 is directed against false leaders of the community (making comprehensible Matthew's redactional work in 7:15-20), it must still be

---

121. So Robinson, "'LOGOI SOPHON,'" 94-95.

122. See the discussion in Smith, *The Jesus of the Parables*, 188-91.

123. That a break occurs here is widely recognized. See, e.g., Grundmann, "Die Bergpredigt," 187; Schürmann, "Die Warnung des Lukas," 57-81. Smith (*Tannaitic Parallels*, 91-92) even considered—and rejected—the possibility that Luke 6:39-49 represents a "separate collection of sayings"; Smith notes that with Luke 6:39 "the sequence of thought is completely broken." The ingenious but overly subtle attempt by Bartsch ("Feldrede und Bergpredigt," 14-15) to show a continuity of thought between Q 6:37-38 and 6:39 is not convincing.

admitted that not everything in the section fits this interpretation well. In fact, nearly all of it is comprehensible as inner-community exhortation. This leads to the conclusion that the polemical character of Q 6:39–45 is a redactional feature—that is, that it was redactional already in Q. And this conclusion seems to be justified by further analysis. The sudden shift into polemic which occurs at 6:39 is best understood as a difficulty arising out of redactional activity. Q 6:40 fits only poorly into this polemical scheme, and has no discernible connection with 6:39. In fact, the entire section of the sermon derives its polemical cast from Q 6:39 plus a few minor alterations (perhaps the addition of Q 6:42a; the exclamation "you hypocrite!" in 6:42). It was noted that Q 6:39 takes up an honorific title, "leader of the blind"; the situation is similar in 6:42a, where the image of taking the speck out of another's eye is attested in Jewish sources as an image for the offer of instruction or reproof. Similar polemic is directed against Jewish leaders in the Q material in Luke 11 and Matthew 23. Thus, the Q sermon would seem to have been subjected to redaction; and this redaction is most probably to be attributed to that stage of Q where one finds emphasized the idea that Jesus, rejected by "this generation," was a prophet or messenger of Wisdom.

The redactional work on Q 6:39–45 can, perhaps, also be made visible by considering the pre-redactional stage of the material. The pre-redactional stage would have begun with Q 6:40 (perhaps with some transition from 6:37–38). Q 6:41–42 had to do with a warning against those who presume to help others. When this is seen, the original link to 6:40 is recovered: the disciple needs to know that he cannot presume to teach others till he is fully taught himself. The call for the elimination of the discrepancy in Q 6:42b is then followed by sayings which assert a radical doctrine of wholeness: the external manifestations of a person are to correspond with absolute consistency with one's interior condition (Q 6:43–45). The discrepancy which was dealt with satirically in Q 6:41–42 is here proclaimed to be intolerable, indeed impossible.

It has often been observed that "lord, lord" in Q 6:46 is a form of polite address to a teacher.[124] Understood thus, Q 6:46 closes off this section by an allusion to the disciple fully taught (Q 6:40) and with a final call to become like the teacher and not only to address the teacher with formal politeness. This point would then have been further clinched by the parable in Q 6:47–49.

It should be noted that at the pre-redactional stage, the Q sermon was already split into two parts; however, the separation between them was not as sharp as later. In the first part, there is a call to imitate God and thus become sons of the Most High; in the second part, there is a call to imitate the teacher and become like him. Thus, the second section of the Q sermon (Q 6:39–49) is entirely comprehensible at its conjectured pre-redactional stage; this makes all

---

124. See, e.g., Cullmann, *Christology*, 202, 204–5; Foerster, "κύριος," 1086, 1093; and see above, n. 84.

the more clear the nature of the redactional activity which has transformed that section into polemic.

The sermon as a whole is a collection typical of the wisdom tradition, with a conclusion also typical of that tradition. The concluding parable, moreover, represents Jesus as claiming that his "words" will do what other collections of wisdom material also claim; that is, he appears as a spokesperson of Wisdom.

The Q sermon (Q 6:20b-49) is preserved substantially intact in Luke, at least with respect to the sequence of the material. Analysis of the sermon has shown that it is a collection of small groups of sayings, with three isolated sayings (Q 6:39, 40, 46). Two of these isolated sayings were part of the Q sermon (namely Q 6:40, 46), and though isolated they form part of a coherent unit (Q 6:39-46). The third isolated saying (6:39) was added as part of a redactional alteration of the second part of the sermon in the course of which it was turned into polemic against Jewish "blind" leaders. The redactional alteration of the sermon agrees with two other verses which are clearly redactional, namely Q 6:22-23. From the analysis of this redactional activity, it appears that the Q sermon was subjected to minor changes which altered considerably the meaning of its parts. As it stands now, the redacted sermon contains a series of commands followed by warnings against false leaders, and a concluding call to do Jesus' words.

The Centurion's Servant (Q 7:1-10)

Matthew and Luke agree on the location of this text: it is the first Q material after the sermon in Q 6:20b-49.[125] The wording of the text is more difficult to establish. There is close agreement in the dialogue but only rare agreement in the narrative. There is one particularly striking difference between the Lukan and Matthean versions: Matthew has inserted additional Q material in 8:11-12, recognizable as such by the new quotation formula and by the clumsy change in audience.[126]

Luke's redactional work may have altered the narrative portion of the story radically; this would account for the rarity of verbal agreement with Matthews's narrative. Luke has sought to avoid a direct encounter between Jesus and a gentile, thereby developing the "unworthiness" motif already present in Q 7:6. The centurion is never allowed to meet Jesus. Instead, hearing of Jesus he sends a delegation of Jewish elders (!) to plead on his behalf. Jesus agrees to come, but before he gets to the house the centurion sends another (!) delegation (of "friends") to tell Jesus that he should not come after all, since the centurion is not "worthy." There is no need to come anyway; if only Jesus will

125. The conjecture of Manson (*Sayings*, 63, 65-66), that in Q the story came after Luke 13:27, has no textual support.

126. Most exegetes agree that Matthew's location for these verses is secondary. Whether Luke's location represents Q is another question; it is denied, e.g., by Hoffmann, "Πάντες ἐργάται ἀδικίας," 205-8).

say the word, the servant will be healed. These delegations are surely products of Luke's own mind and hence of his theology.[127]

For our purposes it is not necessary to establish the original wording of the Q text. The distinctive features of the text are to be found in the dialogue portion. Thus the location of the story and its basic character are discernible without a reconstruction of the Greek text. However, on one important point there is no disagreement: the figure in the story is a gentile centurion.

The peculiar features of the Q story can be determined in part by a comparison with the parallel account in John 4:46–54; a similar story is told of R. Hanina ben Dosa in *b. Ber.* 34b.[128] Most obvious is the fact that in Q the miracle itself so far recedes in importance that it becomes unclear whether Q told of a miracle at all.[129] That "the servant was healed at that very moment" (Matt 8:13, lacking in Luke) may be merely a feature typical of healings at a distance (cf. John 4:42–43; *b. Ber.* 34b; Mark 7:30). By comparison with John's account, the Q story has a centurion who is clearly gentile. The Q account also contains other distinctive motifs: "worthiness"; authority; and the title κύριος ("lord") with a more deferential sense than its counterpart in John 4:49. Both John and Q stress the point that the centurion/official believed Jesus' λόγος (word)—the only place in Q that λόγος is used to designate a miracle-working word. A striking difference between the Johannine and Q accounts is the "punchline" in Q: "I tell you, not even in Israel have I found such faith."[130]

The Q account lays stress upon faith in Jesus' word.[131] And as Lührmann noted, it can hardly be an accident that the title κύριος is used in Q only here and in Q 6:46, and that the centurion's faith answers directly to the relation of hearing to doing demanded in Q 6:46.[132] The location of the Q account directly after the sermon is thus fully comprehensible, and the centurion is

---

127. On this, see Jervell, *Luke and the People of God*, 120–21; also 41–74. Luke uses the device of a centurion sending a delegation also in Acts 10. There too the delegation stresses the exemplary piety of the centurion.

The reason for the delegation is explicitly recognized in Acts 10:28. Haenchen (*Acts of the Apostles*, 357–63) notes that in Acts 10 the centurion is a product of Luke's mind (p. 360). The pious centurion whose witness/help comes at strategic moments seems something of a commonplace in early tradition; see Mark 15:39; Acts 10; 21:23; 22:25–26; 23:17, 23; 27:43; 28:16. The Jews' pleading on behalf of a benevolent friend is also typically Lukan (see Stendahl, "Matthew," 781). Also note the delegation in Luke 7:18–23.

128. See Fiebig, *Jüdische Wundergeschichten*, 19–22. Also cf. Mark 7:24–30.

129. That we have a healing at a distance need imply no heightening of the miraculous since it is a motif which could as well be attributed to the fact that a gentile is involved; see Bousset, *Kyrios Christos*, 99.

130. Or, "I tell you, with no one in Israel. . . ." This is the more probable reading in Matt 8:10 (see Metzger, *A Textual Commentary*, 21). However, the Matthean reading is secondary, and Luke more nearly represents Q. Even if "not even in Israel" implies that hitherto the best examples of faith were to be found in Israel, the point is not to extol Israel's faith but to shame Israel for its lack of faith; so Lührmann, *Redaktion*, 57–58, and Schulz, *Q*, 244.

131. See Robinson, "Kerygma and History," 56–58; J. Blank, "Zur Christologie ausgewählter Wunderberichte," 112–17; R. Schnackenburg, "Zur Traditionsgeschichte von Joh 4,46–54," 72–73.

132. Lührmann, *Redaktion*, 58.

therefore portrayed as a paradigm for belief in Jesus' word.[133] However, this does not account for other peculiarities of the account—the fact that a gentile is involved, that his faith stands in sharp and deliberate contrast to the absence of faith in Israel, and that the centurion discusses authority.

The last item may be examined first. Not only does the centurion have faith, he has a certain kind of faith. His chief characteristic is surely a lack of presumption, a humble but firm trust. This absence of presumption is highlighted by the centurion's explanation that he has at his command soldiers and slaves—precisely he submits to Jesus' word. The presumption of faithless Israel is a common theme in Q (3:7-9; 10:15; cf. 6:41-42; 10:21-22; 14:11). Nevertheless, this may be only an accidental implication of Q 7:8; its more basic purpose is probably to show that the centurion recognizes the authoritative character of Jesus' word. The centurion commands and it is done; so too with Jesus' word. Perhaps we are to hear in this an allusion to the creative word of God.[134] If in Q 7:8 the centurion's recognition of Jesus' word implies a correlation between the authority under which the centurion stands and the authority (i.e., God) under which Jesus stands,[135] then the closest parallel in Q to this idea is in Q 10:22 ("all things have been delivered to me by my father...").

If the above features of the Q account of the centurion are somewhat ambiguous in their intent, the same cannot be said for the stark contrast of the believing gentile with unbelieving Israel. It is on this note that the Q account reaches its climax. But this characteristic also accords precisely with the latter part of the Q sermon, which has been edited in such a way as to stress this very point.[136] In fact, by virtue of this redaction, Q 6:46 no longer refers to the wavering believer but to the "blind" Jewish leaders, who address Jesus with formal politeness but do not do what he says. Thus, the peculiarities of the Q account of the centurion's servant over against its Johannine parallel are perfectly understandable in the context of the account in Q.

Q 7:1-10 should not be regarded as evidence that the Q community was engaged in a mission to the gentiles, or that it contained gentile members. The purpose of the gentile in this story is rather to put Israel to shame. Behind the story in its present form stands Israel's rejection of Jesus and his followers and the reflection of the Q community upon these experiences.[137] The motif present here is found elsewhere in Q (e.g., 13:34-35). Of course, the charge

---

133. Lührmann, *Redaktion*, 58. Robinson ("Kerygma and History," 57) also notes the relationship between the account of the centurion and the parable of the houses/builders. Lührmann is in error, however, in holding that the story requires that there were gentiles in the Q community (see Schulz, *Q*, 244 n. 461).

134. Blank ("Zur Christologie ausgewählter Wunderberichte," 115-16) calls attention to Genesis 1 and Ps 33:9, to which Bar 3:33 may be added.

135. Blank, "Zur Christologie ausgewählter Wunderberichte," 116.

136. See the discussion above of the Q redaction of Jesus' sermon.

137. This is noted in Gnilka, *Die Verstockung Israels*, 97-98; the same motif is found elsewhere in Q, as Gnilka notes (pp. 97-102). Steck (*Israel*, 287 n. 2) notes that Q 7:1-10 cannot be taken as evidence of a mission to the gentiles.

that no one in Israel believed Jesus is false; for that very reason, one suspects that Q 7:9 really represents a fixed doctrine concerning Israel's unbelief. Thus when Matthew adds 8:11–12, he is only carrying forward a motif already found in the story.

The discussion of Q 7:1–10 may now be summarized. The distinctive character of the Q account of the centurion and his servant was evident by comparison with its parallel in John 4:46–54. In Q the miracle itself recedes in importance, and is displaced by an emphasis on hearing and doing the word; moreover, a gentile is chosen to illustrate this point, and his belief and absence of presumption are put in contrast to unbelieving Israel. This distinctive character, and the fact that the pericope followed directly after the Q sermon, lead to the conclusion that the account was added to strengthen and illustrate motifs already present in the sermon, especially the use of the title "lord" in connection with hearing and doing (Q 6:46). But Q 7:1–10 develops this point in deliberate contrast to unbelieving Israel; that is, it relates to Q 6:46 in its later, polemical usage. From this we may conclude that Q 7:1–10 shares a point of view with the redactional reworking of the sermon discussed earlier. The view of the centurion's "worthiness" as the absence of presumption, as well as the polemic against unbelieving Israel, also agree with the view expressed in the redactional addition to Q 3:7–9 (i.e., 3:8b).

H John and Jesus (Q 7:18–35)

This long unit of Q material is a composite piece united mainly on the basis of a common theme: John and Jesus. The component parts must be examined separately.

1. John's Question to Jesus (Q 7:18–23)

The Q text is difficult to establish for the dialogue portion of this subunit, i.e., Q 7:19b, 22–23. The framework is even more difficult. Nevertheless, the basic framework is visible in the agreements of Luke and Matthew: John sends his disciples to ask Jesus a question.

In general, Matthew's wording is to be preferred. Lukan redaction is quite visible here, especially in 7:20–21.[138] Luke's intention can probably be sensed outside the unit itself, for in 7:11–17 he has inserted a story in which, on the basis of a miracle, the people cry out, "A great prophet has arisen among us!" (Luke 7:16). Moreover, the story provides an account of the raising of the dead which perhaps Luke preferred not to list in 7:21 as merely one more miracle.

---

138. So Conzelmann, *Theology of St. Luke*, 191–92. Hoffmann (*Studien*, 192–93), Schulz (*Q*, 190–91), and many other exegetes agree. Vögtle ("Wunder und Wort," esp. 219–22) attributes 7:20–21 to Luke's desire to have John's disciples be witnesses of Jesus' works; for this reason also Luke inserts "two" in v. 18 (to have the required number of witnesses) and changes the tense of the verbs of seeing and hearing in v. 22. Cf. also Kümmel, *Jesu Antwort*, 149–51.

In any case, the prefixed story in Luke 7:11–17 shows how Luke understood 7:18–23, namely as attestation by miracles of Jesus' status. This same understanding is reflected in Matthew's redactional work. Matthew delays the account of John's question until he has related the miracles described in Matt 11:5//Luke 7:22.[139]

Bultmann regards this pericope as an apophthegm.[140] He considers the framework (John's question) a later development, and thinks that Q 7:22–23 was a saying which originally circulated independently. That Q 7:22, or 7:22–23, circulated independently is, however, doubtful.[141]

For a number of reasons, Q 7:18–23 represents an erratic block in the context of Q. First, Q 7:22 is dependent upon the LXX,[142] though this in itself is not unusual for Q. What is striking is the citation a few verses later (Q 7:27) which seems to be based upon the Masoretic text of the Old Testament; at least it is not dependent upon the LXX.[143] This suggests that Q 7:18–23 may be somewhat later than Q 7:24–35 or, at the very least, that the two units have a separate origin.

A second eccentric feature is the list of miracles in Q 7:22. Q seems to have little interest in miracles. It has one miracle story (Q 7:1–10), but the nature of the illness is not specified[144]; so no reference to this miracle can be derived from Q 7:22. The one type of miracle in Q linked to the manifestation of the kingdom is exorcism (Q 11:20), and exorcism is not mentioned in Q 7:22! Only in Q 11:14 is there a miracle listed in Q 7:22, namely, the healing of a deaf man; but that miracle is an exorcism. In short, the list of miracles in Q 7:22 bears no relation to the rest of Q.

The oddness of this list of miracles might be accounted for by the argument that no reference was intended to specific miracles of Jesus; rather we have merely a general Isaianic picture of the blessedness of the end-time.[145] But this view cannot be accepted, because not all the miracles listed are derived from Isaiah; at least the cleansing of lepers has been added.[146] Probably the raising

139. See Held, "Matthew as Interpreter of the Miracle Stories," 251–52 and the discussion above, pp. 77–79.

140. Bultmann, *History of the Synoptic Tradition*, 23–24; likewise Lührmann (*Redaktion*, 25) and others.

141. That this is an isolated saying is denied by Vögtle ("Wunder und Wort," 231–36), Schulz (*Q*, 193), and Hoffmann (*Studien*, 210–15).

142. The blind see again (Isa 61:1 LXX; cf. Isa 29:18; 35:5); the poor have good news proclaimed (Isa 16:1 LXX; cf. Isa 29:19); the lame walk (cf. Isa 35:6); the deaf hear (Isa 29:18; 35:5 LXX). And see Johnson, "The Biblical Quotations in Matthew," 145–46, and Stendahl, *School of St. Matthew*, 91.

143. See Stendahl, *School of St. Matthew*, 49–50.

144. Matthew's reference to paralysis in 8:6 is probably redactional; he inserts it in 4:25 also.

145. So Bultmann (*History of the Synoptic Tradition*, 23), Bornkamm (*Jesus of Nazareth*, 67). Lührmann (*Redaktion*, 25–26) follows Bultmann here as elsewhere with respect to Q 7:18–23. For a critique of this position see esp. Robinson, *New Quest*, 116–19.

146. For the rejection of a metaphorical view of Q 7:22–23, see Percy, *Botschaft Jesu*, 187–88. Kuhn's defense of the metaphorical view (*Enderwartung und gegenwärtiges Heil*, 196 n. 4) is unconvincing.

of the dead also derives from the Jesus tradition rather than from Isa 26:19. Q 7:22, then, does not merely present a picture of the end-time salvation painted in Isaianic colors; it was formulated with stories of Jesus' miracles in mind. This being so, grave doubts about the age of this unit in relation to the other Q material must be expressed; it presupposes contact with the traditions of Jesus' miracles. The fact that John is here sharply subordinated to Jesus is another sign of lateness.

A third eccentric feature of this text is the use of the title, the "coming one." It is generally recognized that this was not a current Jewish or early Christian messianic title.[147] In Q the title refers to a figure who will carry out the judgment, probably God.[148] The occurrence here of the title ὁ ἐρχόμενος ("the coming one") is clearly a reference back to the preaching of John (see Matt 3:11, where the wording in Matthew represents Q). Therefore, in Q the title can be understood in no other way than as a reference to the figure announced by John—the end-time judge. However, Q 7:18–23 makes no sense if it presupposed the identification of the "coming one" with the apocalyptic figure of judgment announced by John.[149]

But it was noted in the analysis of Q 3:16–17 that the original Q wording in Q 3:16 must have been, "I baptize with water, but he will baptize with wind and fire." It was also seen that this saying has been broken up by an insertion, best preserved in Matthew, in which John spoke of a "coming one." This insertion reinterprets the original Q saying of John by contrasting the two baptisms; and it links the figure announced by John to Jesus. To be sure, the claim there is somewhat elliptical, just as it is in Q 7:18–23. But it is most probable that at a later stage in the Q tradition the identification of Jesus with the figure announced by John (and designated "coming one") was made. This identification is presupposed in Q 7:18–23. Thus we have here two instances of redactional work which must represent the same late stage in the Q tradi-

---

147. See Vögtle, "Wunder und Wort," 223–27. Vögtle regards the whole pericope as a product of the early church. His arguments are criticized by Kümmel (*Jesu Antwort*, esp. 151–159); Kümmel agrees that ὁ ἐρχόμενος was not a current messianic title, but takes up again the line of argument set forth in his earlier book, *Promise and Fulfilment* (pp. 109–11), that the tradition is authentic precisely because the early church would not have used such a non-title. But this ignores the likelihood that the church needed to claim precisely this title for Jesus in order to reconcile the Baptist tradition with the Jesus tradition (rightly noted by Vögtle, "Wunder und Wort," 225–26). For the view that ὁ ἐρχόμενος was a messianic title, see Stanton, "On the Christology of Q," 29–32; cf. Bultmann, *History of the Synoptic Tradition*, 156–57 n. 3.

148. Rightly noted by Hoffmann, *Studien*, 199–200 and Schulz, *Q*, 194. See also Bretscher, "'Whose Sandals'?"

149. It is often held that the title "coming one" refers to an eschatological prophet. See Meyer, *Der Prophet aus Galiläa*, 26–28 and F. Hahn's appendix to his *Titles of Jesus in Christology* ("The Eschatological Prophet," 352–406, esp. 380). But this is far from certain. Hoffmann (*Studien*, 204–9) notes that the Jewish sources dealing with eschatological prophets have to do with miracles that imitate past salvific miracles, not with healings. Healings are mentioned in rabbinic sources in relation to the end-time salvation, but they are not linked to prophets. Only in the final component (preaching good news to the poor) is it possible to see evidence of the idea of the end-time prophet.

tion. The relationship of this "redactional stage" to other stages in the history of the composition of Q will be described later.

We have not yet considered Q 7:23, the beatitude which concludes this pericope. Presumed in this beatitude is a disparity between John's expectation of a "coming one" who is an eschatological judge, and the character of Jesus as summarized in Q 7:22. The beatitude affirms those who see no problem claiming that Jesus was nevertheless the "coming one" announced by John. If the argument is correct that this pericope is a late addition to Q, then it must have been created to claim Jesus' sanction for appropriating the figure of John and his message for the followers of Jesus. It does not directly make John bear witness to Jesus, but it warns those with lingering ties to John not to be concerned about the apparent disparity between John's preaching and Jesus' activity.

In conclusion, Q 7:18–23 must be regarded as a late addition to Q. It appeals to Jesus' miracles as attestation of his status as "coming one"—yet Q itself provides none of this crucial evidence. Moreover, the pericope emphatically subordinates John to Jesus, which is not typical of most of Q. Its identification of Jesus' with the "coming one" announced by John is probably to be understood as evidence that it belongs to the same redactional stage observed in Q 3:16–17. It was also noted that the dependence upon the LXX in this pericope sets it in contrast with Q 7:24–35 where (in 7:27) dependence is rather upon the Masoretic text. Finally, the concern with Jesus' christological status sets this pericope off from most of Q.[150]

2. Jesus and John (Q 7:24–28; 16:16)

The text of Q for most of this material is not difficult to establish, at least for Q 7:24–27. Luke is responsible for some changes in 7:25b.[151] Otherwise, Luke and Matthew are almost verbatim in Q 7:24–27. The Q introduction is relatively long: "(Jesus) began to say to the crowds concerning John. . . ." The reference to "crowds" is abrupt and unexpected. The nearest previous reference to "crowds" was in Q 7:1, where it refers to those who heard Jesus' sermon. The words ἄνεμος (wind) in Q 7:24 and σαλεύειν (to shake) in Q 7:24 also occur in Matt 7:25, 27 and in Luke 6:48 respectively, and thus could be Q language in the parable of the houses/builders (Q 6:47–49); that is, there may be a catchword link between Q 7:24–27 and 6:47–49. This is especially interesting because the two intervening pericopes (Q 7:1–10, the centurion's servant; Q 7:18–23, John's question to Jesus) may both be later additions (the latter pericope being the more recent addition).

Jesus' speech about John resembles John's own first preaching: both are addressed to the crowds, and both use rhetorical questions as well as the λέγω

150. Hoffmann (*Studien*, 210–12) notes that Q 7:18–23 may be compared with Q 10:23–24, but holds that the former must be regarded as later than Q 10:23–24.

151. So Hoffmann, *Studien*, 187, and Schulz, *Q*, 229.

ὑμῖν ("I say to you") formula. Thus even the formal features of Jesus' sayings about John reinforce the recollection of the initial Q section on John.

The artfully-constructed threefold rhetorical question, "What did you go out to see?" is designed to elicit the agreement of the hearers that something extraordinary was to be seen. It is doubtful whether the suggested foolish responses are meant to suggest anything specific.[152] In any case, the rhetorical questions are used in such a way as to make emphatic the correct response: they went out to see a prophet! Indeed, just as Jesus is "more" than Solomon and "more" than Jonah (Q 11:29–32), so John is "more" than a prophet. This "more" is then explained by the use of an Old Testament citation, a composite of Exod 23:20 and Mal 3:1.

Exegetical attention is usually directed primarily to the second part of the citation, that from Mal 3:1, where an allusion to Elijah might be seen (cf. Matt 11:14–15, a redactional addition by Matthew).[153] But it may be asked whether there is any interest here in defining John's role, aside from the idea that John "prepared the way," a point also made in the citation of Isa 40:3 in Q 3:4.[154] The emphasis seems to be placed more on the first part of the citation (Exod 23:20 LXX). That this is so seems evident not only from the apparent lack of interest in defining specifically John's function, but from other factors as well. For example, the formula ἰδοὺ (ἐγὼ) ἀποστέλλω ("behold, I send") is striking because it appears at other important points in Q.[155] Moreover, one could argue that the mere fact of divine accreditation is the crucial point in this context, because it shows that John is "more than a prophet" and that rejection of him has eschatological significance. Perhaps Exod 23:21 was in mind: "Take heed to yourself and hear him (*sc.* the "angel/messenger" of Exod 23:20) and do not disobey him, for he will not shrink back from you, for my name is upon him." That this Old Testament citation can occur at this place in Q, and thus speak of John's work of preparing the way as still having validity *during* the ministry of Jesus, shows a very different view from that of Mark. In Mark, Mal 3:1 and Isa 40:3 (which refer to preparing the way) occur at the beginning, *before* Jesus' ministry; and John's preparatory work reaches its goal

---

152. The first response, "A reed shaken by the wind?" is usually taken to refer to a trivial, everyday phenomenon, though other suggestions are made. The parallels do not support this view, however, but suggest rather a person shaken by adversity or by God's wrath, perhaps one who has been made a spectacle in his decimation (see 3 Kgdms 14:15; 3 Macc 2:21; *b. Ta'an.* 20a [Strack-Billerbeck, *Kommentar*, 1. 596–97]). This would also fit as a contrast to one in soft clothes, i.e., one who experiences good fortune. But if this contrast is intended, its purpose is still unclear.

153. That Q saw John as Elijah is unlikely. Friedrich, et al. ("προφήτης," 841) notes that Matt 11:14 shows the newness of that doctrine. In any case, Mal 3:1 is here used to designate John as forerunner of Yahweh, as in Luke 1:17, 76 (cf. H. Thyen, "ΒΑΠΤΙΣΜΑ ΜΕΤΑΝΟΙΑΣ," 156 n. 118). See esp. Steck, *Israel*, 213.

154. The ὁδός that is prepared in Q 3:4 is the Lord's, in Q 7:27 the people's. The two passages have been harmonized in Luke 1:17: ἑτοιμάσαι κυρίῳ (cf. Q 3:4) λαὸν κατεσκευασμένον (cf. Q 7:27).

155. Q 10:3; 11:49. So Seitz, "The Commission of Prophets," 236–40.

when Jesus arrives on the scene. Mark has no room for John's preparing the way as an activity *during* the ministry of Jesus. That Q does is remarkable.

The high estimate of John in Q 7:24–27 is altered in the next verse, often regarded as a later addition:[156] "I tell you, among those born of women none[157] is greater than he." Since we hear at a number of places in the synoptics discussions about who is greatest, as well as the idea that the humble servant is the greatest (Mark 9:33–37; 10:15, 42–45; Luke 14:11; 18:14 [=Matt 23:12]; Matt 23:11), we may suspect that the entire verse (Q 7:28) is a late creation; at least Q 7:28b stands out as a later addition.[158]

We come now to one of the most difficult passages in the synoptics: Q 16:16. Although the wording of this saying differs in Matthew and Luke, the basic structure of the saying is quite clear. There is a contrast between two aeons, a former aeon characterized by the law and the prophets and a later one characterized by the kingdom of God. At the turning point between the aeons stands John. The latter aeon, however, is also characterized by violence of some sort.

The wording of Q 16:16a is especially difficult to reconstruct. There is considerable scholarly support for the Lukan reading.[159] Matthew's two characterizations of the aeons in Matt 11:12a and 11:13 arouse suspicion, in part because they are in reversed order and in part because of evidence of Matthean redaction.[160] On the other hand, Luke apparently understood the phrase "the law and the prophets were until John" to mean that John is included in the aeon of the law and the prophets, whereas the succeeding phrase ("from that time the kingdom of God is proclaimed") seems to exclude John from the

---

156. Q 7:28b is recognized as secondary by Robinson (*New Quest*, 117 n. 1); Wink (*John the Baptist*, 24–25). Lührmann (*Redaktion*, 27) regards at least Q 7:28b as secondary, and probably the whole verse, a view held more emphatically by Schulz (*Q*, 233–34). Hoffmann (*Studien*, 218, 230) regards Q 7:28a as original and Q 7:28b as secondary. Haenchen (*Der Weg Jesu*, 316) notes that the identification of the kingdom with the Christian community shows how late the addition is; he apparently regards the whole verse as secondary. See also W. C. Robinson, *The Way of Lord*, 20–22.

157. The addition of προφήτης in Codex Bezae is secondary. It serves to prevent comparison of John to Jesus by declaring that John is the greatest prophet but setting Jesus in a different category altogether. See Dibelius, *Täufer*, 9.

158. The occurrence of the motif of the least/greatest in the kingdom is probably a sign of lateness; cf. Matt 5:19. This motif is, for example, present in the Markan version of the parable of the mustard seed (Mark 4:30–32) but absent in its Q counterpart. Also cf. Mark 10:40; 10:42–45 and parallels.

159. Those who regard Luke 16:16a as original include Käsemann ("The Problem of the Historical Jesus," 42); Kümmel (*Promise and Fulfilment*, 122); Trilling ("Die Täufertradition," 278); Barth ("Matthew's Understanding of the Law," 63–64); Wink (*John the Baptist*, 29); Jüngel (*Paulus und Jesus*, 191); Schnider (*Jesus der Prophet*, 179–80); Percy (*Botschaft Jesu*, 192); Polag (*Fragmenta Q*, 74); Marshall (*Luke*, 628); Catchpole ("Law and Prophets," 95–96). Arguing for the priority of Matthew are Friedrich ("προφήτης," 839–40); Hoffmann (*Studien*, 51–52); Meyer ("The Community of Q," 37); Jeremias (*New Testament Theology*, 46–47); Schenk (*Synopse*, 43–44); and Kloppenborg (*Formation*, 114).

160. See Schulz, *Q*, 261–62; Kloppenborg, *Formation*, 114. Since ἄρτι is demonstrably Matthean (only he of the synoptists uses it), and since it is essential to the construction of 11:12a, it should probably be seen as Matthew's signature on this minor literary creation (i.e., 11:12a). Matthew has inserted προφητεύειν in 11:13, in accordance with his view that scripture is prophetic.

proclamation of the kingdom. This may reflect Luke's view that, as Jeremias put it, "the time of salvation began after the death of John the Baptist (Acts 1:5; 10:37; 13:24–25; 19:4)."[161] By contrast, Matt 11:12a locates John at the beginning of a period during which the kingdom has suffered violence. Insofar as this saying identifies John as the inaugurator of a new aeon, it contradicts the general tendency to consign John to the old aeon and for that very reason may be original.[162] However, it should be noted that Matt 11:12a does not say that the kingdom began with John, only that the kingdom began to suffer violence with John. It seems probable Matthew has preserved the original sense of Q 16:16a, but Luke has preserved the original structure of the saying, which begins with a characterization of the aeon.

In the case of Q 16:16b there is widespread support for the Matthean reading, i.e., Matt 11:12b.[163] Matthew has certainly preserved the more difficult reading. Luke has substituted $\epsilon\dot{v}\alpha\gamma\gamma\epsilon\lambda\dot{\iota}\zeta\epsilon\sigma\theta\alpha\iota$ (to proclaim good news) for $\beta\iota\dot{\alpha}\zeta\epsilon\sigma\theta\alpha\iota$ (to use force or violence), and has instead used the latter verb in a positive sense, to describe an intense effort to enter the kingdom (cf. Luke 13:24).[164]

Gottlob Schrenk presented the classic argument concerning the meaning of $\beta\iota\dot{\alpha}\zeta\epsilon\sigma\theta\alpha\iota$ in this passage,[165] and there is now widespread agreement on this point.[166] Schrenk's argument considers two factors in particular: (1) contemporary usage of the verb, which relates to hostile force, and (2) the relationship between the last two parts of the sayings (Q 16:16a and 16b). On the latter point, Schrenk noted that both $\dot{\alpha}\rho\pi\dot{\alpha}\zeta\epsilon\iota\nu$ (to snatch away) and $\beta\iota\alpha\sigma\tau\dot{\eta}s$ (violent, impetuous man) refer to hostile actions and so require the same meaning of $\beta\iota\dot{\alpha}\zeta\epsilon\sigma\theta\alpha\iota$, which they serve to interpret. He concludes that the verb must be understood as passive, and used in a negative sense. Thus "to use force or violence" refers "to the enemies of the divine rule, i.e., that it is contested, attacked or hampered by contentious opponents."[167] And $\dot{\alpha}\rho\pi\dot{\alpha}\zeta\epsilon\iota\nu$ means here that "violent enemies close the kingdom to men, not allowing those who desire to enter to do so (Matt 23:13)."[168] Since it is generally agreed that Matthew's text in 11:12—at least his use of $\beta\iota\dot{\alpha}\zeta\epsilon\sigma\theta\alpha\iota$, $\beta\iota\alpha\sigma\tau\dot{\eta}s$, and $\dot{\alpha}\rho\pi\dot{\alpha}\zeta\epsilon\iota\nu$

161. Jeremias, *New Testament Theology*, 47.

162. See Käsemann, "Problem of the Historical Jesus," 42–43.

163. Käsemann, "Problem of the Historical Jesus," 42; Kümmel, *Promise and Fulfilment*, 122; Creed, *Luke*, 207; Percy, *Botschaft Jesu*, 121; Kloppenborg, *Formation*, 113–14.

164. The verb $\epsilon\dot{v}\alpha\gamma\gamma\epsilon\lambda\dot{\iota}\zeta\epsilon\sigma\theta\alpha\iota$ occurs ten times in Luke, only once in Matthew (11:15= Luke 7:22, probably from Isa 61:1 LXX). Had Matthew read this word in his source, he would probably not have omitted or changed it since he speaks often of "the gospel of the kingdom" (4:23; 9:35; 24:14). So $\epsilon\dot{v}\alpha\gamma\gamma\epsilon\lambda\dot{\iota}\zeta\epsilon\sigma\theta\alpha\iota$ must be Lukan. Luke's interest in the abundant response to missionary preaching lies behind his adaptation of Q 16:16b in a positive sense, i.e., "everyone is forcing their way into it." Danker, however, argues that $\beta\iota\dot{\alpha}\zeta\epsilon\sigma\theta\alpha\iota$ in Luke 16:16 must be interpreted in a negative sense ("Luke 16:16—An Opposition Logion").

165. Schrenk, "$\beta\iota\dot{\alpha}\zeta o\mu\alpha\iota, \beta\iota\alpha\sigma\tau\dot{\eta}s$."

166. For different views see, e.g., Percy, *Botschaft Jesu*, 191–97, who thinks of the kingdom as that which does the violent acting.

167. Schrenk, "$\beta\iota\dot{\alpha}\zeta o\mu\alpha\iota$," 611. See also Turner, *Grammatical Insights*, 60.

168. Schrenk, "$\beta\iota\dot{\alpha}\zeta o\mu\alpha\iota$," 611.

—is more original, we arrive at a meaning such as this: ". . .the kingdom is hampered (or suffers violence), and men of violence seize it (from others)."

Critical to the interpretation of this saying is the observation that the saying contained two parallel statements, and that Matthew has preserved this parallelism.[169] The occurrence of ἁρπάζειν in the second line provides strong support for the claim that βιάζεσθαι in the first line must be interpreted in a negative sense. The second line also identifies who it is that causes the violence, and it specifies the kind of violence as "snatching away." Precisely what this means is, however, very difficult to say. It may be that the key to the interpretation is Q 11:52, which says that the opponents neither enter (the kingdom) themselves nor allow others to enter. Hoffmann, in particular, has argued that in Q the messengers of the kingdom are identified with the presence of the kingdom, so that violence directed at the messengers can be said to be directed at the kingdom.[170] There is ample evidence in Q of the theme of violent opposition to the messengers, so it may be the community which is experiencing sharp opposition. But whether this interpretation is justified must remain uncertain.

We turn now to the problem of the location of Q 16:16 in Q. We have seen that, with the exception of the first part of Luke 16:16, Lukan redaction is plainly in evidence. The reason for Luke's alterations is generally recognized to be his missionary interest. That is, Luke has interpreted βιάζεσθαι in a good sense: the kingdom of God is proclaimed, and the masses are pressing to get in! Indeed, W. C. Robinson believes that Luke 16:16 is "a thematic statement for

169. The parallelism is emphasized, e.g., by Schrenk ("βιάζομαι," 611) and Kümmel (*Promise*, 122–23).

170. Hoffmann, *Studien*, 50–79. Hoffmann puts it this way: "When opponents persecute the messengers and hinder them in their activity the kingdom itself suffers violence, and when they—as one might possibly render the special nuance of the second statement [Matt 11:12b]—illicitly seize the goods (*Sache*) of the kingdom which are entrusted to the messengers of God alone, and when they carry on in false ways, they, like a robber, snatch the kingdom for themselves. In the background of the second, more difficult statement must therefore stand divergent understandings of the proclamation of the kingdom and of the authorization for it, which leads to conflict with the opponents, indeed to persecution. That was the occasion for Q to reproach the opponents for 'usurpation' of the kingdom-goods [*Basileia-Sache*]" (p. 71).

Hoffmann proceeds to explain that this saying is a concrete interpretation of a very specific historical period, from John to the present. This was a period of ferment in Palestine (Hoffmann refers esp. to Josephus, *War* 4.128–34), when Christians of the Q group took a stand against insurrectionists. They saw the period as the time of the messianic woes, and they charged their opponents with "robbing" the kingdom in that they claimed authority for their violent view of the kingdom (in contrast to the non-violent view of the Q group).

Hoffmann's interpretation is attractive, but it cannot be accepted in the present case. First, the Matthean text in 11:12a (which Käsemann regarded as secondary) is an uncertain witness to Q. (For Hoffmann's view of the priority of Matthew, see *Studien*, 51–52). This is particularly true of ἄρτι (which occurs nowhere in Luke-Acts) as a precise time-designation. Second, and more seriously, Hoffmann's interpretation does not fit the saying in its Q context, which is correctly preserved by Matthew, as will be shown later. In the context, the "violent ones" cannot refer to a competing form of kingdom-proclamation but only to those who reject the message of John and Jesus.

For other criticism of a presumed zealotic background for Q 16:16, see Percy, *Botschaft Jesu*, 195, and Hahn, *Titles of Jesus in Christology*, 151–52.

the rest of Luke and Acts."[171] Schrenk had noted that "ἐυαγγελίζεσθαι [to proclaim good news] is a characteristic of the new age with its conversion of the heathen. With joyful pathos the character of the εὐαγγέλιον [gospel] is revealed through this πᾶς. . . . It assures to everyone an entry unhampered by any restrictions."[172] Why then, if this is the case, does Luke say in the very next verse that "it is easier for heaven and earth to pass away, than for one dot of the law to become void" (Luke 16:17)?

Schrenk is right that Luke had altered the Q saying, and that his changes reflect his missionary intent. But he is wrong in stressing (in paulinizing fashion) that, as it were, Christ is the end of the law. Luke's view is entirely different. Luke's view is that "many will seek to enter and will not be able" (Luke 13:24). For though indeed many are pressing to get in, not just anyone can get in. There are conditions. This is clear already when one observes the progression of thought: (a) the law and the prophets were until John; (b) since then the good news of the kingdom is preached, and everyone presses to get in; but (c) it is easier for heaven and earth to pass away, than for one dot of the law to become void. This is followed by the saying on divorce which says that remarriage constitutes adultery. Then follows the parable of the rich man and Lazarus, which concludes by saying, "If they do not hear *Moses and the prophets*, neither will they be convinced if someone should rise from the dead" (Luke 16:31).

The placement by Luke of Q 16:16 in a context dealing with the validity of the law reflects Lukan theology. Here we see at work the same author who created, or at least placed great emphasis upon, the story of the apostolic decree from the Jerusalem council in which some conditions were imposed on gentiles who wanted to press into the kingdom.[173]

The conclusions concerning Q 7:24-27; 16:16 may now be summarized. We saw that Q 7:24-27 may originally have been joined, by catchwords, directly to the end of Q's sermon by Jesus. This observation corresponds to the conclusion that both Q 7:1-10 and 7:18-23 were added to Q later (though not at the same time). The composite Old Testament quotation in Q 7:27 seems to use Mal 3:1 not as an allusion to an Elijanic messenger but simply to refer to one who prepares the ὁδός (way), as in Q 3:4. The first part of the citation is from Exod 23:20, and, since it is from the LXX, may be later than the citation of Mal 3:1. Here we noted the use of the formula ἰδοὺ (ἐγὼ) ἀποστέλλω ("behold I send") which is found elsewhere in Q. John thus emerges as "more than a prophet"—as a divinely accredited messenger. His work of preparing a way continues to have validity even during Jesus' public ministry.

171. W. C. Robinson, *The Way of the Lord*, 101.
172. Schrenk, "βιάζομαι," 612.
173. See Haenchen, *Acts of the Apostles*, 457-72. Haenchen regards the council and its decree as a creation by Luke; however, the decree, he says, probably reflects real conditions in a diaspora community. A much more optimistic view of the historical reliability of the account is provided by Lüdemann (*Early Christianity*, 166-73).

Q 7:28 (or Q 7:28b) was shown to be a later addition which subordinates John to Jesus; it dissociates John from the kingdom while the next verse (Q 16:16) associates John with the kingdom. Q 16:16 was shown to have been moved by Luke from its original Q context, which Matthew has preserved. John is here located at the shift of the aeons. This saying may mean that the community is suffering violent opposition, though the saying itself does not allow us to state precisely how this opposition is expressed.

Seen as a whole, this pericope begins with Jesus' saying that John is "more than a prophet" (given emphasis by introductory rhetorical questions). This "more" is explained in Q 7:27 with an Old Testament quotation stressing that John is indeed God's messenger. Then follows the statement that with John comes the shift in aeons—but also violent opposition. This last point is introductory to the parable of the children's games, where the seriousness of the opposition to the message preached "since John" (i.e., by John and Jesus) is expressed as the rejection of Wisdom.

3. Concluding Parable (Q 7:31–35)

This pericope is the first of the "wisdom pericopes" in Q. It is the only one which takes the form of a parable. Like Q 11:29–32, it deals with "this generation" in its unbelief, and the title "son of man" occurs in both. The theme of prophets sent and rejected, which is only implicit in the parable, becomes explicit in Q 11:49–51 and 13:34–35. The word σοφία (wisdom) occurs here as well as in Q 11:49–51 and 11:29–32. Thus despite its different form this pericope shares a number of features with the other wisdom pericopes.

The interpretation of the parable is problematic at many points. It is usually held that the pericope contains four elements: (a) an introduction in Q 7:31; (b) the parable itself in Q 7:32; (c) an allegorical interpretation of the parable, which follows directly in Q 7:33–34; and (d) another saying in Q 7:35. The problems in this pericope have less to do with reconstructing the Q text than with understanding the interrelationships of the various elements in the pericope.

The introduction contains, in Luke,[174] two rhetorical questions, in a manner typical of rabbinic parables.[175] The introduction to the parable establishes its connection with "this generation."[176] The parable itself comes in Q 7:32. It

---

174. The Lukan form probably represents Q. So Hoffmann, *Studien*, 196; Schulz, *Q*, 379; Linton, "The Parable of the Children's Game," 160. A fuller discussion is found in Arens, *The HΛΘON-Sayings*, 224 n. 8.

175. McNeile, *St. Matthew*, 157; Jeremias, *The Parables of Jesus*, 100–103. Dibelius says that the double form is typical of Q, arguing that Luke 7:31 and Luke 13:18, 20 preserve the Q versions as against Matthew (*Täufer*, 15 and n. 2).

176. The synoptic epithet "this generation" is correctly regarded as a *terminus technicus* (Meinertz, "'Dieses Geschlecht,'" 285; cf. Polag, *Christologie*, 138). The usage in Q shows considerable uniformity; it occurs in the genitive (τῆς γενεᾶς ταύτης) in Q 7:31; 11:31, 32, 51. In addition, there are cases of single attestation where Q may be strongly suspected: Luke

consists of two parts: a brief narrative (or apophthegmatic) setting and a brief saying with parallel members. Whether this is really a parable seems debatable. The heart of the "parable" is a saying, hence the justification of speaking of an apophthegmatic introduction. The saying itself may be a common Jewish proverb.[177]

Most of the text of the parable can be established without too much difficulty.[178] Among the most difficult differences are ἀλλήλοις ("to each other") and τοῖς ἑτέροις ("to the others") (Luke 7:32//Matt 11:16) and ἃ λέγει ("what [one] says") and λέγουσιν ("saying," or "they say") (Luke 7:32//Matt 11:17).[179] The difficulty here lies in determining the point of the comparison. Luke's text assumes a group of children divided into two sets who shout accusations at each other. This means that in Luke "this generation" is compared to quarreling children. Matthew's text assumes that "this generation" is compared to one group of children, who have tried in vain to get another group of children to play, first at weddings, then at funerals; they take the initiative but get no response. A decision between these alternatives may be delayed for now,

---

11:30 (dative), 11:50 (genitive) and Matt 12:45 (dative). A deviant form occurs in Q 11:29 (γενεὰ πονηρά), but here there is a Markan parallel (8:12) and the saying defines "this generation" as evil. The Markan usage is less uniform: Mark 8:12, 38; 9:19; 13:30. Luke 17:25 is probably a redactional insertion, and Luke 16:8 is a different usage.

It is remarkable that the epithet "this generation" is found almost exclusively in the synoptics; elsewhere in the NT it is found only in Acts 2:40; Phil 2:15 (Deut 32:5); Heb 3:10 (Ps 94:10 LXX). The term never occurs in the Fourth Gospel or in the Gospel of Thomas.

There can be little doubt about the importance of the epithet in Q. This was shown by Lührmann (*Redaktion*, 24–48). However, Lührmann does not deal at length with the term itself (see pp. 30–31). Meinertz ("'Dieses Geschlecht'") did not recognize its importance in Q.

In the OT, "this generation" can be found with a generic sense in Gen 7:1; Ps 12:7 (11:7 LXX); Jer 8:3; Wis 3:19. However, often specific reference is made to the wilderness generation, with emphasis on its unfaithfulness which led God to punish it by, among other things, not allowing it to enter the Promised Land. This theme, along with the "generation" terminology, occurs in Num 32:13; Ps 77:8 LXX (and see 77:9–37, 40–58); Ps 94:7b–11 LXX. However, no terminological consistency can be observed in these passages, though there are a couple of references to a "perverse" generation (Deut 32:55; Ps 77:8 LXX). A tendency may be noted to use the theme of the rebellious wilderness generation to characterize Israel at different points in its history (Deut 32:5, 20; Jer 2:31; 7:29 and perhaps most clearly Ps 94:7b–11 LXX). This use of the "this generation" epithet, implying that a contemporary group is like the faithless wilderness generation, is what we find in Q. It is present in Mark too (8:12, 38; 9:19), but it is more nearly a theme in Q.

The OT parallels to "this generation" suggest that its roots are in the deuteronomistic tradition; further evidence of this is found in Jubilees 23 (note esp. vv. 14, 15, 16, 22; and see Steck, *Israel*, 162 n. 1).

177. See Ehrhardt, "Greek Proverbs in the Gospel," 51–53.

178. The plural ὅμοιοι in Luke 7:32 is the result of Luke's secondary insertion of τοὺς ἀνθρώπους in Luke 7:31, possibly caused by the two instances of ἄνθρωπος in Q 7:34. Linton notes a similar instance in Q 11:31 ("The Parable of the Children's Game," 160). Matthew's plural, ἐν ταῖς ἀγοραῖς, is secondary (so Schulz, *Q*, 379; Linton, "The Parable of the Children's Game," 161; Arens, *The* ΗΛΘΟΝ-*Sayings*, 224 n. 8). Matthew's ἐκόψασθε (11:17) is original. On a possible Aramaic paronomasia underlying Matt 11:17, see Black, *An Aramaic Approach*, 161.

179. Linton ("The Parable of the Children's Game," 161–62) discusses the alternatives at length, but is unable to come to a firm decision.

though it may be noted that in this case word statistics are ambiguous and cannot decide the matter.

The next element in the pericope is the allegorical interpretation. That the interpretation is, in fact, allegorical has not been demonstrated; that is, it cannot simply be assumed that there is a one-to-one correspondence, so that playing at funerals=John's fasting, and playing at weddings=Jesus' behavior. But this too may be passed over for now. Normally, the interpretation of a parable is not directly attached to the parable itself, as is the case here; this could mean that the parable and its interpretation were composed at the same time. The Matthean text (11:18–19) represents the Q text, as is generally recognized. It reads, "for John came ($\mathring{\eta}\lambda\theta\epsilon\nu$) neither eating nor drinking, and they say, 'He has a demon!' The son of man came ($\mathring{\eta}\lambda\theta\epsilon\nu$) eating and drinking, and they say, 'Look! A glutton and wine-bibber, a friend of tax collectors and sinners!'"

The contrast between John and Jesus is strictly in terms of not eating/not drinking and eating/drinking. What is implied, no doubt, is more than just personal idiosyncrasies. This is clear already from the (perhaps secondary) reference to Jesus as a "friend of tax collectors and sinners." It is illegitimate to interpret this text by means of Mark 2:15–22. That is, it cannot be presumed without further ado that Jesus, being the bridegroom, does not fast, while it is proper for John to do so because he is still "in waiting."[180] In any case, the primary contrast is not that of John to Jesus but that of "this generation" to both John and Jesus.

Nevertheless, the relationship between John and Jesus requires attention. The interpretation (Q 7:33–34) is given in the form of parallel statements about John and Jesus. In each case the person is named, a brief characterization in terms of eating/drinking is given, then the response is quoted in the form, "they say. . . ." The parallelism suggests the close relationship between John and Jesus, and the response by "them," though different in each case, is one of rejection in both instances. The common fate suffered by John and Jesus is, in fact, the chief point; the insults are merely expressions of rejection. Nothing is said which explicitly disturbs this parallelism. Even $\mathring{\eta}\lambda\theta\epsilon\nu$ ("he came"), a word with possible epiphanic overtones, is used of both John and Jesus.[181] Nor is there any implication that Jesus' behavior was superior to John's fasting; on the contrary, John's fasting must be valid or else its rejection

---

180. That Matthew and Luke both saw this pericope in relation to Mark is shown by the 'corruptions' in their parallels to the Markan text. Matt 9:15 speaks of the wedding guests *mourning* while they wait for the bridegroom, while Luke 5:33 speaks of John's disciples fasting while "yours *eat and drink.*"

181. Note Bousset's comment (*Kyrios Christos*, 36) that "the oft-recurring formula $\mathring{\eta}\lambda\theta\epsilon\nu$ ὁ υἱὸς τοῦ ἀνθρώπου from the outset creates the impression of a specifically hieratic stylizing." Bultmann (*History of the Synoptic Tradition*, 156) argued that the $\mathring{\eta}\lambda\theta o\nu$ sayings were created by the early church "to gather up the significance of the appearance of Jesus as a whole." Arens suggests that the use of $\mathring{\eta}\lambda\theta o\nu$ with participles places the emphasis not on the sheer fact of coming but on the manner of coming (*The* ΗΛΘΟΝ-*Sayings*, 242).

would be meaningless. There are only two factors which suggest that greater weight is given to Jesus. First, the insult hurled against him is longer, though this could be to provide a certain balance to the doublet form of the children's taunts. Second, the designation "son of man" might imply Jesus' superior status.

The meaning of the title "son of man" is much disputed. However, the reference cannot be to an apocalyptic figure because in apocalyptic texts the "son of man" is a future figure, not one who "has come," and because the mundane activities of eating and drinking are inappropriate to an apocalyptic figure. Either the title had lost its apocalyptic connotations, much as "christ" became a second name for Jesus, or else the phrase "son of man" could be used without any apocalyptic meaning. I consider the latter to be the more probable in this instance; it seems to be simply an elliptical way of saying "I."

What is most striking, then, about the interpretation of the parable in Q 7:33–34 is its willingness to see John and Jesus as belonging to a common front. There is even a curious interchangeability in the charges against John and Jesus. John is charged with having a demon—a charge otherwise reserved for Jesus (Mark 3:21–22, 30; John 7:20; 8:48, 52; 10:20; cf. Q 11:15). On the other hand, John is said to have attracted tax collectors and sinners (Luke 3:12; 7:29); Q does not describe Jesus as a friend of tax collectors.

The relation between the interpretation (Q 7:33–34) and the parable and its introduction is problematic. This has been an important factor in regarding the interpretation as secondary.[182] The interpretation seems to direct attention away from what the parable is supposed to be about, namely, "this generation," and to focus on Jesus and John. That the interpretation is to be regarded as an allegorical interpretation is probable, because it is difficult to deny some relationship, however clumsy, between John's fasting and the playing at funerals, and between Jesus' meal fellowship and celebrative behavior and the playing at weddings. The principal objection to this would be that the action of the parable is conceived as a whole. There is some justification for this view.[183] But it is more probable that the interpretation does have an allegorical relationship to the parable, and so is a later addition to it.

The final element is the saying about Wisdom, which is probably intended as part of the interpretation. It has already been noted that in Q 7:33–34 John and Jesus form a common front against "this generation." When Q 7:35 is

---

182. Hoffmann (*Studien*, 227), Schulz (*Q*, 380–81) and others regard this interpretation as secondary. Mussner ("Der nicht erkannte Kairos") regards the whole pericope as authentic Jesus material, a view I do not share.

183. The justification is that John's and Jesus' action may not be intended to correspond to the children's piping and lament songs. The introduction to the parable compares "this generation" to the children who do the piping and wailing, not to the sulky children. This is usually regarded as a mistake. However, Linton argues that what is in mind is this: "this generation" has set its religious agenda and complains because neither John nor Jesus will follow their agenda ("The Parable of the Children's Game," 171–79). This would imply that there is no intention of linking John's and Jesus' behavior directly to that of the children; their behavior is simply one of noncompliance.

considered, and it is noted that both John and Jesus seem to be regarded as messengers of Wisdom, then it is clear that it is not a new relationship between John and Jesus that is being asserted; their relationship is being clarified in terms of their mutual origin.[184] Moreover, in contrast to the children who are compared to "this generation," we now hear of another group of "children"— those who, it is implied, "justify" Wisdom by acknowledging her messengers. Thus Q 7:35 functions as further interpretation. The fact that it is not really in tension with Q 7:33–34 suggests that it is not a still later addition but was of a piece with the interpretation (Q 7:33–34) from the outset.

The precise meaning of the Wisdom saying is, however, subject to some dispute. We can accept as well-established the reading of the text itself: καὶ ἐδικαιώθη ἡ σοφία ἀπὸ τῶν τέκνων αὐτῆς[185] ("but Wisdom is justified by her children"). There is also general agreement that the καί (and) is adversative, and that ἀπό (from) should be understood in the sense of ὑπό (by).[186] The interpretation of ἐδικαιώθη is only occasionally disputed. There are three alternatives: (1) the simple past tense: "was justified"; (2) the gnomic aorist: "is (always) justified"; (3) an implied future: "will be justified (at the End)."[187] The third alternative may be dismissed.[188] The gnomic aorist interpretation ignores the fact that, in the context, what is at stake is not just the normal procedure ("Wisdom is invariably justified by her children") but a special case: John and Jesus are rejected by some, and (implied) received by others. Thus we are left with the simple aorist.

It is clear that Wisdom in Q 7:35 is personified: she has children![189] What it means that she is justified by them, however, is less clear. The sense is probably that she is vindicated, as δικαιοῦν is used in *Pss. Sol.* 2:15; 3:3, 5; 4:8; 8:7, 23, 26; 9:2; cf. Luke 7:29. That she is vindicated, however, means that some action or message from Wisdom must be understood. Since the "children" of 7:35 are presumably opposite to the "children" of 7:32, they must be

184. See Robinson, "Jesus as Sophos and Sophia," 5: "It is precisely in relation to Sophia that John and Jesus stand parallel. . . ."

185. Luke's πάντων is redactional (Schulz, *Q*, 380 and the majority of interpreters). That Matthew has replaced τέκνων with ἔργων is generally agreed; the most important argument is put forth by Suggs (*Wisdom, Christology and Law*, esp. 55–58). The view of Leivestad ("An Interpretation of Matt 11:19," 179–81) that Matt 11:19 is a Jewish proverb is mistaken; he has no evidence of such a proverb and he must assume the secondary Matthean text to be primary.

186. So, e.g., Schrenk and Quell, "δικαιόω," 214 n. 13. On the causal use of ἀπό, see Blass-Debrunner-Funk, *A Greek Grammar*, §210; cf. Isa 45:45.

187. Wilckens ("σοφία," 516 n. 351) says that the meaning is "eschatologically 'justified'" and adds, "It is the passive of the factitive or declarative active δικαιόω = צרק."

188. Hoffmann (*Studien*, 229 n. 138) rightly notes: "This interpretation is not justified by the context, which presupposes an acknowledgement which Wisdom has already been given."

189. For Wisdom's children, see Sir 4:11; Prov 8:32. In Sirach, the "children" are those who seek wisdom. Bultmann ("Der religionsgeschichtliche Hintergrund," 19) argued that the τέκνα θεοῦ of John 1:12 has its analogue in Q 7:35. He rejects Sir 4:11 and Prov 8:32 as parallels because here "children" is simply "catechetical terminology" (p. 19 n. 17); see Suggs, *Wisdom, Christology and Law*, 38–48; Robinson, "Jesus as Sophos and Sophia." The view of Christ (*Jesus Sophia*, esp. 74–75) that Jesus is identified with Wisdom in this passage is certainly in error.

those who respond to John and Jesus and who, by doing so, vindicate Wisdom. This means that John and Jesus in some sense represent Wisdom, presumably as bearers of her message, so that Wisdom is vindicated when people respond affirmatively to her messengers, John and Jesus.[190] Luke 7:29-30 may provide some insight into the meaning of this statement. There, to "justify" God means to accept the βουλή (purpose) of God, i.e., to respond to John's call to repent and be baptized. Whether this claim about Wisdom's children justifying her means further that those who responded to John and Jesus (above all, the Q group itself) understood themselves as "children of Wisdom" is not clear; however, this may be implicit in the "babes" of Q 10:21. It may be asked further what specifically was the message of Wisdom which John and Jesus delivered; we may probably assume that it was not an esoteric revelation but a public call for repentance and renewal. This means that Wisdom is understood to be the source of a prophetic call, as she is in Prov 1:20-33.

It is important to note the joining together here of various elements: rebuke of "this generation," the figure of Wisdom, the announcement of judgment, the call to repentance, the messengers of Wisdom. This combination is probably best understood in terms of the deuteronomistic tradition. What is implicit in Q 7:31-35 becomes explicit, and is thus confirmed, in the other Q wisdom pericopes.

The First Section of Q as a Compositional Unit

The order of the pericopes in the first part of Q can be established with relative certainty; it was shown that Luke has preserved this order best. Since the order is roughly chronological, one may assume at least a limited historical interest. However, this historical interest is purely secondary; there is no attempt in Q to compose a connected narrative account of Jesus. That is, the first section of Q has the miscellaneous character of a sayings collection. Yet it may be regarded as a compositional unit because of two factors: a certain thematic unity was given the unit through editorial work, and the material concerning John the Baptist was used to form compositional clamps holding the material together.

We may now review, in reconstructed sequence, the contents of the first section of Q.

190. For the idea that Wisdom sends prophets and envoys, see Robinson, "Jesus as Sophos and Sophia"; Bultmann, "Der religionsgeschichtliche Hintergrund," 22-27; Suggs, *Wisdom, Christology, and Law*, 38-48. Also see Q 11:49; 13:34; 2 Esd 1:32; and the agraphon cited in Resch, *Agrapha*, 184-85: καὶ ἐν τῷ εὐαγγελίῳ ἀναγέγραπται· καὶ ἀποστέλλει ἡ σοφία τὰ τέκνα αὐτῆς [and in the gospel it is recorded: and Wisdom sends her children]. For a contrary view, see Marshall Johnson, "Reflections on a Wisdom Approach," 45-53.

The messengers sent by Wisdom are called prophets and apostles (Q 11: 49; 13:34; cf. Q 6:23c). The messenger formula is used of John in Q 10:3 and of others in Q 11:49. Another Q passage, 12:10, seems to presuppose the idea that Jesus is Wisdom's messenger; so Schweizer, *Matthew*, 288, 447.

John the Baptist	Luke 3:1–6	Matt 3:1–6
John's preaching	Luke 3:7–9, 16–17	Matt 3:7–12
Temptations	Luke 4:1–13	Matt 4:1–11
Jesus' preaching	Luke 6:20b–49	Matt 5:3–7:27
Centurion's servant	Luke 7:1–10	Matt 8:5–13
John's question to Jesus	Luke 7:18–23	Matt 11:2–6
John and Jesus	Luke 7:24–27	Matt 11:7–10
	Luke 7:28	Matt 11:11
	Luke 16:16	Matt 11:12
Wisdom pericope	Luke 7:31–35	Matt 11:16–19

The Stages in the Composition of the First Section

In the course of this investigation it became evident that some material was added later, and that some of these additions shared a common point of view even though they are widely separated in the text of the gospels. Further, some additions seem very late and others not so late. It is probable, therefore, that Q underwent a series of revisions. The attempt had to be made to sort out these additions and assign them, if possible, to a stage in the history of the composition of Q. Naturally, such a list of the stages in the composition of Q is a hypothetical construction, useful if it can coordinate the evidence discovered and provide insight into the evolution of the Q material.

The stages are given as (a) final redaction, that is, the latest stage of Q available to us; (b) the intermediate redactional stage; and (c) the compositional stage. It may be assumed that there were stages prior to these. However, this investigation extends only to that level at which it seemed possible to find a tendentious editing of Q which imposed a largely consistent point of view upon the sayings material which was assembled. This stage may be called the "compositional stage" because, though earlier stages of composition are assumed, it was at this stage that it was possible to locate the reworking of Q which underlies the later redactional activity. In the following, an attempt is made to sort the additions into stages and to review the results of the investigation thus far.

1. The Final Redaction: Q 4:1–13

This pericope represents a scribal debate in which Jesus is portrayed as a Jewish scribe who is able to repulse the devil with biblical quotations. Signs of lateness, besides the style, include the use of the title "son of God"; the summary character of the pericope, in that it seems to allude to other material in Q; evidence of contact with a tradition of Jesus' miracles which is not evidenced elsewhere in Q (except 7:18–23); and apparent anti-enthusiastic polemic which presupposes the emergence of tendencies in the community which require the correction being made. The pericope reflects a community which maintains the Jewish confession of one God and understands Jesus as a model scribe who demonstrates complete fidelity to God. In general, the Q temptation account seems to presuppose, but pointedly reject, certain tendencies which will appear in the later material in Q.

2. Intermediate Redaction: Q 3:16c; 7:18-23; 7:28

Q 3:16c interrupts and reinterprets the contrast saying by John concerning two baptisms. John spoke of a baptism with water and a baptism with fire and wind. Q 3:16c was inserted in the middle of this saying, causing John to speak no longer of the coming of Yahweh for judgment but of Jesus, and altering the original baptisms of repentance and judgment into a contrast of John's old (water only) baptism and Christian baptism. The original meaning of the contrast saying is evident especially in the vestigial phrase, "and fire," which relates to judgment, not to Christian baptism. Moreover, the insertion breaks up the flow of thought from Q 3:7-9 to Q 3:16-17; all this material deals exclusively with the coming judgment except for the addition in Q 3:16c.

In Q 7:18-23 Jesus appears in the new aeon, attested by miracles, while John looks on from the old aeon, uncomprehending. But the miracles have to do not merely with a new aeon but with Jesus specifically as the "coming one" (cf. Q 3:16c), so that the miracles attest Jesus. Elsewhere Q shows little interest in miracles. The one type of miracle which is regarded in Q as a manifestation of the kingdom, namely exorcism (Q 11:20), is missing from Q 7:18-23, while none of the miracles to which appeal is made is given elsewhere in Q.

At least Q 7:28b is generally regarded as a later addition. This saying clashes with its context, in which John appears as "more than a prophet," by introducing the old and new aeon contrast—the least in the kingdom is greater than John. In short, we have noted here a series of passages which stand out from their contexts but which share a common point of view. Q 3:16c, 7:28, and 7:18-23 all seek to subordinate John to Jesus. John is relegated to the old aeon; correspondingly, Jesus' superior status is attested by miracles (Q 7:18-23).

3. The Compositional Stage: Q 3:8b; 6:23c; 6:39, 42; 7:1-10; 16:16; 7:31-35

Q 3:8b directs John's preaching against the Jewish leaders rather than the people generally. The imagery of the tree and its fruits is broken up though the theme of repentance is continued. The idea of presumption as a cause of impenitence is also found in Q 10:13-15.

Q 6:23c is distinguished from Q 6:22-23b by the fact that it stems from the deuteronomistic tradition about the violent fate of the prophets, whereas Q 6:22-23b stems from the tradition of the suffering of the righteous. The parallels to Q 6:22-23 in GThom 68 and 1 Pet 4:14 lack this fragment, helping to confirm the finding about the lateness of Q 6:23c.

The addition of Q 6:39 serves to turn the second part of Jesus' sermon into polemic against the unbelieving Jewish leaders. This polemic is continued in Q 6:42—an addition to Q 6:41, as can be seen from the independent attestation of the saying in GThom 26 (which has a parallel to Q 6:41 but not to Q

6:42). The addition of Q 6:42 indicates a pointed rejection of the Jewish leadership, and accuses them of blindness. Some evidence of polemic also seems to be present in Q 6:43–45, though more clearly in the Matthean than the Lukan version of the saying.

The parallel in John 4:46–53 helps to reveal what is distinctive of Q 7:1–10, the story of the centurion's servant. In Q, the healing itself is not emphasized; rather, the power of Jesus' word comes to the fore. But, in addition, the centurion serves as an example in two respects: (a) his understanding of the relationship between hearing and doing (Q 7:8) illustrates and strengthens the point made at the end of Jesus' sermon (Q 6:46, 47–49); and (b) his faith is used to shame Israel for its lack of belief.

Q 16:16 may have been added by whoever composed Q. It says that John is the turning point of the aeons, and that with this turning there also came an intensification of violence. This saying, whose location in Q is represented by Matthew, serves as a transitional statement between the statements about John and the statements which follow about "this generation."

The parable and its interpretation in Q 7:31–35 reflect the deuteronomistic and wisdom traditions. The views it expresses coincide with those found elsewhere in the compositional stage of the first section of Q: John and Jesus are placed on the same level, both are rejected, and there is polemic against "this generation." But this pericope goes beyond the previous material in showing how John and Jesus are related, namely, as messengers of Wisdom. This pericope thus provides the theological basis for the composition of the whole first section of Q. The "children" of Wisdom are those who, in contrast to "this generation," respond to the call to repentance issued by John and Jesus, and who thus "justify" Wisdom. Thus, Q 7:31–35 brings to clearer expression the tendencies at work in the composition of this whole section of Q.

Most of the material in the first section of Q recognized the important role of John, proclaimed him as a prophet, and (in contrast to Mark and John) gave space to his preaching. John's preaching continues to play a role even during Jesus' public ministry, and rejection of him is no less serious than rejecting Jesus. To be sure, John and Jesus are distinguished; however, they represent a common front. This tendency runs through most of the material, except for certain additions which contradict this tendency and which also stand out for other reasons (e.g., by breaking up the contrast saying in Q 3:16c).

It was noted that the first section of Q is clamped together by material dealing with John (Q 3:7–9, 16–17 and Q 7:24–35). Moreover, these two sections are related: both contain an Old Testament quotation which speaks of John preparing a "way"; both use Old Testament citation formulas which are nearly the same (elsewhere in Q, such formulas are not used); and the two sections share a common view of John as prophet.

Finally, we saw evidence of original connections between material separated by what have been identified as later additions to Q. First, the reference in Q 7:24 to "crowds" is abrupt and unexpected after Q 7:18–23 (a later addition); the nearest reference to "crowds" occurred in Q 7:1. This provides some evidence of a better connection between Q 7:1–10 and 7:24–35 when the intervening material (Q 7:18–23, conjectured to be a later addition) is removed. Second, there may have been catchwords linking Q 7:24–35 to the end of Jesus' sermon. They are ἄνεμος (wind) in Luke 7:24 and in Matt 7:25, 27 (the latter occuring in the parable of the houses/builders, Q 6:47–49), and σαλεύειν (to shake) in Q 7:24 and in Luke 6:48. Since the story of the centurion's servant (Q 7:1–10) was probably added during the compositional stage of Q, these catchwords may point to an even more primitive connection between the end of Jesus' sermon and the material on John (Q 7:24–35). Thus the original seams by which Q was sewn together seem still visible when the later additions are removed.

6
Mission
The Second
Section of Q
and Reception

It will be argued in this chapter that Q 9:57–60; 10:1–12, 13–15, 16, 21–22 represents a compositional unit or "section." Like the first section, it culminates in a wisdom pericope, in this case Q 10:21–22. Discipleship and mission are what unite the material in this chapter from the point of view of subject matter; but the question of the reception of this mission is so basic that we must speak of all three topics—discipleship, mission and reception—to characterize adequately the content of this section. As we did in chapter five, we will again reconstruct the sequence of the Q material, then move to an analysis of each pericope.

The Sequence of the Second Section

1. Following Jesus (Q 9:57–60a)

Luke and Matthew do not place the double apophthegm in Luke 9:57–60a//Matt 8:19–22 in the same location with respect to other Q material. Matthew's location for this pericope was shown to be redactional in one of the earliest redaction critical studies, Bornkamm's essay on "The Stilling of the Storm."[1] However, it is not the case that Matthew has moved the apophthegms or chreiai themselves. Rather, he has moved the storm miracle out of its Markan location (Mark 4:35–41) to its present position after the chreiai (i.e., at Matt 8:23–27).[2] The chreiai in Matthew come directly after the story of the centurion's servant (only Matt 8:14–17 [Markan material] separates the two pericopes). The location of the chreiai in Matthew thus agrees with Luke's placement of the pericope just before the mission charge, except that the Q material dealing with John and Jesus (Luke 7:18–35) is interposed in Luke between the story of the centurion's servant (Luke 7:1–10) and the chreiai in Luke 9:57–60a. When, however, we recall that Matthew was shown to have dislocated the Q material on John and Jesus (Matt 11:2–19//Luke 7:18–35; see

---

1. See also Held, "Matthew as Interpreter of Miracle Stories."
2. Had Matthew followed Mark in his location of the storm miracle, it would have come in Matthew 13 after a series of parables whose parallels are in Mark 4.

above, chapter five), it can be seen that the evidence in both Matthew and Luke agrees in placing the chreiai in Q 9:57–60a directly after the account of John and Jesus (Q 7:18–35).

In Luke, the chreiai in 9:57–60a directly precede the mission charge (10:2–12). In Matthew, though no Q material intervenes between the two pericopes, a series of miracle stories does intervene, including the stilling of the storm, as noted above. Matthew, as is well known, has assembled a group of miracles in chapters 8 and 9. Thus the evidence for the connection of the chreiai and the mission charge is very good, and so a second link is established.[3]

2. The Mission Charge (Q 10:2–12)

In Luke, the Woes over the Galilean Cities (10:13–15) follow directly after the mission charge. Since no direct connection exists in Matthew, we shall have to consider whether or not Luke's connection is likely to represent the original order of Q. The problem is more complicated now because much of the material between the two pericopes in Matthew is from Q, as can be seen in the following table.

Matt 9:35–10:16		Luke 10:2–12 (Mission Charge)
Matt 10:17–21	Mark 13:9–12	Luke 21:12–16; 12:11–12
Matt 10:22–23		
Matt 10:24–25a		Luke 6:40
Matt 10:25b		
Matt 10:26–33		Luke 12:2–9
Matt 10:34–36		Luke 12:51–53
Matt 10:37–38		Luke 14:26–27
Matt 10:39	cf. Mark 8:35	Luke 17:33
Matt 10:40	cf. Mark 9:37	
Matt 10:41–42	cf. Mark 9:41	
Matt 11:1		
Matt 11:2–19		Luke 7:18–35
Matt 11:20–23a		Luke 10:13–15 (Woes)

Suspicions as to the presence of Matthean compositional activity arise immediately because all of the material after the mission charge has to do with discipleship,[4] at least until Matt 11:1, where Matthew marks the formal conclusion to his discourse. What then follows (i.e., Matt 11:2–19) was already shown to have been dislocated by Matthew. Other parts, including Matt 10:17–21, 24–25a, 40–42, are also quite clearly out of place. The material in Matt 10:26–33 (=Luke 12:2–9) has also been dislocated by Matthew,[5] who has moved it into his discourse on discipleship (Matthew 10).

Matthew seems to preserve an indication of his awareness of the original

3. See Taylor, "Original Order," 116.
4. The whole section is regarded by Bornkamm as a product of Matthew's compositional activity ("End-Expectation and Church," 17–19); likewise, Taylor, "Original Order," 104–7.
5. So Lührmann, *Redaktion*, 50; Easton, *Luke*, 199; Manson, *Sayings of Jesus*, 106.

integrity of the Q section as given in Luke 10:2-16. First, the saying about Sodom which concludes the Q mission charge (Luke 10:12) and serves as a transition to the woes (Luke 10:13-15) also serves as the conclusion to Matthew's mission charge (Matt 10:15). This same saying about Sodom is given again by Matthew in 11:24 at the end of his version of the woes (Matt 11:20-24 [=Luke 10:13-15]). The repetition of the saying about Sodom shows that Matthew was aware of the original connection between the mission charge and the woes.[6] A second observation provides further evidence for this point. The whole section in Q (i.e., the mission charge and the woes) concluded with the saying in Luke 10:16. A variant of this saying is used by Matthew to conclude his whole discourse on discipleship (Matt 10:40). That is, Matthew seems to have expanded the Q mission charge by adding on related material; but he retained the Q conclusion to the whole discourse in 10:40.

The connection of mission charge to woes preserved by Luke in 10:2-12 is, furthermore, a good connection. The formal similarity between Luke 10:12 and Luke 10:14 must derive from Q, since the sayings are attested by both Luke and Matthew; that they were near each other in Q is probable. So this further strengthens the argument for the connection between the mission charge and the woes.

3. Woes over Galilean Cities (Q 10:13–15) and Jesus' Thanksgiving (Q 10: 21–22)

The linkage here of the woes to Jesus' thanksgiving is very well attested. They are immediately joined in Matthew, and in Luke only a small passage of Lukan special material (Luke 10:17-20) intervenes.

4. Other Material Possibly in the Second Section

The second section of Q seems to have ended with Jesus' thanksgiving or, prior to its addition, the woes and saying in Q 10:13-16. For reasons that will be elaborated in the next chapter, Blessed are the Eyes (Q 10:23-24) is assigned to the third section of Q. At this point, I note only that I regard Q 10:21-22 as a very late addition to Q, so that the connection often detected between Q 10:21-22 and 10:23-24 need not be original. This observation requires that the role of Q 10:23-24 be reexamined. Matt 11:28-30, which is sometimes attributed to Q, is probably not to be so attributed.[7]

Luke 10:25-28 also offers some evidence that it may have belonged to Q; moreover, its location seems to represent a deviation from the Markan framework generally followed by Luke (cf. Mark 12:28-31). However, the evidence for Q in the wording of the pericope is very uncertain.[8]

---

6. Lührmann, *Redaktion*, 62-63.
7. See Betz, "Logion of the Easy Yoke," 10-24.
8. This pericope (Luke 10:25-28) is not usually attributed to Q in recent studies. But see, e.g., Fuller, "Das Doppelgebot der Liebe".

5. Conclusions

A second unit of Q extends from Q 9:57 to Q 10:22, and again ends in a wisdom pericope (Q 10:21–22). The concern in the analysis to follow will be to determine the role of Wisdom in the composition of this Q material, and to determine the relationship between the wisdom pericope and the rest of the material.

Analysis of the Second Section of Q

1. Following Jesus (Q 9:57–60a)

Here we have two chreiai.[9] Each chreia begins with a would-be volunteer who comes forward to follow Jesus and is met with an odd, if not brusque, response. Since many also assign Luke 9:61–62 to Q,[10] we must first pause to ask whether that is the case. The presumption must be that it is not from Q, since it is not attested by Matthew; but arguments for or against its inclusion in Q are inconclusive. And since its absence would not substantially affect the interpretation of Q 9:57–60a, we shall not include it in our discussion of that text. However, it should be noted that Luke 9:61–62 has to do with being "suitable" or "qualified" ($\epsilon \ddot{v} \theta \epsilon \tau o s$) for the kingdom of God. It thus assumes the equation, following Jesus=fit for the kingdom. This equation is not impossible in the context of Q, but we are not justified in using a singly-attested saying as evidence for such an equation. Thus we shall limit ourselves to the two chreiai in Q 9:57–60a.

The next problem to be faced is the divergent readings in Matthew and Luke for the second chreia. Luke 9:59–60 reads:

"And he [Jesus] said to another, 'Follow me.' But he said, 'Permit me first, having departed, to bury my father.' But he said to him, 'Leave the dead to bury their own dead, but you go and proclaim the kingdom of God.'"

Matt 8:21–22 reads:

"And another of the disciples said to him, 'Sir, permit me first to go and bury my father.' But Jesus said to him, 'Follow me, and leave the dead to bury their own dead.'"

We can begin by eliminating Luke 9:60b ("but . . . go . . . proclaim . . .") as a Lukan addition. Not only is it unattested by Matthew, but it transforms the

---

9. Jeremias (*Parables*, 90) includes Q 9:58 in an extensive list of "paired parables and similes." These are treated more fully by Steinhauser, *Doppelbildworte*; Q 9:58 is treated on pp. 96–121. Bultmann (*History of the Synoptic Tradition*, 28–29) includes the pericope as a whole among the "biographical apophthegms," a form more widely attested in rabbinic literature (pp. 57–61). However, rabbinic literature does not offer the closest parallels; see Betz, *Nachfolge und Nachahmung*, 10–13, and Hengel, *Charismatic Leader*, 50–57. Note that in Q this double apophthegm followed directly after the double parable in Q 7:31–35.

10. On the division of opinion about Luke 9:61–62, see Kloppenborg, *Q Parallels*, 64.

saying into a call narrative which begins with "follow me" and ends with an assignment. Further, its addition was probably occasioned by the addition of Luke 9:61–62, which also concludes by referring to the kingdom of God. In any case, Luke 9:60b assumes a positive interest on the part of Q in the calling of disciples, and there is no reason to make that assumption. Matthew, on the other hand, describes the volunteer as a "disciple." Thus redaction by both Matthew and Luke is clearly in evidence.

The problem that remains in interpreting Q 9:57–60a is whether in Q Jesus began by telling the anonymous volunteer, "follow me" (as in Luke), or whether this came later (as in Matthew). Matthew's is certainly the more difficult reading because it has the volunteer giving excuses before he has even been asked (or has offered) to follow. It is more difficult, too, in being unlike the call stories where Jesus takes the initiative (Mark 1:16–20; 2:13–14; cf. 3:13; 6:7). This would be the only instance in Q of such a call story. It is preferable, therefore, to take Matthew's harder reading, minus the redactional additions ("of the disciples" and "sir") as the text of Q. Indeed, it is very probable that Matthew's redactional additions were an effort to deal with the clumsiness of the Q text. By describing the volunteer as a disciple, Matthew obviated the problem that the volunteer offers excuses before he is called.

Q 9:60a ("let the dead bury their own dead") is often interpreted to mean, "Let the spiritually dead bury the physically dead." But even if this was Q's meaning, the saying must not be thought of as a new rule but as a sarcastic remark which means, in effect, "Forget about your dead father!" Jewish precedent for calling the living the "dead" need hardly be sought, so common must such a locution have been.[11] More pertinent is the way the saying consigns "my father" to "the dead"[12]; thus, in its very phraseology, the saying severs the relationship between the volunteer son and his dead father.

The paradoxical nature of "let the dead bury the dead" must surely be intended. Of course, the dead cannot bury the dead! But the very offensiveness of the saying, which gets diluted with the spiritual interpretation, needs to be retained. Its callousness mirrors the callousness it seeks to engender. The heart of the saying, in fact, is precisely the comic incongruity of the dead burying their own dead. It is a shocking denial of filial piety: this important matter is shrugged off with biting humor. The most solemn filial duty is dismissed as a laughing matter. The radicality of the saying is rightly stressed by Hengel[13] and E. P. Sanders,[14] but they fail to see the comic nature of the saying, and thus generalize about Jesus' attitudes toward Jewish piety and the Torah (Sanders) or Jesus' "messianic authority."[15] We have here not a rule for

11. Cf. Strack-Billerbeck, *Kommentar*, 1. 489.
12. Note that "the dead" (τοὺς νεκρούς) is plural. The father has become simply a member of the realm of the dead. The use of "their own" (ἑαυτῶν) makes clear that the dead belong to this separate realm.
13. Hengel, *Charismatic Leader*, 5–15.
14. Sanders, *Jesus and Judaism*, 252–55.
15. Hengel, *Charismatic Leader*, 15.

the community but, as Robert C. Tannehill has observed, a "focal instance," a saying of such specificity and extremity that it undermines one's understanding of how the world works.[16]

We turn now to Q 9:57–58. Here a volunteer comes forward and promises, "I will follow you wherever you go." Jesus' puzzling reply is, "Foxes have dens and birds of the sky have lodgings, but the son of man has not where he may lay the head." This response is a carefully structured unit, as Tannehill has shown.[17] It is, in this respect, quite unlike Q 9:60. The saying is schematized by Tannehill in the following way:

Foxes	holes	have
and birds	of the sky	lodgings
but the son	of man	has not
where	the head	he may lay[18]

This carefully structured saying, with its alliterative ending ($\kappa\epsilon\phi\alpha\lambda\grave{\eta}\nu$ $\kappa\lambda\acute{\iota}\nu\eta$), contrasts wild animals and the human, using specific residents of land and sky to push the mind toward generalization. The point of comparison is the provision of shelter. Probably we are to think not of places built by animals (holes dug by foxes, nests built by birds, as implied in the *RSV*) but naturally provided shelter.[19]

The contrast between the shelter enjoyed by foxes and birds and the absence of shelter for the son of man is clearly meant to imply that even the animals have shelter yet, shockingly, the son of man has none. One is led to ask, "Why does the son of man have nowhere to rest?" Indeed, the language used ("nowhere to lay his head") seems intended to elicit one's sympathy, just as the oft-cited parallel in Plutarch *Vita Tiberii Gracchi* 9 (828C) seeks to elicit sympathy for those fighting for Italy by comparing them with the wild beasts, which have holes to sleep in:

> The wild beasts that roam over Italy have their dens and holes [$\phi\omega\lambda\epsilon\acute{o}s$] to lurk in, but the men who fight and die for our country enjoy the common air and light and nothing else. It is their lot to wander with their wives and children, houseless and homeless, over the face of the earth.

The structure of the saying does not permit us to think of elective homelessness. The homelessness of the son of man is thrust upon him; it is unnatural, unjust. It ought not to be. But if that is so, how does a statement about the injustice of the homelessness of the son of man respond to the volunteer's assertion that he will follow wherever Jesus goes? The saying, frankly, does not

---

16. For the concept and definition of "focal instance," see Tannehill, *Sword of His Mouth*, 71–72. For the present saying as a "focal instance," see pp. 77, 162–63. However, I do not agree with Tannehill's nonliteral interpretation of the word "dead."

17. Tannehill, *Sword of His Mouth*, 157.

18. Tannehill, *Sword of His Mouth*, 161.

19. On "lodgings" ($\kappa\alpha\tau\alpha\sigma\kappa\eta\nu\acute{\omega}\sigma\epsilon\iota s$), see Moulton and Milligan, *Vocabulary*, *s.v.* $\kappa\alpha\tau\alpha\sigma\kappa\acute{\eta}\nu\omega\sigma\iota s$ (332).

fit very well as a response to the volunteer. The volunteer says, "I will follow you wherever you go"; Jesus responds, in effect, "Consider how unjust it is that the son of man has no place to sleep; why even wild animals are able to find shelter." This, then, is a saying that does not fit its context, and that, moreover, has nothing to do with discipleship. This also helps to explain why the volunteer's promise to go anywhere, which hardly seems like an inadequate offer, fits so poorly with the response by Jesus.

The conclusion to which these reflections lead is that Q 9:58 is a later addition to Q 9:59–60, that Q 9:57 has been created to adapt the saying in Q 9:58 to the context of discipleship, and that the real function of Q 9:58 is to speak about the son of man, not about discipleship. We saw earlier that structurally Q 9:58 and 9:60 are very different. More critically, Q 9:60 is a sarcastic dismissal of filial piety, and thus an expression of elective homelessness. But Q 9:58 cannot be interpreted as recommending elective homelessness. The tension between these two sayings, therefore, is rather severe. The older is likely to be Q 9:60. Thus Q 9:58 appears to be an addition.[20] The likelihood that this is so is greatly strengthened by the fact that Q 9:58 is attested independently in GThom 86, which reads, "Jesus said: [The foxes have their holes] and the birds have [their] nest, but the son of man has no place to lay his head and rest."

Thus it would appear that Q 9:59–60a represents the nucleus of the brief collection dealing with "discipleship." Q 9:58 was added later, and Q 9:57b was created as the means by which to insert Q 9:58; it established the context as that of following Jesus, so as to create the link with Q 9:59–60a. But, as we have seen, Q 9:57b and 9:58 do not really fit together very well; this means that the context is artificial. Indeed, by having the person volunteer to go "wherever you go," instead of having him simply be asked to follow, the redactor has intensified the emphasis on rejection in Q 9:58. Jesus' response acquires the rather brusque character that was noted earlier. Thus, the addition of Q 9:57b makes sense from the point of view of the redactor's aim, even though Q 9:58 ends up as an apparent non sequitur.

It is interesting to observe that, given the context of Q 9:57–58 (i.e., immediately following Q 7:31–35), it is entirely possible that Wisdom's futile search for rest may stand in the background (cf. 1 Enoch 42). At the very least, the notion that Wisdom sends prophets and messengers who are rejected may lie behind this saying, especially since it is a notion attested elsewhere in Q (11:49–51; 13:34–35).

Before moving on, we may briefly consider an apparent anomaly. Q 7:34 is, as is well known, often cited as evidence of Jesus' more celebrative, non-ascetic lifestyle. He goes out to the public, eating and drinking, while John eschews these, living his ascetic wilderness life. Conversely, Q 9:58 is often

---

20. So Kloppenborg, *Formation*, 190–92. Note, however, that Kloppenborg's interpretation of the saying diverges sharply from mine. He maintains that "Q 9:57–58 says nothing of rejection . . ."; I have argued that rejection is exactly its point.

cited as evidence of Jesus' voluntary homelessness, or the homelessness he endures in his solidarity with the poor of Israel. In short, cheek by jowl in Q we find proof-texts for apparently opposite lifestyles. In fact there is no anomaly, because Q 9:58 does not have to do with elective homelessness but with rejection, and Q 7:31-35 also has to do with rejection.

2. The Mission Charge (Q 10:2-12) and Woes (Q 10:13-15 [16])

The Q mission charge has almost nothing in common with modern missionary methods, so speaking of "mission" can be misleading.[21] In fact, the mission charge should not be understood as an evangelizing mission but, as we shall see, an errand of judgment. What is related is a remarkable process which, apparently counting on few positive results, has "laborers" sent out for the purpose of distinguishing, merely by their reception, between the elect and the damned.

The historicity of the mission charge is questionable.[22] Bultmann says that it "must . . . be included among the regulations of the church."[23] But this position is vulnerable because of the scanty evidence that early church practice is reflected here.[24] The argument that the mission charge was indeed a product of the early church has been advanced by Käsemann.[25] In fact, Käsemann thinks that the mission by the oldest Jewish Christian community—a mission limited to Palestine and seeking the eschatological renewal of the covenant— may have been "the original *Sitz im Leben* of the logia source."[26] Theissen, on the other hand, apparently takes the mission charge to be authentic Jesus material. He argues that "wandering charismatics" took these sayings literally.[27] However, we shall see that there are serious difficulties with an interpretation of the Q mission charge as a charter for a real mission. To be sure, it is possible that behind the account there may be an actual mission, namely, a call for repentance issued to Israel. But the historicity of the mission charge can only be properly evaluated when its nature and purpose are examined more carefully.

(a) *The Origin of the Mission Charge.* The mission instructions in Q 10:2-16 are a Q sayings composition. The original Q sequence is best preserved by

21. Cf. Schürmann, "Mt 10,5b-6," 146-47; Steck, *Israel*, 287; Schulz, *Q*, 410-13.

22. See Beare, "Mission of the Disciples," 1-13.

23. Bultmann, *History of the Synoptic Tradition*, 145.

24. The "mission" described here was antiquated already for Matthew and Luke, each of whom solved the problem in his own way, Matthew with his post-resurrection extension of the mission (cf. Matt 28:16-20 with 10:5-6), Luke by having Jesus explicitly annul the previous instructions (cf. Luke 22:35-38 with 10:1-16). The "mission" is thus a well-attested instance of the evangelists retaining primitive material by limiting its validity to a segment of the historical past; see Hoffmann, *Studien*, 261.

25. Käsemann, "Primitive Christian Apocalyptic," 112-13.

26. Käsemann, "Primitive Christian Apocalyptic," 112. Steck (*Israel*, 288) holds that Q must have been a collection of sayings for the instruction of early Jewish Christian preachers, whose message to Israel was couched in the terminology of the deuteronomistic view of history.

27. Theissen, "Wanderradikalismus." See also Theissen, "Legitimation"; "'Wir haben alles verlassen'"; and *Sociology, passim.*

Luke. The usual judgment has been that Matthew has conflated the Markan account (Mark 6:6b–13) with the Q account (see Matt 9:35–10:16), whereas Luke's two accounts (9:1–6; 10:1–16) keep Q and Mark separate, the latter account being from Q. This assumption has much to recommend it, even though, as Hoffmann has reminded us, we cannot simply assume that Luke's second account is from Q.[28]

The versions in Mark and Q have enough in common to say that they share a common origin or that they represent a common pattern.[29] Thus mission instructions antedate the redaction of Q, and the mission charge is not simply the creation of the Q redactor.

(b) *Reconstruction of Q 10:2–11:16.* The number of disagreements between Matthew and Luke in the wording of Q 10:2–11, 16, as well as the importance of this text generally, require that we seek to reconstruct the text. Below is given a reconstruction of the text, giving only those portions which belong to the mission charge proper (i.e., Q 10:2–11, 16).[30]

10:2   [καὶ λέγει αὐτοῖς·]
          ὁ μὲν θερισμὸς πολύς,
          οἱ δὲ ἐργάται ὀλίγοι·
          δεήθητε οὖν τοῦ κυρίου τοῦ θερισμοῦ
          ὅπως ἐκβάλῃ ἐργάτας εἰς τὸν θερισμὸν αὐτοῦ·

10:3   ὑπάγετε·
          ἰδοὺ ἀποστέλλω ὑμᾶς
          ὡς ἄρνας ἐν μέσῳ λύκων.

10:4   μὴ βαστάζετε βαλλάντιον,
          μὴ πήραν,
          μὴ ὑποδήματα·
          [καὶ μηδένα κατὰ τὴν ὁδὸν ἀσπάσησθε.]

10:5   εἰς ἣν δ᾽ ἂν εἰσέλθητε οἰκίαν,
          πρῶτον λέγετε· εἰρήνη τῷ οἴκῳ τούτῳ.

28. Hoffmann, "Lk 10,5–11." Luke, says Hoffmann, has added 10:8, 11b; has rearranged the Q material so as to place the mission in cities in last and emphatic position; and has made the mission to houses into a search for quarter. Hoffmann contends that in Q the missionary activity was directed to houses, even though Luke 10:13–15 assumes a mission to whole cities (and Matthew himself seems aware of this in 10:14). Hoffmann's claim that Luke's compositional activity is responsible for the clumsy situation in which the messengers enter a house before entering the city is dubious. This apparent clumsiness may instead show Luke's primitiveness, since the order houses/towns seems to be present in Mark too. Cf. Schulz, *Q*, 404; Hoffmann, *Studien*, 263–86.

29. The question whether Mark had access to Q for his account of the mission is left undecided here. For the view that Mark used Q, see Grant, "Mission of the Disciples." Lührmann (*Redaktion*, 59–60) rightly notes that the mission in Mark is also eschatological, but less strongly so than in Q.

30. This reconstruction is indebted to the work of Sellew ("Early Collections," 103–42). But Sellew regards Q 10:2–16 as a coherent composition, a position which does not do justice to the tensions within the composition. For example, he regards Q 10:3 as a clarification of 10:2 (p. 145), a view I cannot accept. For another recent reconstruction, see Uro, *Sheep Among the Wolves*, 73–96. Except for Q 10:6, 16, my reconstruction is similar to that of Schulz (*Q*, 404–7) and Laufen (*Doppelüberlieferungen*, 205–33).

10:6   καὶ ἐὰν μὲν ᾖ ἡ οἰκία ἀξία,
        ἐπαναπαήσεται ἐπ᾽ αὐτὴν ἡ εἰρήνη ὑμῶν·
        εἰ δὲ μὴ ᾖ ἀξία,
        ἐφ᾽ ὑμᾶς ἀνακάμψει.
10:7   ἐν αὐτῇ δὲ τῇ οἰκίᾳ μένετε,
        ἐσθίοντες καὶ πίνοντες τὰ παρ᾽ αὐτῶν·
        ἄξιος γὰρ ὁ ἐργάτης τοῦ μισθοῦ αὐτοῦ.
        [μὴ μεταβαίνετε ἐξ οἰκίας εἰς οἰκίαν·]
10:8   καὶ εἰς ἣν ἂν πόλιν εἰσέρχησθε καὶ δέχωνται ὑμᾶς,
        ἐσθίετε τὰ παρατιθέμενα ὑμῖν,
10:9   καὶ θεραπεύετε τοὺς ἐν αὐτῇ ἀσθενεῖς,
        καὶ λέγετε αὐτοῖς·
        ἤγγικεν ἐφ᾽ ὑμᾶς ἡ βασιλεία τοῦ θεοῦ.
10:10   εἰς ἣν δ᾽ ἂν πόλιν εἰσέλθητε
        καὶ μὴ δέχωνται ὑμᾶς,
        ἐξελθόντες εἰς τὰς πλατείας αὐτῆς εἴπατε·
10:11   καὶ τὸν κονιορτὸν τὸν κολληθέντα ἡμῖν
        ἐκ τῆς πόλεως ὑμῶν εἰς τοὺς πόδας ἀπομασσόμεθα ὑμῖν·
        [πλὴν τοῦτο γινώσκετε ὅτι ἤγγικεν ἡ βασιλεία τοῦ θεοῦ.]
10:16   ὁ ἀκούων ὑμῶν ἐμοῦ ἀκούει,
        καὶ ὁ ἀθετῶν ὑμᾶς ἐμὲ ἀθετεῖ·
        ὁ δὲ ἐμὲ ἀθετῶν ἀθετεῖ τὸν ἀποστείλαντά με.

Translation:

10:2   [And he said to them,]
        The harvest is indeed great,
        but the laborers are few.
        Pray, therefore, the lord of the harvest
        that he send laborers into his harvest.
10:3   Go!
        Behold, I send you as lambs in the midst of wolves.
10:4   Carry no purse,
        no bag,
        no sandals;
        [and salute no one along the way].
10:5   And whatever house you enter,
        first say, "Peace be to this house!"
10:6   And if the house is worthy,
        your peace will rest upon it;
        but if it is not worthy,
        it (namely, your peace) will come back upon you.
10:7   And remain in the same house,
        eating and drinking what is provided by them;
        for the laborer is worthy of his reward.
        [Do not itinerate from house to house.]
10:8   And when you enter a city, and they receive you,
        eat what is set before you,
10:9   and heal those sick within it,

and say to them,
"The kingdom of God has come near to you."

10:10   And whatever city you enter and they do not receive you,
when you go into its streets, say,

10:11   "Even the dust from your city that clings to our feet
we wipe off against you.
[Nevertheless know this, that the kingdom of God has drawn near.]"

10:16   Whoever hears you, hears me,
and he who rejects you, rejects me;
and whoever rejects me,
rejects the one who sent me.

The introduction to the mission instructions is no longer recoverable. Only a brief "and he said to them" can be said to have probably been present in Q. When we turn to the instructions themselves, we encounter problems first in Q 10:3. If word statistics ever show a clear preference, it would be this instance: Luke does not use ὑπάγειν (to go) in the imperative. Thus its occurrence here is best understood if we assume it was in Q. That Matthew is responsible for the alteration of "lamb" (ἀρήν) to "sheep" (πρόβατον) is probable because of his use of "sheep" in 9:36 and 10:6.[31] Matthew is also responsible for moving this verse from the beginning to the end of the mission charge, to serve as the transition to 10:17–25 (Matthean special material) and perhaps because it would fit poorly in close proximity to Matt 10:6.

The briefer reading in Luke 10:4 is to be preferred. Matthew has expanded here upon Mark 6:8–9. The occurrence of "silver" (ἀργύριον) in Luke 9:3 and in Matt 10:9 (ἄργυρος) is intriguing, but it is also a common word and need not be taken as evidence of Q. Matthew's prohibition of "two tunics" (δύο χιτῶνες) and a staff (ῥάβδος) come from Mark 6:8–9.[32] The prohibition of greeting anyone along the way is included in Q 10:4 by almost all scholars, yet it has no Matthean parallel. Still, it is hard to see why Luke would have invented it, and a reason for Matthew's lack of it may perhaps be found in Matt 5:47: "If you salute (ἐὰν ἀσπάσησθε) only your brethren, what more are you doing than others?"[33] Nevertheless, the prohibition against greeting is only singly attested.

31. See further, Sellew, "Early Collections," 115–16.

32. The prohibition of a staff (ῥάβδος) occurs in Luke 9:3 and Matt 10:10 and could derive from Q, since in Mark 6:8 the staff is permitted as an explicit exception to the rule, "Take nothing. . . ."

33. Moreover, Matthew uses the verb "greet" (ἀσπάζεσθαι) in 10:12 ("As you enter the house, salute it"), so he may have retained the term but transformed it to conform to typical early Christian usage (cf. Acts 18:22; 21:7, 19, and frequent references in the letters, especially Romans 16); see Schulz, Q, 406. It is very strange that Matthew seems not to have understood the nature of this greeting, since it is not merely the greeting even gentiles give to strangers (Matt 5:47). The real character of the greeting can be seen in Q 10:6, where the "peace" greeting is a word of power. As Uro puts it (Sheep Among the Wolves, 137), "the greeting of the messengers relies on the idea of the dynamistic power of the uttered word manifested, e.g., in the blessings and curses." Similarly, the kingdom of God comes upon one (Q 11:20). Paul may well reflect this concept when, using language untypical for him, he says that "the kingdom of

Although the wording of Q 10:5a is probably best preserved by Luke, the wording of Q 10:5b is more difficult. Most commentators take the Lukan reading as Q. However, if we accept Matthew's reading, then we have an interesting relationship between Q 10:4 (". . . and salute no one along the way") and Q 10:5 ("but whenever you enter a house, salute it"). And we could explain Luke's adding "first say, 'Peace be to this house!'" as an effort to explain the curious greeting ritual. Nevertheless, because Matthew's redactional activity is more clearly in evidence in shaping his mission charge, and because of the parallel syntactic structure of Luke 10:10 (cf. Matt 10:14), I regard the Lukan reading as more likely that of Q.

The basic structure of Q 10:6 and much of its wording are preserved by both Matthew and Luke. But the wording is suspect in both cases. Matthew's worthiness motif is usually regarded as secondary (cf. Matt 10:37–38; 22:18), though worthiness language is introduced by Luke in 7:4, and is known in Q (10:7; cf. 3:8). In favor of Matthew's wording it may be noted that Matt 10:13 fits poorly in its present context. Matthew has clearly composed Matt 10:11, not noticing that by identifying who is "worthy" already in 10:11 he has rendered 10:13 superfluous, and for that reason one may argue that 10:13 represents Q. But this does not necessarily decide the case in favor of the motif of worthiness. Luke 10:6 is also problematic, however, because it individualizes the greeting of peace. The context has to do with approaching a house, not with individuals within it. This individualizing occurs in Matt 10:11 too, and is secondary there, as Matt 10:13 shows. Luke 10:5 concludes with "peace be to this house"; likewise, Matt 10:12 requires that the house be saluted. Matthew's wording in 10:13 is to be preferred to the extent that it too is oriented to the house, not to individuals. On the other hand, Luke is probably more original in preserving the rather shamanistic understanding of "peace," which "rests upon" and thereby identifies the righteous, and which can also "return" to its sender.[34] Matthew has weakened this by using imperative verbs. Luke 10:7 assumes that the greeting ritual has identified the worthy house, and thus continues the house locus while assuming that "peace" seeks out the righteous. In sum, the worthiness motif remains questionable as the Q reading, but the net result of these deliberations is to suggest that the least unsatisfactory reading is that quoted above as Q 10:6.

Although Q 10:7 is attested for the most part only by Luke, it is probable

God is not in word but in power" (1 Cor 4:20; cf. 2:4). The prohibition of the greeting, thus, is to be linked to its power, which is not to be exercised indiscriminately. The notion that the greeting was prohibited due to the extreme urgency of the mission (Schulz, *Q*, 216; Polag, *Christologie*, 67–68) is rightly rejected by Hoffmann (*Studien*, 298 n. 33; cf. Uro, *Sheep Among the Wolves*, 135). The view of O'Hagen ("'Greet no one on the way'") that the omission of the greeting should be seen as a gesture of hostility is probably correct, although many of his arguments are fanciful.

34. On the strange and powerful notion of "peace" here, see, in addition to the previous note, Windisch, "ἀσπάζομαι," 498–99; Käsemann, "The Beginnings of Christian Theology," 103.

that it was the victim of Matthew's authorial scissors. The proverb about the laborer being worthy of his wages or food (Q 10:7b) certainly belongs to the mission charge, since it is also attested in Matthew; and it is hard to imagine a better place for it than that provided by Luke. The Matthean location is certainly secondary; he has used it to rationalize the puzzling instructions about equipment (Matt 10:10). So it seems likely that Luke has preserved the Q reading here, though "and drinking" may be Lukan, since he uses the combination "eating and drinking" quite often. The command not to go from house to house is not attested by Matthew; it must be regarded only as possible Q material.

Q 10:8 is only partially attested by Matthew (cf. Matt 10:11 but also Mark 6:10), but it is independently attested in GThom 14, and thus cannot be a creation by Luke. Neither does it derive from Mark. A rule similar to Luke 10:8 was known to Paul and used to counsel the setting aside of food laws for the sake of mission (1 Cor 10:27). But it is not likely that Luke introduced the saying at this point with the same goal, because according to Luke food laws were rescinded only later, and then only partially (Acts 15:20, 29; Acts 10:1–16 is not interpreted by Luke as implying the rescinding of food laws). So no motive for Luke's insertion of a non-Q independent saying can be found. Moreover, Luke seems puzzled by the whole ritual of reception. Rather than making internal changes, he simply provides an interpretive framework: Jesus sent the messengers ahead to prepare for his arrival (9:51, 52; 10:1).

The wording of Q 10:9 is not too difficult to recover, and instances of uncertain wording are not materially significant. Matthew is certainly responsible for the expanded list of miracles in 10:8; likewise the Matthean location for this material is secondary. The ritual of testing whether the house or city is worthy makes no sense unless the preaching and healing are confined to those places that are worthy. Matthew, by contrast, begins with the command to preach and heal, making the followers' mission parallel to Jesus' own (cf. Matt 4:17, 23). The woes in Q 10:13–15 also contradict the Q mission instructions, because they assume that mighty works are done without the testing ritual. It is unlikely that Luke would have invented such an odd procedure as we find here, so it is best to assume that he has preserved the Q location and, probably, wording too.

Q 10:10–11 is parallel in structure to Q 10:8–9, but it treats cases of non-reception rather than reception. Again, the Matthean parallel has been reworked, as can be seen by the combination "house or city." The instructions are appropriate for a city but not for a house. Matthew has shortened Q 10:11 so as to diminish its incongruity with his "house or city" context. The form and the wording of Matt 10:14 have been strongly influenced by Mark 6:11. Luke's wording is, therefore, to be preferred. However, it is not clear whether the final statement, "Nevertheless know this, that the kingdom of God has drawn near," belonged in Q, because it is not attested by Matthew. Since his editorial work is only too evident, it is quite possible that Matthew lopped this off too.

The wording of Q 10:16 is not easy to reconstruct. A preference for "receive" (δέχεσθαι) as in Matt 10:40 is encouraged by its use in Q 10:10 (and see Luke 10:8). The fact that Luke shows a greater preference generally for δέχεσθαι than does Matthew argues for the Lukan wording. Further, it is difficult to see why Luke would have changed "receive" to "hear" because, in addition to his proclivity toward "receive," that word would have fit his context better: Luke 10:13–15 speaks of "mighty works" being done, not of preaching in the Galilean cities, and in Luke 10:17–20 the mission of the seventy is characterized not by preaching but by exorcisms. Moreover, Luke obviously knew a variant form of the saying using "receive" (9:48), so his use of ἀκούειν (to hear) is difficult to explain except as a survival of the wording of Q. Luke's liking for the word "hear" explains nothing,[35] because Matthew likes it equally well. In addition, Justin attests a form of the tradition using "hear,"[36] and Matthew seems to preserve some recollection of "hearing" as an alternative reading (Matt 10:14, "And whoever does not receive you and does not *hear* your words . . .").[37] Further, it must be noted that Matthew's location makes his wording suspect. Although Matthew might have known a version of the saying which began with δέχεσθαι, his location for the saying would have provided him an excellent reason for altering 10:40b so as to eliminate the idea of rejection. In sum, the Lukan wording of Q 10:16 is to be preferred.[38] The positive and negative formulation in Luke is also likely to be primary; Luke shows no preference for "reject" (ἀθετεῖν), and the double form reflects the mission charge itself.

(c) *Redaction of the Mission Charge.* As can be seen by comparing the Markan and Q versions of the mission charge, a common tradition lies behind them.[39] Yet the Markan mission charge differs from that of Q in several particulars. Peculiar to Mark are these features: the Twelve as recipients of the instructions; the two-by-two sending; the granting of authority over demons; the permission to carry staff and sandals; and the report of a successful mission. Peculiar to Q are these features: the generally negative character of the material and the emphasis upon judgment; a sending statement in direct speech; a saying about being sent out like lambs in the midst of wolves; the prohibition of staff, sandals, and greeting anyone along the way; proclamation of the kingdom of God and of judgment; woes; and a messenger saying (Q 10:16).

The "completely eschatological perspective" of the Q mission charge has

---

35. Against Sellew, "Early Collections," 140.
36. Justin *1 Apol.* 16:10; 63:5.
37. This is true even though Matthew has clearly been influenced by Mark 6:11.
38. So Kloppenborg, *Formation*, 196 n. 111, and Uro, *Sheep Among the Wolves*, 86–88.
39. See, e.g., Hahn, *Mission in the New Testament*, 43–44; more recently, Sellew, "Early Collections," 65–93, and Uro, *Sheep Among the Wolves*, 26–39, 98–110.

been noted by Dieter Georgi,[40] who compares the Q account with the "entirely different picture" that we meet in Mark 6, where "the eschatological tension has almost completely vanished."[41] In Mark 6, "the missionary, the apostle, no longer proclaims the imminent end but the present power."[42]

The Q account of the mission charge is an especially important text because it offers the best glimpse that we have into the self-understanding and actual behavior of Jesus' early followers. Not surprisingly, this is the basic text for attempts to describe the sociology of the Jesus movement. It may represent the self-understanding and behavior of only one part of the Jesus movement, but it is presumably the part that is responsible for Q, although it is difficult to know to what extent the redacted mission charge reflects praxis still current in the community. It will be argued below that the redaction, in fact, reflects the failure of the mission, so it may already have been abandoned. In any case, the Q mission charge contains some very old material. As Kloppenborg rightly notes, "the radical comportment of Q is usually taken as a sign of its antiquity."[43]

If, however, the Q mission charge is a window through which we can see the earlier Jesus movement, we are confronted with a complex picture. Such categories as Cynic[44] or, as Kloppenborg seems to accept, sapiential, do not seem adequate, though there is truth in both. For example, the "laborers" spread an odd sort of shalom, announce the nearness of the kingdom of God, and heal the sick, activities not easily subsumed under the categories of Cynic teacher or wise person. Eschatology is clearly present in the mission charge.[45] Scholars often characterize Jesus as a prophet,[46] and there is certainly evidence that the members of the Q community (or its leaders) understood themselves as prophets (cf. Q 6:23). Theissen's composite picture of Jesus as prophet, wisdom teacher, poet, and martyr[47] could well be used of Jesus' earliest followers: in the mission charge, and elsewhere in Q, we seem to have a

40. Georgi, *Opponents of Paul*, 165.

41. Georgi, *Opponents of Paul*, 167.

42. Georgi, *Opponents of Paul*, 167.

43. Kloppenborg, *Formation*, 195.

44. For a brief description of the Cynic movement, see Meeks, *Moral World*, 52–56. See further Malherbe, "Cynics," "Self-Definition," and *The Cynic Epistles*, as well as O'Neil, *Teles*. Parallels between the messengers of the Q mission charge and Cynic teachers were noted by Hengel, *Charismatic Leader*, 27–33; cf. Mack, *A Myth of Innocence*, 67–69, and Downing, *Jesus and the Threat of Freedom*. This relationship is disputed by Horsley, *Jesus and the Spiral of Violence*, 228–31, and *Sociology*, 46–47, 116–18.

45. See, e.g., Schulz (*Q*, 410): "The presence of mission activity in Israel is therefore already an apocalyptic end-time event." It may be recalled that Albert Schweitzer, who held that eschatology and ethics were mutually exclusive, turned to the mission charge as evidence that ethical teaching played no role in Jesus' mission (*Mystery of the Kingdom of God*, 87), or more precisely that ethical teaching must be subsumed under the call to repentance (89–97).

46. See, e.g., E. P. Sanders, *Jesus and Judaism*, 237–40. Sanders prefers Hengel's term, "eschatological charismatic" (see Hengel, *Charismatic Leader*, 18–24).

47. Theissen, *Biblical Faith*, 89–104.

combination of several traditions, including prophetic, sapiential, eschatological/apocalyptic, and charismatic.

When we turn to look for evidence of redaction in the Q mission charge, we note that its ending is clearly Q 10:16. This means that the unit we are considering is Q 10:2–16. But having noted that, we can see quite clearly that Q 10:13–15 did not originally belong with the mission charge. These woes, uttered over Chorazin, Bethsaida and Capernaum, three villages on the north side of the Sea of Galilee, are directly addressed to the cities, and thus represent an abrupt shift in audience. Moreover, as noted earlier, Q 10:13–15 presupposes that Jesus and/or his followers performed mighty deeds and then were rejected. But this contradicts the procedure outlined in the mission charge, according to which the "laborers" are first to determine whether the city is worthy, and only then to preach and heal the sick. Further, Q 10:13–15 interprets the mission specifically as a call for repentance. This is probably implicit in the mission charge, but it is not made explicit. Lührmann was correct in seeing Q 10:12 as a redactional creation by the composer of Q, created as a link to the woes in Q 10:13–15.[48] Thus, the Q redaction of this material is characterized by an emphasis upon judgment. The positive instructions for mission are overshadowed by massive denunciations. The addition of the woes shows, in fact, that the mission had come to be understood by the redactor as an errand of judgment.

Since Q 10:3 forms an *inclusio* with Q 10:16 (note the repeated "send," ἀποστέλλειν), it is likely that these verses were added at the same time. Q 10:16 played no role in the tradition common to Mark and Q, whereas much of Q 10:4–11 has a parallel in Mark 6:8–11. We have every reason, therefore, to suspect that Q 10:16 is a redactional addition and, since both Q 10:3 and 10:16 use the verb "to send,"[49] that they were added at the same time.

Q 10:3 could be an ironic use of a Jewish metaphor: Israel as lambs among the gentile wolves.[50] But I now regard this as unlikely.[51] The text of the

48. Lührmann (*Redaktion*, 62) contends that this saying was created during the redaction of Q and was formed by analogy with Q 10:13–15. If Q 10:13–15 refers to the mighty deeds of Jesus, then the consequence of rejecting him is the same as that of rejecting the messengers; this, in any case, seems clearly to be implied here. The addition of Q 10:12 will have been to provide a transition to Q 10:13–15 (cf. Hoffmann, *Studien*, 303–4). What is implied here concerning the disciples is made explicit in Q 10:16, as Hoffmann notes.

49. The sending formula occurs in Q 7:27; 10:3; and 11:49; in 11:49, Wisdom is the sender. According to Steck (*Israel*, 286–87 n. 9), Jesus in 10:3 stands in the place of Wisdom; that is, John and Jesus are messengers of Wisdom, but the messengers are actually sent by Jesus. Steck and Schulz (*Q*, 412–13) judge that Jesus is identified with Wisdom here, and that therefore the continuity between John and Jesus is broken. However, in the present context the identification of Jesus with Wisdom is not clear, because at the end of the mission charge (at Q 10:16), we again encounter the chain of envoys, which seems more typical of Q. Indeed, if Q 10:3 and 10:16 were added at the same time, they very likely both assume the same chain of envoys.

50. In Jewish apocalyptic literature, a similar image is used to refer to Israel (sheep) among the hostile nations (wolves); e.g., 1 Enoch 89:13–27; 55; Tanḥuma Toledoth 32b; cf. *Pss. Sol.*

mission charge does not encourage this interpretation, because it does not deal with hostility to the "laborers" but with their reception or rejection. More likely is the view that Q 10:3 is meant simply as a metaphor for vulnerability. In this case, it fits nicely with Q 10:4, which expresses this vulnerability in concrete terms: no purse, bag, or sandals.[52] The theme of dependence upon God is prominent in Q (see Q 4:1–13; 6:20–21, 38; 11:3–4, 9–13; 12:4–7, 11–12, 22–31, 33–34; 17:5–6, 33). Thus there is considerable warrant for interpreting Q 10:3 as a metaphor for vulnerability rather than as a sarcastic inversion of a traditional image. Given this interpretation, Q 10:3 could have been added at the same time as the rest of the mission instructions were added.

Q 10:16 provides a theological interpretation of Q 10:3–11. It does not openly contradict the mission charge, but it does go well beyond it. It focuses attention on the messengers in a way that simply does not happen in the mission charge proper (i.e., Q 10:3–11). In fact, Q 10:16 operates within a different conceptual universe from that of Q 10:3–11. In the latter, the messengers are mainly vehicles for divine power, but in 10:16 they are emissaries of Jesus who is in turn the emissary of God. The focus upon the fate of the person, rather than on the kingdom which manifests itself through the messengers, represents an important shift in emphasis. Although the specific terminology and themes of the deuteronomistic tradition are not present in Q 10:16, it is possible to make that connection because of the emphasis upon the consequences of hearing or rejecting the one sent, and because of the emphasis upon rejection. The point of Q 10:16 is not so much divine authorization for the messengers as the seriousness of rejecting them.

It is not clear what is the conceptual background of Q 10:16. One may hear in it echoes of the Jewish institution of the "agent" (שליח),[53] of the notion of the prophet,[54] the deuteronomistic tradition,[55] and the tradition of hospitality.[56] The last has been too little emphasized, yet it is clearly evident in the tradition, such as in the sayings attached to Matt 10:40, the variant saying in Mark 9:37 par., Matt 25:31–46, and elsewhere. The importance of hospitality is emphasized by noting that the identity of the guest is not as it appears on the surface; for "some have entertained angels unawares" (Heb 13:2, alluding to Abraham in Genesis 18–19; cf. Matt 25:31–46). This suggests that "hear" in Luke 10:16a is probably not just a translational variant of "receive." Luke's

---

8:23; 4 Ezra 5:18. However, the image can also be used to speak of the treachery of leaders: Ezek 22:27; Zeph 3:3; Prov 28:15 LXX; Matt 7:15; John 10:12; Acts 20:29; Did 16:3; IgnPhil 2:2; 2 Clem 5:2–4; Justin *1 Apol.* 16:13; *Dial.* 35:3; 81:2. The image of wolf and sheep is, of course, a very common one, and not only in Jewish tradition; see Bornkamm, "λύκος," 308–11, and Bauer, *s.v.* ἀρήν. See also Hoffmann, *Studien*, 294–95; Schulz, *Q*, 412–13.

51. Contrary to the view I expressed in "Wisdom Christology in Q," 151 n. 32.

52. See Kloppenborg, *Formation*, 194. Concerning the purse, bag, and sandals, see further Sellew, "Early Collections," 77–88, 122–24, and Uro, *Sheep Among the Wolves*, 117–34.

53. See Kloppenborg, *Formation*, 197.

54. See Boring, *Sayings of the Risen Jesus*, 148.

55. Steck, *Israel*, 286–87 n. 9; Schulz, *Q*, 458.

56. On this topic, see esp. Koenig, *New Testament Hospitality*.

formulation, which is probably that of Q, reflects more the vocabulary of prophetic mission than of hospitality. This, coupled with the peculiarly negative formulation in Q, strengthens the claim that Q 10:16 is consonant with the deuteronomistic tradition. The negative formulation of Q 10:16 accords with the negative emphasis in the larger Q mission complex, namely 10:2–16.

We have not yet treated Q 10:2. This verse is not likely to have been added at the same time as Q 10:3, because the former speaks of asking God ("the lord of the harvest") to send "laborers" whereas the latter has Jesus do the sending. Since Q 10:2 can hardly have served as an adequate introduction to the mission charge, and since the common tradition visible behind Mark and Q probably had a statement about sending, it seems likely that Q 10:3 was the earlier introduction to the mission charge, and that Q 10:2 was a subsequent addition.

The usual interpretation of Q 10:2, that many souls await reaping (=conversion) but there are too few missionaries to reap this harvest, is untenable. If it were correct, it would certainly clash with Q 10:3–11, which provides no warrant for such an interpretation. On the contrary, harvest is a common metaphor for judgment in Jewish writings,[57] and it would seem to preferable to interpret Q 10:2 as a saying about judgment, particularly since harvest as a metaphor for judgment is found elsewhere in Q. In that case, we would expect the great harvest in Q 10:2 to refer to the task of cutting the grain and then separating the wheat from the straw and chaff. The greatness of the harvest is probably relative, not absolute: it represents an enormous task given the small number of "laborers." But if harvest is a metaphor for judgment, then it is an unusual use of the metaphor, because the "laborers" can hardly be thought of as anything other than human beings, not angels, as for example, in Matt 13:39, 41, or the one like a son of man and his angels, as in Rev 14:14–20 (cf. Joel 3:13). Yet the image is peculiarly apt for describing the Q mission, which in fact does involve a separation of the righteous from the wicked; precisely in the reception or non-reception of the "laborers" this winnowing is going on.

Given what has been said concerning Q 10:2, it would seem best to assume that the harvest is indeed a metaphor for judgment. The saying itself came from the tradition, as the parallel in GThom 73 shows, and thus cannot be the product of the Q community. Curiously, the Gospel of Thomas has joined three sayings (73, 74, 75) which are parallel in structure and seem intended to interpret each other; if so, the meaning must be that "harvest" is a state of blessedness, and the "laborers" are the few to attain to it. Thus, Thomas either

---

57. See Isa 18:3–6; 24:13; Jer 51:33 (=28:33 LXX); Joel 3:13 (=4:10 LXX); Mic 4:11–13; 4 Ezra (=2 Esdras) 4:28–32; 2 Bar 70:2; Matt 13:39; Mark 4:29; John 4:35; Rev 14:15; and esp. Q 3:17; cf. Q 3:9. The image of "harvest" is an Old Testament and apocalyptic image for judgment, but the idea of sending human laborers to reap that harvest seems to derive from the deuteronomistic tradition (Schulz, *Q*, 411–12). If at one time the idea was that of gathering the eschatological people of God, as Schulz (*Q*, 411) and Hoffmann (*Studien*, 290–91) argue, this meaning was lost when the mission charge was turned into a statement about judgment for Israel.

does not know or rejects the association of harvest and judgment. But even in Q the harvest is boldly interpreted as occurring through the activity of the messengers.

The stages in the literary growth of the material analyzed here are difficult to determine with confidence. However, a probable sequence can be determined. First, we have seen that Q 10:13–15 is a late addition. It is more likely that it was inserted before Q 10:16, creating an abrupt change in audience, than that Q 10:16 was added later. Q 10:16 quite clearly belongs with the mission charge. It forms an *inclusio*, as noted, with Q 10:3. Q 10:12, as stated earlier, was a redactional creation, designed to provide a transition from Q 10:11 to Q 10:13–15, and thus was added at the same time as 10:13–15. Second, since Q 10:3 and Q 10:16 form an *inclusio*, it is likely that they were added at the same time. They represent a logical beginning and conclusion to the discourse. Thus Q 10:4–11, or at least part of those verses, represents the earliest stage of the discourse. Third, Q 10:2 was added later than Q 10:3, as argued earlier. Since these two verses clash with each other, it is highly unlikely that they were added at the same time. Moreover, while Q 10:3 would have made a very good introduction to the discourse, Q 10:2 would not have. Hence Q 10:2 is a later addition. But how late? We have noted that Q 10:2 introduces the theme of judgment, a theme clearly evident again in Q 10:12–15. Indeed, without Q 10:2 one would not think to interpret the mission as an "errand of judgment." With it, however, the whole discourse is shifted into the context of judgment. It is likely, therefore, that Q 10:2 was added at the same time as Q 10:12–15. Thus, the order in which we may conclude that the discourse was put together is (a) Q 10:4–11; (b) Q 10:3, 16; and finally (c) Q 10:2, 12–15. It is certainly possible that earlier stages existed, prior to Q 10:4–11; but our interest is not in that earlier history but in its later redactional history.

The relation of this material to Q 9:57b–60a needs to be considered in this context. It was observed that Q 9:59–60a is the nucleus to which Q 9:57b–58 was later added; especially striking were the differences between Q 9:58 and 9:60a. In particular, Q 9:58 speaks of involuntary homelessness, while Q 9:60 calls for elective homelessness. The radicality of Q 9:60a, we may now add, is mirrored by the radicality of the material in the mission charge, especially Q 10:4. It seems entirely likely, in fact, that Q 9:59–60a was already connected with the mission charge before the intrusive addition of Q 10:2, 12–15. Likewise, it is possible to see a continuity between Q 9:58 and the additions in Q 10:2 and especially Q 10:12–15. Both concern the rejection of the messenger. The link to Q 7:31–35 also becomes clear: Q 9:58 picks up not only the theme of rejection but also the term "son of man." And both may, as again noted earlier, involve the notion of Wisdom as the sender of messengers; this is explicit in Q 7:31–35, and is possibly implied by Q 9:58.

Finally, although the deuteronomistic perspective is not directly evidenced in this material, it was noted that Q 10:2, 12–15 are highly congruent with that tradition, and thus it may be supposed that Q 10:2, 12–15 were added at the same time as other Q material which also reflects the perspective of the deuteronomistic tradition. The same is true of Q 9:58.

3. Jesus' Thanksgiving (Q 10:21–22)

We have seen that Jesus' thanksgiving followed immediately upon the mission charge (Q 10:2–16) in Q. This means that the change in mood is quite astonishing. We pass from the bitter denunciations in the mission complex to a joyful gratitude in Jesus' thanksgiving. Whereas that portion of Israel which rejected the messengers had just been denounced and consigned to hell for their failure to respond, now it is said that God's revelation was hidden from the "wise and understanding." This sudden and total change of perspective can only be understood as a reinterpretation of the failure of the mission. Rather than anger and disappointment at the failure of the mission, we now have the view that God in fact intended this failure, that the light was deliberately withheld from all but the little fellowship of "babes."[58] Worse yet, most of Israel is said to have no knowledge of God, since this is known only to the son and to those to whom he wishes to reveal the father. This appears to be the expression of a radically sectarian group whose alienation from their own people exceeds anything found anywhere else in Q.

It is noteworthy that the deuteronomistic perspective has been completely left behind in Q 10:21–22. More precisely, the deuteronomistic perspective is contradicted, since there is no place in the deuteronomistic tradition for a thanksgiving for Israel's unbelief. The expectation of Israel's repentance found elsewhere in Q presupposed Israel's knowledge of God, which is here denied.

Wisdom is understood differently in Q 10:21–22 as well. Elsewhere in Q there is a tendency to relativize the status of Jesus by placing him in a series of prophets or messengers; but, to the extent that it is present, the wisdom tradition here functions to absolutize the status of Jesus. Moreover, rather than being an emissary of Wisdom, Jesus is here said to mediate revelation directly.[59] In fact, Robinson has argued that here for the first time in Q we have the identification of Jesus with Sophia, and thus the emergence of a "Sophia christology" in the strict sense.[60] The new status of Jesus is clearly reflected in the "father/son" terminology, which is not found elsewhere in Q. Further, the identity of the son is now said to be hidden: no one knows who the son is except the father. The language of direct address to the father is new as well, and has its only Q parallel in the Our Father (Q 11:2–4), but there the

58. Fitzmyer (*Luke*, 873) correctly observes that this text "ascribes to God an activity similar to the hardening of Pharaoh's heart (Exod 7:3)."
59. Cf. Haenchen ("Gnosis," 1653) who observes that in Q 10:21–22 Jesus speaks "like a Gnostic redeemer."
60. Robinson, "Jesus as Sophos and Sophia," 9–10. For a contrary view, see Kloppenborg, "Wisdom Christology in Q."

speaker is submerged in the plural "us" and "we." Again we see the sharp differences which separate this pericope from the rest of Q, differences which must not be minimized.

The sharp contrast between Q 10:21-22 and 10:2-16 is acknowledged by Kloppenborg, but he seeks to overcome this problem by setting it "in the context of the group self-definition and polemics of cults under pressure."[61] But this solution does justice neither to the dramatic shift in vocabulary in Q 10:21-22 to something unlike anything else in Q, nor to the way that Q 10:21-22 seems designed as a comment on 10:2-16. If a parallel is to be sought, it would seem preferable to note the way in which the alienation of the Johannine community from their fellow Jews gave rise to, or was at least accompanied by, claims to be the exclusive recipients of divine revelation. In fact, the "Johannine" nature of Q 10:21-22 has long been noted. This fact encourages one to seek in the Q community a development parallel to that in the Johannine community. One finds echoes of this language also in the Gospel of Thomas (especially sayings 61-62), including an apparently more modest claim: "I was given some of the things of my father."

It has often been argued that Q 10:21 and 10:22 were originally independent sayings, or at least have a different origin.[62] The former is a thanksgiving, the latter a claim to be the exclusive source for the revelation of God. The two sayings do share a common vocabulary (father, son [implied in 10:21]); both reveal a general concern for knowledge, indicated by "wise and understanding" in 10:21 and "know" in 10:22; and both use language about divine favor. Yet 10:22 asserts the exclusiveness of Jesus' knowledge of the father in a way that is not present in 10:21. Robinson has noted the tension between the esotericism of Q 10:22 and the apparent rejection of esotericism in 10:21 (the pointed exalting of the "babes" over the "wise and understanding").[63]

It is not likely that "all things" ($\pi\acute{a}\nu\tau a$) in 10:22 refers to the mission complex in Q 10:2-16, both because of its position—it would be more appropriate as a reference to 10:21 than to 10:2-16—and because it is the logical basis for 10:22b and 10:22c: the son has received "all things" and therefore controls access to the father. Thus "all things" has to do with knowledge of God and the mysteries of God. The reference cannot be to the kingdom of God or to eschatological secrets because of the radicality of the claim: there is no knowledge of God except through him to whom "all things" have been delivered.

Stages in the Composition of the Second Section

The "second section" of Q shows evidence of significant redactional activity. In particular, Q 9:59-60a seems to have belonged with the mission

61. Kloppenborg, *Formation*, 202.
62. See Robinson, "Hodajot-Formel," 226-28.
63. Robinson, "Hodajot-Formel," 228.

charge, either in its earlier form in Q 10:4–11 or, more likely, in its somewhat later form as Q 10:3–11, 16. The next stage in the composition of the material seems to have been the addition of Q 9:57b–58 and 10:12–15. The intrusiveness of these verses was noted, as well as the fact that they have much in common, in particular an emphasis on rejection and judgment. In addition, Q 9:57b–58 establishes a link with and is thematically congruent with Q 7:31–35, probably the nearest previous pericope in Q. Both speak of the son of man, both dwell upon the rejection of the son of man, and in the background of both seems to be the deuteronomistic and wisdom traditions.

A quite new redactional stage is encountered in Q 10:21–22. Conceptually, these two verses stand virtually alone in Q. But they stand out equally because they represent a 180-degree change in perspective from the mission charge to which they were attached. Whereas the mission charge had been turned into an errand of judgment by the addition of Q 10:2, 12–15, and we hear bitter attacks on those Jews who failed to respond to the Q messengers, the mood switches abruptly in Q 10:21–22. Now God is thanked for withholding the divine revelation from the "wise and understanding" and for having reserved it for the "babes," which presumably means the Q community. Q 10:22 goes even further: the rest of Israel is in total darkness, not even knowing God, while the privilege of divine revelation is reserved exclusively to the Q community. Nowhere else in Q do we catch sight of such a dramatic reversal. It would appear that the failure of the mission, presupposed already by the stage of redaction which included the addition of Q 9:57b–58 and 10:2, 12–15, has ceased to be a matter of deep pain and anger. Q 10:21–22 reflects a very different attitude, one of having left that pain and anger behind to become a self-satisfied conventicle, a conventicle convinced that it alone has access to the truth and that all others vainly grope in the darkness.

7

The Third Section of Q

Against This Generation

The third section of Q contains sayings compositions whose theme may be described as a disputation against "this generation." In the third section of Q are Blessed are the Eyes (Q 10:23–24), the Lord's Prayer (Q 11:2–4), Answer to Prayer (Q 11:9–13), the Beelzebul Controversy (Q 11:14–20, 23), the Odyssey of the Unclean Spirit (Q 11:24–26), the Sign of Jonah (Q 11:29–32), the Lamp on a Stand (Q 11:33), the Sound Eye (Q 11:34–35), and the Woes (Q 11:46, 42, 39–41, 44, 47–48, 49–51, [43, 52]).

The third section of Q opens with Q 10:23–24, Blessed are the Eyes. Although these sayings are often seen as the continuation of Q 10:21–22, one must recall that Q 10:21–22 has been identified as one of the latest additions to Q. Therefore, one needs to imagine what the text of Q would have been like prior to its addition: Q 10:23–24 will have followed the mission charge and preceded the Beelzebul Controversy. It is quite possible that the content of Q 10:23–24 prompted the insertion of Q 10:21–22.

It will be argued here that Q 10:23–24 represented a transition from 10:13–16 to a new section. It will be further argued that Q 11:2–4, 9–13 are also later additions, even though they are old material. What Q 10:23–24 asserts is that Jesus' followers live in a privileged moment in history. They must, it is implied, be among those to take advantage of this moment, recognize the divine presence turning toward God's own at this time, and thus be found on the right side. The Beelzebul Controversy illustrates this very point; Q 11:23 makes it clear that what side one is on is precisely the issue. A similar point is made in Q 11:29–32: a greater than Solomon and Jonah is here, and "this generation," which failed to recognize this, will be condemned by those gentiles who responded to Jonah's kerygma and Solomon's sophia. The collocation of prophet and king in Q 11:29–32 recalls, interestingly, what was said in Q 10:24, that many prophets and kings longed to hear what Jesus' followers are now privileged to see and hear. Similarly, the blessing upon the eyes in Q 10:23 finds its echo in 11:34–35. Reproof of this generation continues in Q 11:24–26, and becomes more specific in 11:39–51.

Again and again the abysmal insensitivity of "this generation" is illustrated and denounced, and the call sounded to be found on the right side, the side of those attuned to the new movements of God. The two reinforce each other: the future plight of the obdurate gives urgency to the receptive, and the blessedness of the receptive intensifies the guilt of the obdurate.

The Sequence of the Third Section

The third section of Q contains a fairly lengthy tract of material, whose sequence can be established with some certainty. Whether this section of Q was a self-enclosed unit in Q is not so clear. We shall see that it contains a nearly sustained block of deuteronomistic material, which does tend to suggest that it was a unit. But it lacks the clear structure of the first section. The second, third and fourth sections are less clearly compositional units, but there is a certain thematic unity.

1. Blessed are the Eyes (Q 10:23-24)

Matthew has inserted this little pericope (Matt 13:16–17) into the section of his parable chapter that dwells on why some hear and others are deaf. The context is entirely derived from Mark; therefore, Matthew provides no evidence for the Q location of this text.

The Lukan location for the text gives little evidence of tendentious editing. The connection of Luke 10:23–24 to 10:25–42 is hardly obvious. Luke treats these pericopes as a string of anecdotes linked only by Jesus' chance encounter with a lawyer and his visit to the house of Martha and Mary. Therefore, there seems to be no particular reason for rejecting Luke's sequence as that of Q as well.

2. Lord's Prayer (Q 11:2-4) and Answer to Prayer (Q 11:9-13)

The location of Q 11:2-4 and Q 11:9-13 is difficult to establish because Luke and Matthew disagree on the location of both pericopes. However, there are a number of catchwords, which not only link the two pericopes internally but also provide links to the material which, in Luke, stands before and after the two pericopes. These catchwords are "father" ($\pi\alpha\tau\eta\rho$): Q 10:21 (twice), 22 (twice); 11:2, (11), 13; "son" ($\upsilon\iota\dot{o}\varsigma$): Q 10:22 (twice); 11:11, 19; cf. "babe" ($\nu\eta\pi\iota\sigma\varsigma$) in Q 10:21 and "children" ($\tau\epsilon\kappa\nu\alpha$) in Q 11:13; "to give" ($\delta\iota\delta\dot{o}\nu\alpha\iota$): Q 10:22; 11:3, 9, 11, 13; "all/everything" ($\pi\hat{\alpha}\varsigma$): Q 10:22; 11:4, 10, 17; "kingdom" ($\beta\alpha\sigma\iota\lambda\epsilon\dot{\iota}\alpha$): Q 11:2, 17, 18, 20; "bread" ($\ddot{\alpha}\rho\tau\sigma\varsigma$): Q 11:3, 11 (Matthew); "heaven" ($\sigma\dot{\upsilon}\rho\alpha\nu\dot{o}\varsigma$): Q 10:21; 11:2 (Matthew), 13, (16). As can be seen, there is an abundance of catchwords, especially linking Q 10:21-22; 11:2-4 and 11:9-13. There are catchword connections to Q 11:14-20, 23, but they are fewer and limited largely to "every" and "kingdom." Thus there seems to be a particularly strong linkage among Q 10:21-22; 11:2-4 and 11:9-13. It will be argued later that all of these are later additions.

However, the linkage in Matthew of the saying against giving what is holy to the dogs and against throwing pearls to the swine (Matt 7:6) to the sayings in

Matt 7:7-11 may be traditional. It is attested in the Gospel of Thomas (sayings 92-94). Luke may have omitted the saying in Matt 7:6 because it had come to be used by Jewish Christians to combat the mission to the gentiles.[1] Thus the possibility must at least be considered that Matt 7:6 is a saying from Q omitted by Luke.

3. Beelzebul Controversy (Q 11:14-20, 23), Odyssey of the Unclean Spirit (Q 11:24-26), Blessing Upon Hearers (Luke 11:27-28), and Sign of Jonah (Q 11:29-32)

The sequence of this material is the same in Luke and Matthew except for Q 11:29-32 (Sign of Jonah). The agreement on sequence is vitiated somewhat by the inclusion in Matthew of some material which is located in different contexts in Luke (Matt 12:31 [=Luke 12:10]; Matt 12:34 [=Luke 6:45]). Luke, in these instances, has probably preserved the correct sequence of Q. Matthew altered the sequence of Q because he followed the Markan conclusion to the Beelzebul Controversy (in that he included Matt 12:31-32 [=Mark 3:28-29]), and he then attached some other material dealing with confession (including 12:31, 34-35). Here Matthew's compositional activity seems quite clearly in evidence; the only serious problem, therefore, is the location of the Sign of Jonah pericope.

A firm decision on the location of the Sign of Jonah pericope is difficult. Fortunately its exact location does not significantly affect its interpretation; it is clear at least that it is linked to the Beelzebul pericope and to the Odyssey of the Unclean Spirit. Most interpreters assume that Luke, as usual, has preserved the sequence of Q better than has Matthew.[2] However, this assumption must be doubted. Luke is probably responsible for the insertion of 11:16 (cf. Matt 12:38). This insertion has the effect of creating two audiences as a means of unifying the various units which follow. One group charges that Jesus casts out demons by Beelzebul; this charge forms the introduction to the Beelzebul Controversy. The other group demands a sign from heaven; this prepares us for the Sign of Jonah pericope. A second bit of Lukan redaction is evident in Luke 11:21-23. Luke has rewritten the (Markan) parable of the strong man (Luke 11:21-22 [=Mark 3:27]), and the resulting parable bears formal resemblances to Luke 11:24-26—both begin: ὅταν, . . . and they are of similar length.[3] The apparent formal assimilation of the two parables shows that Luke

1. Schweizer (Matthew, 169-70) holds that the saying was used in this way, but that Matthew did not so understand it. Neither did the Didache; see Did 9:5. Cf. Grundmann, Matthäus, 221-22. Luke also omits the story of the Syrophoenician woman (Mark 7:24-30), which contains the saying about throwing bread to the dogs. However, this story was omitted along with a number of other Markan pericopes in Luke's "greater omission."

2. For example, Bultmann, History of the Synoptic Tradition, 14, and Edwards, Sign of Jonah, 91. However, see Carlston, Parables, 69.

3. Word statistics support the view that Luke 11:21-22 is the result of Lukan composition: "peace" (εἰρήνη; Matthew: three times; Luke: thirteen; Acts: fourteen; cf. Hawkins, Horae

understood the second (Luke 11:24–26) simply as a piece of demonological material illustrating the reverse of 11:21–22. Since he could make sense of it only as demonological material, he altered the Q sequence by attaching the Odyssey of the Unclean Spirit to the Beelzebul Controversy. But earlier, in 11:16, Luke tips his hand to reveal his awareness that the Beelzebul Controversy and the Sign of Jonah pericope belong together.

Matthew, on the other hand, has probably preserved the Q sequence. Had the Odyssey of the Unclean Spirit been attached to the Beelzebul Controversy in Q, it is hard to see why Matthew would have altered the sequence of these stories. Likewise, it is difficult to understand why Matthew, who seems to prefer to bring thematically similar material together, would separate two pieces of demonological material. Whether Matt 12:45d ("so shall it be with this generation") is Matthean redaction or not, it reveals Matthew's awareness that the Odyssey of the Unclean Spirit belongs with the Sign of Jonah, not with the Beelzebul Controversy. Note the formal similarity of Matt 12:45d to Matt 12:40 and especially its Lukan parallel in 11:30! I take this to mean that Matt 12:45d was probably in Q. Of course, there is also a verbal (catchword?) connection between Matt 12:45d and Matt 12:39 (=Luke 11:28). Finally, it should be noted that although both Q 11:24 and 11:14–23 can be described as demonological material, the former speaks of "unclean spirit" while the latter uses the word "demon." Thus there is no original connection between the two pericopes, a point suggesting that Matthew's, not Luke's, sequence is that of Q.

The Aland and Huck-Greeven synopses give the impression that Luke 11:27–28 is Lukan special material.[4] However, Luke 11:27–28 contains a saying about hearing and doing which is parallel to Mark 3:35//Matt 12:50 (cf. Luke 8:21). Moreover, Matthew, like Luke, has this saying directly after the parable of the Unclean Spirit. This striking agreement[5] cannot be fully accounted for by the fact that Mark has the saying in his pericope of True Relatives (Mark 3:31–35), which also follows the Beelzebul pericope; it does not account for the fact that Matthew and Luke both introduce the saying precisely after the Odyssey of the Unclean Spirit (even though they present this parable in somewhat different locations). Matthew, it is true, follows the Markan wording. Luke (8:21) has a separate version of the Markan True Relatives pericope, and the wording of 8:21 shows obvious influence from 11:28, or vice versa. "Word of God" is a favorite phrase of Luke's (see Luke

---

Synopticae, 17); "goods" or "possessions" (τὰ ὑπάρχοντα; Matthew: three; Luke: eight; cf. Hawkins, *Horae Synopticae,* 23); φυλάσσειν in the sense of "guarding" (Matthew: none; Luke: four); "to take away" (παραδιδόναι; Matthew: none; Luke: two); "to overcome" (νικᾶν; elsewhere in the synoptics: Luke 1:22); "whenever" (ἐπάν; redactional in Luke 11:22, 34).

4. Aland, *Synopsis Quattuor Evangeliorum* and Huck (rev. Greeven), *Synopse der drei ersten Evangelien.*

5. See Streeter, *Four Gospels,* 278–79, and Bacon, "The Redaction of Matthew 12," 29–30.

5:1; 8:11, 21; Acts 4:31; 6:2, 7; 8:14; 11:1; 12:24; 13:5, 7, 44, 46, 48; 17:13; 18:11). Note further that Luke 11:27 has parallels in Luke 1:42 and 23:29, and thus is suspect of being Lukan redaction. The fact that Luke 11:28 is attested in GThom 79 does not, in this case, argue against Lukan redaction, because GThom 79 is not an independent saying; it is a particularly artificial construction of two clearly Lukan sayings, Luke 11:28 and 23:29. Thus although examination of the sequence of the material suggests that Luke may have independently preserved a Q saying omitted by Matthew, examination of the wording of the saying raises grave doubts regarding the Q wording, since Lukan redaction is all too evident.

The synopses are misleading in one other detail. The true verbal parallel to Luke 11:14 is not Matt 12:22-24, as it is given in the synopses, but the doublet which occurs in Matt 9:32-34. Matt 12:22-24 is important because it witnesses the agreement between Matthew and Luke on the order of the material.

Finally, the whole string of pericopes in Q 11:14-32 can now also be linked to the end of the second section of Q. In Matthew, no Q material at all intervenes between the end of the second section of Q (Matt 11:24-27//Luke 10:21-22) and the third section of Q (Matt 12:22-30//Luke 11:14-23). In Luke, only Luke 11:2-4, 9-13 intervenes.[6] Although this last material is probably old, there is evidence that it was not added until later, at which point it was attached to Q 10:21-22 at the end of the second section of Q.

4. Lamp on a Stand (Q 11:33) and Sound Eye (Q 11:34-35)

We have here, in all probability, two separate sayings: Luke 11:33//Matt 5:15 and Luke 11:34-35//Matt 6:22-23.[7] The location of Matt 5:15, however, is probably due to Matthew, not Q.[8] Matthean redaction is probably also responsible for the location of Matt 6:22-23.[9] The Lukan placement of Q 11:33-35 probably represents the original Q location.[10] However, since Luke probably altered the location of Luke 11:29-32, as noted earlier, and since Luke 11:27-28 may represent Q, the following sequence seems probable:

6. This means that Q 9:57-10:22 was, as a section, followed immediately by Q 10:23-24 and 11:14-20, 23. We have observed that Q 10:21-22 is a later addition. Thus Q 10:2-16 would, at the compositional stage of Q, have been followed directly by 10:23-24. It is important to note that in these two portions of Q (i.e., Q 10:2-16; 11:14-20, 23) we encounter the idea of the kingdom as power ("peace" in Q 10:5-6; "spirit" or "finger" of God in Q 11:20). In both cases, this power is transferable; envoys have this power in Q 10:2-11; Jewish exorcists in Q 11:19; see also Q 11:23. There is, therefore, a certain theological continuity between the two sections.

7. With Q 11:33 cf. Mark 4:21; Luke 8:16; GThom 33. With Q 11:33-36 cf. GThom 24b and 61; Teach Silv 88,25-89,1; also see GThom 70.

8. Cf. Schnackenburg, "Salz der Erde," 177-200; Davies, *Setting*, 249-50; Schneider, "Bildwort von der Lampe," 199-202. The fact that both Matt 5:15 and Luke 11:33 are linked to their contexts by catchwords is used by Jeremias (*New Testament Theology*, 39) as an argument against Q. However, Matthew used catchwords as a compositional technique; see Lohr, "Oral Techniques," 422-24.

9. Cf. Hahn, "Worte vom Licht," 124-25.

10. So Grundmann, *Lukas*, 241.

Blessed are the Eyes	Luke 10:23–24	Matt 13:16–17
Beelzebul Controversy	Luke 11:14–20, 23	Matt 12:22–28, 30
Sign of Jonah	Luke 11:29–32	Matt 12:38–42
Unclean Spirit	Luke 11:24–26	Matt 12:43–45
Lamp on a Stand	Luke 11:33	Matt 5:15
Sound Eye	Luke 11:34–35	Matt 6:22–23

5. Woes (Q 11:46, 42, 39–41, 44, 47–48, 49–51, [43, 52])

We have here a series of accusations against Jewish leaders. The sequence of the individual accusations is not the same in Matthew and Luke, but this need not be examined in detail at this point. That the accusations belong together is shown by the fact that Matthew has them together in Matthew 23 and Luke has them together in Luke 11. The question at this point is whether in Q these accusations came after Q 11:33–35. This cannot be answered with any certainty. However, probability is on the side of Luke; Matthew seems to have followed the Markan sequence, inserting the Woes where Mark has some warnings about scribes (Mark 12:37b–40; before and after the Woes, Matthew follows Mark). However, Matthew does not simply expand Mark, but seems rather to have developed a discourse which he inserts at this point. There is, on the other hand, no obvious reason why Luke has inserted the Woes in Luke 11. He has been following Q at least since 11:9, and he can be shown by comparison with Matthew to have followed closely the original sequence of Q for the earlier sections (i.e., Luke 14–23), so one may assume that he is also following the order of Q at this point.

Analysis of the Third Section

1. Blessed are the Eyes (Q 10:23–24)

It was argued earlier that Q 10:23–24 is a transitional text, i.e., it marks the transition from the end of the Mission Charge (Q 10:13–16) to our "third section," and especially to the Beelzebul Controversy.

The wording of Luke 10:23 is more likely to represent Q than is that of Matt 13:16. Matthew has assimilated this pericope to the Markan context by speaking of the mere fact of seeing and hearing. Luke preserves the point in Q: *what* is seen, not *that* it is seen, is the basis for the blessing.[11] The emphasis on *what* is seen and heard is preserved by both Matthew and Luke in the following saying (Matt 13:17=Luke 10:24). Nevertheless, Matthew has probably added the parallel blessing on the ears. It fits his context (13:15, though note also 13:17 [=Luke 10:24]).

Luke's reference to "kings" in 10:24 is likely to represent Q. We find this linking of prophets and kings elsewhere in Q, namely in 7:25–26 (cf. 11:31–32). Matthew, on the other hand, links prophets with the righteous also in

---

11. Schulz, *Q*, 419. Cf. Fitzmyer, *Luke*, 867; however, Fitzmyer sees Lukan redaction here.

23:29, and frequently uses the word, "righteous." Luke's "wish" (θέλειν) is attested elsewhere in Q (6:31; 13:34 [twice]), and thus is likely to represent Q. "Truly" (ἀμήν) is very likely a Matthean addition.

The blessing in Q 10:23 has, as noted, to do with what is seen. Therefore, we probably do not have to do with revelation vouchsafed only to the elect (according to Q 10:21, the "babes" [νήπιοι]), but to something in principle visible to all, though not until just now. This means that the connection between Q 10:23–24 and 10:21–22 is more apparent than real. It also means that the antecedent connection is with Q 10:13–15, not with 10:21–22. Chorazin, Bethsaida, and Capernaum had the chance to see what prophets and kings wished to see, but these villages could see nothing. Similarly, we now have a good connection with Q 11:14–20, 23, where again discernment of what is going on is the key.

Q 10:23–24 does not seem to be self-referential. Jesus does not speak to magnify his own importance but to call attention to what is happening, of which he, of course, is an important part. The fact that Q 10:23–24 does not lead to any christological conclusions should come as no surprise.

2. The Lord's Prayer (Q 11:2–4) and Answer to Prayer (11:9–13)

It is commonly stated that the sayings in Q 11:9–13 have to do with prayer. However, the history of the interpretation of these sayings shows that they were understood in a variety of ways.[12] Through much of this history they circulated independently; as they stand in Q they are already a small collection of originally independent sayings.[13] Since the sayings in Q 11:11–13 have to do with asking and receiving, the main concern when the sayings were brought together was with asking/receiving rather than seeking/finding. The sayings exude remarkable confidence: "*Everyone* who asks receives" (πᾶς γὰρ ὁ αἰτῶν λαμβάνει). There are no conditions mentioned here as there are, for example, in 1 John 3:22: "and we receive from him whatever we ask, because we keep his commandments. . . ." The simile in Q 11:11–12 is also remarkable.[14] It implies that the father might not give "good things." Luke may have understood this in relationship to the Beelzebul Controversy, which in his gospel follows next (Luke 11:11–23), since he has changed "good things" to "holy spirit."[15] He may have thought that God would no more send an unclean

---

12. For the history of the interpretation of these sayings in the early church and in gnostic writings, see Brox, "Suchen und Finden," and Minear, *Commands of Christ.*

13. See Bultmann, *History of the Synoptic Tradition*, 87. Jeremias (*Parables*, 144–45) also notes that Q 11:11–13 was originally separate from Q 11:9–10. There is a change in Q 11:11 from the second to third person. Also, τίς ἐξ ὑμῶν; ("who among you?") is often used to introduce parables addressed to opponents; this, says Jeremias, would fit with the words ὑμεῖς πονηροὶ ὄντες ("you who are evil"). He concludes (p. 45) that Q 11:11–13 is "a saying of Jesus directed against the misinterpretation of his words and acts." See also the discussion of Q 11:9–13 in Crossan, *In Fragments*, 95–104, and Piper, *Wisdom in the Q Tradition*, 15–24.

14. With the strange expression, "If you, then, who are evil, . . ." cf. *Corp. Herm.* frag. 11.2.48 (cited in Dibelius, *James*, 103 n. 177): "What is God? An unchangeable good. What is the human being? A changeable evil (κακός)."

15. Jeremias, *Parables*, 145; Schulz, *Q*, 162.

spirit than Jesus would cast out demons by Beelzebul. But the idea that the father might not give good things may relate instead to the Lord's Prayer (Q 11:2–4) which concludes with the request to the father that the utterer not be led into temptation. That such a question could arise is shown by Jas 1:13: "Let no one say when he is tempted, 'I am tempted by God' . . ."; for God "tempts no one" but is rather the source of "every good and perfect gift" (Jas 1:17).[16] Since Q 11:11–13 denies that God can give anything evil, it may have functioned as exposition of the Lord's Prayer, exposition which takes up a dualistic position attested elsewhere (e.g., James 1; cf. 1 John 1:5: "God is light and in him is no darkness at all").

It is probable that the Lord's Prayer was part of the secret teaching of the early church, reserved for the "mature."[17] In fact, the Lord's Prayer together with its exposition in Q 11:9–13 may have been secret teaching already in Q. It would be among "these things" which according to Q 10:21 are now revealed to "babes" by the son who alone has access to the father and mediates the knowledge of God to whomever he wills (Q 10:22). This, at least, might be inferred from the relationship among Q 10:21–22, 11:2–4 and 11:9–13, if they formed a unit as the above has sought to show. Just as Jesus can address God as "father" (Q 10:21), so now the "babes" are allowed to enter this special relationship and to address God as "father" (Q 11:2). The meaning of this relationship to the father is drawn out in Q 11:9–13, which speaks of the boundless care of the father for his own. Anything that is requested will be given.

The inferences above are, to be sure, based on the verdict that Q 10:21–22, 11:2–4 and 11:9–13 belonged together in Q. When this material is removed from its present synoptic context, so that the sayings can mutually interpret one another by their context in Q, then the interpretation given here is at least plausible. The fact that such themes were under discussion in the early church tends to strengthen the case for this interpretation (see, for example, 1 Cor 3:21–23; John 3:34–35; Rom 8:15–17, 32).

The striking parallelism between the temptation account and the material in Q 10:21–22; 11:2–4, 9–13 should also be noted. The title "son of God," rare in Q, occurs in both; we hear of stones and bread in Q 4:3 as well as in Q 11:11 (Matthew). Q 4:9–12 presupposes such boundless confidence in the father's care as Q 11:9–13 may have inspired. And of course Jesus is, in effect, led into temptation. The Q temptation account thus counters tendencies which I have contended are to be found in Q 11:9–13. The various expressions of the view that all things are possible for the son are put on the devil's tongue; Jesus, however, is steadfastly obedient to the father.

What do these observations mean for the history of the composition of Q? We have already observed that Q 10:21–22 is a late addition, and that it represents a basic shift in the theology of the group which stands behind Q. Its

16. On this passage as an answer to the concern whether God can be the source of both good and evil or of good only, see Dibelius, *James*, 99–103.
17. Manson, "The Lord's Prayer," and, following Manson, Jeremias, *Prayers of Jesus*, 82–85.

addition perhaps occasioned the introduction of material understood as the special revelation of the son concerning the father, and hence dealing with the status of the community members as "babes" and "sons." The material introduced is old, to be sure; the Lord's Prayer is the chief addition. But it is accompanied by an interpretation (Q 11:9–13) which presents the sharing of sonship with Jesus as a sharing in his reception of "all things" from the father, and which denies that any evil gift comes from the father. Such boundless confidence points to a kind of religious enthusiasm which we rarely find elsewhere in Q.

It is possible that other material that bears a similar stamp was introduced into Q at this stage. The saying about faith that does the impossible (Q 17:6; cf. Mark 11:23; 1 Cor 13:2) probably comes from this enthusiastic tendency. As Mark 11:23–24 shows, this faith was associated with asking and receiving whatever was asked.[18] Matthew (17:20) has the most radical form of the saying; it concludes with the promise that "nothing will be impossible to you!" Other material introduced at this stage may include Q 7:18–23 which, as noted earlier, showed a shift in the understanding of Q (miracles attest him as the "coming one"), and also presupposed that an infusion of miracle stories had entered the community.

3. Beelzebul, the Unclean Spirit, Jonah and Solomon (Q 11:14–32)

(a) *Beelzebul Controversy (Q 11:14–20, 23)*. Since Mark has a version of the Beelzebul Controversy (Mark 3:19b–27), it is useful to compare it with the version in Q. In Mark one is given the impression of a flurry of activity by Jesus, of his darting here and there. Whenever people hear of him, they are drawn to him; he appears among them charged with power. There is the congestion of crowds, jostling and milling about. But there is opposition too, and Mark 3:19b–27 is an instance where the opposition surfaces. "Those with him" (Mark 3:21), apparently Jesus' family,[19] regard him as crazy (ἐξιστάναι) and act to have him seized (κρατεῖν, "forceful arrest," as in Mark 6:17; 12:12; 14:1, 44, 46, 49, 51). That seizure is contemplated shows that it is not just a case of embarrassment caused by Jesus' eccentricity, but a case of insanity; it is probably implied that he is a demoniac. The family treats him as unclean and sends others to seize him, later (Mark 3:31) standing outside the house calling to him. Meanwhile, scribes from Jerusalem arrive with the official diagnosis: "He is possessed by Beelzebul, and by the ruler (ἄρχων) of the demons he casts out demons" (Mark 3:22).

The scribal accusation actually contains two charges[20]: that Jesus is a demo-

18. On this saying, see Fridrichsen, *Problem of Miracle*, 82–83, and J. M. Robinson, "Kerygma and History," 41.

19. That οἱ παρ' αὐτοῦ refers to "family, relatives" (Bauer, *s.v.* παρά §I.4.b.β) can be inferred from Mark 3:31–35. Early readers understood the idiom this way, as we can see from attempts by copyists to substitute a less embarrassing reading (see Metzger, *Textual Commentary*, 81–82).

20. See Haenchen, *Der Weg Jesu*, 145.

niac, and that he is used by the ruler of the demons to cast out lesser demons. The first charge accords with the judgment of the family and with the view of the charge in the Markan framework (Mark 3:30). It is only the second charge, however, that is answered in Mark 3:23–27, i.e., in the Beelzebul Controversy proper. This means that Mark has placed traditional material in a new context. Mark's understanding is that Jesus is charged with being a demoniac. This charge is answered in material which Mark has added to the Beelzebul controversy, namely, Mark 3:28–30. Mark shows that Jesus is possessed by the holy spirit,[21] not by the ruler of the demons.

The point of view expressed in the traditional material (Mark 3:23–27), however, is different. There the charge against Jesus was that he is an instrument of Satan. The first response (Mark 3:23b) assumes a monolithic view of the demonic world. That Satan could be opposed to Satan[22] is absurd, as is shown by the use of a rhetorical question.[23] The image of civil war in the examples of the kingdom and the house (Mark 3:24, 25) awakens memories of nations and families torn by internal strife. If Jesus is thus part of a demonic civil war, there is no cause for alarm; it means that the demonic world is about to self-destruct. In contrast to these negative statements, Mark 3:27 introduces a positive interpretation: the "strong man" has been bound and now his "goods" can be plundered. This probably means that Jesus has bound Satan and is now liberating his captives.[24]

The Q version of the Beelzebul pericope is quite different from the traditional material in Mark, and from Mark's interpretation of it. In fact, Q has in common with the Markan version only the example of the kingdom divided, and even that in a different form. The differences between the Q and Markan versions of the Beelzebul Controversy may now be noted:

- the Q version is introduced by a miracle story (Luke 11:14–15//Matt 12:22–24; 9:32–34)[25];
- in Q, Jesus is said to know the thoughts of his opponents (Q 11:17)[26];

21. Probably for that reason he adopts new terminology in 3:30—the "unclean spirit" stands in contrast to the holy spirit.

22. This would be akin to the dualistic rift within the godhead in Valentinian Gnosis (see Jonas, *Gnostic Religion*, 174–79).

23. This assumes what is not entirely clear, namely that this rhetorical question is an independent argument rather than the introduction to the "parables" of the kingdom and the house.

24. See J. M. Robinson, *Problem of History*, 28–32; Tannehill, *Sword of His Mouth*, 182.

25. The miracle story reflects popular demonology: demons are associated with specific physical impairments rather than with moral evils or temptations. The discourse which follows gives quite a different view of exorcism. The linking of miracle story and discourse occurs in some synoptic apophthegms where a miracle is the setting (Mark 3:1–6 par.; Luke 13:10–17; 14:1–6; cf. Bultmann, *History of the Synoptic Tradition*, 209). However, the Q Beelzebul Controversy differs from these in that it discusses the nature of the miracle itself. In this respect the Q account is closer to the Johannine miracles with appended discourses (e.g., John 6), where the discourse plumbs the deeper meaning of the miracle.

26. This note is strange. Jesus hardly needs to discern their thoughts, since they have just openly expressed them. It is true that the evidence for a Q version of the accusation is slim

- the form of the Q example of the kingdom divided differs from the Markan version[27];
- Q lacks the example of the divided house;
- Q contains a rhetorical question referring to the "sons" (perhaps meaning "disciples") of the opponents;
- Q speaks of Jewish exorcists who will judge their "fathers";
- Q contains the saying, "If I by the finger (or: spirit) of God cast out demons, then the kingdom of God has come upon you ($\check{\epsilon}\phi\theta\alpha\sigma\epsilon\nu$ $\dot{\epsilon}\phi$ ' $\dot{\nu}\mu\hat{\alpha}s$)" (Q 11:20);
- Q lacks the example of the strong man bound[28];
- Q lacks a saying concerning blaspheming the holy spirit (Mark 3:28–29);
- the conclusion to the Q Beelzebul pericope is the saying, "He who is not with me is against me, and he who does not gather with me scatters" (Q 11:23).

Thus, there are far-reaching differences between the Markan and Q versions of the Beelzebul pericope. The most intriguing difference comes in sayings introduced by Q in 11:19–20:

But if I cast out demons by Beelzebul,
By whom do your sons cast them out?
Therefore, they will be your judges!
But if I cast out demons by the finger (or: spirit) of God,
then the kingdom of God has come upon you.

It is widely held that these sayings cannot belong together since, as Easton noted, "as the two verses stand at present the Jewish exorcisms could be taken as proofs of the advent of the Kingdom."[29] Käsemann, who also noted the logical inference that must be drawn from the linkage of these two sayings, complained:

But the logical result conceals the theological dubiousness of the argument. The eschatological uniqueness of Jesus is not preserved if one compares him to Jewish exorcists; moreover, if the facticity of the miracle is a criterion for divine legitimation, then the ambiguity of all mere facts is completely misunderstood.[30]

(though note "*in* Beelzebul" in Q 11:15 in contrast to Mark 3:22; the preposition also occurs in Q 11:19); also that Luke 11:18b might be construed as an effort to supply the missing accusation. However, it is probable that Q did have the accusation, and that "knowing their thoughts" is primarily a transition from the miracle to the discourse. For the clairvoyance of "divine men," see Schulz, *Q*, 208.

27. See Linton, "Q-Problem," 52–54. According to Linton, "Lk. deduces his conclusion from a *general rule* concerning kingdoms, Mk. from *two samples*, $\beta\alpha\sigma\iota\lambda\epsilon\acute{\iota}\alpha$ [kingdom] and $o\mathrm{i}\kappa\acute{\iota}\alpha$ [house]" (p. 53). Similarly, Jülicher, *Gleichnisreden*, 2. 221–22. Linton takes Luke's reading, including "house falls on house," to be the more likely Q reading (likewise Easton, "Beezeboul Sections," 61–62). The fall of houses would merely illustrate the decimation of the kingdom. In support of this is the use in Q of the verb $\dot{\epsilon}\rho\eta\mu o\hat{\nu}\nu$ in 11:17 to describe what happens to the kingdom; this word means "to lay waste, depopulate" (Bauer, *s.v.* $\dot{\epsilon}\rho\eta\mu\acute{o}\omega$); by "fall," Mark means roughly what in modern idiom is meant by a "toppled administration."

28. For the division of opinion, see Kloppenborg, *Q Parallels*, 92. For an argument that it was in Q, see Sellew, "Early Collections," 42–44.

29. Easton, "Beezeboul Sections, " 64.

30. Käsemann, "Lukas 11,14–28," 244.

The theological quandary posed by the juxtaposition of these two sayings in Q 11:19–20 has usually received some such answer as Käsemann's, often with the conclusion that Q 11:19 and 11:20 do not belong together.[31] Other scholars have emphasized that while Jesus and the Jewish exorcists both exorcize through the power of God, only Jesus' exorcisms have eschatological significance.[32] Bent Noack, on the other hand, has argued that the coming of the kingdom (and the overthrow of Satan) is the presupposition of both Jesus' exorcisms and those of other Jewish exorcists. Jesus is different only in that he knows why the demons are subject to him and to other Jewish exorcists, namely, because of the arrival of the kingdom of God.[33]

The basic problem with Q 11:19–20, then, seems to be theological. However, the "you" ($\dot{v}\mu\hat{a}s$) in Q 11:20 is also difficult, since in the context it must refer to the opponents. That is, it would speak of the kingdom of God coming upon the opponents. Yet even this is not impossible in the context of Q, since something very close to that is said in Q 10:11.

Q 11:19–20 implies that the other Jewish exorcists do indeed cast out demons by the power of God; this must be so, otherwise Jesus' answer to his opponents is not valid. Jesus and they stand, therefore, on much the same level. When the opponents reject Jesus' exorcisms, they also reject the power at work in their own disciples, namely, God. Therefore, "they" (the Jewish exorcists) will stand in judgment on the "fathers" (cf. Q 12:53). This is quite remarkable. Yet it has a close parallel in the next pericope, the Sign of Jonah, where it is said that the Queen of the South and the men of Nineveh will arise in the judgment to condemn "this generation" (Q 11:31, 32).[34]

Without question the juxtaposition of Q 11:19 and 11:20 jeopardizes the eschatological uniqueness of Jesus. But we have seen elsewhere in Q that this was apparently no problem. No christological screen apparently existed to filter out statements which jeopardize Jesus' uniqueness. In this instance, exorcism, whether by Jesus or other exorcists, is construed as evidence of the presence of God's kingdom and of God's spirit.

This interpretation appears to collide with the saying in Q 11:23: "He who is not with me is against me, and he who does not gather with me scatters." This saying seems to be formulated in a more exclusivistic fashion than its counterpart in Mark 9:40. Yet Q 11:23 must be understood in the context of the Beelzebul account.

31. So Bultmann, *History of the Synoptic Tradition*, 14, 162; Kümmel, *Promise and Fulfilment*, 105–6; Schweizer, *Matthew*, 284; McNeile, *Matthew*, 175–76; Haenchen, *Der Weg Jesu*, 148; Perrin, *Rediscovering*, 63–64; Lorenzmeier, "Mt 12,28; Lk 11,20."

32. Thus Schulz, *Q*, 212; Grundmann, *Matthäus*, 329; Percy, *Botschaft Jesu*, 180.

33. Noack, *SATANÁS und SOTERÍA*, 70–72.

34. Of course, the Ninevites and the Queen of the South merely respond to the kerygma and sophia while the Jewish exorcists are instruments of power or spirit. However, all of these stand in judgment over unbelieving Israel. That the Jewish exorcists will stand in judgment over their fathers implies that in some sense they too respond in a way that their fathers did not.

The Beelzebul pericope in Q brings into view two kingdoms: that of God (Q 11:20) and that of Satan (Q 11:18).[35] Jesus denies that his exorcisms can be manifestions of the kingdom of Satan, for that would mean division within the demonic world; the rule is that "every kingdom divided against itself is laid waste" (Q 11:17). Jesus contends that his exorcisms, like those of the other Jewish exorcists, are manifestations of the kingdom of God. But the principle initially put forth holds good here too: a kingdom divided against itself will be laid waste. Q 11:23 expresses this point with respect to the kingdom of God. Neutrality has ceased to be possible: "He who is not with me is against me. . . ." It is a question of which side one is on. But since neutrality is impossible, the situation can actually be formulated in seemingly opposite ways: he who is not with me is against me (Q 11:23); he who is not against us is for us (Mark 9:40).[36]

Q 11:23, however, contains a phrase not present in Mark 9:40: "and he who does not gather with me scatters." Here again it is a question of whose side one is on. But now it is clearer than it was in Q 11:23a that Jesus' uniqueness is not what the saying wishes to express. There is a "gathering" ($\sigma\nu\nu\acute{\alpha}\gamma\omega\nu$) in which others can participate. The addition of Q 11:23b probably shows the direction in which 11:23a was interpreted. The "gathering" is not explained. From the immediate context (Q 11:19), as well as from the more distant context (i.e., Q 10:2–16, which, with the Woes, was probably joined directly to the Beelzebul pericope in the composition of Q), one will think of an eschatological "harvest."[37] Those who share in Jesus' gathering activity are presumably the "laborers" of Q 10:2, 7 who function as messengers and in response to whom the eschatological fate of the hearer is decided as much as it is in response to Jesus himself.[38]

(b) *The Sign of Jonah (Q 11:29–32)*. The Sign of Jonah is a composition by the compiler of Q.[39] There were at least three stages in its growth: (1) Luke

35. Note also the parallel formulation of Q 11:19 and 11:20, which produces the contrast, $\dot{\epsilon}\nu$ $\beta\epsilon\epsilon\lambda\zeta\epsilon\beta o\acute{\nu}\lambda$ / $\dot{\epsilon}\nu$ $\delta\alpha\kappa\tau\acute{\nu}\lambda\omega$ $\theta\epsilon o\tilde{\nu}$ ("by Beelzebul"/"by the finger of God").

36. In both pericopes containing a version of this saying (Mark 9:38–40 and Q 11:14–20, 23) there are Jewish exorcists who are not followers of Jesus but whose exorcism is regarded as valid.

37. "Gathering" here probably has nothing to do with joining Jesus in his work of liberating Satan's captives by means of exorcism; for then "scattering" would not be done by the one who "gathers," but by Satan. The image implied is probably that of the shepherd and the sheep (see Jer 23:1–3; Ezekiel 34; John 10:1–18; and note Q 15:3–7), though these verbs can be used non-metaphorically, as in Ezek 11:16–17; Tob 13:5; John 11:52. "Gathering" the scattered people is frequently used to describe God's saving acts (e.g., Jer 23:1–3; Ezek 11:16–17; 20:33–35, 41; 28:25; 34; Tob 13:5; John 11:52). In Q 11:23 there may be an implicit charge against the current "shepherds" of Israel.

38. The view of Jülicher (*Gleichnisreden*, 2. 233), that Q 11:23 is a call for decision and is inappropriate where sides have long since been taken, is mistaken. It is not a question of a gathering with respect to Jesus, but of a gathering in which Jesus is involved, and thus a gathering/scattering of Israel. There is no call to decision; rather, the consequences of rejecting what comes to expression through Jesus are stated: the Jewish leaders are scattering Israel.

39. It seems to have been an apophthegm (so Lührmann, *Redaktion*, 36, and Schulz, *Q*, 250–51, 253), though there is no actual verbal agreement between Luke 11:16 and Matt 12:38 (cf. Matt 16:1–4).

11:29b//Matt 12:39b; (2) Luke 11:30//Matt 12:40; (3) Luke 11:31-32//Matt 12:41-42. The core for the composition is certainly the first saying (Q 11:29b), which is independently attested in Mark 8:12. It probably read, "An evil generation seeks a sign, but no sign will be given it except the sign of Jonah."[40] It is not clear whether the Markan or Q version of the saying is older. The most notable difference between them is the presence in the Q version of "except the sign of Jonah." Some have held the Q version to be older in part simply because "sign of Jonah" seems the *lectio difficilior*.[41]

Q 11:29b differs from Mark 8:12 not only in its reference to the "sign of Jonah" but also in speaking of a generation which is "evil" ($\pi o\nu\eta\rho\dot{\alpha}$). Moreover, in Matthew's version of the saying, which probably more faithfully reproduces Q, the denial of a sign is punitive. This opens up the possibility that the exception of the "sign of Jonah" corresponds to the punitive nature of the denial of signs. That is, if the "sign of Jonah" refers to Jonah's announcement to Nineveh of the impending judgment, it may have been added in Q to express what now awaits "this generation." No "sign" will be given to "this generation" except the announcement of impending judgment. In what sense, if any, such an announcement could be called a "sign" is not clear. However, in Q the "sign" is not a sign to legitimate Jesus but a sign of the end.[42] Thus there is a very real possibility that the exception of a "sign of Jonah" belongs together with other differences observable in the Q saying, in contrast to its Markan counterpart.

The second saying (Q 11:30) is an explanation ("for . . ." [$\gamma\dot{\alpha}\rho$]) of what the sign of Jonah is—not of why no sign is given (which reason is stated in Q 11:29). The original Q wording for this saying has been lost. Therefore, despite the great weight of significance often attached to this saying, its meaning remains uncertain because its original wording is unknown. There can be little doubt, however, that Luke's version is to be preferred to Matthew's.

Assuming Luke 11:30 to be more original than Matt 12:40, the next question concerns the identity of the "son of man." The presence of the future, "will be" ($\ddot{\epsilon}\sigma\tau\alpha\iota$), could require that the son of man be an agent of apocalyptic judgment; however, this "will be" merely answers to the "shall be given" ($\delta o\theta\dot{\eta}\sigma\epsilon\tau\alpha\iota$) in the previous verse.[43] Further, if "son of man" designates an agent of apocalyptic judgment, then comparison with Jonah becomes difficult.

40. For a reconstruction of this saying, see Schulz, *Q*, 251, and P. D. Meyer, "Community of Q," 8 n. 1. Matthew's version is more original than Luke's. It is especially important to note that Q had the simple "evil generation" ($\gamma\epsilon\nu\epsilon\dot{\alpha}$ $\pi o\nu\eta\rho\dot{\alpha}$), not Luke's "this generation" ($\dot{\eta}$ $\gamma\epsilon\nu\epsilon\dot{\alpha}$ $a\ddot{\nu}\tau\eta$), which is from Mark. This means that the catchword linkage of Q 11:31-32 is to Q 11:30, not to Q 11:29.

41. Bultmann (*History of the Synoptic Tradition*, 118 n. 1) suggested this, and he is now followed by Vielhauer ("Jesus und der Menschensohn," 150); likewise, Perrin, *Rediscovering*, 192-93. However, it is not certain that the Q version is the older; see Edwards, *Sign of Jonah*, 75-77.

42. So Schulz, *Q*, 254 n. 537 and 255-56.

43. So Vielhauer ("Jesus und der Menschensohn," 151-52), who notes that "will be given" ($\delta o\theta\dot{\eta}\sigma\epsilon\tau\alpha\iota$) "in no way designates the eschatological future."

How could an apocalyptic judge be to "this generation" what Jonah was to the Ninevites? In what sense is the apocalyptic son of man a "sign"? The difficulties with this interpretation have led a number of scholars to argue that "son of man" cannot refer to an apocalyptic judge.[44] For whatever reason the title "son of man" may have been introduced, therefore, the meaning seems to be that Jesus or his preaching is what is compared to Jonah before the Ninevites.

For our purpose it is crucial to determine the relationship between Q 11:29–30 and 11:31–32. For it is in Q 11:31–32 that we encounter wisdom material,[45] and its relationship to the rest of the pericope is a matter of great interest. It is true that Q 11:31–32 may have been attached to 11:29 by catchword ("Jonah," Ἰωνᾶς), and that Q 11:30 may have been the last saying added.[46] It is more likely, however, that the verses that appear to have been tacked on at the end were indeed tacked on. A number of observations point in this direction. The terms "wisdom" (σοφία) and "preaching" (κήρυγμα) in Q 11:31–32 may indicate later tradition.[47] The stronger catchword connections with Q 11:31–32 are not in 11:29 but in 11:30 (in addition to "Jonah" [Ἰωνᾶς], also "this generation" [ἡ γενεὰ αὕτη] and "Ninevite" [Νινευίτης]). In addition, it is difficult to explain the saying about the "wisdom" (σοφία) of Solomon except as a later addition. And Q 11:29 (and 11:30) seems to allow at least some chance yet for "this generation" to repent, something that is no longer the case in Q 11:31–32. It seems unlikely, therefore, that Q 11:30 was added after Q 11:29 and 11:31–32 had been brought together. The latest stage in the growth of this composition was therefore the addition of sayings in Q 11:31–32 which bear the imprint of the wisdom tradition.

Since, as I have argued, Matthew has preserved Q's location for the Sign of Jonah pericope (i.e., immediately following the Beelzebul Controversy), we must ask whether any connections exist between these two pericopes. The primary connection appears, as might be expected, in the more recently redacted part of Q 11:29–32, namely 11:31–32. These sayings envision a judgment scene in which those who expect exoneration are condemned by others. This is also what we have in Q 11:19. If this thematic association was the work of whoever added Q 11:31–32, then what he or she regarded as common to each pericope also becomes evident: the judgment and the condemnation of the opponents.

It must be added that Q 11:31–32 operates on different premises than Q 11:29–30. In Q 11:29–30 the *preaching of Jonah* was the salient feature; in Q 11:31–32 Jonah himself recedes in importance and the *response of the Ninevites* comes to the fore. Moreover, the temporal framework has been broken.

---

44. For example, Vielhauer, "Jesus und der Menschensohn," 151–52, and Schulz, *Q*, 256.
45. Lührmann, *Redaktion*, 38–39.
46. That Q 11:30 is a redactional addition is the view of Edwards, *Sign of Jonah*, 80–89; Lührmann, *Redaktion*, 41. The latter, in contrast to Edwards, regards Q 11:31–32 as also important evidence of the redaction of Q.
47. Schulz, *Q*, 253–54 n. 534.

In Q 11:29–30 Jonah and the men of Nineveh remained firmly in the past; their relationship to the present is only comparative. Now, however, the Ninevites have, so to speak, leapt out of the past to stand as accusers of "this generation." It is true that a general resurrection effects this rupture of the temporal framework. Yet a fundamental change has occurred. The Ninevites are no longer actors in an historical anecdote but, one might say, participants in a redemptive history. The distance between Jesus and Jonah which is preserved in a comparison now collapses[48]—what took place in Jonah's preaching is fundamentally similar to what takes place in Jesus's preaching.[49] Yet there is, after all, a difference between Jonah and Jesus: Jesus is "greater."[50] It is striking that the tradition is satisfied with this rather modest claim; yet, in its context, the function of this statement is not to promote a christological claim but to intensify the guilt of "this generation."

That a new view of things is pushing its way to the surface here can be seen also in the addition of material which is related only formally to Q 11:32. The addition of Q 11:31 did not change the subject (Jonah and Nineveh); but now, quite unexpectedly, we hear of the "wisdom" ($\sigma o\phi\acute{\iota}a$) of Solomon (Q 11:32). No doubt the fact that the Ninevites were gentiles has something to do with the introduction of another gentile witness against "this generation." But it does not explain the addition of precisely the Queen of Sheba, much less the "wisdom" of Solomon. No doubt "wisdom" answers to "preaching"; but the designation in Q 11:31 of Jonah's message as "preaching" (i.e., "kergyma," $\kappa\acute{\eta}\rho\upsilon\gamma\mu a$) is also new vis-à-vis Q 11:29–30.[51]

What has made possible this further expansion, i.e., the inclusion of the wisdom (sophia)[52] of Solomon as well as the Queen of the South who, like the Ninevites, takes her place among the elect who rise up to condemn "this generation"? It could be a sense that the male Ninevites needed to be matched by the female Queen of the South. But beyond that, the expansion is made possible by the perception of a fundamental continuity, not only between Jonah and Jesus but throughout history. This is best understood in relation to the idea that Wisdom has continually sent prophets and messengers, as in Q 11:49–51 and 13:34–35.

In Q 11:31–32, then, we can detect the influence of the wisdom tradition. At

48. Thus the view of Käsemann ("Beginnings of Christian Theology," 95–96), that Q 11:31–32 embodies the apocalyptic principle that the end corresponds to the beginning, does not apply here. The "beginning" and the "end" here are not compared, but stand face to face in the judgment.

49. Cf. the allusion to Wis 12:10 in connection with a citation of the Sign of Jonah pericope in 1 Clem 7:5–7.

50. Since the comparison involves the "wisdom" ($\sigma o\phi\acute{\iota}a$) of Solomon and the "proclamation" ($\kappa\acute{\eta}\rho\upsilon\gamma\mu a$) of Jonah, we should not interpret the "greater" in strictly personal terms. Jesus is greater because of the eschatological finality of his call.

51. The juxtaposition of "wisdom" and "kerygma" is very rare; on its occurrence in 1 Cor 1:18–31 see J. M. Robinson, "Kerygma and History," 42.

52. 1 Kgs 10:4, 6, 7, 8 have "wisdom" (חכמה); the LXX has "understanding" ($\phi\rho\acute{o}\nu\eta\sigma\iota\varsigma$) (3 Kgs 10:4, 6, 8).

first glance, however, it would seem that the deuteronomistic view of history is absent here. Yet it is echoed in the reference to "this generation," regarded as utterly impenitent. Instead of a history of Israel's persistent rejection of God's messengers, we have here the beginning of a counter-history of gentiles who believed.[53] Like figures out of the night, gentiles loom up out of Israel's (alleged) faithless past to condemn "this generation." Here the deuteronomistic view of history stands in the background rather than the foreground.

It is also important to note that in Q 11:31–32 sophia and kerygma are not only juxtaposed but functionally identified. A positive gentile response to one as surely condemns "this generation" as does a positive response to the other. The juxtaposition of sophia and kerygma implies a *communicatio idiomatum* between them.[54] But this relationship between sophia and kerygma is only another expression of the fact that Wisdom has taken the place of God as the sender of prophets (Q 11:49–51; cf. Proverbs 1–9). Now sophia seems to be regarded as a call to repentance, because the Queen of the South's response to sophia has been introduced as a factor in shaming "this generation."

Q 11:31–32 presupposes the view that the son of man was a "sign" because he, like Jonah, issued an eschatological warning, but also because he had imparted wisdom. So wisdom and prophecy are not only identified but are used to characterize Jesus' ministry. Here we have a clear picture of the categories which the Q community used to interpret Jesus. And, as noted earlier, this fits well with the view expressed in Q 11:49–51, that Wisdom sends prophets who utter eschatological warnings.

It is useful to pause here to ask about the historical basis for the allegation that "this generation" asked for a sign. Who specifically asked for a sign, and why? Why was such a request generalized and attributed to "this generation"? This is not a tradition limited to Q. It is independently attested in Mark 8:11–12, where "the Pharisees" ask the question; in John 6:30, where the crowds who follow Jesus ask for a sign; and in 1 Cor 1:22, where Paul states that "Jews demand signs." In no case are the interlocutors identified with any specificity. This suggests that the disputes that we hear about concerning "signs" as well

53. Here as elsewhere in Q the response of gentiles is used to shame Israel; cf. Q 7:29 and 10:13–15 (also Q 7:35, which provides the theological basis for why "this generation" stands condemned while others become the elect). See P. D. Meyer, "Gentile Mission," 405–17.

The deuteronomistic view of history, while enabling sharp attacks on Israel's impenitence, does not elsewhere serve as the foundation for the sort of revisionist salvation history that seems to emerge in Q 11:29–32. Here we are not far removed from a gnostic reinterpretation of the OT. The OT is not given an eccentric interpretation, as in much gnostic exegesis, but the radical selectivity which fastens onto two examples of gentile belief serves a similarly provocative purpose. Whereas the potential receptivity of Tyre and Sidon can be contrasted with that of Bethsaida and Chorazin, a much more radical example is given when Sodom is regarded more hopefully than "this generation."

54. As Lührmann (*Redaktion*, 39) comments, "This juxtaposition is made possible by the fact that in the later wisdom tradition, [wisdom] became a sacred doctrine, no longer simply a specific endowment bestowed upon humans by God." Lührmann refers to the Wisdom of Solomon and Sir 51:13–30.

as Jesus' "authority" are questions put to the early followers of Jesus, not to Jesus himself.

It is beyond doubt, therefore, that questions about signs and authority were raised, in all probability by Jewish religious authorities concerned about what were perceived as the excesses of popular religion. The authority of priest, scribe, Pharisee, or other individual could not be presumed decisive. It was possible to imagine that some locally popular figure was a legitimate religious authority (cf. Mark 11:30; Acts 23:9). Even to be open to this possibility means that the Judaism in Jesus' time was no monolithic entity, a point widely agreed upon today.

Presumably the request for a sign came, as suggested above, from religious authorities. It is they primarily who must be meant by "this generation" in Q 11:29, even though no specific identification of these leaders is possible. In any case, they are not impressed by Jesus' signs. Perhaps one is to imagine either a local sanhedrin's decision on this matter, or simply a consensus among the religious leaders that Jesus was no genuine religious authority. If we can judge by the apparent failure of Jesus to gain a numerically significant following among his fellow Jews, the judgment of the Jewish authorities must have been, if not influential, at least not out of touch with popular sentiment.

In every case the demand for a sign is taken as evidence of the unbelief of those who ask the question; this is true of Q, Mark, John, and Paul (1 Cor 1:22). This rather impudent refusal contrasts with other parts of the gospel tradition, which are quite anxious to display Jesus' signs and wonders. Here too we can see how different Q 7:18–23 is from the dominant perspective in Q, and why this pericope must be seen as a later addition. Interest in Jesus' signs and wonders seems to be something that emerges at secondary levels of the tradition, such as the speech attributed to Peter which introduces Jesus of Nazareth as "a man attested to you by God with mighty works and wonders and signs . . ." (Acts 2:22). By contrast, Q 11:29 says that "no sign shall be given . . . except the sign of Jonah."

(c) *The Odyssey of the Unclean Spirit (Q 11:24–26).* The Lukan version of this pericope, which agrees closely with Matthew's, reads:

> When the unclean spirit has gone out of the person, he passes through waterless places seeking rest (ἀνάπαυσις); and finding none he says, "I will return to my house from which I came." And having come, he finds (it) swept and adorned. Then he goes and brings seven other spirits more evil than himself, and they enter and dwell there; and the last state of that person becomes worse than the first.

We saw earlier that the Odyssey of the Unclean Spirit followed the Sign of Jonah pericope in Q, as it does it Matthew; further, that it is interpretatively associated with the Sign of Jonah rather than with the Beelzebul Controversy. That is, in Q the Odyssey of the Unclean Spirit was not treated as demonological material. Its point, therefore, is not likely to have to do with exorcism.

Probably the most common interpretation of this parable[55] is that one's house (=heart, life) should not remain "empty." Something (the holy spirit, the kingdom, or God) must take the place of the departed evil spirit, else the last state will be worse than the first. But this interpretation runs into difficulties at two points. First, Q probably did not have the word "empty" at all, since the manuscript evidence shows that Luke 11:24 did not include the word. Second, the subject is not guilty merely of spiritual sloth in failing to advance beyond the evacuation of evil; rather, this person positively *invites* the unclean spirit.

On the face of it, the parable of the unclean spirit could be propaganda against exorcism, since it appears to claim that a demon returns to the one who has been exorcised, and the person ends up being worse off than before the exorcism. This interpretation would certainly be remarkable, since the parable follows hard on the heels of the Beelzebul pericope, where it is stated that the kingdom is manifest in exorcisms! Such an anti-exorcistic interpretation cannot be excluded, but it is unlikely. Further along these lines we may note that the Unclean Spirit pericope was immediately preceded by the statement, "Behold, a greater than Solomon is here" (Q 11:31c). Since Solomon was widely associated with exorcism,[56] it could be argued that the point of the Odyssey of the Unclean Spirit is that exorcism by itself is not enough, and hence that Jesus is greater in the sense that he goes beyond mere exorcism. But if this is the point, it is certainly not emphasized, and Matt 12:45d argues against it.

The anti-exorcistic interpretation of the parable of the Unclean Spirit is promoted by Jeremias[57] who, following previous interpreters, solved the problem by reconstructing an Aramaic conditional clause beneath the Greek of Matt 12:44–45[58]: "*If* the unclean spirit, when he returns, finds the house empty, ... then he goes ... (and finds his comrades)." But it is not certain that the subordination is conditional; it may equally be temporal,[59] as is suggested by Matthew's "then" (τότε).[60] Moreover, the net effect of the conditional inter-

55. Most interpreters regard the story as a parable. Thus Jülicher, *Gleichnisreden*, 2. 233–38; Cadoux, *Parables*, 160–61; Jeremias, *Parables*, 197–98; Carlston, *Parables*, 69; C. W. F. Smith, *Jesus of the Parables*, 149–52. Fitzmyer (*Luke*, 924–25) designates it a "minatory saying." Bultmann (*History of the Synoptic Tradition*, 164) treats the pericope in a supplement to his subsection on "I-Sayings," but notes that "in style it is more closely related to a parable. ..." However, Schulz (*Q*, 477, 574) prefers to call it a *Warnrede* ("warning speech").

56. See Josephus *Ant.* 8.45–49 and esp. the Testament of Solomon. On this tradition, see Duling, "Testament of Solomon," 944–51, 57.

57. Jeremias, *Parables*, 197–98 and *New Testament Theology*, 153–54.

58. Jeremias attributes this insight to Nyberg ("Zum grammatischen Verständnis"). However, basically the same point had been made by McNeile (*Matthew*, 183), and even earlier by Gould ("Matt. xii.43–45," 62). The construction noted by Nyberg also occurs in Greek; see Blass-Debrunner-Funk, *Grammar*, §471.3. The portion of text involved occurs in Matt 12:44b–45: καὶ ἐλθὸν εὑρίσκει σχολάζοντα [καὶ] σεσαρωμένον καὶ κεκοσμημένον. τότε πορεύεται. ...

59. Cf. John 10:12, and discussion in Blass-Debrunner-Funk, *Grammar*, §471.3.

60. Neither Nestle-Aland (26th ed.) nor Greeven (in Huck-Greeven, *Synopse*) takes account

pretation of Q 11:25–26 is to reinstate the traditional interpretation, which has other problems in the text, as already noted.

The critical weakness in the usual interpretation of the pericope as a parable about spiritual sloth or inadequate repentance is the fact that the anonymous "person" actually welcomes the unclean spirit. Jeremias himself had observed this:

> The comparison of a possessed person to the "house" of a demon is still common in the East. The house is "empty, swept, and garnished," i.e. prepared for the ceremonious reception of a guest.[61]

The fact that the "house" is "swept"[62] and "decorated,"[63] that a festive welcome is prepared, is actually the turning point of the parable. The unclean spirit has found a place to "rest," and so goes and calls his friends to join him. What is at issue is not merely spiritual sloth, or the vulnerability of the novice penitent to returning evil powers, but a damning instance of welcoming the unclean spirit. The story, on this reading, is sarcastic and accusatory, not merely admonitory.

Q 11:24–26 is unique in the gospels. Though it deals with demons, it is not an account of an exorcism (the "first" state of the person is mentioned in 11:26 but never described). As Bultmann observed, it is formally a parable,[64] but it is unlike other parables in having a demon as its protagonist.

On the one hand, the story incorporates a good deal of popular demonological lore. Demons do not like water, and thus haunt the desert.[65] When evicted from their host, demons wander about seeking a new home. "Unclean spirit" is a typically Jewish designation for a demon. Spirits often come in groups of seven.[66] The plot for this vignette may also be folkloric. A similar plot is found in 2 Esdr 7:78–87, though there we have spirits of the dead instead of demons. That the seventh demon is the worst recalls the worse state of the person in Q 11:26. The common image of the well-tended garden (or city or fortress) ending up forsaken and inhabited by wild and/or demonic creatures (see Isa 34:9–14; Prov 24:30–31; Isa 13:19–22; Jer 50:35–40) may

---

of a conditional or temporal paratactic construction; both have a period at the end of Matt 12:44.

61. Jeremias, *Parables*, 197. However, Jeremias still speaks of the dangers of a merely "empty" house.

62. In the NT, "to sweep" (σαροῦν) occurs only here and in Luke's parable of the lost coin (Luke 15:8). Sweeping can also be preparation for a festive occasion, as in Herm Sim 9.10:2–3.

63. The verb is κοσμεῖν. The *RSV* translation, "put in order," is apparently based on the notion that the sweeping, etc., is the means by which the unclean spirit is expelled, thus not part of the welcoming process; but it is more natural to translate the word "decorate," and see it as part of the welcoming process.

64. Bultmann, *History of the Synoptic Tradition*, 164.

65. See Lev 16:10; Isa 13:21; 34:14; TestSol 5:11; Bar 4:35; Mark 1:12–13; Rev 18:2.

66. Cf. the seven spirits before the throne of God in Ezek 9:1–2; Tob 12:15; 1 Enoch 20:1–7; Rev 3:1; 4:5; 5:6; 8:2, 6; seven demons in TestRub 2:1; Luke 8:2 (=Mark 16:9). See further M. Smith, *Jesus the Magician*, 202.

also lie in the background; a midrash on Prov 24:31 shows how this image could suggest a plot like that of our story:

> As if a king went into the steppe, and found dining halls and large chambers, and went and dwelt in them. So with the evil inclination; if it does not find the words of the Law ruling (in the heart), you cannot expel it from your heart.[67]

On the other hand, Q 11:24–26 is unlike the popular demonology reflected in the Greek magical papyri,[68] the Testament of Solomon, and other sources available to us. The motifs and themes assembled by Theissen in his analysis of miracles stories provide no parallel to Q 11:24–26.[69]

Probably the house that is swept and adorned (Q 11:25) is a comic feature; it is difficult to explain any other way, for example, as an element from popular demonology. But a certain mischievous demonological humor is not unknown elsewhere: the name "Beelzebul" (probably the appellation for a Canaanite deity, transferred to a leader of demons); accounts of exorcism such as Acts 16:16–18 and 19:13–17; and perhaps the demonic possession of swine in Mark 5:11–13. Also unusual for demonological material is the novelistic treatment in Q 11:24–26 of the adventures of the unclean spirit and the irony of an unclean spirit inhabiting a newly cleaned "house." These unusual features, along with the swept and adorned house, are best understood not as typical demonological elements but as clever features of a story meant to ridicule and chastise someone—presumably "this generation."

It seems likely that the well-ordered state of the "house"—swept and adorned—is intended as a caricature of "this generation." The latter has sought to exorcise evil from their midst and has maintained itself in a state of readiness; but when a greater than Jonah or Solomon is in its midst, it does not welcome him. Like the man in the story, "this generation" will end up infested with spirits worse than those evicted. Whether there is an allusion in the phrase "swept and adorned" to the preoccupation of "this generation" with purity and cleanness cannot be determined; it is certainly possible (cf. Q 11:39–40, 44).

4. Lamp on a Stand (Q 11:33) and Sound Eye (11:34–35)

The original Q wording of Q 11:33 is uncertain. Many prefer the Matthean version (Matt 5:15).[70] However, Luke's wording ("in a cellar" [εἰς κρύπτην] and "that those who enter may see the light" [ἵνα οἱ εἰσπορευόμενοι τὸ φέγγος

---

67. Midrash on Prov 24:31, quoted in Montefiore and Loewe, *Rabbinic Anthology*, 124.

68. See Betz, *The Greek Magical Papyri*, PGM IV.86–87 (p. 38); IV.1227–64 (p. 62); IV.3007–86 (pp. 96–97); LXXXV.1–6 (p. 301); LXXXIX.1–27 (p. 302); XCIV.17–21 (p. 304); CXIV.1–14 (p. 313).

69. Theissen, *The Miracles Stories of the Early Christian Tradition*, 47–80, 84–90.

70. So, e.g., Schneider, "Das Bildwort von der Lampe," 184–86; Schulz, *Q*, 474–75; Carlston, *Parables*, 90.

βλέπωσιν]) is also attested in GThom 33.[71] Of course, the saying in Thomas may depend on Luke.[72] But if Thomas follows Luke, it is strange that he follows *Matthew* in linking the light saying with the saying about the city set on a hill (GThom 32//Matt 5:14; GThom 33b//Matt 5:15), but *Mark* (4:21) in identifying two places where one would not put a lamp. On the other hand, commentators typically note that Matthew's saying presupposes the simple Palestinian one-room house, where a lamp could illuminate all in the house, whereas Luke assumes hellenistic architecture. However, the basic thrust of the saying is discernible whichever reading one follows: it is ridiculous to light a lamp and then to prevent anyone from benefiting from its light.

In the case of Q 11:34-35 the wording in Matthew (6:22-23) is probably to be preferred over the longer Lukan version.[73] Luke 11:36 is probably a Lukan composition, v. 36b serving to link the two lamp sayings (Luke 11:33, 34-35). Matthew's location for Q 11:33 (i.e., Matt 5:15) is secondary, but it does show that Matthew did not interpret the "light" christologically. Rather, the disciples are the light which is not to be hid. Luke gives no evidence of knowing a christological interpretation either.[74] Moreover, neither Matthew nor Luke knows of an interpretation according to which "light" refers to the message of Jesus. The Lukan context again shows no signs of tendentious editing. As noted earlier, however, in Q, 11:33-35 followed the Odyssey of the Unclean Spirit (Q 11:24-26) rather than the Sign of Jonah (Q 11:29-32). The most natural interpretation of Q 11:33 within its Q context, therefore, is that the foolishness of concealing light refers to the folly of this generation in not recognizing what is going on in its midst.[75]

Q 11:34-35 is attached to Q 11:33 by the catchword, "lamp" (λύχνος).[76] These verses do not develop further the thought of Q 11:33. As Betz has shown, these verses, puzzling in their Matthean wording, show awareness of, but reject, Greek philosophical theories of vision, which are basically physiological.[77] Accordingly, perturbations of vision are also physiological. But Matt

---

71. Both Schneider ("Das Bildwort von der Lampe," 206-7) and Hahn ("Die Worte vom Licht," 113-14) hold that the Gospel of Thomas has used Luke. For the contrary view, see Montefiore, "Comparison," 68-69.

72. See Kloppenborg, *Formation*, 135 n. 144.

73. So Schulz, *Q*, 469; however, cf. Hahn, "Die Worte vom Licht," 127-34.

74. A christological interpretation of the Q light sayings depends upon their connection to Q 11:29-32; see Grundmann, *Lukas*, 243; Hahn, "Die Worte vom Licht," 132-34; Schneider, "Das Bildwort von der Lampe," 204; Krämer, "Ihr seid das Salz der Erde," 144 n. 17; 151. Schulz (*Q*, 475-76) declares that the saying in Q 11:33 cannot be interpreted on the basis of its context, but proceeds to interpret the light "in the [general] context of Q" as referring to the proclamation of the kingdom, which is accessible to everyone. Kloppenborg (*Formation*, 138) rightly interprets the text within its Q context.

75. Krämer ("Ihr seid das Salz der Erde," 144) correctly notes that "the negative formulation of the saying points to a polemical situation."

76. Kloppenborg (*Formation*, 135) adds that there is also a "logical parallel" between the lamp which gives light to the house and the eye/lamp which gives light to the body.

77. Betz, "Matthew 6:22-23."

6:22–23 (which probably preserves the wording of Q) asserts instead that "the ethical disposition of a person determines whether or not the eyes function properly."[78]

Considered as an isolated saying, Matt 6:22–23 (=Luke 11:34–35) does seem to function as Betz suggests, namely to leave one wondering whether "my inner light is darkness" and "How can it be made bright again?"[79] However, within the context of Q as I have reconstructed it, the saying is no longer directed at the hearer/reader but at the opponents, whose inability to see is attributed to lack of moral soundness. But it goes beyond that to assert that if this lack of moral soundness has impaired their vision, this means that there is a terrible darkness within these people, a depth of depravity that will shortly be described in the Woes (Q 11:39–52). In short, the saying about vision is an excellent transition to the Woes.

5. The Woes (Q 11:39–52)

The order of the Q material in the Woes section varies so widely between Luke and Matthew that it appears that its original order cannot be reconstructed. However, such an attempt at reconstruction may not be so hopeless as is often supposed. First, some of the material already stands in a common sequence:

Luke 11:39–40	Matt 23:25–26
Luke 11:44	Matt 23:27
Luke 11:47–48	Matt 23:29–32
Luke 11:49–51	Matt 23:34–36

This still leaves the following unaccounted for:

Luke 11:42	Matt 23:23
Luke 11:43	Matt 23:6–7
Luke 11:46	Matt 23:4
Luke 11:52	Matt 23:13

The meal scene in Luke 11:37–38 is probably a Lukan creation, perhaps based on Mark 7:1–5.[80] As in Mark, the meal scene leads naturally to a discussion of clean/unclean. It is to be suspected, therefore, that Luke selected the woe most appropriate for the meal setting (i.e., Luke 11:39–40) as his first woe (he probably also eliminated the "woe" cry). Therefore, Matthew's first woe (Matt 23:4//Luke 11:46) was probably the first woe in Q. Matthew has no opening scene except for the general "crowds and disciples"; his first saying (Matt 23:2–3) must have been taken up from his tradition. Thus, although

---

78. Betz, "Matthew 6:22–23," 85.
79. Betz, "Matthew 6:22–23," 87.
80. Bultmann, History of the Synoptic Tradition, 334. Grundmann (Lukas, 245) mentions other such Lukan scenes: Luke 5:29; 7:36; 10:38. Cf. also POxy 840, the Greek text of which is in Aland, Synopsis, 280; ET in Cameron, The Other Gospels, 53–54; Hennecke-Schnee-melcher, New Testament Apocrypha, 1. 92–94; Jeremias, Unknown Sayings, 47–60.

Matthean composition is certainly to found in this section,[81] it is not obvious in the setting itself.

Between Luke 11:44 and 11:47–48, and between Matt 23:27 and 23:29–32, there are catchword connections. In Luke it is "grave" or "tomb" (μνημεῖον), just as in Matthew it is "grave" or "tomb" (τάφος). The two woes stand together in Matthew but not in Luke. However, what comes between them in Luke is a rather clear instance of Lukan redaction: Luke has divided the woes into those directed at Pharisees and those directed at lawyers. Luke 11:45 marks the transition from one group to the other. But while Lukan redaction seems clear here, Matthew shows signs of being particularly faithful to Q: he has a cluster of Q woes whose order in large part agrees with Luke's. Here again, a reason why Luke might have altered the location of Q 11:46 can be seen.

The two woes suspected of having been dislocated in Luke (11:39–41 and 11:46) form the opening woes for the two parts of his "Woes" section. Luke appears to have moved 11:39–41 to fit the meal scene he constructed. Then he took what had been the first woe in Q (Matt 23:4//Luke 11:46) and recognized its priority by placing it at the beginning of his second series of woes.[82]

Another woe, Luke 11:42//Matt 23:23, can now be seen to be in the same relative position in Matthew and Luke, once Q 11:39–41 and 11:46 have been placed in their proper locations. We then have the following expanded sequence of material:

Luke 11:46	Matt 23:4
Luke 11:42	Matt 23:23
Luke 11:39–41	Matt 23:25–26
Luke 11:44	Matt 23:27
Luke 11:47–48	Matt 23:29–32
Luke 11:49–51	Matt 23:34–36

Most of the material in the "Woes" section has now been placed in its probable Q sequence. Matthew seems to have preserved the Q order of woes better than Luke. There remain Luke 11:43//Matt 23:6–7 and Luke 11:52// Matt 23:13. The difficulty in locating these sayings may be due to the fact that they were floating sayings (with Q 11:43 cf. Mark 12:38–39; with Q 11:52 cf. GThom 39; Justin *Dial.* 17.4). Q 11:52 appears to dangle at the end of the non-Q material. However, Q 11:43, though it cannot be placed exactly, obviously stood near the beginning of the "Woes" section since Matthew and Luke both

---

81. See Haenchen, "Matthäus 23" Pesch, "Theologische Aussagen"; Kümmel, "Die Weherufe"; Strecker, *Der Weg*, 137–43; Schweizer, *Matthew*, 427–46.

82. Luke seems to distinguish between the Pharisees and lawyers. When legal questions arise, lawyers are on hand (Luke 14:3; cf. 10:25). Jesus eats with Pharisees, never lawyers (Luke 14:1; 7:36; 11:37). A Pharisee comes to warn Jesus about Herod (13:31). In the woes, the Pharisees are linked by Luke to ceremonial hypocrisy, while legal matters are limited to the woes on lawyers. The most damning woes (including 11:49–51) are directed exclusively at lawyers, not Pharisees.

have it near the beginning.[83] Thus only one verse cannot be located in the original sequence of Q, namely 11:52 (=Matt 23:13).[84]

We next observe that in the "Woes" section there are two basic types of material: woes and the saying by the sophia of God (Q 11:49–51). The formal difference is matched by a marked material difference. The oracle by Wisdom speaks of blood-recompense extracted from "this generation," because it continues the age-old pattern of killing the prophets of Wisdom. The "Woes," on the other hand, deal with various accusations involving infidelity to the Law. Only one woe deviates from this pattern: Q 11:47–48. But this woe is directly attached to the oracle of Wisdom and belongs with it materially as well.

The dislocation of Luke 11:46 was noted above. Its removal brings to light a catchword connection between Luke 11:44 and 11:47–48 ("grave" [$\mu\nu\eta$-$\mu\varepsilon\hat{\iota}o\nu$]); the parallel sayings in Matthew are joined directly, and are linked by a catchword as well ("grave" [$\tau\acute{\alpha}\phi o\varsigma$]). When now we examine the reconstructed sequence of Q, bearing in mind the division of the material into two types, the compositional activity that has taken place becomes evident. Two types of material have been stitched together: Luke 11:44 with 11:47–48, and Matt 23:27 with 23:29–32. The old "Woes," which may in some form go back to Jesus,[85] have been attached to material which bears the clear imprint of the combined wisdom and deuteronomistic traditions. It is probable that the "Woes" (except for Q 11:47–48) had already been drawn together before the compositional stage of Q.[86] During what has been called here the "compositional stage" of Q, the material influenced by the wisdom/deuteronomistic tradition was added.[87]

It is possible that the addition of Q 11:49–51 caused distortion of other sayings in the section. Luke 11:39//Matt 23:25 speaks rather incongruously of "extortion" ($\dot{\alpha}\rho\pi\alpha\gamma\acute{\eta}$) and either "wickedness" ($\pi o\nu\eta\rho\acute{\iota}\alpha$, Luke 11:39) or "rapacity" ($\dot{\alpha}\kappa\rho\alpha\sigma\acute{\iota}\alpha$, Matt 23:25) being either inside of a cup (Matthew) or inside the Jewish leaders (Luke). Luke's more logical location, however, is probably secondary. In any case, we may suspect that the saying has been distorted by the introduction of violent language, and that such language was introduced because of a tendency, traceable to Q 11:47–51, to view the Jewish leaders as not just hypocritical but treacherous.

---

83. Cf. Crossan (*In Fragments*, 171–73), whose sequence is the same as mine. However, he simply places Q 11:43 as the second woe, hence "near the beginning," as I have indicated. He notes that this produces a group of woes—which he calls a "formal cluster of woes"— culminating in the wisdom oracle. Kloppenborg's sequence (*Formation*, 139–40) differs only in the location of Q 11:46.

84. We shall return to this woe in chap. 8. Crossan (*In Fragments*, 173), who follows the Matthean sequence of the woes, lists Q 11:52 as the third woe, but Matthew does not represent Q either; see Kloppenborg, *Formation*, 139–40.

85. On the antiquity of the woes see, e.g., Bultmann, *History of the Synoptic Tradition*, 147.

86. A similar view is taken by Bultmann (*History of the Synoptic Tradition*, 113–14). Lührmann (*Redaktion*, 45) thinks all seven woes formed a unit in the tradition underlying the redaction of Q.

87. Similarly, Lührmann, *Redaktion*, 45; however, Lührmann attributes only Q 11:49–51 to the "redaction of Q," which for him occurred all at once, not through successive stages.

We will now consider the material in the Woes, beginning with the oldest material, the woes themselves. These woes are very different from the woes in Luke 6:24–26, which speak of an eschatological reversal (except Luke 6:26). The woes in Q 11:39–52 give the woe-cry, the addressee (the original form of which, aside from "you," is difficult to determine) and the accusation introduced by "for" (ὅτι). There is a tendency to expand the woes with parenetic additions (Luke 11:41//Matt 23:25; end of Luke 11:42//Matt 23:23) which may be introduced with exclamations such as "You [blind] fools!" The use of this epithet, widespread in Matthew, may already have started in Q (Luke 11:40//Matt 23:26). The Q woes resemble the woes in the Old Testament, except that the Q woes are in direct speech whereas Old Testament woes usually have the woe-cry followed by a participle addressing the one doing evil.[88]

It is important to observe that the woes, despite their bitter tone, are the product of *inner-Jewish debate*.[89] The validity of the Law is assumed, and the only issue is its correct interpretation. Schulz has noted that it is precisely because the Q community and their Jewish opponents both saw the Law as their foundation that the struggle between them was so fierce.[90] Similar inner-Jewish invective can be found in Testament of Moses 7 and Psalms of Solomon 4.

We come now to Q 11:47–48 and 11:49–51. I have contended that these were added as a unit to the end of the older series of woes during the compositional stage of Q. This contention must now be examined further. Q 11:47–48 reflects the deuteronomistic view concerning the violent fate of the prophets.[91] Schulz, who assigns the woe (Q 11:47–48) and the Wisdom oracle (Q 11:49–51) to different levels of the Q tradition, agrees nevertheless that the deuteronomistic view of the prophets is strongly in evidence in both.[92] It is possible that an old woe did inveigh against the practice of building (or decorating) monuments to the prophets,[93] and that only the strained explanation of how this is evidence of the Jewish leaders' complicity in the prophet-murders of their fathers was added later. I think this is unlikely, because the explanation does not seem accidental; it is designed to prepare for the oracle of Wisdom in Q 11:49–51. But to assume that only the explanation (Q 11:47b–48) was added to an existing woe encounters the difficulty of understanding how a woe against building/decorating prophets' tombs could have existed without some explanation.[94] Moreover, the above reconstruction of the se-

---

88. See Westermann, *Basic Forms*, 190–94.
89. Rightly emphasized in Schulz, *Q*, 94–114; Schillebeeckx, *Jesus*, 234–35.
90. Schulz, *Q*, 99.
91. See Steck, *Israel*, 28–33.
92. Schulz, *Q*, 108–10 (for Q 11:47–48) and 336–45 (for Q 11:49–51).
93. On such tombs or monuments see Jeremias, *Heiligengräber in Jesu Umwelt*, with reference in particular to the tombs of Isaiah and Zechariah, son of Jehoiada in Jerusalem (pp. 61–72).
94. Cf. Derrett, "You Build the Tombs of the Prophets." Derrett suggests various possible word-plays, but does not emerge with a coherent and convincing explanation.

quence of the Q material in the Woes pericope makes it possible to see a compositional "seam," where new material has been stitched on to the old.

Q 11:47–48 and 11:49–51 belong together, not only by virtue of physical proximity and common theme but by direct linkage: "therefore" (διὰ τοῦτο). It is by no means uncommon to find "therefore" following a woe or series of woes in the prophets (e.g., Isaiah 5). The woe is often found linked, in this or other ways, to other material, particularly threats.[95] These combinations of prophetic materials do not follow steryotyped patterns whose formal characteristics one might list. However, as Gerstenberger has noted:

> There can be no doubt that in the present prophetical context the combination of two or more form elements after the introductory woe-cry is meant as a kerygmatic unit.[96]

Indeed, it is not unusual to find the view expressed that "therefore" (διὰ τοῦτο) has the effect of drawing together the woe as a reproach (*Scheltwort*) with the threat (*Drohwort*), i.e., the woe and the oracle of Wisdom.[97] Thus there is at least no formal objection to the linking of a woe with other material.[98] As we shall see, there are other reasons for viewing Q 11:47–48 and 11:49–51 as a unit. Here we may add that there is only one woe that has any logical relationship to Q 11:49–51, and therefore can be considered as the antecedent to "therefore" (διὰ τοῦτο), namely Q 11:47–48.

I have argued that "therefore also the Wisdom of God said" (διὰ τοῦτο καὶ ἡ σοφία θεοῦ εἶπεν)[99] is a typical prophetic messenger formula.[100] The Hebrew equivalent to "therefore also . . . he said" (διὰ τοῦτο καὶ . . . εἶπεν) is the prophetic formula (יהוה) לכן כה אמר, often used to introduce oracles.[101] Therefore, we do not have here a citation formula referring to some lost apocryphal wisdom book, as is sometimes supposed.[102] In contrast to the Old Testament prophetic messenger formula, however, the speaker now is Wisdom, and Jesus is her messenger.

---

95. Gerstenberger, "Woe-Oracles," 252–53.
96. Gerstenberger, "Woe-Oracles," 253.
97. So, e.g., Steck, *Israel*, 51–52, 281–82.
98. Of the instances of this type listed by Gerstenberger, some are particularly interesting because they, like Q 11:49, include a "therefore" with the messenger formula: Jer 22:13–19; 23:1–4; Ezek 13:3–8; 24:6–14.
99. The Lukan wording is generally accepted as that of Q; cf. Steck, *Israel*, 29–30 n. 3; Schulz, *Q*, 336. It should be noted that Steck's reconstruction of Q is sometimes tendentious and arbitrary; his reconstructed text fits only too well his presuppositions about the deuteronomistic view of history.
100. This view is shared by Lührmann, *Redaktion*, 46; Steck, *Israel*, 51–52; Schulz, *Q*, 341; Schnider, *Jesus der Prophet*, 139; Müller, *Prophetie und Predigt*, 54–55, 176–77; and Sato, *Q und Prophetie*, 152 ("a modified messenger formula").
101. Steck, *Israel*, 52; see esp. n. 6, where Steck observes that "εἶπεν corresponds to the Qal perfect of אמר in the messenger formula." Early Christian prophets seem to have taken up the messenger formula; see, e.g., Acts 21:11; IgnPhil 7.
102. Schulz (*Q*, 341 n. 145) lists a number of scholars who have taken this view; to which add Suggs, *Wisdom*, 16–20.

Interpreting the message is difficult. The Q wording is generally agreed to have been best preserved in Luke.[103] There are a number of details on which certainty concerning the wording is hard to attain; but the basic structure of the message is clear. The Lukan version of the text (Luke 11:49–51a) is as follows:

> Therefore also the Wisdom of God said: "I will send them prophets and apostles, and some of them they will kill and persecute, so that the blood which has been shed by all the prophets from the foundation of the world may be required of this generation, from the blood of Abel to the blood of Zachariah who perished between the altar and the sanctuary."

It is often asserted that Wisdom is speaking at the dawn of time.[104] The problem of the standpoint from which Wisdom speaks is, in fact, an exegetical crux. There are a number of problems which attend the view just mentioned; indeed, they are so serious that the usual opinion about the standpoint from which Wisdom speaks must be abandoned. If Wisdom stands at the dawn of time, it becomes difficult to understand why she speaks of blood which *has been* shed,[105] or how she can speak of "this generation."[106] The most natural interpretation is that Wisdom stands in the present, confronting "this generation." The other interpretation seems to derive chiefly from the judgment that the prophets Wisdom will send must of necessity be the Old Testament prophets. But this means that the prophets Wisdom *will* send are the same prophets whose blood *has been* spilled. It is rather that Wisdom will send prophets to "this generation"; and some of these prophets[107] will be murdered and persecuted by "this generation." The killing or persecution of *these* prophets incurs guilt for the blood of all the Old Testament prophets which has been shed since time began.[108] This is also the way in which Matthew understood

103. See, e.g., the reconstructions of the text by Schulz, *Q*, 336–38, and Polag, *Fragmenta Q*, 56.

104. E.g., by Suggs: "It is clear that the Wisdom of God speaks 'before the beginning of the earth' (Prov. 8:23)" (*Wisdom*, 21). The role of Wisdom in this pericope is discussed more fully in Christ, *Jesus Sophia*, 121–35; Kloppenborg, "Wisdom Christology in Q"; and J. M. Robinson, "Jesus as Sophos and Sophia."

105. Matthew's present participle is secondary; Luke's perfect participle (ἐκκεχυμένον) is to be preferred. So rightly Steck, *Israel*, 31 n. 8; Schulz, *Q*, 338.

106. Suggs (*Wisdom*, 22) concedes that "it is logical the pre-existent Wisdom should not speak of the final generation [in the remote future] as 'this generation'. . . ." Suggs's solution is not convincing even to him; he attributes this failure of logic to "the inconsistency of apocalyptic literature in matters of this kind." Steck (*Israel*, 32 n. 1) wants to eliminate the phrase "from this generation" (ἀπὸ τῆς γενεᾶς ταύτης); his suggestion is rightly rejected by Lührmann (*Redaktion*, 47 n. 1) and Schulz (*Q*, 338).

107. It is probable that Luke's "and apostles" (11:49) was in Q (cf. Schulz, *Q*, 336–37). Matthew, who also understood the text to refer to contemporary prophets, has inserted the names of others he regards as sent to "this generation" (i.e., the "wise" and "scribes"). This is simply an adaptation of the text to his own community, not a fundamental change in interpretation. In Q there was probably little if any distinction between "prophets" and "apostles."

108. I leave undecided here the question of the identity of the Zechariah mentioned here. Steck (*Israel*, 33–40) is probably correct in judging that in Q the Zechariah in 2 Chron 24:17–22 was meant. Manson (*Sayings of Jesus*, 103–5) came to the same conclusion. Abel's blood

the oracle; though he has changed it in various ways, Matthew was faithful to the original meaning of the text. The most spectacular change Matthew made was the substitution of Jesus for Wisdom.[109]

The conjunction "so that" (ἵνα) in Luke 11:50 (cf. Matt 23:35: ὅπως) is another source of difficulty. It is natural to take it as final, as translators regularly do. But this results in a quite remarkable assertion. Wisdom would then speak of sending prophets to "this generation" for the sole purpose of making it answerable for the blood of all the murdered prophets. It is true that there is a semitic tendency to refuse to distinguish between purpose and result,[110] and thus the final force of the "so that" (ἵνα) may not have been intended. Bauer says that "purpose and result are identical in declarations of divine purpose."[111] Yet the fact remains that the most natural interpretation grammatically is to take the "so that" (ἵνα) as final; it states why the prophets will be sent. If this is so, a vast and terrible mystery is locked up in the simple "so that" (ἵνα). Lührmann's interpretation would then be mild: "This announcement of judgment no longer envisions the conversion of Israel; for it [Israel] there yet remains only judgment."[112] If indeed "so that" refers to Wisdom's purpose, we would seem to have the perspective of a group radically alienated from its Jewish heritage.[113] Israel's God has vanished in the darkness of a terrible necessity that lies upon "this generation."

But will "this generation" kill or persecute Wisdom's prophets, as she prophesies? It is taken for granted that "this generation" will act as predicted. The reason for this is that the woe in Q 11:47–48 had already made the situation clear: "this generation"[114] is no different from its prophet-murdering forefathers. The prophesied prophet-murders are not actually said to occur; instead there is the strange allegation that building or decorating the tombs of the prophets establishes the solidarity of guilt of the sons with their murdering fathers. To these sons Wisdom then says that she will send prophets, with the expected result that the prophets will be persecuted or killed. But with these

cried from the ground (Gen 4:10; note Matthew's insertion of "ground" in 23:35), and the Zechariah in 2 Chron 24:22 called to the Lord to "require" (שׁדר) his blood. Thus Abel and Zechariah provide instances of blood which has been shed, of which note is made that it will be "required." These figures stand at the beginning and end of the Hebrew Bible, if we can assume that 2 Chronicles already stood at the end of the canon (cf. Schulz, Q, 344–45 n. 164); hence the sweeping phrase, "all the prophets from the foundation of the world." Abel, however, was hardly a prophet, and the opening was probably created for Matthew's view that the "righteous" are the ones in view.

109. See esp. Suggs, Wisdom, 58–61.
110. See Moule, Idiom-Book, 142–43.
111. Bauer, s.v. ἵνα II.2.
112. Lührmann, Redaktion, 47.
113. Miller has objected to my claim about radical alienation ("The Rejection of the Prophets in Q," 232; he refers to Jacobson, "Wisdom Christology," 191). Miller argues that such "radical alienation" is really quite traditional, namely the alienation one finds among prophets. I agree completely. I had not made sufficiently clear that the Q community of which I spoke was a Jewish community. I can see no basis for claiming it to be "Christian."
114. This epithet is not found in Q 11:47–48, but may be assumed to be the "them" mentioned there.

last prophets the end of the line has been reached, and the accumulated guilt of centuries will fall on "this generation." Here we can see that the internal, if grotesque, logic of Wisdom's oracle requires its association with the preceding woe. The prophets persecuted by "this generation" are none other than the members of the Q community, as Robert Miller has recently noted.[115]

A fragment of the oracle remains: "Yes, I tell you, it will be required of this generation" (Luke 11:51b//Matt 23:36). This is the application of the oracle to "this generation"; presumably now Jesus himself speaks (through a prophet). It is difficult to say whether this application was originally joined to the oracle. It does not correspond to Old Testament usage. The best parallels seem to be in Q itself. In Luke 7:26//Matt 11:9b, "yes, I tell you" ($\nu\alpha\grave{\iota}\ \lambda\acute{\epsilon}\gamma\omega\ \acute{\upsilon}\mu\hat{\iota}\nu$) comes (as in Q 11:51b) at the end of a brief speech (about John), and serves to provide an authoritative conclusion: "Yes, I tell you, and more than a prophet."[116] Another parallel is found in the lament over Jerusalem, which also ends with "I tell you" ("And I tell you, you will not see me until you say, 'Blessed is he who comes in the name of the Lord'" [Q 13:35]). Yet this parallel is mainly formal: an "I tell you" ($\lambda\acute{\epsilon}\gamma\omega\ \acute{\upsilon}\mu\hat{\iota}\nu$) formula at the end of an oracle. The closest parallel may be Luke 10:12//Matt 10:15: "I tell you, it will be more tolerable on that day for Sodom than for that town." Here the "I tell you" ($\lambda\acute{\epsilon}\gamma\omega\ \acute{\upsilon}\mu\hat{\iota}\nu$) formula comes at the end of a section on "mission" (Q 10:2–11), and it pronounces an eschatological verdict on those who reject those sent to them. And though it comes before the woe in Q 10:13–15 it was probably created later in imitation of Q 10:13–14, to serve as a link between the "mission" and the woe. That is, it in effect applied the woe in Q 10:13–15 to a different situation. In any case, in Q 11:49–51 Jesus acts as messenger of Wisdom to "this generation"; he concludes by affirming that what Wisdom has said will indeed come true for "this generation."

The Third Section: A Deuteronomistic Stratum

The reconstructed sequence of the third section of Q is given here (Q 11:43 and 11:52 are omitted because they cannot be placed in their Q sequence).

Blessed are the Eyes	Luke 10:23–24	Matt 13:16–17
Lord's Prayer	Luke 11:2–4	Matt 6:9–13
Answer to Prayer	Luke 11:9–13	Matt 7:7–11
Beelzebul Controversy	Luke 11:14–20, 23	Matt 12:22–28, 30
Sign of Jonah	Luke 11:29–32	Matt 12:39–42
Odyssey of the Unclean Spirit	Luke 11:24–26	Matt 12:43–45
Lamp on a Stand	Luke 11:33–36	Matt 5:15; 6:22–23

---

115. Miller's examination of the logic of this Q pericope ("The Rejection of the Prophets in Q," 229–31) correctly notes that there is a missing premise: "*The missing premise is that 'this generation' is persecuting the bearers of the Q tradition*" (p. 230, Miller's emphasis). That is why the building of monuments for dead prophets is hypocritical.

116. See above, chapter 4, pp. 61–62.

Woes	Luke 11:46	Matt 23:4
Woes	Luke 11:42	Matt 23:23
Woes	Luke 11:39–41	Matt 23:25–26
Woes	Luke 11:44	Matt 23:27
Woes	Luke 11:47–48	Matt 23:29–32
Woes (Oracle of Sophia)	Luke 11:49–51	Matt 23:34–36

The material in this section of Q does seem to cohere. However, no story develops, and there is no geographical or historical movement; rather there is a piling up of indictments against "this generation." Within this section, however, some material stands out as later additions, namely Q 11:2-4, 9-13. This is probably quite old material, but I have argued that it represents a perspective different from most of the Q materials, and probably was added after the deuteronomistic compositional level.

Q 10:23-24 has already been identified as the point of transition from the second section of Q to the third section. It speaks of the privilege of seeing now what prophets and kings longed to see but could not. If this is a blessing for those who see, it is judgment for those who do not see. This theme is developed, with particular attention to the damning obduracy of "this generation."

The Beelzebul Controversy has Jesus answer the charge that he casts out demons by Beelzebul by saying that only two sides exist, the kingdoms of God and Satan. What is manifested in exorcism, therefore, is not the kingdom of Satan but the kingdom of God. The kingdom of Satan is not divided against itself but is being assailed by God. The "sons" of the opponents make themselves instruments of God's kingdom; Jesus and they stand on the same side. Any other position is a position of opposition to God's kingdom. The Jewish leaders, by their opposition, demonstrate that they are blind leaders, unable to distinguish between the spirit at work in their midst and the ruler of the demonic world.

The Sign of Jonah pericope, in its present form, was shaped by the wisdom tradition, though the deuteronomistic view of history stands in the background providing the history of Israel's persistent unbelief. But now, in contrast to the Jewish leaders, we hear of gentiles in Israel's history who responded to the sophia and kerygma addressed to it by Wisdom's prophets. These gentiles, selected as part of a new "counter-history" of Israel, will rise up to condemn "this generation," which is blind to the greater than Jonah/Solomon in its midst.

The Odyssey of the Unclean Spirit intensifies the polemic against "this generation." "This generation" is like a man exorcised who thereafter prepares a welcome for the unclean spirit and ends up being infested with evil. The lamp sayings continue this indictment. A light has been lit in the midst of Israel, yet "this generation" absurdly seeks to hide this light. This failure of vision is traced to moral depravity, a charge that is then elaborated upon in the Woes.

The indictments are thus spelled out in a collection of old woes. Appended to them, however, is the most terrible judgment of all. Wisdom declares through Jesus that she will send prophets to "this generation" but that they will kill and persecute them, and thereby fall heir to and be required to pay for the full enormity of Israel's guilt in killing the prophets Wisdom has sent from the dawn of time. The indictments may reach a climax here. Of course, the guilt of Israel is stupendous precisely because Israel is the elect of God, the people through whom God has chosen uniquely to act in the world. This is never stated; it is merely presupposed. But now the situation has reached crisis proportions; there seems to be not even a shred of hope for the conversion of Israel, for its reawakening. The polarization of "this generation" and Wisdom's children seems to be understood in terms of God's judgment, in terms of the separation even now of those who respond from those blind ones who remain in darkness; but this polarity is close to becoming dualism. The fact that Q, in contrast to Mark, is able to speak (in the Beelzebul Controversy) of two kingdoms, God's and Satan's; that there is only for and against; and that there is either light or darkness, wisdom or folly, holy spirit or Beelzebul—all this smacks of dualism. Moreover, "this generation" seems to have been consigned totally to the realm of darkness: it is blind, resistant to the light but audaciously providing a welcome for the unclean spirit.

Aside from a later addition (Q 11:2–4, 9–13), all the material in this section seems to bear the stamp of the deuteronomistic tradition, either in the content of the sayings themselves or by virtue of their context in Q. To be sure, at times it is possible to identify earlier and later strata in the sayings compositions. Thus, Q 11:31–32 was identified as a later addition to 11:29–30, and Q 11:47–48, 49–51 was identified as a later addition to the woes in 11:39–40, 42, 43, 44, 46. But it is only in the woes that anything approaching an earlier identifiable stratum becomes evident. What we see there is a lively inner-Jewish debate. Only in the deuteronomistic stratum does this debate degenerate further into violent denunciation. What is striking, therefore, is the large block of material, virtually an entire section, which reflects deuteronomistic tradition. This tends to vindicate the designation of this stratum as the "compositional level of Q," i.e., the stratum in which Q received its basic shape.

8
To the
The Last Community
Part of Q

From Q 12:2 to the end of Q, following the Lukan order, one is hard pressed to discern any literary unity or structure. Indeed, at the outset I shall not designate this material "the fourth section of Q" because I have reserved the term "section" to refer to coherent literary units.

Some indications of literary intentionality are, however, present. For example, a significant amount of material containing eschatological themes is to be found in the last part of Q, including the so-called "Q apocalypse" in Q 17:23–37. More intriguing is the fact that many of the Q parables occur in this material. Although metaphorical sayings can be found in the first three sections of Q, only three sayings in these sections are commonly reckoned to be parables: Q 6:47–49 (Builders); Q 7:31–35 (Children in the Market Place); and Q 11:24–26 (Unclean Spirit). But in the rest of Q are to be found a number of parables or parabolic sayings: Q 12:39–40 (Thief); 12:42–46 (Faithful and Wise Servant); 12:54–56 (Interpreting the Sky); 12:58–59 (Reconciliation with Accuser); 13:18–19 (Mustard Seed); 13:20–21 (Leaven); 14:16–24 (Banquet); 15:4–7 (Lost Sheep); and 19:12–27 (Talents/Pounds). We shall see that sayings with deuteronomistic themes are also common. Finally, much of the rest of Q is directed toward the community itself.

Within the rest of the Q material clusters of sayings may be frequently observed, and among these a number can be shown to be linked in various ways. We turn now to an examination of this material.

If the Lukan order can be trusted, the end of the Third Section was Q 11:52, the last of the woes.[1] Luke's version reads:

> Woe to you lawyers, for you have taken away the keys of knowledge ($\gamma\nu\hat{\omega}\sigma\iota\varsigma$);
> for you did not enter, and you hindered those entering.

This woe, which seems strangely anticlimactic after the prophecy in Q 11:49–51, accuses the opponents of hindering those who seek to enter. The

---

1. In the previous chapter an effort was made to locate Q 11:52 among the woes, since Matthew and Luke differ as to its location. No decision could be reached. In favor of Luke's position it may be noted that it is hard to explain why Luke would have put it there if it were not already there, since it is so anticlimactic and follows so poorly after 11:49–51.

use of "enter" with no object seems peculiar, and yet in the context of Q it is not, since we encounter it again in Q 13:24. But in Q 11:52 there is an identification of that which is entered. According to Matthew (23:13), it is the "kingdom of heaven"; according to Luke (11:52), it is "knowledge." Most commentators have judged that Luke's reading is secondary. Schulz is typical; he regards Luke's reading as secondary "on material grounds,"[2] presumably on the assumption that neither Jesus nor Q would have spoken of the "keys of gnosis." Yet the Lukan reading, "keys of knowledge," is found in the Coptic GThom 39 and perhaps in its probable Greek antecedent (POxy 655). This can hardly be explained as due to gnostic influence, since the saying reads, "The Pharisees and scribes have taken the keys to knowledge and have hidden them." Even (or especially) if the Gospel of Thomas is held to be gnostic, a claim that others have the keys to knowledge would be quite remarkable!

If, as now seems possible, Q 11:52 used the word "knowledge," then a connection becomes visible with the saying which seems to have followed 11:52, namely Q 12:2. The two sayings were connected with catchwords: "to know" (γινώσκειν) in Q 12:2 echoes "knowledge" (γνῶσις) in Q 11:52. Indeed, the possibility needs to be considered that we have more than a catchword link, that, in fact, Q 12:2-3 is to be interpreted as the continuation of Q 11:52, as already suggested by Manson.[3] In that case, we have the following:

Q 11:52	Woe to you . . . for you have taken away the keys of knowledge. You did not enter, and you hindered those who were entering.
Q 12:2	Nothing is covered up that will not be revealed, or hidden that will not be known.
Q 12:3	Whatever you have spoken in the dark shall be heard in the light, and what you have whispered in private rooms shall be proclaimed upon the housetops.[4]

If Q 11:52 did not conclude Q 11:49-51 but rather introduced Q 12:2-3, the interpretation of these verses must change accordingly. Now they say that what the opponents have concealed will be made public. Yet there are difficulties with this. First, in this case Q 12:4 must represent a shift in audience (as indeed is the case in Luke), and second, we would have to explain the remarkable coincidence that neither Matthew nor Luke associated Q 12:2-3 directly with Q 11:52 and, further, that both associated Q 12:2-3 instead with Q 12:4-9. The second, much more difficult problem, does have an explanation, however. It is that Q 12:2 was known in a different form by both Matthew and Luke, a form in which it was applied not to opponents but to the

2. Schulz, *Q*, 110.
3. Manson, *Sayings*, 105-6; cf. Friedrich, "κηρύσσω," 705.
4. Luke preserves the future passive in Q 12:3 as in 12:2; Matthew has altered Q 12:3 (=Matt 10:27) into an admonition. Also, Luke has probably preserved the Q parallelism: in the dark/in the light; in chambers/on rooftops. Cf. "chamber" (ταμεῖον) in Q 17:23, where Matthew has probably preserved Q's wording.

proclamation of the community. This form is found in Mark 4:22 (=Luke 8:17). Luke seems to have made a break in Q between the woes (11:39–51) and the other sayings which followed, the first of which he had already given in its Markan context. It thus seems plausible that, in Q, 11:52 belonged with 12:2–3, and that the last part of Q began with Q 12:4. Q 11:52 and 12:2–3 served as a transition from the woes to the new section.

Unlike previous chapters where the sequence of Q was worked out at the beginning, here we will proceed text by text, examining both the order and the composition for each as they arise.

A Call to Courage Q 12:4–12

Luke 12:4–12	Matt 10:28–33; 12:32; 10:19–20
⁴I tell you, my friends, do not fear those who kill the body and after that have no more that they can do.	²⁸And do not fear those who kill the body but cannot kill the soul;
⁵But I will warn you whom to fear: fear him who, after he has killed, has power to cast into hell; yes, I tell you, fear him!	rather fear him who can destroy both soul and body in hell.
⁶Are not five sparrows sold for two pennies? And not one of them is forgotten before God.⁵	²⁹Are not two sparrows sold for a penny? And not one of them will fall to the ground without your father's will.
⁷Why, even the hairs on your head are all numbered. Fear not; you are of more value than many sparrows.	³⁰But even the hairs on your head are all numbered. ³¹Fear not, therefore; you are of more value than many sparrows.
⁸And I tell you, every one who owns up to me before people, the son of man also will own up to before the angels of God;	³²So every one who owns up to me before people, I also will own up to before my father who is in heaven;
⁹but he who denies me before people will be denied before the angels of God.	³³but whoever denies me before people I also will deny before my father who is in heaven
¹⁰And every one who speaks a word against the son of man will be forgiven; but he who blasphemes against the holy spirit	12 ³²And whoever says a word against the son of man will be forgiven; but whoever speaks against the holy spirit

5. Note that confidence in God's providence (12:6–7) exists side by side with the motif of fearing the heavenly judge (12:5).

will not be forgiven.	will not be forgiven, either in this age or in the age to come.
[11]And when they bring you before synagogues and the rulers and the authorities, do not be anxious how or what you are to answer or what you are to say;	10[19]When they deliver you up, do not be anxious how you are to speak or what you are to say; for what you are to say will be given to you in that hour; [20]for it is not you who speak,
[12]for the holy spirit will teach you in that very hour what you ought to say.	but the spirit of your father speaking through you.

This cluster of sayings has a similar sequence in both Luke and Matthew, except for Q 12:10. Matthew locates this saying in quite a different context, a much better context, but one based on Mark. Matthew, therefore, provides no evidence for the Q location of this saying. Luke's context could, in fact, be that of Q, since we can note a catchword connection between Q 12:10 and 12:11–12, namely "holy spirit."

1. Q 12:4-7 as the Core of the Composition

Kloppenborg rightly contends that the kernel of this composition is Q 12:4–7.[6] Here we find several sayings linked by the catchword "fear" ($\phi o \beta \epsilon \hat{\iota} \nu$). Q 12:4–5 belong together, as do Q 12:6–7. However, the logical transitions are not smooth. Essentially each "aphoristic compound," to adopt Crossan's terminology,[7] approaches the situation from a different perspective. Q 12:4–5 exhorts people to fear God rather than human beings, who can inflict less serious damage. Q 12:6–7, on the other hand, appeals to God's solicitude for even the more insignificant things. The strategies differ, but the goal is the same: to disperse fear. The presumed context is some sort of persecution ("kill the body").

2. The Link with Q 12:11-12

The persecution context reappears in Q 12:11–12, and also becomes more explicit. Here we have, apparently, local authorities (only Luke identifies them) before whom the presumed audience is hauled and told to give testimony. The logical connection between Q 12:4–7 and 12:11–12, thus, is quite satisfactory.

6. Kloppenborg, *Formation*, 208. Piper (*Wisdom*, 51–61) sees Q 12:4–7 as the nucleus of an "aphoristic collection" to which Q 12:2–3 and 12:8–9 were simultaneously added later. Kloppenborg, however, argues that Q 12:8–9 would not have been added at the same time as 12:2–3. Piper stretches the point when he argues that Q 12:2–3, like 12:8–9, deals with open confession.

7. Crossan, *In Fragments*, chap. 4.

3. The Meaning of Q 12:8-9 and 12:10 in Context

Although Q 12:4-7 presupposes a context of persecution, it is very vague as to the reasons for it. The addition of Q 12:8-9 has the effect of defining this context: a trial before Jewish elders (?) in which the addressees are told to renounce Jesus, or at least to admit that they are followers of Jesus. It would appear that Q 12:8-9 was added during a period in which the Q community was a secret Jewish group whose outward life differed in no way from that of other Jews; hence the necessity of a legal process for identifying dissidents. But presumably in secret they maintained their fellowship. Yet they could not have been so anonymous, so concealed and so innocent that the Jewish gerousia (elders) would have had no reason to be worried. There would have to have been some reason why authorities would need to identify these dissidents in their community.

Q 12:10 is usually seen as contradicting Q 12:8-9.[8] In its present context, the "son of man" in Q 12:10 can only be the heavenly son of man mentioned by Q 12:8. In neither instance is this "son of man" identified with Jesus. It has been argued, for example by Barnabas Lindars,[9] that in the original Aramaic the saying contained a simple contrast between slandering humans, which would be forgivable, and blaspheming God, which would not. But the Greek text, which is all we have, does not permit such a contrast; "son of man" does not mean "humans." Moreover, if Q contained so simple a contrast, it is very difficult to understand why it was placed in its present context.

Q 12:10 is a bipartite saying in which the second strand intensifies the first. The vague "speak a word against" in Q 12:10a becomes "blaspheme" in 12:10b, and "son of man" gives way to "holy spirit." On this interpretation, "speak a word against" is not a technical term for some special type of speech; it is simply a less radical act. The saying should be seen as marking a dividing line on a continuum: many things are forgivable, even speaking a word against the son of man, but blaspheming the holy spirit crosses the line and is unforgivable. The saying is misunderstood if it is taken to imply that speaking a word against the son of man is something of little importance. The point seems to be that the holy spirit is constitutive for the community in a way that the heavenly prosecutor, the son of man (Q 12:8-9), is not. Moreover, as Q 12:11-12 makes clear, blaspheming the spirit robs members of the one last resource upon which they may rely in time of persecution. Such reliance upon the spirit marks this as a prophetic community, but we have noted evidence of this elsewhere in Q.

Thus, Q 12:10 can in fact be related to its context. It does not contradict Q 12:8-9, because in both the son of man is simply the heavenly prosecutor who argues the case before the divine judge. But neither in Q 12:8-9 nor in 12:10 is Jesus identified with this heavenly prosecutor figure. Since we know that

---

8. E.g., Kloppenborg, *Formation*, 211-12.
9. Lindars, *Jesus*, 34-36.

elsewhere in Q the identification of Jesus with the son of man has occurred, we may conclude that this identification is relatively late, and that both Q 12:8–9 and 12:10 are relatively early. Further, we saw above that Q 12:8–9 presumes an early stage, in which the Q community was a secret Jewish group externally indistinguishable from other Jews. Correspondingly, the whole unit, Q 12:4–12, must be early relative to other Q material encountered in sections one to three. It could be argued, nevertheless, that Q 12:10 was added to this unit later than Q 12:8–9. The main reason for this is that these were originally independent sayings, as their parallels show. But that does not necessarily argue against seeing Q 12:8–9 as part of a Q compositional unit.

That the Lukan context of Q 12:11–12 represents that of Q is suggested by the fact that Luke has used this saying twice, once in its Markan context (Mark 13:11//Luke 21:14–15) and the present instance, presumably the Q context.

In spite of evidence that Q 12:4–12 has behind it a compositional history, nevertheless it represents a single block of material whose purpose it is to give courage to a community facing real and daunting dangers.

Against Anxieties (Q 12:22b–31)

Luke 12:22–32	Matt 6:25–34
22And he said to his disciples, "Therefore I tell you, do not be anxious about what you eat nor about [your] body, what you wear.	25"Therefore I tell you, do not be anxious about your life what you eat [or what you drink], nor about your body, what you wear.
23For the soul is more than food and the body is more than clothing.	Is not the soul more than food and the body more than clothing?
24Consider the ravens, for they neither sow nor do they reap; for them is neither storehouse or barn, yet God feeds them. You are of far more value than birds.	26Consider the birds of the sky, for they do not sow, neither do they reap, nor do they gather into barns, yet your heavenly father feeds them. Are you not superior to them?
25And who among you is able by being anxious to add a cubit to his span of life?	27And who among you is able by being anxious to add one cubit to his span of life?
26If then you cannot do the slightest, why are you anxious about the rest?	
27Consider the lilies, how they neither spin nor weave; but I tell you, not even Solomon in all his glory was clothed like one of these.	28And why are you anxious about clothing? Consider the lilies of the field, how they grow; they neither toil nor spin; 29but I tell you, not even Solomon in all his glory was clothed like one of these.
28But if God likewise clothes	30But if God likewise clothes

the grass in a field	the grass of the field
which is here today	which is here today
and tomorrow is cast into a furnace,	and tomorrow is cast into a furnace,
how much more you,	will he not much more clothe you,
deficient in trust!	deficient in trust?
29And you, do not seek	31Therefore do not be anxious saying,
what you will eat	'What shall we eat?'
or what you will drink,	or 'What shall we drink?'
and do not be worried.	or 'What shall we wear?'
30For all the nations of the world	32For all the nations
seek these things,	seek these things.
and your father	For your heavenly father
knows that you need these.	knows that you need all of these.
31But seek his kingdom	33But seek first the kingdom
	and its justice,
and these will be added to you.	and all these will be added to you.
32Fear not, little flock,	34Therefore do not be anxious
	about the morrow,
for your father takes delight	for the morrow is anxious of itself;
to give you the kingdom.	sufficient for the day
	is the evil thereof.

This sayings composition continues the general theme of courage noted above in Q 12:4–12. While there are important differences between 12:4–12 and 12:22–32, continuity is still evident. The composition is linked by catchword ("do not be anxious") to Q 12:11. We can thus reconstruct this much of the rest of Q, namely 12:4–12, 22–31.

Some, such as Kloppenborg, would include Luke 12:13–14, 16–21 in Q, even though it is attested only by Luke.[10] The presence of "therefore" in Q 12:22b could lend credence to this, and there are some catchword connections (barn, soul, eat, drink). But the absence of a Matthean parallel creates a presumption against assigning this material to Q. Moreover, these verses have no particular connection with Q 12:4–12, nor do they fit especially well with Q 12:22b–31. The purpose of Luke 12:13–14, 16–21 is to warn against thinking that life consists of possessions, whereas Q 12:22b–31 addresses an audience with the opposite problem, of wondering where their next meal will come from. Moreover, as Hoffmann notes,[11] Lukan redaction is abundantly evident in Luke 12:13–21, and therefore these verses are best left out of consideration.

If a juridical context was presupposed in Q 12:4–12, a quite different context is assumed in Q 12:22b–31. Here the concerns of followers about food and clothing are addressed. Perhaps this reflects a situation in which an austere lifestyle, devoted to God, is being defended before those invited to adopt this lifestyle. The addressees may already have joined the community and need this assurance that the austere lifestyle they have chosen will not leave them

10. Kloppenborg, Q Parallels, 128.
11. Hoffmann, "Sprüche vom Sorgen," 132.

unduly exposed to danger. This composition, therefore, is not as radical as Q 9:57a-60a, for there the call to an austere lifestyle is not cushioned with assurances that the risk taken will not, after all, involve any real danger. Q 12:22b-31 could well be the product of a community which, however small, was able to supply the minimal needs of life, or which at least had sufficiently good relations with its larger community that it could count on their support.

Q 12:22b-31 gives the appearance of a carefully constructed sayings composition. And yet there is such clear evidence of literary disunity that we can observe a process of literary growth.

Q 12:22b-23 contains an admonition followed by a reason. The admonition is not to be anxious about your life or your body. The reason (Q 12:23) is that life is more than food and the body more than clothing. This unit is essentially complete and could have stood alone. It is quite possible that Q 12:25, which is widely regarded as an ill-fitting fragment, was the original conclusion to Q 12:22b-23. Like those verses, it focuses on anxiety but promises no satisfaction of one's needs. It simply pokes fun at the inability of anxiety to change one's situation, and like Q 12:22b-23 it says nothing of God's providential care.

Q 12:24 and 12:26b-28 are parallel formulations designed to reassure would-be followers that God will provide both food and clothing just as God does for birds and lilies. This argument against anxiety is quite different from the one in Q 12:22b-23 and 12:25. In the former, God's providential care is invoked, and the new thought is introduced that the risks entailed in austere discipleship are not so great after all, because of the care that is assured. Because of these differences, it is probably best to regard Q 12:24, 26b-28 as later additions to 12:22b-23, 25. The wording of Q 12:26b is probably best preserved by Matthew; Luke has tried to provide a transition from Q 12:25, which seemed to him as out of place as it does to us.

Q 12:29-31 appears to be another independent saying. Matthew has more carefully integrated these verses into his composition by introducing a "therefore" in 6:31 and by repeating the admonition not to be anxious. But Luke preserves the earlier and clumsier paratactic construction and the original verb: "and do not seek. . . ." This verb, "seek," is repeated in Q 12:31. Luke has also preserved the original food and drink, whereas Matthew has again adapted the saying to its context by adding the question about clothing. Luke's "nor be of anxious mind" is a later addition, as the phrase "these things" in Q 12:30 makes clear: an anxious mind cannot be included among "these things." The argument in Q 12:29-31 is different from the other arguments against anxiety. Now we are told that the gentiles concern themselves with food, but the addressees are to seek God's kingdom, and in doing so they will find that their needs are met anyway.[12]

It is likely, therefore, that Q 12:22b-31 went through the following stages of

---

12. This is a very old theme. See, e.g., the Babylonian Theodicy, lines 240–42: "He that bears his god's yoke never lacks food, though it be sparse. Seek the kindly will of the god; what you have lost over a year you will make up in a moment" (Lambert, *Babylonian Literature*, 85).

growth: (a) Q 12:22b-23, 25, to which (b) Q 12:24, 26b-28 was added, and then (c) Q 12:29–31.[13] The probably playful recurrence of "added on to you" ($\pi\rho\sigma\tau\epsilon\theta\dot{\eta}\sigma\epsilon\tau\alpha\iota\ \dot{\nu}\mu\hat{\iota}\nu$) in Q 12:31 (cf. 12:25) suggests that Q 12:29–31 presupposed 12:25. On the other hand, the whole unit is sufficiently well constructed that we should probably not assume a lengthy process of literary growth. Indeed, it is quite possible that the three constitutive units (Q 12:22b-23, 25; 12:24, 26b-28; and 12:29–31) were brought together all at once.

Treasures (Q 12:33–34)

Luke 12:33–34

[33]Sell your possessions and give alms.

Make for yourselves purses
that do not deteriorate,
an unfailing treasure in the heavens,
where a thief does not approach
nor a moth destroy.

[34]For where your [sing.] treasure is,
there will your heart be also.

Matt 6:19–21

[19]Do not treasure for yourselves
treasures on earth
where moth and corrosion disfigure,
and where thieves penetrate and thieve.
[20]But treasure for yourselves

treasures in heaven,
where neither moth nor corrosion disfigures,
and where thieves do not penetrate
nor do they thieve.
[21]For where your [plur.] treasure is,
there will your heart be also.

Although Matthew locates these verses in his Sermon on the Mount, the Lukan location for them is probably that of Q. It should be noted, however, that Matthew places these verses (Matt 6:19–21) in close proximity to the composition on anxiety (Matt 6:25–33), so the two pericopes were probably linked in Q as well.[14] In the opinion of many commentators the wording in Matthew is to be preferred to that of Luke.[15] However, it is not obvious that Luke 12:33a was composed by Luke and reflects his special concerns. The association of alms with heavenly treasures is a traditional theme (see, e.g, Sir 29:11–13; Tob 4:8–11; 12:8–9; cf. TestLevi 13:5–9; 2 Apoc Bar 14:12; 24:1; 1 Enoch 38:2; 4 Ezra 7:77; 8:33; Pss. Sol. 9:5; Mark 10:21; 1 Tim 6:19); sometimes such treasures are contrasted with corruptible, earthly treasures (see 2 Enoch 50:5; Jas 5:2–3; Philo de Cherub. 48; cf. Pindar frag. 22). Further, that Luke 12:33b is not likely to be simply a Lukan abbreviation of Matt 6:19–20 is shown by the parallel in GThom 76b. And, as Crossan has noted, the Lukan version has an integrity of its own and hence a claim to priority.[16] However, Justin (1 Apol 15.11) may provide evidence that Matthew's version was also traditional. Moreover, Q 12:34 presupposes alternative locations for treasure, and thus it may assume the Matthean wording in Q.

---

13. See the analysis of Piper, *Wisdom*, 24–36.
14. So Hoffmann, "Sprüche vom Sorgen," 132.
15. E.g., Schulz, *Q*, 142–43.
16. Crossan, *In Fragments*, 128–31.

Q 12:33 and 12:34 are probably originally independent sayings which have been attracted to each other by the catchword, θησαυρός ("treasure").[17] However, the connective "for" (γάρ) indicates that the editor regarded Q 12:34 as a motive for 12:33. That is, one should seek heavenly rather than earthy treasures because "where your treasure is, there your heart will also be." But Q 12:33 does not need this motive; it can stand alone, as can 12:34.

The addition of Q 12:33–34 to 12:22b-31 provides another motive for not being anxious: the fact that earthly treasures are so vulnerable. It also strikes out in a new direction, invoking the old motif of treasure in heaven to urge the pointlessness of being preoccupied with worldly things. Q 12:33–34 looks very much like a pious addition to Q 12:22b-31 which, though designed to strengthen this discourse, actually obscures its point by introducing new considerations. The fact that it uses traditional language means that it is probably hazardous to propose that it reflects some special circumstance in the life of the community. In fact, there seems to be nothing in the saying which would help locate it within the compositional history of Q.

Being Ready (Luke 12:35–38)
and Faithful Servant (Q 12:39–40, 42–46)

Luke 12:35–38 ³⁵Stand, your loins being girded and the lamps burning, ³⁶and be like people waiting for their master when he returns from the wedding feast, so that when he comes and knocks, you may immediately open to him. ³⁷Blessed are those slaves who when the master comes he finds watching. Amen, I say to you, he will gird himself and will make them recline and, approaching, he will serve them. ³⁸And if he comes in the second or the third watch and finds them so doing, blessed are they.

Luke 12:39–40, 42–46	Matt 24:43–51
³⁹But know this,	⁴³But know this,
that if the master of the house	that if the master of the house
had known at what hour	had known at what watch
the thief would come,	the thief would come,
he would not have allowed	he would have watched and not permitted
his house to be broken into.	his house to be broken into.
⁴⁰ You also must be prepared,	⁴⁴Therefore you also must be prepared,
for the son of man comes at an hour	for the son of man comes at an hour
you do not expect.	you do not expect.
⁴¹But Peter said, "Sir,	
do you speak this parable to us	
or also to everyone?"	
⁴²And the master said,	
"Who then is the faithful,	⁴⁵Who then is the faithful
prudent steward whom the master	and prudent slave whom the master

17. Q 12:33 is attested as a saying separate from 12:34 in GThom 76b; cf. Justin, *1 Apol.* 15.11, 16b.

will set over his servants	will set over his household slaves
to give the ration on time?	to give them food on time?
43Blessed is that slave	46Blessed is that slave
whom his master, when he returns,	whom his master, when he returns,
finds performing in this manner.	finds performing in this manner.
44Truly I say to you that he will	47Amen, I say to you that he will
set him over all his possessions.	set him over all his possessions.
45But if that slave says in his heart,	48But if that bad slave says in his heart,
'My master is delayed,'	"My master is delayed in coming,"
and begins to beat the menservants	49and begins to beat
and the maidservants,	his fellow slaves,
to eat and to drink	and he eats and drinks with those
and to get drunk,	who are drunk,
46the master of that slave will come	50the master of that slave will come
on a day he does not expect	on a day he does not expect
and at an hour he does not know	and at an hour he does not know
and he will rip him apart,	51and he will rip him apart,
and cast his lot with the unbelievers."	and cast his lot with the hypocrites.
	There will be weeping
	and gnashing of teeth in that place.

These verses are often assigned to Q,[18] but they present a very complicated situation, as we shall see. Luke 12:35–38 is frequently treated as parallel to Mark 13:33–37. In both pericopes we have an admonition followed by a parable and, at the end, references to various watches of the night. Verbal parallels between them are few. Both make a comparison with a "person" or "persons" (ἄνθρωπος in Mark, ἄνθρωποι in Luke). In both, the returning master "comes" and "finds" someone waiting. Mark 13:34 mentions a "door-keeper," while this figure is only implied in Luke 12:35–38.

On the other hand, Mark 13:34 is also parallel to Luke 19:12–13//Matt 25:14–15. Here, in contrast to the marriage feast setting of Luke 12:35–38, we have "a person" who goes on a journey. Further, the departing master assigns tasks to "each" slave to perform in his absence (Mark 13:34; Luke 19:13; Matt 25:14b-15). In the Q parable, the assignment is to increase the money entrusted to the slaves; in Mark, it is to do some unspecified task. It is striking that these work assignments in Mark 13:34 play no role in the admonitory elaboration of the parable in Mark 13:35–37, where only the motif of watching is emphasized. Equally striking is the fact that the "doorkeeper" seems like an addition to Mark 13:34, both grammatically and thematically, but it is the doorkeeper who is necessary to the admonitory elaboration in 13:35–37. So Mark 13:34 seems to contain a parable which may be related to the parable in Q 19:12–27. This is not to be taken to mean that Mark depended upon the Q parable, however, because the parallel is only to the very beginning of the Q parable (19:12–13).

18. See Kloppenborg, Q Parallels, 136.

Crossan, however, asserts that Luke 12:35–38 contains the "debris" of the doorkeeper parable also found in Mark 13:33–37, and that Matt 24:42 and Did 16:1 are even more fragmentary versions of the same parable.[19] Crossan does not deal with the relationship between Luke 12:35–38 and the Q parable in 19:12–27. Instead, he treats the differences between Mark 13:33–37 and Luke 12:35–38, which one might see as evidence of a relationship to Q 19:12–27, simply as less primitive features of a basic doorkeeper story. So for Crossan the marriage feast of Luke is to be preferred to Mark's journey setting, Mark's single servant to Luke's plural servants, and the time of the return in Luke to that of Mark. Neither does Crossan speculate as to why Matthew would have eliminated the sayings attested in Luke 12:35–38, if indeed they were in Q. It is sometimes argued that Matthew omitted these sayings and used instead a related but longer unit, Matt 25:1–13. However, this is at best only a possibility.

Crossan argues further that Luke 12:35–38 should be assigned to Q. The primary observation upon which this claim is based is the formal parallelism between Luke 12:35–38 and 12:42–46, namely the unusual insertion of a beatitude into the middle of a parable.[20] Since the parallel to Luke 12:42–46 in Matt 24:45–51 has a beatitude inserted into a parable, this pattern must have been in Q. Second, Crossan takes Matt 24:42 to be a brief, aphoristic version of the parable in Luke 12:35–36, 38a. This means that each unit in Luke 12:35–46 has a parallel in Matthew (Luke 12:35–38//Matt 24:42; Luke 12:39–40//Matt 24:43–44; Luke 12:42–46//Matt 24:45–51), and they are in the same sequence. Crossan offers a third observation as well. Luke 12:35–38 also has a parallel in Did 16:1, and again the version in the Didache is a brief, aphoristic version of Luke 12:35–38. What is striking about the Did 16:1 parallel is that it is the only instance of a saying in the Didache which is attested only in the special Lukan material. In this instance, Crossan agrees with Richard Glover that the source of this saying must have been Q.[21]

Other reasons, in addition to those adduced by Crossan for assigning Luke 12:35–38 to Q, may also be noted. That these verses are not simply Lukan redaction is suggested both by the parallel to 12:35 in Did 16:1 and by the fact, noted by I. Howard Marshall, that the verses betray features not typical of Luke: the use of "truly" ($\dot{a}\mu\dot{\eta}\nu$) in 12:37, the "Semitizing style," and the use in 12:38 of the Jewish system for reckoning time.[22] Francis W. Beare has called attention to the likelihood that "servant" ($\delta o\hat{v}\lambda os$) is a catchword linking the various sayings in 12:35–38, which suggests that they were part of one source.[23] Finally, the introductory "but know" (. . . $\delta\grave{\epsilon}\ \gamma\iota\nu\dot{\omega}\sigma\kappa\epsilon\tau\epsilon$) attested in both Luke 12:39 and Matt 24:43 makes more sense as a transition from Luke

19. Crossan, *In Parables*, 99; *In Fragments*, 59.
20. Crossan, *In Fragments*, 58.
21. Crossan, *In Fragments*, 59.
22. Marshall, *Luke*, 536–37.
23. Beare, *Earliest Records*, 169.

12:35–38 (as a Q passage) than as a transition from Q 12:33–34. Taken together, these observations suggest that Luke 12:35–38 should be assigned to Q.

If we maintain that Luke 12:35–38 was in Q, then we need to note further that redactional levels can be discerned within this pericope. As Crossan notes, we have here a parable (Q 12:35–36, 38a) and a beatitude (12:37) chiastically expanded in 12:38b.[24] After each beatitude is a statement beginning, "I tell you." This combination is also found in Q 10:23–24, but nowhere else in the New Testament. This gives added reason for assigning Luke 12:37 to Q, although it is certainly possible, if not probable, that Lukan redaction is also present here (cf. Luke 17:8; 22:27). In any case, the beatitudes in Luke 12:37 and in 12:43 probably represent later additions in Q. The first beatitude (12:37a) does not add substantially to the sayings in 12:35–36. The purpose of the "I tell you" saying which follows in 12:37b is not clear; if it is meant as an allusion to an eschatological meal, then it is at best a rather clumsy addition. The meal is served wherever the servants are presumed to be, and the servants must admit the master to the place where the meal is to be held! It may be that the beatitudes were added in order to elaborate on the idea of having one's heart focused on the right object (Q 12:34) by stressing constant vigilance.

An earlier level of Q redaction is encounted in Q 12:39–40. Kloppenborg has argued that Q 12:40 must be a later addition to 12:39,[25] but it must already have been added before 12:39–40 was joined to 12:42–46 because the basis for joining the latter to the former is found in 12:40 (cf. 12:46), not 12:39.[26] The parousia at this level (that is, Q 12:40) is of the "son of man," and it is portrayed as rather ominous, like a thief in the night.

The original core of this unit was Q 12:39. This saying occurs without the parousia interpretation in GThom 21, and in a somewhat different version (as a beatitude) in GThom 103. The comparison of the parousia to the intrusion of a thief was widespread in the early church; versions of it also occur in 1 Thess 5:2; 2 Pet 3:10; Rev 3:3; and Rev 16:15. It is unclear whether this early and widespread tradition prompted the interpretation of the parable in Q by the addition of Q 12:40, or whether Q itself lay at the basis of this development.

It is important to note that a catchword connection exists between Q 12:39 and 12:33, namely "thief" ($\kappa\lambda\acute{\epsilon}\pi\tau\eta\varsigma$) and perhaps also "dig through" ($\delta\iota\sigma\rho\acute{\upsilon}\sigma\sigma\epsilon\iota\nu$), though the latter wording is attested only by Matthew (10:43). Thus, Luke 12:35, which I have assigned to Q, must have been added to Q at a point

---

24. Crossan, *In Fragments*, 58–59.

25. Kloppenborg, *Formation*, 149. Fleddermann ("Householder," 24) notes that the parable indicates that one cannot know when a thief will come, so one can do nothing; but the application insists one must be ready.

26. Kloppenborg, *Formation*, 149–50. Fleddermann ("Householder," 25) takes the opposite approach: Q 12:40 was formulated as an introduction to 12:42–46.

when Q 12:34 was directly followed by 12:39.[27] Very likely the same redaction is responsible both for the parallel structure in 12:35–38 and 12:42–46 and for the transitional phrase in 12:39, "but know this. . . ." No doubt other changes were made as well, perhaps including the addition of Q 12:40. However, at this point, the redactional history of Q becomes murkier and it is difficult to see deeper into the layers of redaction.

Luke has provided a question in 12:41 which provides a transition from Q 12:39–40 to 12:42–46. The answer to the question, however, is not fully given until Luke 12:47–48. There is thus no reason to suppose that Luke 12:41 belonged in Q.[28]

In Q 12:42–46 we again have a parable followed by a beatitude, an "I tell you" saying, and a warning. The beatitude and the "I tell you" saying have the faithful servant rewarded by being placed over all the master's possessions. The beatitudes in Luke 12:37 and 43 and the "I tell you" sayings which follow go beyond the exhortation to be ready for an unexpected master; both hold out a reward for faithfulness. But unfaithfulness appears to be the greater concern, as can be seen both by the length of the saying (Q 12:45–46) and by its severity. It is difficult to imagine to what circumstances Q 12:45–46 might refer. It is unlikely that it is directed against violence or dissipation within the community—problems not mentioned elsewhere in Q. The beating of slaves calls to mind instead the violence of "this generation" against God's messengers (e.g., in Q 11:49–51), while dissipation calls to mind the behavior of "this generation" condemned in the Q "apocalypse" (17:27). Correspondingly, the reward to the faithful in Q 12:44 probably has its closest parallel in Q 22:28–30. In other words, Q 12:42–46 appears to be aimed at Israel, and to distinguish the "faithful and wise servant" (no doubt the Q group) from their faithless detractors. It thus appears that a warning which is thematically consonant with the deuteronomistic tradition has been adapted to later eschatological concerns, especially the delay of the parousia. It may be noted that the excuse that the master is delayed (Q 12:45) is hardly reason to beat one's follow servants, and thus appears to be foreign to its context; however, the delay as such need be no later addition, since the slave must be given time to exhibit faithless behavior so as to reap the storyteller's censure.[29]

The analysis above suggests that three stages in the compositional history of Q are discernible here: (a) an early stage when Q 12:33 and 12:39 were directly attached, (b) a later stage when Luke (=Q) 12:35–38 was added, and (c) a stage

27. The catchword connection between 12:33 and 12:39 renders problematic Kloppenborg's assignnment of 12:33–34 to the later, apocalypticized recension (*Formation*, 20 n. 11).

28. However, Crossan "rather tentatively" assigns Luke 12:41 to Q (*In Fragments*, 60).

29. Scott treats this parable as one of a group of patron and client parables, and more specifically one of several parables of departure and return. He notes the motif common to these that "the master's departure is the occasion for a test of the servant" (*Hear Then the Parable*, 211).

when 12:39 and 12:42–46 were added. It was only at this last stage that the
delay of the parousia of the son of man made its appearance.

Not Peace but a Sword (Q 12:49–53)

Luke 12:49–53	Matt 10:34–36
⁴⁹I came to cast fire upon the earth, and how I wish it were already kindled! ⁵⁰I have a baptism in which to be baptized, and how I am stifled until it is accomplished! ⁵¹Do you think that I came to give peace on the earth? No! I tell you, but rather dissension.	³⁴Do not think that I came to scatter peace upon the earth. I did not come to scatter peace but a sword.
⁵²For from henceforth five will be in dissension in one house, three being divided against two and two against three,	
⁵³father against son and son against father, mother against daughter and daughter against mother, mother-in-law against her daughter-in-law and daughter-in-law against the mother-in-law.	³⁵For I came to divide a man against his father, and a daughter against her mother, and a daughter-in-law against her mother-in-law. ³⁶And a person's enemies will be members of his household.

Luke 12:49 has no parallel in Matthew, so it is questionable whether it
belongs in Q at all. So striking is the similarity between this saying and Matt
10:34 (=Luke 12:51), however, that two assessments seem justified: (a) Luke
12:49 was in Q, and (b) Luke is responsible for the wording of Luke 12:51. In
the case of the latter, Matthew's "Do not think..." ($\mu\dot\eta$ $\nu o\mu\dot\iota\sigma\eta\tau\epsilon$) may not be Q
(cf. Matt 5:17), but it seems clear that Luke's "Do you think..." ($\delta o\kappa\epsilon\hat\iota\tau\epsilon$) is
Lukan redaction, as is "I came" ($\pi a\rho\epsilon\gamma\epsilon\nu\acute o\mu\eta\nu$ instead of $\hat\eta\lambda\theta o\nu$) and "give"
($\delta o\hat\upsilon\nu a\iota$) instead of "scatter" ($\beta a\lambda\epsilon\hat\iota\nu$). And yet one cannot depend entirely on
the Matthean wording either, given the similarity of Matt 10:34 to 5:17.

The connection between Q 12:49–53 and what precedes it is probably not
just topical. The verb "to come" ($\check\epsilon\rho\chi\epsilon\sigma\theta a\iota$) appears as a kind of leitmotiv (Q
12:39, 40, 43, 45 [?], 49), and perhaps "cut in two" ($\delta\iota\chi o\tau o\mu\epsilon\hat\iota\nu$) in Q 12:46 was
associated with "divide" ($\delta\iota\chi\acute a\zeta\epsilon\iota\nu$) in Matt 10:35 (=Q 12:53). Luke 12:50 has a
rough parallel in Mark 10:38, and thus could be from Mark. But Q 12:51 is
formulated in antithesis to 12:49, so that Luke 12:50 seems like an intrusion.

Kloppenborg, who also regards this verse as Lukan, compares it in terms of function to Luke 17:25.[30]

The rest of the unit, namely Q 12:51–53, presents some other problems. In particular, Luke 12:52 has no parallel in Matthew. Yet, since it is independently attested in GThom 16, it is probably not Lukan, and thus can be assigned to Q with some probability. Q 12:53 is based on Mic 7:6, and 12:52 presupposes this allusion. But its wording is somewhat suspect, especially the important temporal note, "from henceforth" (ἀπὸ τοῦ νῦν; cf. Luke 1:48; 5:10).

This is a particularly telling text. The admonition, "Do not think that I have come to bring peace on earth," suggests that some people thought that Jesus' mission was to bring peace. If we ask who might have construed Jesus' mission as a mission of peace, we have to look no further than the Q group itself. There is certainly a great deal in the Q tradition, especially in Jesus' inaugural sermon, which would support such an interpretation. But now this interpretation, that Jesus came to bring peace, is being rejected. We seem to encounter a stage of the tradition where the peaceful interpretation of Jesus' mission has proven no longer useful.

There is, in fact, a curious relationship between this text and the mission discourse in Q 10:2–16.[31] There, the "laborers" are to say "peace to you" to each "house." Yet the mission discourse is redacted in such a way as to put particular emphasis upon the division that occurs, so much so that I have already proposed calling that pericope not a mission discourse but an "errand of judgment." Q 12:54–56 coheres remarkably well with 10:2–16, and thus probably represents the same redactional layer. But beyond that, Q 12:54–56 reveals an important division within the Q community, between those who emphasize Jesus' mission as peaceful (and who probably use the Sermon on the Plain/Mount as their text), and those who see his mission rather as the winnowing of wheat from chaff, the separation of the righteous from sinners. Here, indeed, may be evidence of a basic change within the Q community. This might explain why the Sermon on the Mount was preserved as a separate entity, then edited in Q into the larger context of John's and Jesus' confrontation with "this generation." It is unclear what caused this reinterpretation of the earlier message of peace, but it probably has little to do with the question of war or guerilla movements versus pacifism. The following verse (Q 12:53) makes it plain that the issue concerns peace versus division within families.

It will be recalled that the Q "mission discourse" was subjected to a deuteronomistic redaction in which the "mission" became one of separating the righteous from the unrighteous. But this redaction was performed on material already existing, material which called for an austere, itinerant life-

---

30. Kloppenborg, *Formation*, 151 n. 213.
31. Note that Matthew includes this text in his larger mission discourse.

style, but which also entailed an explicit message of peace (Q 10:5–6). At this earlier stage, rejection of the laborers and their greeting of peace was not to be met with any vindictive act, but simply with abandonment of the rejectors. The redaction, however, severely condemned those who reject the messengers. The conclusion emerges that (a) reflected in the earlier level of the Q "mission discourse" is precisely the sort of orientation to peace which seems presupposed in Q 12:51, and (b) a reinterpretation of the failure of this mission under the influence of the deuteronomistic tradition took place. That has probably happened also in Q 12:51, 53. Here, however, what is reinterpreted is the itinerant lifestyle and the tensions within families that it must have entailed: these tensions are now seen as something inevitable, as part of a divine separation of the righteous and the unrighteous. Thus, Q 12:51, 53 may be assigned to the deuteronomistic redaction of Q.

The fact that the Sermon is included in Q probably means that it was taken over and claimed by the same group which had earlier treated the Sermon as the gospel of peace. That is, we are dealing not with two successive groups but with one group which experienced an internal transformation, retaining its old gospel (the Sermon) and putting it into a new context.

Interpreting the Times (Q 12:54–56)

Luke 12:54–56	Matt 16:2–3
[54]And he also said to the crowds,	[2]And answering he said to them,
"When you see a cloud	"When evening comes,
rising in the west,	
immediately you say,	you say,
'A rainstorm is coming,'	'Fair weather, for the sky is red.'
and so it happens.	
[55]And when the south wind is blowing,	[3]And in the morning,'It will be stormy,
you say, 'There will be scorching heat,'	for the sky is fiery and overcast.'
and so it happens.	
[56]Hypocrites!	
You know how to read	You know how to interpret
the face of the earth and the sky,	the face of the sky,
but you do not know how	but you are not able
to read this present time?"	to interpret the signs of the times?"

Since many early manuscripts lack Matt 16:2–3, serious questions may be raised about its inclusion in Q. However, Crossan has shown how improbable these verses are as scribal insertions, and therefore affirms that this text was not a later addition.[32]

Matthew has placed these sayings in a Markan context (Matt 16:1–4//Mark 8:11–13), and thus has not preserved the Q context. The catchword link

---

32. Crossan, *In Fragments*, 247–48.

between Matt 16:1 and 16:2–3 ("heaven," οὐρανός), noted by Polag[33] and Crossan,[34] is intriguing. Nevertheless, it is very odd to have Jesus refer to weather conditions in response to a request for a "sign from heaven." If one could find other instances of such ironic editing in Matthew, one might be inclined to attribute it to sheer editorial playfulness. Indeed, there is some evidence of deliberate playfulness: the Matthean version differs from the Lukan in speaking only of sky conditions, whereas Luke mentions the "south wind" and later speaks of "earth [with its wind] and sky [with the rain-bearing clouds from the west]." That is, the Matthean sky-oriented version has been made to correspond more directly to the introductory "sign from heaven" mentioned in 16:1. So it appears that we have no mere catchword link but a play on "a sign from heaven." The logical connection, however, is so obscure that one can understand the scribal solution—simply to omit the offending verses—as in Vaticanus, Sinaiticus, and other manuscripts.

The verbal agreement between Matthew and Luke in these sayings is not great. Evidence of Matthean redaction is present ("when evening comes," ὀψίας γενομένης, and "signs," σημεῖα). However, clear evidence of Lukan redaction is hard to find. It is hardly likely that Luke deliberately introduced this text at this point, so poorly does it fit. Luke has solved the problem of discontinuity between 12:51–53 and 12:54–56 by a simple expedient: he understands these words as addressed to a different audience, the uncomprehending "crowds" (12:54). The vocative, "hypocrites!" (ὑποκριταί), has perhaps been added to strengthen that interpretation, though it is hardly appropriate here because the ability to predict weather, in contrast to inability to understand the present, is scant evidence of hypocrisy!

Given the interpretation of Q 12:49–53 suggested above, Q 12:54–56 also needs to be seen in a new light. It can, at least, be interpreted as a rebuke to members of the community who fail to grasp that "new occasions teach new duties," that the situation of division must be seen not as the failure of the gospel of peace, since Jesus did not, after all, come to bring peace.[35] On this interpretation, Luke has misinterpreted the text by having it directed to outsiders, "the crowds."

Handling Accusers (Q 12:58–59)

Luke 12:58–59	Matt 5:25–26
[58]For as you go with your accuser before a magistrate,	[25]Make friends with your accuser quickly,
on the way	while you are on the way with him,
try to get him to drop the charges,	
lest you be dragged before the judge,	lest the accuser hand you over to the judge

33. Polag, *Christologie*, 66–67.
34. Crossan, *In Fragments*, 249.
35. On how Q 12:54–56 "works," see Tannehill, *Sword*, 128–34.

and the judge hand you over	and the judge
to the bailiff	to the assistant,
and the bailiff throw you into prison.	and you be thrown into prison.
[59]I say to you,	[26]Truly, I say to you,
you will not get out of there	you will not get out of there
until you have paid back	until you have paid back
the last little coin.	the last cent.

Q 12:58–59 is an ill-fitting sequel to 12:54–56; it is linked neither by catchword nor by theme. Moreover, Q 12:54–56 is in the plural, whereas 12:58–59 uses the second person singular. So the location of this pericope within Q is a puzzle which the evangelists do not help us to solve. Nevertheless, Luke is the more likely to have preserved the text in its Q context. By his context Matthew indicates how he understands this admonition, namely as an injunction to reconcile oneself with others. He apparently wished to complement the saying about reconciliation with the brother in 5:21–22 by adding the admonition about handling one's accuser. The text, however, is not an apt example of reconciliation. It is strictly prudential advice to debtors. Luke, on the other hand, has simply attached 12:57–59 to 12:54–56, assuming it to be accusatory speech consistent in tone with 12:56. Luke therefore adds the question in 12:57 ("And why do you not judge for yourselves what is right?"), which implies that the hearers cannot, in fact, judge what is "right" or "just" ($\tau\grave{o}$ $\delta\acute{\iota}\kappa\alpha\iota\upsilon\upsilon$). So Luke, unlike Matthew, finds no positive message in this parable, and treats it instead as accusatory speech.

The admonition is expanded dramatically, and clinched with a warning. Considering the mundane point, the dramatic expansion seems overly elaborate: the accuser will hand you over to the judge, the judge to the bailiff, and the bailiff will throw you into prison. And yet the phrase "on the way" suggests just such a progression. The reason for this progression is rhetorical. The fact that things go from bad to worse makes the point very clearly: the earlier one reaches agreement the better. The progression strengthens rhetorically the force of the injunction by forcing the hearer to visualize each fateful step, each consequence of inaction. Not until the end of the saying is it clear that the presumed "you" who has been put into prison is a debtor: he won't get out until he pays the last little copper coin. So the release "on the way" is a reprieve from debt. One is enjoined to work out a payment schedule with one's creditor now; if not, one will have to pay anyway, but from jail. This small pericope probably was not intended simply as an injunction to debtors to settle up before they started down the slippery slope to ruin. Rather it was intended to be metaphorical, and Luke has correctly sensed that it should be treated as a rebuke for failure to understand what is going on. Therefore, it is functionally consistent with Q 12:54–56.[36]

The analysis thus far indicates that Q 12:49–53 as well as 12:54–56 should

---

36. See Dodd, *Parables*, 105–8.

be assigned to the deuteronomistic redaction of Q. We have seen, further, that Q 12:40, 42–46 were post-deuteronomistic additions to Q. This means that prior to the deuteronomistic redaction, the next previous material before Q 12:58–59 was 12:39. Indeed, a catchword connection exists between Q 12:39 and 12:58–59, namely "watch" or "prison" ($\phi\upsilon\lambda\alpha\kappa\acute{\eta}$).[37]

Mustard Seed and Leaven (Q 13:18–19, 20–21)

Luke 13:18–19, 20–21	Matt 13:31–32, 33
[18]He said therefore,	[31]Another parable he put before them,
"To what is the kingdom of God similar	"The kingdom of heaven is similar to
and to what may it be compared?	
[19]It is like	
a grain of mustard seed	a grain of mustard seed
which a person took	which a person took
and threw into his garden,	and sowed in his field,
	[32]that is the smallest of all seeds,
and it grew	but when it has grown
	is the largest of herbs
and became a tree,	and becomes a tree,
and the birds of the heaven	so that the birds of the heaven
nested in its branches."	come and nest in its branches."
[20]And again he said,	[33]He told them another parable:
"To what will I compare	
the kingdom of God?	
[21]It is like leaven	"The kingdom of heaven is like leaven
which a woman having taken hid	which a woman having taken hid
in three measures [a bushel] of wheat	in three measures [a bushel] of wheat flour
until it was all leavened."	until it was all leavened."

Here we have the paired parables of the mustard seed and the leaven. Verbal agreements between Matthew and Luke in the case of the mustard seed parable are few, yet they are striking enough to make it highly probable that the parable, also attested in Mark 4:30–32 and GThom 20, was in Q. As for the parable of the leaven, there can be no doubt that it was in Q. The fact, moreover, that these parables are linked both by Matthew and by Luke makes their derivation from Q virtually certain. A catchword also joins these parables to the previous pericope, namely "throw" ($\beta\acute{\alpha}\lambda\lambda\epsilon\iota\nu$).

The parallels between the parables of the mustard seed and leaven are several: both are parables of the kingdom; both involve growth; both contain the phrase "which a person/a woman took . . ."; both involve the act of placing one thing into another; and both involve exaggerated amounts (tree, bushel of flour). Whether they are meant to interpret each other, however, is uncertain.

---

37. Only Matthew attests $\phi\upsilon\lambda\alpha\kappa\acute{\eta}$ for Q 12:39 (=Matt 24:43), but it is highly likely that Matthew's wording is that of Q. Luke has assimilated 12:39 to 12:40 by substituting "hour" for "watch" (Schulz, *Q*, 268).

The fact that the parallelism breaks down—one can expand on "tree" in a way one cannot on "bushel of flour"—suggests at least that the two parables have different origins.

Each parable has one or more features which distort reality. Only a single mustard seed is planted, which is odd. Even more odd, this tiny seed becomes a "tree" ($\delta\acute{\epsilon}\nu\delta\rho\sigma\nu$) in which birds come to nest. In the case of the parable of the leaven, the odd and perhaps telling note is that the leaven is "hidden," though the amount of flour leavened is also very large. In the parable of the mustard seed, the image of the tree is almost certainly a traditional one. As Nils A. Dahl has noted, "the figure of the great tree giving shelter to the birds of the air is a traditional picture of a great kingdom," for example in Dan 4:11, 18 (Theod 4:12, 21); Ezek 31:6; Judg 9:15; Lam 4:20; Bar 1:12; and Sir 14:26.[38] The parable picks up this traditional image, but twists and plays with it by claiming that this great "tree" has grown from a single mustard seed. The point of the parable has to do with the almost comic disparity between the minuscule mustard seed and the great "tree." Since the tree was a traditional symbol for a great kingdom, it is quite natural that the "kingdom of God" is likened to a tree. What is said of this tree is that the birds of the air make nests in its branches. Possibly these birds are gentiles, who find refuge in God's kingdom.[39] But whoever it is that finds refuge in the kingdom, the image itself is appropriate in the context of Q, because in only a few verses we will be told that "people will come from east and west [and north and south] and sit at table in the kingdom of God" (Q 13:29). A similar point was made in Q 11:52. It is important to underline this proximity in Q of the mustard seed and the leaven parables (Q 13:18–21) to the saying about the streaming in of people to sit at table in the kingdom of God (13:28–29). Only a few verses intervene, namely Q 13:24–26, and they dwell on the same theme.

What then is the point of the parable? It is to assert that the hoped-for kingdom, to which diaspora Jews (or perhaps gentiles) will come streaming, is present even now but in almost unrecognizable insignificance. The Q people are probably the mustard seed which will become a tree; they are the kingdom.

A thematic relationship may be noted between Q 12:49–56 and 13:18–21. In the former, the existence of painful divisions within families is reinterpreted. It is not a sign of the failure of the gospel of peace. Rather, the gospel of peace had been misunderstood; precisely this division within families was intended by Jesus. Next, those who misconstrue the present time are rebuked. They can tell what weather is brewing, but they cannot discern what is going on in the present social context. The parable of the mustard seed continues this explication of the real meaning of the present. Hidden but active in the present is none other than the kingdom of God.

The parable of the leaven makes a similar point. The odd feature here too is the contrast between the small handful of sourdough ("leaven") and the huge

38. Dahl, "Parables of Growth," 147.
39. Manson (*Teaching*, 133 n. 1) cites 1 Enoch 90:30, 33, 37, and the midrash on Ps 104:12.

To the Community 205

amount of flour into which it is mixed. The contrast is what is in focus here. A tiny amount, apparently insignificant, indeed something reckoned to be an agent of putrefaction,[40] transforms a huge mass of dough into the staff of life. Not only is the contrast made between an insignificant thing and the daunting size of the end result, but the suggestion is made that something very small can transform the larger mass, a point not made by the parable of the mustard seed. Further, the paradox that something one associates with putrefaction is able to lead to life-giving bread reminds one of the similarly paradoxical effect of the Jesus movement, which causes division within the society and yet is the kingdom hidden in the present. It seems likely therefore that Q 13:18-21 belongs to the deuteronomistic redaction of Q.

Who Is In and Who Is Out? (Q 13:24-30)

Luke 13:24-30	Matt 7:13-14, 22-23; 25:10b-12; 8:11-12; 19:30//20:16
[24]Struggle to enter through the narrow door, for	[13]Enter through the narrow gate; for wide is the gate and commodious the road which ushers into destruction,
many, I tell you, are seeking to enter	and many are those entering through it. [14]For narrow is the gate and crowded the road that ushers into life,
and are not able. [25]When once the master of the house has risen and closed the door, then you will begin to stand outside the door and to knock on the door saying, "Sir, open to us!" And answering, he will say to you,	and few are those finding it. 25[10b]and the door was shut. [11]And later the remaining virgins come saying "Sir! sir! Open to us!" [12]But answering, he says, "Truly I say to you,
"I do not know where you are from." [26]Then you will begin to say, "We ate in your presence and we drank, and you taught in our streets." [27]But he will speak, saying to you, you,	'I do not know you.'" 7[22]Many will say to me in that day, "Sir! sir! Did we not prophesy in your name and cast out demons in your name, and do many miracles in your name?" [23]And then I will announce to them,

40. The ceremonial prohibition of leaven (Exod 12:15-20) suggests that leaven (i.e., sourdough) was regarded as an agent of corruption, fermentation being a form of corruption. See Mitton, "Leaven," 339-40. This view of leaven lies behind its metaphorical use in Mark 8:15 par.; Matt 16:11-12; 1 Cor 5:6-8; Gal 5:9; Justin *Dial.* 14.2; Ps.-Clem. *Hom.* 8.17. The point is made clearly by Plutarch: leaven is "from corruption" (ἐκ φθορᾶς) and it "corrupts" the dough (*Roman Questions* 289F; cf. *Table Talk* 659B).

"I do not know where you are from.	"I have never known you!
Depart from me	Depart from me,
all workers of injustice!	you who produce lawlessness!"
28There will be weeping	811I say to you
and gnashing of teeth	that many from east and west
when you see	will be present and they will recline
Abraham and Isaac and Jacob	with Abraham and Isaac and Jacob
and all the prophets	
in the kingdom of God,	in the kingdom of the heavens.
but you are thrown out."	
29And they will be present	
from the east and west	12But the sons of the kingdom
and from north and south,	will be thrown into the outer darkness.
and they will recline	In that place there will be weeping
in the kingdom of God.	and gnashing of teeth.
30And behold,	
there are last ones who will be first,	
and there are first ones who will be last.	1930But many of the first will be last,
	2016So the last will be first and the first last.

Once the parables of the mustard seed and the leaven are placed in their Q contexts and interpreted accordingly, the logical connection to the next verse in Q 13:24 becomes evident. For there the idea of "entering" suddenly surfaces. One will certainly think of "entering" the kingdom, which is the subject at hand. Indeed, this becomes inevitable when, in Q 13:28–29, we hear of people streaming into the kingdom.

This is a puzzling group of sayings. The initial problem is whether they constituted a unit in Q. The parallels in Matthew are certainly striking; but they are also random, scattered over four different chapters; but the question whether this material was in Q cannot be solved simply by examining parallels. The literary integrity of the material in Luke must be carefully studied to determine whether we are dealing with Lukan redaction or with a composition available to him basically as we have it. If we are dealing with a pre-Lukan sayings composition rather than Lukan redaction, then we must accept the weight of the Matthean parallels and assign the material to Q.

In Luke, there are two units of material: an admonition in 13:24 and a form-critically odd unit in 13:25–30, which begins like a parable, but then quickly shifts to dialogue in direct speech. Both parts of Q 13:25–30 deal with the same theme: some are allowed in while others are excluded.

The admonition in Luke 13:24 shares only a few words with Matt 7:13–14, and the sayings are different in many details; yet they are recognizably the same material.[41] Matthew's version consists of an injunction followed by two

---

41. *Pace* Schulz, *Q*, 424. The words "and shut the door" are echoed in Matt 25:10. "Where you come from" in 13:35 is probably a Lukan addition; see Koester, *Synoptische Überlieferungen*, 83. The second half of 13:25 is clearly from Q. I do not think that the saying in Luke 13:25 is a fragment of a Q parable more fully developed in Matt 25:1–13.

parallel reasons. It envisions two paths, probably paths leading out of, or perhaps into, a city. The gate opening up to one path is narrow, the other wide. Correspondingly, the first road is commodious while the second is narrow and constricted. The first road leads to destruction, the second to life. And yet the problem seems not to be that many choose the commodious path, but rather that few can "find" the "life" to which the narrow road leads. The Matthean version prepares us for a conclusion different from the one we get, because it encourages us to suppose that most people choose the spacious, easy road instead of the difficult, narrow road. Therefore, "those who find it are few" comes as a surprise, even though it balances "those who enter by it are many" in 7:13. These internal tensions are probably the product of Matthean redaction: Matthew has adapted the Q saying to his contrast of "many/few" (Matt 22:14; cf. 7:22; 8:11). Probably the common Jewish and later Christian "Two Ways" metaphor, with its accompanying moralism, has imposed itself on the saying.

Luke is unable to see any connection between the saying (13:24) and the preceding parables (13:18–21), and so has added his own introduction (13:22–23). Luke sets up the admonition in 13:24 by having "someone" ask Jesus, as he travels toward Jerusalem, "Sir, will those who are saved be few?" Luke envisions not a narrow gate but a narrow door. And, unlike Matthew, he affirms that many try to enter it and fail. Entering is a struggle, so Luke has inserted the imperative, "Struggle to enter. . . ." We are not told why the many are unable to enter. Luke's version shows signs of his redactional activity, and yet it is probably closer to Q than is Matt 7:13–14.[42]

The construction of the Greek in Luke 13:25–26 is certainly problematic. It appears to be one sentence whose apodosis begins either with "(then) he will answer you" in v. 25, or with "then you will begin to say" in v. 26. But this difficulty, which does not substantially affect the interpretation of the saying, is not the only problem here. Equally puzzling is the transition from third person description ("When once the householder has risen and closed the door") to direct address in v. 25 ("then you will begin to stand outside . . ."). More consistent stylistically is Matthew, who has parabolic description without the odd transition to direct speech (Matt 25:1–13), while keeping in direct speech what it makes sense to have in direct speech (Matt 7:22–23). The sheer difficulty of the Lukan version argues for its originality vis-à-vis Matthew.

The Lukan version, however, has a certain logic to it. The master of the house shuts the door, apparently, when he knows all the guests have arrived. Others seek to get in but the master of the house will not acknowledge them. They appeal to him on the basis of their earlier companionship with the

---

42. "We ate . . . and we drank" in 13:26 is attested in Justin (*1 Apol.* 16.9; *Dial.* 76.5), but this is not independent attestation. However, 13:27 is independently attested in 2 Clem 4:5b. Koester (*Synoptische Überlieferungen*, 84–85) is probably correct that, in Q, 13:27b was an exact citation of Ps 6:9 LXX, which both Matthew and Luke altered.

master of the house, who is now intended to be none other than Jesus. The master of the house again rebukes the unwanted guests, this time more severely and with the epithet, "producers of lawlessness!" The next verses (13:28–30) continue this rebuke. At the same time, Luke 13:28–29 implies that the house of which Jesus is master is really the "kingdom of God." Luke 13:28 implies, given its present context, that the unwanted guests can peer into the house and see Abraham, Isaac and Jacob in the house/kingdom. The "you yourselves" who are thrown out must be other Jews who thought that they would enter the kingdom.[43] Worse, others—outsiders (gentiles?)—will stream in from east and west and sit at table in the kingdom.

The fact that Luke has treated these sayings as parts of a single unit (13:25–30) suggests that he found them as a unit, even though the connections among them are not very good. It is easy to understand why Matthew took them as discrete sayings which could be used to better advantage in different contexts. But despite their hard connections they probably belonged together in Q. Especially striking is the nice irony that those who claim to have eaten and drunk with Jesus before are now excluded from the house, and thus from the meal. Likewise, those who claim to have heard his teaching are derided as "producers of lawlessness."

However, Q 13:28–29 is inappropriate in this context because it is addressed more widely to Israel in general, or more precisely to "this generation."[44] It appears to be a later addition, one which reinterprets the parable of the banquet as applying to the failure of Israel to respond to the Q mission.[45] It invokes the deuteronomistic tradition, according to which Israel's election is not unconditional: if Israel does not obey, God will turn away from her. But the prophetic oracle in 13:28–29 is also appropriate at this point in that it trades upon the meal image, only now it is the eschatological meal "in the kingdom of God."[46] The addition of 13:28–29 may have been accompanied by alterations in 13:25–27 and its attendant problems.

Reflected in this pericope seems to be division within the Q community or within the Jesus movement. At issue is the question of the boundaries of the movement—who is in and who is out. Some claim to have been companions of Jesus and to have heard him teach (13:26). It is implied—in fact, charged—that they are hypocrites because they are "producers of lawlessness." A similar problem in the community is reflected in Q 6:46, and it forms the substance of John's preaching in Q 3:7–9.

43. In Matthew (7:22) they are Christians who prophesied and did miracles in Jesus' name.
44. The words "this generation" do not occur, but since the patriarchs (and all the prophets) are at the banquet, we may take it that the excluded ones are "this generation."
45. The parallel to Q 13:28–29 in 5 Ezra 1:38–40 is striking. Although often taken to be a Christian writing, 5 Ezra may be pre-Christian; see the discussion of 13:34–35. If 5 Ezra 1:38–40 does not depend on Matthew, Luke, or Q, as I believe probable, then we have striking evidence of a common tradition upon which both 5 Ezra and Q drew.
46. The wording of this oracle is better preserved by Matthew than by Luke. On this see Kloppenborg, *Formation*, 226–27, although "all the prophets" (Luke 12:28) was probably in Q.

Lament over Jerusalem (Q 13:34-35)

Luke 13:34-35	Matt 23:37-39
[34]Jerusalem, Jerusalem,	[37]Jerusalem, Jerusalem,
killing the prophets	killing the prophets
and stoning those sent to her, how often	and stoning those sent to her, how often
I wanted to gather your children	I wanted to gather your children
just as a hen gathers her brood	just as a hen gathers her brood
under her wings,	under her wings,
and you would not.	and you would not.
[35]Behold, your house is left to you.	[38]Behold, your house is left to you,
	a desolation.
And I tell you,	[39]For I tell you,
by no means will you see me	by no means will you see me
until the time comes when you say,	until the time comes when you say,
"Blessed is the one coming	"Blessed is the one coming
in the name of the Lord."	in the name of the Lord."

There are numerous problems in the interpretation of this text: its context in Q; its form; the identity of the speaker or speakers; the unity of the text; its tradition history; its origin; and the meaning of key phrases. Establishing the location of this text in Q is the first difficulty.[47] In Matthew, it directly follows the Wisdom oracle in 23:34-36 (=Q 11:49-51). The themes in it and in 23:37-39 (=Q 13:34-35) are very similar: prophets being sent and killed, and consequences described. And since the speaker in Q 13:34-35 appears to be a suprahistorical figure who, over the centuries, sent many prophets, the connection to the Wisdom oracle would be very good: both would have the same speaker. But there are problems: (a) the vantage point of the speaker in Q 11:49-51 is the dawn of time, looking into the future, while the speaker in 13:34-35 looks back from the present into the past[48]; (b) the threats issued are very different: a bloody recompense to be exacted from "this generation" in Q 11:49-51,[49] and the abandonment of "your house" in 13:34-35; and (c) the addressees are different: "this generation" in Q 11:49-51 and Jerusalem in 13:34-35.

On the other hand, Luke's location for the text is problematic. Conzelmann has noted how Luke constructed his journey to Jerusalem and passion motifs,[50] and hence that redactional activity is evident. For Luke the oracle in 13:34-35 is a prediction by Jesus of the fate to befall Jerusalem as a result of her failure to recognize the "time of her visitation" (Luke 19:39-44). Luke's

47. The options are discussed in Schulz, *Q*, 347-48 n. 184; Steck, *Israel*, 45-46; Kloppenborg, *Q Parallels*, 158; Suggs, *Wisdom*, 64-66; and Garland, *Intention*, 187-97.

48. Haenchen, "Matthäus 23," 47.

49. Garland (*Intention*, 195), rightly noting differences in emotional tone (anger in 11:49-51, sorrow in 13:34-35), also draws attention to the call for "active revenge" in 11:49-51 in contrast to "passive abandonment" in 13:34-35.

50. Conzelmann, *St. Luke*, 63-65, 132-35, 139.

redactional activity is also evident in his insertion of 13:31-33. For Luke, the cry, "Blessed is the one coming in the name of the Lord" (13:35b), looks ahead to Jesus' triumphal entry into Jerusalem (Luke 19:28-38). All this does not prove that Luke's location is secondary, however. Indeed, he may have inserted 13:31-33 where he did precisely because he found 13:34-35 at this point in Q, and adapted it to his broader scheme.

Finally, we need to note two other arguments.[51] The first is that Q 13:34-35 can be seen as a fitting sequel to 13:25-29 (30). Q 13:28 refers to "prophets" (the Lukan wording is not echoed by Matthew, but is probably that of Q), and the general context in 13:25-29 is that of a "house." Both of these are found in 13:34-35. Moreover, the deuteronomistic tradition is evident in both 13:25-29 and 13:34-35. Garland also notes the continuity between 13:25-29 and 13:34-35.[52] Second, Garland argues that Luke, in relocating the Q oracle, has violated his journey scheme. The oracle, from Luke's historicizing perspective, is a speech addressed by Jesus to Jerusalem. But Jesus is not yet in Jerusalem. Worse, the oracle assumes that Jesus has been there many times ("how often..."), even though he is still, by Luke's scheme, in Galilee and has not yet been to Jerusalem.[53] We are therefore led to the conclusion that Luke's location of Q 13:34-35 has good claim to be that of Q, though the matter is far from certain.

From a form-critical point of view, Q 13:34-35 is a prophecy of disaster.[54] A prophecy of disaster has typically the following components: (a) introduction; (b) indication of the situation; (c) prediction of disaster; and (d) concluding characterization. These are present in Q 13:34-35 as follows:

(a) introduction	13:34a	"O Jerusalem, Jerusalem ..."
(b) indication of situation	13:34b	"How often I wanted ..."[55]
(c) prediction of disaster	13:35a	"Behold, your house ..."
(d) concluding characterization(?)	13:35b	"And I tell you. ..."

The Q prophetic oracle lacks a formal introduction, but the repeated address, "Jerusalem, Jerusalem," seems to serve one of the functions of the typical introduction, namely to appeal for attention. Although Aune regards Q

---

51. A third additional argument is Sato's claim that 13:28-29 and 13:34-35 are similar in "Gattung" or form; see *Q und Prophetie*, 42.

52. See especially Garland (*Intention*, 193 n. 99) who emphasizes a thematic continuity: the theme of rejection.

53. Garland, *Intention*, 189. Miller ("Rejection of the Prophets in Q," 237) also notes the clumsiness of Luke's location of the text, but does not suspect that this clumsiness is due to Luke's having preserved the oracle in its Q context.

54. On this form see Koch, *Growth of the Biblical Tradition*, 191-94, 210-13; Westermann, *Basic Forms*, 142-63, 169-76; March, "Prophecy," 159-62; and Aune, *Prophecy in Early Christianity*, 92. Miller ("Rejection of the Prophets in Q," 233-34) emphasizes the mixture of traditional prophetic traits with what he calls "innovative Christian" features.

55. The present tense in "is abandoned" (ἀφίεται) seems to have a future sense here (a "prophetic present").

13:35b as a prophecy of salvation,[56] such a characterization, as Sato notes,[57] fails to take seriously either the mournful lament, "Jerusalem, Jerusalem," or the nature of the prophecy of disaster form. Q 13:35b is a warning, "you will not see me until . . ." and as such implies a call for repentance. Whether it is to be regarded as a "concluding characterization" or a part of the prediction of disaster is not clear, although a "concluding characterization" can simply spell out further the disastrous consequences described in the prediction. An analysis of the structure of the oracle may help clarify its function. However, it may first be noted that the "contrast motif," which Claus Westermann finds to be a common part of the announcement of disaster, occurs in Q 13:34b ("How often I . . . but you would not").[58]

The oracle is constructed so that the two characterizations of the situation (13:34a and 34b) are matched by two predictions of disaster (13:35a and 35b). In each case the first element (13:34a, 35a) has a divine passive (a passive verb used as a circumlocution for an implied divine actor) and the second element (13:34b, 35b) is in the first person. This parallelism is not accidental. It implies (a) that 13:35b is a second threat, and (b) that 13:35b is part of a unified oracle and not a later addition, as often supposed.[59] It may also be that the "contrast motif," which Westermann describes as part of the announcement of disaster, occurs in Q 13:34b.[60]

On the basis of this structure noted above, it would be possible to read the threat in 13:35a as a response to the accusation in 13:34a, and the threat in 13:35b as a response to the complaint in 13:34b. But it is also possible, and perhaps better, to see here a chiastic structure: the accusation in 13:34a finds its response in 13:35b, and the complaint in 13:34b finds its response in 13:35a, so that gathering the children relates to the "house," and killing the prophets to welcoming the prophets.

We may return briefly to Q 13:35b, "You will not see me until you say, 'Blessed is the one who comes in the name of the Lord.'" The quotation is taken verbatim from Ps 117:26a LXX. It is generally agreed that the "me" in this saying is not the "I" who sends prophets and wants to gather the children of Jerusalem (13:34), so the only way of seeing this as related to Jesus is to see it as a later addition to the oracle. The fact that the story of the entry into Jerusalem also uses this quotation from Ps 117:26a might seem to support this view. However, Did 12:1 attests the use of the quotation in precisely the way suggested here, namely as the words one is to use in welcoming prophets. Moreover, there are at least two problems in seeing Q 13:25b as a Christian

---

56. Aune, *Prophecy in Early Christianity*, 158.
57. Sato, *Q und Prophetie*, 158.
58. Westermann, *Basic Forms*, 155–58.
59. E.g., by Kloppenborg, *Formation*, 228. Kloppenborg's claim that "I say to you" (λέγω ὑμῖν) introduces a change in speaker, here and in Q 11:51, is not justified. "I tell you" in Q is not used in this way; rather, it is a compositional device used to bring emphasis or to expand upon a previous saying.
60. Westermann, *Basic Forms*, 155–58; so also Sato, *Q und Prophetie*, 157.

addition: (a) as an addition meant to clarify or apply the oracle it is remarkably obscure; and (b) this interpretation focuses attention on the christological content of the text rather than on its function within the oracle as a whole. On the other hand, Q 13:35b is untypical of most of Q in that it uses a direct citation of scripture. The phrase "the coming one" (ὁ ἐρχόμενος) occurs elsewhere in Q (3:16; 7:19).

Q 13:35–35 is usually described as an oracle of Wisdom.[61] The fact that it is a prophetic oracle does not jeopardize this identification, for wisdom and prophecy are often found together in Jewish tradition. On the other hand, there is nothing in the oracle that specifically refers to or requires its interpretation as a Wisdom oracle. Yet in the context of Q, there can be little reason to doubt that Wisdom is regarded as the sender of prophets and "those sent," just as she was in Q 11:49–51. In any case, the use of the divine passive in Q 13:35a means that God can hardly be the speaker in 13:34, whereas Wisdom would fit quite nicely. The claim sometimes made, that Q 13:35a refers to the Shekinah (or Wisdom as Shekinah),[62] cannot be accepted, because we have no proof that the Shekinah tradition antedates the destruction of the Temple.[63]

Wisdom, then, has again and again sent prophets to Jerusalem (i.e., to Israel as a whole; see, e.g., Isa 49:14–21; 51:17–20; 54), but she has rejected them (Q 13:34a). The purpose of Wisdom is elaborated in Q 13:34b: it was to "gather the children of Jerusalem." A common prophetic theme is the gathering of the exiles from out of the nations and their return to Jerusalem (e.g., Isa 11:12; Jer 23:8; Joel 3:1–3). But a different type of "gathering" is meant here, because it is a kind of gathering that can be refused; implicit in this is that the "gathering" is a call to repentance. Here the deuteronomistic tradition is evident (see, e.g., Deut 4:25–31; 30:1–5; Neh 9:6–37; Dan 9:4b–19; Zech 7:4–8:17; Bar 1:15–38; Tobit 13).[64] According to Q, Jesus engaged in such "gathering" (11:23; cf. 14:16–24) but, as 11:23 illustrates, this was an activity in which others were involved too. This fits Q 13:34 nicely, and it places the "gathering" activity within a much larger context. The deuteronomistic tradition is reflected too, of course, in the motif of the violent fate of the prophets (13:34), and in the assumption that the presence or absence of God (or Wisdom) is dependent upon a willingness to hear and obey God's messengers.

This oracle has often been regarded as a citation from a separate pre-Christian source,[65] but the arguments for this are not convincing. Q itself is "pre-Christian," and it stands within Jewish traditions, including the deuteronomistic tradition, just as much as other Jewish documents. What we have is

61. See Bultmann, *History of the Synoptic Tradition*, 114–15; Suggs, *Wisdom, Christology and Law in Matthew's Gospel*, 63–70; Steck, *Israel*, 227–39; Schulz, *Q*, 346–60; Boring, *Sayings of the Risen Jesus*, 171–73; Kloppenborg, *Formation*, 227–29; Sato, *Q und Prophetie*, 156–60.
62. See, e.g., Strecker, *Der Weg*, 113.
63. See Goldberg, *Untersuchungen über die Vorstellung über die Schekhinah*, esp. 409–13.
64. See Steck, *Israel, passim*.
65. See the arguments adduced by Christ, *Jesus Sophia*, 138–40.

a prophetic oracle, and we probably have no further to look for its origin than the Q community itself.[66] It is not a saying of the risen Lord. That would require that Wisdom be identified with the risen Lord, but there is no evidence for this in Q. What we have, rather, is a prophetic saying in which Wisdom, who spoke through the prophets of old as well as through John and Jesus, continues to speak through her prophets.[67] Neither can it be attributed to the historical Jesus (*pace* Aune),[68] because we cannot demonstrate that sayings which reflect the deuteronomistic tradition originated with Jesus. This tradition seems rather to have come into play in response to the failure of the Q mission to the Jews.

Nevertheless, because of parallels in 5 Ezra 1:30a and 1:33a, a pre-Q origin for Q 13:34–35 cannot be excluded. While 5 Ezra (=2 Esdras 1–2=4 Ezra 1–2) has been edited by Christians, its indebtedness to the New Testament gospels has not yet been demonstrated conclusively.[69] Crossan has argued that Q and 5 Ezra are both dependent upon "Christianized Deuteronomic traditions."[70] Robert A. Kraft, who has recently examined the "Ezra" materials,[71] notes that there were two traditions about Ezra, one as priest and one as prophet, and that the latter appears to be either earlier than or at least independent of, the former.[72] Examination of the text of 5 Ezra 1:30a, 33a yields no evidence which requires dependence upon Matthew, Luke, or Q. Thus the suggestion of Klaus Berger and Carsten Colpe, that Jewish rather than Christian tradition underlies 5 Ezra 1:30a, 33a, gains in credibility. But if this is the case 5 Ezra is an extremely important witness to the Jewish tradition to which it and Q were both heirs.

66. So Boring, *Sayings of the Risen Jesus*, 171–73; Sato, *Q und Prophetie*, 159.

67. Miller ("Rejection of the Prophets in Q," 235–39) argues that the speaker is the risen Jesus, and apparently understands that the risen Jesus was identified with Wisdom. Sometimes a prophecy attributed to Yohanan ben Zakkai, a contemporary of Jesus, is cited as a parallel. Aune, for example, cites it (*Prophecy in Early Christianity*, 144): "Galilee, Galilee, you hate the Torah. Your end will be to fall into the hands of the conductores [large-scale tenant farmers]." However, Neusner doubts the authenticity of this saying, noting that it is cited only in *y. Sabb* 16:8 and is in Aramaic "while all Yohanan sayings are cast in good Mishnaic Hebrew" (*Development of a Legend*, 133), so its relevance as a parallel to Jesus' saying is dubious.

68. Aune, *Prophecy in Early Christianity*; see also Boring, *Sayings of the Risen Jesus*, 175–76.

69. The extant manuscripts are rather late and are in Latin; see Bensly, *The Fourth Book of Ezra*. On the question of Jewish or Christian origins, see Kraft, "Towards Assessing the Latin Text of '5 Ezra.'" Stanton ("5 Ezra and Matthean Christianity") argues that 5 Ezra represents "a continuation into the second century of Matthean Christianity" (p. 80). J. Daniélou ("Le Vᵉ Esdras et le Judéo-christianisme Latin au Second Siècle") finds the themes in 5 Ezra best situated in an apocalyptic Christianity of the second century C.E. Kraft notes both the general assertion of the Christian origin of 5 Ezra and the tenuousness of the evidence for that conclusion. See also Bergren, "The 'People Coming from the East' in 5 Ezra 1:38."

70. Crossan, *In Fragments*, 139–42. A similar view is taken by Berger and Colpe (*Religionsgeschichtliches Textbuch*, 111), though they regard it as Jewish rather than Christian.

71. Kraft, "'Ezra' Materials."

72. Kraft, "'Ezra' Materials," 134.

Work on the Sabbath (Luke 14:5//Matt 12:11-12)

Luke 14:5	Matt 12:11-12
[5]And he said to them,"	[11]But he said to them,
"Who of you	"What person would there be among you
if a son [or: ass] or an ox	who having one sheep, even if this
should fall into a well	fell into a pit
	on the sabbath,
will not immediately draw it out	will not grab it and raise it?
even on a sabbath day?"	
	[12]How much more, then,
	a person matters than a sheep!"

There is some textual basis for assigning this to Q. Its structure is the same in Matthew and Luke, and seven Greek words are similar. The saying may be given in its Lukan version, but omitting all words that are not in common and emphasizing words that are identical: "Which *of you* . . . falls *into* . . . not . . . of the sabbath?" The saying is inserted in similar contexts in Matthew (12:9-12) and Luke (14:1-6), namely a healing on a sabbath. There are some slight verbal agreements between Matthew and Luke against Mark in these stories (Luke 14:2: "And behold a person"; 14:3: "Is it permitted to heal. . .?"). Moreover, the healing controversy makes such an abrupt appearance—in the context of a meal, Luke 14:1!—that it seems at first unlikely to be purely Lukan redaction. However, Luke uses this meal scene rather artificially to string together a series of sayings. The important thing for him, perhaps, is that "lawyers and Pharisees" (14:3) are at hand.

A proverbial saying such as Luke 14:5//Matt 12:11 could easily have floated freely in the tradition. It would quite naturally be attracted to a Sabbath healing story. So while there are enough indications to make it plausible that Luke 14:5 (or 14:1-6) could be Q, they are not fully persuasive. It is more likely that Luke constructed the account on the pattern of the Markan story in 3:1-6 (=Luke 6:6-11),[73] abbreviating Mark 3:4 to yield the question in 14:3. The combination "lawyers and Pharisees" is Lukan (cf. 7:30), as is the silence of the same (14:4a; cf. Acts 11:5; 21:14). Even if the saying belonged in Q, its location cannot be established, so it is best left out of consideration.

The Banquet (Q 14:15-24)

Luke 14:15-24	Matt 22:1-10
[15]When one of those who sat at the table with him heard this, he said to him,	[1]And answering, Jesus again spoke in parables to them, saying,
"Blessed is he who shall eat bread in the kingdom of God!"	
[16]But he said to him,	[2]"The kingdom of the heavens may be compared to a person,

---

73. On this, see Neirynck, "Jesus and the Sabbath," 230.

"A certain person prepared
a great banquet
and invited many,
¹⁷and at the hour for the banquet
he sent his servant
to say to those invited
'Come, for it is already prepared.'
¹⁸And they all alike began
to make excuses.
The first said to him,

a king who prepared
a wedding feast
for his son.

³And he sent his servants
to call those invited
to the wedding feast,
and they did not want to come.

⁴Again he sent other servants,
saying, 'Say to those invited,
"Behold, I have made ready my meal,
my bulls, and the fatted cattle
which have been slaughtered,
and everything is ready.
Come to the wedding feast."'
⁵But paying no heed they went away,
one to his farm,

'I have purchased a farm,
and I must go out to see it.
I ask you consider me excused.'
¹⁹And another said,
'I have bought five yoke of oxen,
and I go to examine them;
I ask you, consider me excused.'
²⁰And another said,
'I have married a wife,
and so it is not possible to come.'
²¹And coming, the servant
reported these things to his master.
Then, enraged, the master of the house

and another to his business.

⁶And the others,
seizing his servants,
mistreated and killed them.

⁷And the king was enraged, and,
dispatching his troops,
killed those murderers
and burned their city.
⁸Then he said to his servants,
'The wedding feast is ready,
but those invited were not worthy.
⁹Go therefore to the outskirts of town,

said to his servant,

'Go out quickly into the streets
and alleys of the city,
and bring to this place the poor

and whomever you find invite
to the wedding feast.'

and the crippled and the blind
and the lame.'
²²And the servant said,
'Sir, what you ordered has been done,
and yet there is room.'
²³And the master said to the servant,
'Go out into the roadways and hedges
and compel them to come in,

¹⁰And when those servants went
into the roadways,
they gathered all whom they found,

so that my house may be filled. ²⁴For I tell you that none of those who were invited shall taste my banquet.' "	wicked as well as good; and the wedding hall was filled with guests."

Concerning this text, the basic questions for our purposes are: (a) Did a version of this parable stand in Q? (b) If it did, where was it? (c) What did it mean in its Q context? It seems clear that Luke 14:15–24 and Matt 22:1–10 are related parables. The existence of a probably independent version in GThom 64 shows that the parable took different forms. A parable, particularly a longer parable and a parable built on an image of such powerful metaphoric resonance as a feast to which invitees refuse to come, is likely to be subject to performancial variation. The fact, therefore, that the verbal agreements between Matthew and Luke are relatively sparse is no surprise and thus also less worrisome as evidence for the existence of a Q version.[74] Furthermore, difficulties internal to the Matthean as well as the Lukan performances of the parable force virtually every interpreter to seek some underlying "skeleton"[75] or "original content and structure."[76]

Matthew's location for the parable is not that of Q. He places it in a Markan context remote from other Q material, and in a string of parables (Matt 21:28–32; 21:33–43; 22:1–14) which all have the same point, namely the replacement of Israel by others. Luke's context also has elements of artificiality, especially the meal context (Luke 14:1–24). However, it is placed near other Q material, so we have no alternative but to suppose that Luke has preserved the context better just as he has preserved the parable itself better.

The text of the parable is best preserved in Luke. It is possible to imagine that the Matthean version developed from the Lukan, but not the converse. Several correspondences between Luke and the probably independent parable in GThom 64 suggest that these cannot be attributed to Luke and probably were in Q: the identity of the host ("a man"), the single slave, the type of meal ($\delta\epsilon\hat{\iota}\pi\nu o\nu$, i.e., the main or evening meal), narrated excuses, and substitute guests. The identity of the substitute guests is unclear. Luke's "the poor and the crippled and the blind and the lame" (14:21) is probably Lukan redaction, since the same list occurs in 14:13. In this instance, Matthew's "whomever you find" (22:9) is to be preferred; the Gospel of Thomas—which can hardly be said to follow Matthew's version—similarly has, "those whom you happen to meet" (GThom 64 [44,33]). So the emphasis seems not to have been on the wretched state of the substitute guests but rather upon their random availability. Luke may also be responsible for the more elaborate description of where the substitute guests were to be found. The one site that is clear is

---

74. Schottroff ("Gleichnis vom grossen Gastmahl," 193) provides a list of both verbal and material agreements which make more evident their common ancestry.

75. Schottroff, "Gleichnis vom grossen Gastmahl," 194.

76. Funk, *Language* 182; cf. the term "originating structure" in Scott, *Hear Then the Parable*, 166–68.

"roads" (ὁδοί; Matt 22:10//Luke 14:23).[77] Luke may not have understood why two expeditions were needed to search for substitute guests, and thus explained this by having the slave search in different locations, within the city and outside the city.

The Q version of the parable probably had three excuses, the last of which was definitive. The last person has no request to be excused; he simply says, "It is not possible to come" (Luke 14:20; cf. Matt 22:3). The three excuses were probably matched by three expeditions. We need not assume, even for Luke, that allegorical interests are behind these three expeditions.[78] Matthew has four expeditions, but the third is a punitive military expedition, secondary to the narrative. However, in both Matthew and Luke one expedition is occasioned by the anger of the host (Matt 22:7/Luke 14:21).

The introduction to the Q parable, if there was an introduction, has not been preserved. The fact that both Matthew and Luke, however, make reference to "kingdom" (Matt 22:1; Luke 14:15) may mean that Q had an introduction similar to the one in Matthew ("The kingdom of heaven may be compared to . . ."). But, given the uncertainty about this matter, such a possible introduction can play no role in the interpretation of the parable in its Q context. The conclusion of the parable is also uncertain. Matthew's conclusion (22:11–14) is secondary. Luke's conclusion (14:24) gives scant evidence of Lukan redaction except the opening, "I say to you [plur.] that . . ." (λέγω . . . ὑμῖν ὅτι). Luke introduces this quotation formula in two other Q parables (15:7; 19:26), and it occurs in several parables from the Lukan special material (11:8; 16:9; 18:8; 18:14).[79] Despite the lack of parallel wording, there is good reason to attribute Luke 14:24 to Q: (1) it forms an *inclusio* with 14:16; (2) it can be understood fully within the plot of the parable and thus is no allegorical addition; and (3) "my dinner" in 14:24 is parallel to "my house" in 14:23.[80] Thus, we may judge that Luke 14:24—without the "I say to you that" quotation formula—was in Q, perhaps introduced by "for." This also means that the switch from the second person singular in 14:23 to the plural in 14:24 is attributable to Luke, and that 14:24 was also directed to the slave; further, this means that "my banquet" is that of the host, not that of the Lord.

The distinctive character of the Q version of the parable may be glimpsed more clearly by comparison with the version in Thomas. Though Thomas's parable is an independent version, it is not without signs of redaction. The four excuses arouse suspicion simply on the basis of the ubiquity of threesomes. There is, as Crossan has noted, reason to doubt the originality of the second excuse because of its formal difference from the others.[81] However, at least the

---

77. Cf. GThom 64:11 and 9:2 (=Mark 4:4), where the same Coptic word (ϩⲓⲏ) occurs as a translation of ὁδός.
78. See Funk, *Language*, 183–85.
79. Neirynck ("Study of Q," 63–64) argues that λέγω ὑμῖν is Lukan.
80. On the last point, see Schulz, *Q*, 397.
81. Crossan, "Hermeneutical Jesus," 240.

first excuse is also suspicious because it fits only too well with the parable's redactional ending: "Businessmen and merchants [will] not enter the places of my father." Crossan takes it that the host in Thomas suddenly decides to hold a banquet, in which case the excuses would be quite plausible since the prospective guests had no advance notice.[82] However, the wording of Thomas leaves this matter unclear. The parable begins, "A man was having visitors. . . ." The verb is the imperfect of "have" (oγnta) and would seem to imply that the visitors were already at his house. They are not simply townspeople, because "visitor" (ϣⲙⲙⲟ) in Coptic refers to a stranger, and so the "visitors" will probably have come to town before preparations for the dinner began, even if it was an impromptu affair.[83] The banquet is thus an act of hospitality to strangers, making their excuses all the more offensive. But the most striking feature of the Thomas parable is that substitute guests are summoned, but there is no reason within the parable why this should be done, and its conclusion is a moral or ascetic point: commercial activity is incompatible with seeking the kingdom. Since the guests refuse to come, they can hardly be insulted by the substitution of other guests! Thus in Thomas the substitute guests are a vestigial feature. The preservation of this feature may be due not only to its being traditional but also to the nice parallelism which existed between the slave's report about "those whom you invited" (ⲛⲉⲛⲧⲁⲕ ⲧⲁϩⲙⲟⲩ [44,30]) and the host's command to bring in "those whom you happen to meet" (ⲛⲉⲧⲕⲛⲁϩⲉ ⲉⲣⲟⲟⲩ [44,33]).

In contrast to the Thomas version, three features of the Q parable stand out: the three expeditions by the slave, the emphasis at the end on the exclusion of the original guests, and the anger of the host. These three features are connected. Two expeditions to find substitute guests are needed to emphasize the point that the dining hall must be completely filled so that there is no room left for the original guests. But neither in Thomas nor in Q is the identity of the substitute guests of any particular interest, as it is in Luke. Another feature of the Q parable also stands out—the anger of the host (Q 14:21), which is not mentioned in Thomas. This too is related to the theme of exclusion: the host is determined to get back at the original guests by arranging to have the dining hall full when—as must be assumed—they finally arrive. And with this, we reach a critical point in the interpretation of the parable.

Eta Linnemann has called attention to a matter of fundamental importance, namely that the whole parable makes much more sense if the excuses are seen as polite requests to come late rather than as outright refusals.[84] On this

82. Crossan, *In Parables*, 72–73; "Hermeneutical Jesus," 239–40.
83. Regarding both the use of the imperfect and the meaning of "visitor," see the translation in Layton, *Gnostic Scriptures*, 391 ("A man was receiving out-of-town visitors"), and his footnoted alternative translation of the imperfect, "had a habit of receiving."
84. Linnemann, *Jesus of the Parables*, 88–90. For an example of late arrival at a banquet, see the parable attributed to R. Jose bar Ḥanina (*Midr. Ps.* 25:9 [in Braude, *Midrash on Psalms*, 1. 352]).
Frequent reference is made to a connection between the excuses and the laws for

reading, the host, stunned by the requests of *all* the guests to come late, quickly arranges to have substitute guests rounded up so that when the original guests finally arrive there will be no room left for them. This would explain why his action must be taken quickly (Luke 14:21); why there is a double expedition to make sure the hall is full; why the host can say, with evident satisfaction and without hint of allegory, "None of those people who were invited shall taste my banquet" (Luke 14:24); and above all why there are substitute guests in the first place. The substitute guests are a basic feature of the parable; they appear to be needed only if the original guests do in fact wish to come, albeit late.

Linnemann's proposal, by which the various parts of the parable are part of a plot that is meaningful on its own terms, obviates the need for allegorical interpretation. Such allegorical interpretation has a long history. The most unfortunate chapter is surely Augustine's interpretation of "compel them to come in" (Luke 14:23) with reference to the Donatists.[85] An allegorical interpretation yields rather unsatisfactory theological results. For example, it implies that Jesus or God turned to the lower classes only after having been rebuffed by the leading people, and, further, did it out of spite and anger! Thomas, to be sure, was able to find a moral lesson in the excuses, but these excuses are difficult to explain allegorically because they imply that Jesus' message was rejected for venial reasons, something that the gospels do not say (though such a point is perhaps conceivable in Q; 17:26–27).

Unfortunately for Linnemann's argument, however, the last excuse is a flat refusal, even if the first two could perhaps be seen as reasons for late arrival. Kenneth E. Bailey is probably correct: such excuses would have been seen as insults and gross social blunders.[86] Nevertheless, Linnemann has pointed to the key to the interpretation of the parable. That the excuses offered by the prospective guests are so flimsy as to be socially inconceivable is no problem, however, if one reads the parable somewhat differently, but assumes Linnemann's plot structure. On this alternative reading, the substitute guests remains a key feature. The parable asks us to imagine a kind of summons which brooks no delays, a situation in which the giving of excuses, moreover, can lead to being excluded altogether. On this reading, it makes no difference whether the excuses are plausible or not. If they are plausible, or if one or more of them are, than we can see that even good excuses (as in Q 9:59–60a) are unacceptable. If the excuses are perceived to be in scandously bad taste, then it

conscription and exemption for war in Deut 20:5–8 and 24:5; see, e.g., Ballard, "Reasons for Refusing." These were, in fact, discussed a good deal (cf. Judg 7:3; 1 Macc 3:56; *m. Soṭa* 8:7; *b. Soṭa* 43a–44b; for Qumran, see Yadin, *Scroll of the War*, 65–86), and at times they have a wider application than war only (e.g., *Sipre Deut.* 193–98 [Neusner]). Precisely because they were a common *topos*, the dissimilarity between these rules and the excuses in the parables becomes so striking as to exclude any connection. Only if the banquet is seen primarily as a metaphor for an eschatological feast, rather than as an element within the parable plot, does the invocation of these rules make sense.

85. On the history of interpretation, see Beare, "The Parable of the Guests at the Banquet," and Norwood, "'Compel Them to Come in.'"

86. Bailey, *Through Peasant Eyes*, 94–99.

is only all the more clear that excuses are unacceptable. Only on this reading, it seems to me, are we able to make sense of the basic plot of the parable.[87]

If the Q parable was not allegorical, and if its focus was upon the exclusion of the original guests, then it fits very nicely into the deuteronomistic perspective which, I have argued, was basic to Q. Indeed, it says in parabolic form what Q 13:28-29 has in oracular form. The parable then is metaphorical, not allegorical.[88] And since its focus is on the exclusion of the original guests, its point cannot have been that which Jeremias, for example, finds for the "original" form of the parable, namely the vindication of Jesus' preaching good news to the poor.[89] That Q 14:24 seems to be directed to a different audience (there is a shift to plural "you" [ὑμῖν]) does not mean that there is a shift to allegory.

Since the emphasis is not upon the inclusion of substitute guests, or upon their identity, but upon the exclusion of the original guests, we may surmise that the parable functioned in Q as a warning: you may be excluded from the kingdom! This was precisely the opening note in Q (3:7-9). But, in addition, we may also detect a recurrence of the envy motif: repentance is urgently needed, or others will take your place! (see Q 7:9; 11:29-32; cf. Rom 11:13-14).

Qualifications (Q 14:26-27; 17:33; 14:34-35)

Luke 14:26-27; 17:33; 14:34-35	Matt 10:37-38, 39; 5:13
[26]If anyone comes to me	[37]The one loving father and mother
and does not hate his father and mother	more than me is not worthy of me.
and the wife and the children	And the one loving son or daughter
and the brothers and the sisters,	more than me is not worthy of me.
yes, even his own life,	
he cannot be my disciple.	is not worthy of me.

87. As already noted, Crossan dealt with the problem of the lame excuses by assuming an impromptu, unannounced dinner. But even if this were true of the "earliest version" of the parable, it would not be true for Q, where the banquet is not an impetuous act. Jeremias tries to solve the problem by establishing a connection between the parable and a story from the Jerusalem Talmud (English text of this story in Scott, *Hear Then the Parable*, 157): Bar Maayan, a rich tax collector, prepared a banquet and invited the town councillors; they all refused to come, so he invited the poor to eat the meal instead. Here, the feeding of the poor is treated as a meritorious deed which Bar Maayan did on the last day of his life, thus making him a righteous man. Jeremias assumes that the "man" in the parable was also a tax collector. But not only is this a dubious assumption, the point of the Q parable is not that inviting substitute guests is a meritorious deed.

88. The identification of the dinner with the eschatological banquet then governs the interpretation of the parable, so that the difficulties in the plot of the parable are ignored (e.g., why substitute guests are summoned, why the parable ends as it does). I do not deny that hearers of the parable would have reckoned with the possibility that the dinner was a metaphor for the eschatological feast. But they would have attended to the parable to learn how—and if—this metaphor was intended. Parable plot governs metaphor, not vice versa.

89. Jeremias, *Parables*, 45, 63-64. Jeremias (p. 176) tries to find in the parable the "note of joy" one would expect to find on his interpretation, but precisely this "note of joy" is missing from Q; see also Funk, *Language*, 175-82.

²⁷Whoever does not bear his own cross
and come behind me
cannot be my disciple.
17³³Whoever seeks to preserve his life
life will lose it,
and whoever loses it
will keep it alive.
14³⁴Salt to be sure is good;
but even the salt if it becomes insipid
with what will it be seasoned?
³⁵It is suitable neither
for the ground nor for a manure pile;
they throw it away.

³⁸And whoever does not take his cross
and follow behind me
is not worthy of me.
³⁹The one finding his life
will lose it,
and the one losing his life for my sake
will find it.
5¹³You are the salt of the earth,
but if the salt becomes insipid,
with what will it be salted?
It is no longer capable of anything but,

being thrown out,
to be trodden upon by people.

These sayings are considered together both because they have a common theme—discipleship—and because they apparently occurred together in Q. Q 17:33 appears to have been relocated by Luke. We can see evidence of this in Luke 14:26, where "yes, even his own life" is listed among the things a disciple must "hate." Comparison with Matt 10:37 shows that this phrase was not in Q. Luke's addition of it here is best understood as tacit admission that he has relocated a saying that in Q came after Q 14:27; he has left behind a kind of summary of it.[90] Matthew has relocated the salt saying (Q 14:34–35) to his Sermon on the Mount, adapting it to its new context with a prefatory announcement, "You are the salt of the world," even though the negative character of the Q salt saying does not lend itself well either to this saying or to its new Matthean context.[91]

1. Rejection of Family (Q 14:26–27; 17:33)

Neither Matthew nor Luke preserves intact the Q text of 14:26–27.[92] But

90. So Schulz, *Q*, 447 n. 327; Kloppenborg, *Formation*, 158–59; Schmithals, *Einleitung*, 221.

91. However, if the Lukan placement of the salt saying is correct, a possible catchword connection between 15:4 and 17:33 (ἀπολλύναι) can be seen.

92. Matthew's "the one loving . . . more than me" is a softening of the harsher language in Luke ("hate"), and is more focused on the person of Jesus ("more than me"). The participial formulation ("the one loving") in Matthew may be that of Q, but in its negative form as in Luke (hence, "the one not hating . . ."). The list of relatives in Luke is probably secondary (cf. Mark 10:29–30); Matthew's shorter list is formally superior, and the parallel in GThom 55 suggests that this formal parallelism was traditional. Matthew's "is not worthy of me" is to be preferred to Luke's "cannot be my disciple." "Disciple" (μαθητής) is clearly attested in Q only twice: in 6:40, where it means "pupil" and has no specific reference to followers of Jesus, and in 7:18, where it refers to John's disciples. Thus, a Q reference specifically to "my disciple" is doubtful for Q. "Worthy" (ἄξιος), on the other hand, is not Matthean (cf. GThom 55), and is attested elsewhere in Q (3:8; 10:7; cf. ἱκανός in Q 7:6).
The evidence does not permit a decision between Luke's "bear" (βαστάζειν) and Matthew's "take" (λαμβάνειν) in Q 14:27. Luke's reading resembles John 19:17. A still different verb, "take up" or "carry" (αἴρειν) is used in Mark 8:34 par. Matthew's "follow" (ἀκολουθεῖν) is perhaps to be preferred over Luke's "come" (ἔρχεσθαι), since Luke used this verb in 14:26 (cf.

Matthew's wording of Q 17:33 probably is closer to that of Q.[93] In Q (and in GThom 55), the cross saying is attached to the saying about hating one's family. The connection is made emphatic by the stong parallelism attested both by Matthew and by Luke and hence deriving from Q. That this connection was not unique to Q is shown by GThom 55. This means that we do not have here merely two separate conditions for following, but two related conditions. Specifically, cross-bearing is not to be understood as suffering in general, but above all as the suffering entailed in division within families, in the loss of community. This, in turn, means that the cross is here a metaphor for rejection and alienation. The death of Jesus probably stands in the background, but it is death understood as rejection, just as it is in Q's deuteronomistic understanding of Jesus as the culmination of a long series of rejected prophets.

We may have in these sayings a window into the history of Q. First, the understanding of Jesus' death implicit in Q 14:26–27 is consonant with the deuteronomistic perspective into which Jesus is set elsewhere in Q. And yet we seem to have two separate strands of tradition here. In one, "following" is in focus, and thus a self-conscious discipleship (though Q does not use the word "disciple"), with the Q group as the implied audience; in the other, deuteronomistic strand, there is a prophetic self-understanding, and the larger Jewish community is the implied audience. Secondly, the rupture of families bulks surprisingly large in Q (note Q 9:57b–60a; 12:51, [52], 53; the eschatological separation in 17:34–35; cf. 6:22–23, and the mission instruction in 10:2–16). This may be a much more important aspect of the social reality of the Q group than generally recognized. Thirdly, the Gospel of Thomas, though lacking the deuteronomistic perspective, has much to say about the dissolution of families (GThom 16, 55, 99, 101, 105; cf. 10, 82, 86, and the notion of the "solitary" in 16, 49, 75) as well as about Jesus' experience of rejection (GThom 52, 68–69a, 64–66, 28; cf. 31 and 113).

It would appear that common to Q and Thomas, and preceding the intro-

---

Luke 6:47!; also see Luke 7:7; Mark 8:34; 10:14), and "follow" occurs elsewhere in Q (7:9; 9:57, 59).

Aland's *Synopsis* and Nestle[26] both read "his own cross" (τὸν σταυρὸν ἑαυτοῦ) in Luke 14:27. However, the IGNTP text (*Gospel According to St. Luke*) reads "his cross" (τὸν σταυρὸν αὐτοῦ), no doubt because of the strong attestation for "his" ($\mathfrak{P}^{45}$, $\mathfrak{P}^{75}$, א et al.). Nestle[26] does not list a variant for "his own," perhaps because αυτου can stand for αὐτοῦ (=ἑαυτοῦ) as well as for αὐτοῦ (see Smyth, *Greek Grammar* §329). Even if Luke did have "his own," it would have to be judged redactional; see Schulz, *Q*, 431 n. 209. So "his cross," as in Matt 10:38, is probably Q.

93. Luke substitutes compound verbs for those in Q. The verb "to find" in Matthew's version occurs commonly in Q (see 7:9; 11:9, 10, 24, 25; 12:43; 15:5), and probably represents Q. Luke has taken over from Mark 8:35 the opening of the saying ("whoever"); so Matthew's participial opening is that of Q (see Crossan, *In Fragments*, 89–90). However, Matthew's "for my sake" is probably from Mark's version of the saying (8:35); see Crossan, *In Fragments*, 90–91. Matthew's chiastic structure also points to the general superiority of his version. Crossan has described the structure of the saying as "inverted antithetical parallelism" (*In Fragments*, 90).

duction of a deuteronomistic perspective into Q, is a tradition in which Jesus' rejection was a major theme, and in which a corresponding experience of rejection and of family disruption was the expected lot of the follower. These themes get elaborated in different ways in Thomas and Q, yet they probably share a common origin. Further, for Q this means that the deuteronomistic perspective is continuous with earlier Q tradition, with its focus on the rejection of Jesus, even though it represents a quite different conceptualization of that rejection. Indeed, this is precisely what we saw in Q 6:22–23, where to 6:22–23b, which embodies the tradition of the suffering of the righteous, was added a deuteronomistic prophetic perspective in 6:23c.

The contrast between Q and Mark with respect to their use of the cross saying should also be noted. In Mark 8:34 the cross saying appears in a different form, in which taking up the cross is interpreted as self-denial: "If anyone wants to come after me, let him deny himself and take up his cross and follow me." Here the cross saying is associated, as in Q, with the "lose your life" saying. However, Mark does not associate cross-bearing with alienation from family (see Mark 10:29–30). Rather, in Mark the cross saying comes first and thus functions as a topic upon which the following verses comment (Mark 8:35–38). Initially, self-denial is set forth as the meaning of taking up the cross. But the concluding saying (Mark 8:38) shifts the focus toward fearless confession. Ultimately, therefore, to take up the cross in Mark is to risk public committment to Jesus.

In Q, as already noted, the topic is hating one's family, and bearing one's cross is one of the comments upon this topic. The other comment comes in Q 17:33, which, I have argued, came after Q 14:27, as it does in Matt 10:37, 38. In Q the point of 17:33 would seem to be that "life" is to be found precisely where it seems to be lost; that is, that the loss entailed in following Jesus—a loss that includes alienation from one's family and community—is not in vain. Indeed, life in some deeper sense is gained. William A. Beardslee, who argues that the idea of losing life to gain it was widespread in hellenistic antiquity, notes that early sayings which contain this thought occur in a context "of the participation of the individual in the struggle of a community for survival."[94] That is also the point in Q 17:33, i.e., it is a call to abandon one's life (specifically, one's old life, one's family and community) to find life in a new community.

Another interesting difference between the cross sayings in Mark and Q may be noted. In Q the saying is formulated as a principle for exclusion ("Whoever does not take up his cross . . . cannot be my disciple") whereas in Mark it is formulated as a principle for inclusion ("If any person wants to come after me, let him take up his cross . . ."). Q 14:26 is also formulated as a principle for

---

94. Beardslee, "Saving One's Life," 61. Seeley ("Was Jesus Like a Philosopher?") argues that Q 14:26–27 is also rooted in Cynic and Stoic traditions.

exclusion ("The one loving father or mother more than me is not worthy of me"). The Markan tradition is aware of the demand to leave one's family, but it focuses on the reward to be gained by it (Mark 10:29-30). In short, sayings about resolute discipleship are used programmatically in Mark to define the Christian way of life.[95] But in Q, they have an intimidating, rather negative, character: there are some who think they are disciples, but unless they can meet these stringent qualifications, they are not. This curious exclusionary formulation in Q 14:26-27 is echoed in 9:57b-60a.

2. Salt Saying (Q 14:34-35)

Whether there is a Q version of the salt saying could be questioned because the verbal agreement between Luke 14:34-35 and Matt 5:13 is limited to a few words. But they are crucial words, especially the odd "become foolish or insipid" ($\mu\omega\rho\alpha\acute{\iota}\nu\epsilon\iota\nu$) and the unusual, uncompounded form, "cast out" ($\beta\acute{\alpha}\lambda\lambda\epsilon\iota\nu + \acute{\epsilon}\xi\omega$). Equally telling is the fact that Matthew and Luke both have a statement about the disposal of bad salt. Moreover, Matthew and Luke agree in omitting Markan material in 9:49-50. In general, Matthew's version of this saying is closer to Q.[96]

The salt saying in Q 14:34-35 has a parallel in Mark 9:50. The differences between the two sayings are striking. Mark begins with "Salt is good," to which is added only a rhetorical question. Q probably did not begin with "Salt is good" but with the rhetorical question, to which is added a statement about disposing of bad salt. There is nothing in Q 14:34 that would seem to require additional comment, so 14:35 is odd. It focuses upon the notion of getting rid of the bad salt, and thus bestows on the Q saying a quite different character and point. Jeremias is correct: the saying conveys a threat.[97]

These observations concerning Q 14:26-27; 17:33 and 14:34-35 underline their peculiar exclusionary character. That, in fact, is one of the primary features they have in common, aside from the presumed theme of discipleship (it is not obvious that this is the theme in 14:34-35). It is not the case that in Q we observe a shift from the banquet parable in 14:16-24 to a new theme, discipleship. Rather, there is remarkable continuity, once the peculiar nature of the Q "discipleship" sayings is noted. Indeed, exclusion is a primary theme for this whole section of Q.

---

95. Note the use of the imperative in 8:34 and the introduction of the element of volition in 8:35 ("wants to save . . .").

96. "Salt is good" in Luke 14:37 is from Mark 9:50. Luke's verb "to season" ($\dot{\alpha}\rho\tau\acute{\nu}\epsilon\iota\nu$) is also from Mark. His references to the ground and to a manure pile probably come from an attempt to figure out what kind of "salt" this was (potash, for example, could be meant), and thus Matthew's simple "it is no longer capable of anything" is probably from Q. However, Matthew's "trampled under foot by people" appears to be an addition.

97. Jeremias, *Parables*, 168-69. Kloppenborg (*Formation*, 233-34) disputes this, observing that "the immediate context of 14:34-35 has more to do with discipleship than judgment." However, we have seen the peculiar way in which these discipleship sayings are used in Q, as principles for exclusion.

Lost Sheep (Q 15:4–7)

Luke 15:4–7	Matt 18:12–14
	[12]What do you think?
[4]What person among you,	If a certain person
having one hundred sheep	has one hundred sheep,
and losing one of them	and one of them was led astray,
does not leave behind the ninety-nine	will he not leave ninety-nine
in the wilderness	on the hills
and go after the lost one	and go and seek the one
until he finds it?	which has gone astray?
[5]and finding it, he will put it	
on his shoulders, rejoicing,	
[6]and coming into the home,	
he calls together friends and neighbors,	
saying to them, "Rejoice with me,	
for I have found my sheep which was lost."	
	[13]And if he should find it,
[7]I tell you that	truly, I tell you
there will be more such joy in heaven	that he rejoices over it more
over one sinner who repents	
than over the ninety-nine righteous	than over the ninety-nine
who have no need of repentance.	which have not gone astray.
	[14]Likewise, it is not the will
	of our father in heaven
	that one of these little ones be lost.

The Q version of the parable[98] of the lost sheep is, with some important exceptions, best preserved in Matthew.[99] There it consists of three parts: (a) introduction, (b) a parable in the form of a rhetorical question, (c) a closing comment introduced by "Truly I tell you."

98. Whether this is a parable or not is left undecided; for purposes of the following discussion it makes no difference.

99. The introductory "What do you think?" is a Matthean locution (see also 17:25; 21:28; 22:17, 42; 26:66); it is not used by Mark or Luke. The opening of the parable is best preserved in Luke's "What person among you . . .?" Matthew's ἐάν construction is secondary. The sheep is "lost" (Luke), not "strayed" (Matthew), for these reasons: (a) Matthew likes the word "stray" (πλανᾶν; cf. 22:29; 24:4, 5, 11, 24); (b) it fits his interpretation better, since for him the one sheep is a strayed Christian, one of the "little ones," not a "lost" Christian; (c) Matthew tips his hand in 18:14 by using "lost"; and (d) Matthew elsewhere uses an image that probably underlies this parable, the "lost sheep of the house of Israel" (Matt 10:6; 15:24). Perhaps Matthew was influenced by Ezek 34:16. The conditional "if he happens to find it" in Matt 18:13 is secondary. The conditional with ἐάν is again Matthean; for hortatory purposes, Matthew wants to introduce an element of uncertainty as to whether the straying Christian will be rescued (*pace* Breech, *Silence*, 79). Luke 15:5–6 is secondary. Luke has introduced the motif of repentant sinners (cf. Luke 5:32). The concluding comment on the parable is best preserved in Matt 18:13 (except the conditional construction, and probably the ending, "which had not gone astray"). Matt 18:14 is Matthean redaction. The Q parable, therefore, probably read: "What person among you having a hundred sheep and losing one of them would not leave the ninety-nine [in the wilderness] and go after the one which was lost until he found it? I tell you, he rejoices more over it than over the ninety-nine [which were never lost]."

The interpretations of this parable by Matthew, Luke, Thomas, and the Gospel of Truth are all very different, and secondary. For Matthew, the parable has to do with the need to seek out straying Christians in the community, and to welcome them back. For Luke, it is about God's joy over sinners who repent. So already, the "lost sheep" has been interpreted in two very different ways, as a straying Christian and as a sinner. For the Gospel of Thomas (107), the one sheep wandered off, but in so doing has separated itself from the unenlightened multitude, represented by the ninety-nine. This one sheep is "large": it knows where the good pasture is, and God loves it accordingly. In the Gospel of Truth (31.35–32.4) the focus shifts from the one sheep to the shepherd. In that respect the Gospel of Truth shares a common, but later, Christian interpretation: the parable is about Jesus as the good shepherd.

None of this is found in Q, which had only a rhetorical question followed by a concluding comment. The comment, moreover, does not go beyond the plot of the parable: "He [the shepherd] rejoices more over it than over the ninety-nine." Luke's version of this comment, which reflects his own interests (cf. Luke 5:32), introduces an application: *God* rejoices over the found sheep. Thus even the concluding comment in Q did not move in the direction of allegory.

Nevertheless, framing the parable as a rhetorical question may have been secondary already in Q. The independent (albeit heavily interpreted) version of this parable in GThom 107 indicates that the "original" parable was a brief narrative whose subject was a shepherd. In any case, the use of a rhetorical question in Q distinguishes its version from that of Thomas in both form and function. As a rhetorical question, it functions as an argumentative device; it seeks to elicit agreement, and thus assumes a questionable position which it is seeking to defend. Presumably, this questionable position was the attention paid to the "lost" and the abandonment of the "normal" community. In the context of Q, this probably means "tax collectors and sinners" (Q 7:35), or the "children" who need to be "gathered" (13:34), or the substitute guests in the parable of the banquet (14:16–24).

The tone in this parable, however, differs from that of much of the rest of Q, in that the ninety-nine are not the subject of denunciation. The comment that concludes the Q parable has a bite to it: "I tell you, he rejoices more over it than over the ninety-nine." Yet the one sheep is lost and the others are not; and, while the wording of Q is uncertain with respect to a concluding characterization of the ninety-nine (such as, "which never went astray"), the ninety-nine are not described as in any way bad or unfaithful. The focus in Q is primarily upon the rescue of the lost sheep. It would appear, therefore, that this parable represents material not yet adapted to the deuteronomistic perspective. It does not continue the theme of exclusion that we have observed in a number of previous Q pericopes. The absence of allegory also points to the relatively primitive character of the parable.

Lost Coin (Luke 15:8-10)

[8]Or what woman having ten drachmas, if she loses one drachma, does not light a flame and sweep the house and search diligently until she finds it? [9]And having found it, she calls together her friends and neighbors, saying, "Rejoice with me, for I found the drachma which was lost!" [10]So likewise, I tell you, there will be joy before the angels of God over the repentance of one sinner.

The lost coin parable is a twin to the parable of the lost sheep, and, though attested only in Luke, is often attributed to Q.[100] There are, in fact, good reasons to think that the parable of the lost coin was in Q: (1) its structure is so similar to that of the lost sheep that it is easy to imagine they were together in Q; (2) Matthew may have had good reason to omit it: he regarded the one sheep as "straying," but a coin could not "stray"; and (3) Q has other twinned sayings (9:57-60; 10:13-15; 11:11-12; 11:31-32; 13:18-21).[101]

On the other hand, there are objections to including the lost coin parable in Q: (1) it is found only in Luke; (2) the lost sheep parable appears in GThom 107 without the Lost Coin, so if they were paired it probably happened in Q, not in the antecedent tradition; if Q was responsible, then a reason for its addition would need to be found; and (3) Luke seems to prefer male/female paired accounts whenever possible (see 2:25-38; 4:25-27; 7:1-17; 17:34-35; 18:1-14; 20:45-21:4).

Unfortunately such considerations do not decide the issue. Reflection upon how the Q version of the parable could be reconstructed, however, is very instructive. First, Luke 15:9 is probably a Lukan addition. Its corresponding member in the parable of the lost sheep was probably due to Lukan redaction, since it is lacking in Matthew's version. Luke 15:9, therefore, can be attributed to Luke or his tradition but not to Q. Secondly, Luke 15:10 is just as clearly Lukan as 15:7. The main difference between the two—the phrase, "before the angels of God"—is probably not a fragment of the conclusion to the pre-Lukan parable, since Luke inserts this phrase redactionally in 12:8-9. So the pre-Lukan parable may have had a concluding comment, but it is not the one we have in 15:10. Likewise, it cannot be Q.

We are left, then, with only Luke 15:8 as possible Q material. But there is an interesting difference between Luke 15:8 and 15:4. The latter has, "What person *among you* . . .?" which I argued was probably the beginning of the parable. But in 15:8, we have "What woman having ten drachmas . . .?" While "among you" could have been in Q and omitted by Luke, we cannot know this. In any case, the result is that the "man" or "person" in 15:4 is a member of the audience who is asked to imagine himself a shepherd, whereas the woman is an actor in the parable, and the audience is not involved. So the parallelism

100. For some of the arguments, see Kloppenborg, *Q Parallels*, 176.
101. But twinned sayings are not peculiar to Q; see, e.g., Matt 13:44-46 (M) and Luke 14:28-32 (L). See Steinhauser, *Doppelbildworte*.

between 15:4 and 15:8 is not as strong as often supposed. Hence, its status as a Q parable, which depends upon that similarity, becomes somewhat dubious. Several conclusions follow: (1) the structural parallelism between the parables is probably due to Luke; (2) the only part of the parable that can come into consideration as Q is 15:8, and that too is doubtful; and (3) to understand what the parable meant in Q, we would have to possess the concluding comment. So it is best simply to leave this parable out of consideration for an understanding of Q.

Miscellaneous Sayings (Q 16:13, 17, 18; 17:3b, 4, 6)

Luke 16:13, (16), 17, 18; 17:3b, 4, 6	Matt 6:24; 5:18, 32; 18:15, 21b, 22, 20
16 [13]It is by no means possible	6 [24]It is not possible
to serve two masters;	to serve two masters;
for either one will hate the one	for either one will hate the one
and love the other;	and love the other;
or one will be devoted to one	or one will be devoted to one
and despise the other.	and despise the other.
It is not possible	It is not possible
to serve God and mammon.	to serve God and mammon.
16 [17]But it is easier	5 [18]For truly I say to you,
for heaven and earth to pass away	until heaven and earth pass away,
than for one serif	one iota or one serif
to fall from the law.	will not fall from the law
	until everything comes to pass.
	5 [32]And I tell you,
16 [18]Everyone who dismisses his wife	everyone who dismisses his wife
	except in the matter of adultery
and marries another	
commits adultery,	causes her to become an adulterer,
and the one marrying someone	and whoever marries one
dismissed from a husband,	who has been dismissed
commits adultery.	becomes an adulterer.
17 [3b]If your brother sins	18 [15]And if your brother sins, go
rebuke him,	discuss it between you and him alone.
and if he repents,	If he listens to you,
forgive him;	you have regained your brother.
	18 [21]Then Peter, coming forward,
	said to him, "Master,
17 [4]And even if he should sin against you	how often shall my brother sin against me
seven times a day and seven	and I forgive him?
times he turned to you, saying,	18 [22]Jesus says to him,
	"I do not say to you
	as many as seven times
"I repent,"	but as many as seventy-seven times."
forgive him.	20 [b]For amen, I say to you,
[6]And the master said,	if you have faith as
"If you have faith as	

a mustard seed,	a mustard seed,
you could say to [this]	you will say to this
mulberry tree, 'Be uprooted	mountain, "Move from here"
and be planted in the sea,'	
and it would obey you.	and it will move,
	and nothing will be impossible to you.

Here we come upon a group of sayings which apparently were in Q but whose context has been lost. Q 16:16 was moved by Luke, as noted earlier; its proper location is (as in Matthew) after Q 7:28. Several sayings have a common sequence in Matthew and Luke (Luke 17:1//Matt 18:7b; Luke 17:3b//Matt 18:15; Luke 17:4//Matt 18:21–22). Further, there are catchword connections between Q 16:13 and 16:16 ("law"); between Q 17:3b and 17:4 ("sin"); and, weakly, between 17:6 and 17:[21], 23 ("there" [ἐκεῖ]). Nevertheless, these sayings do not constitute a coherent unit.

One may speculate that the openness to the non-Law-observant ("the lost") seen, for example, in the previous Q material led to questions about the status of the Law. Perhaps Q 16:17 is to be understood in that context. We saw that Q 15:4–7 reflects a primitive perspective, one in which the sense of alienation had not yet become acute. The ninety-nine sheep were not lost. Q 16:17 reflects this affirmation of the Law.[102] Q 16:18, in fact, reflects a stricter interpretation of the Law, at least with respect to divorce and remarriage. It is possible that this reflects a relationship between Q and the followers of John the Baptist, who criticized Herod Antipas' remarriage, though on different grounds than those in Q 16:18. But this is speculation.

A shift seems evident between Q 16:18 and 17:1, from questions of Law to questions of how to deal with sin in the community; but we cannot know how the transition occurred. Thus while a rationale for the sequence of these sayings can be imagined, we can have little confidence in it because of the fragmentary nature of this part of Q. It is does not seem wise to make inferences about Q based upon these scattered sayings.

The Q Apocalypse (Q 17:[20b-21], 23–24, 26–27, 30, 34–35, 37b)

Luke 17:[20b-21], 23–24, 26–27
30, 34–35, 37b

Matt 24:23, 26–27, 37–41, 28

20b"The kingdom of God
does not come with observation,
21nor will they say,
'Behold, here!' or 'There!'
For behold, the kingdom of God
is within you.

---

102. A different reading of this saying, as an "impossible aphorism," is offered by Dewey, "Quibbling over Serifs." The question here, however, is what the saying meant in its Q context, not what Jesus might have meant.

23And they will say to you,
'Behold, there!' 'Behold, here!'
Do not go out,

neither follow!
24For as the lightning,
flashing forth, lights up
from one place under the heaven
to another place under heaven,
so will be the son of man in his day.
26And as it was in the days of Noah,
so it will also be
in the days of the son of man:

27they were eating, drinking,
marrying and given in marriage
until the day Noah went into the ark,

and the flood came
and everyone perished.
30In like manner will be that day
when the son of man is revealed.
34I say to you, in that night
there will be two upon a bed,
the one will be taken
and the other will be left;
35there will be two
grinding at the same place,
the one will be taken
and the other will be left."
37And answering, they said to him,
"Where, master?" And he said to them,
"Where the body is,
there also the eagles
will be gathered together."

23"Then if someone says to you,
"Behold, here is the messiah!"
or "Here!" Do not believe!
26If therefore they say to you,
"Behold, in the wilderness!"
Do not go out!
"Behold, in the chambers!"
Do not believe!
27For as the lightning
comes
out of the east
and is visible as far as the west,
so will be the arrival of the son of man.
37For just as in the days of Noah,
so will be
the arrival of the son of man.
38For as in [those] days
before the flood
they are eating and drinking,
marrying and giving in marriage
until the day Noah went into the ark,
39and they did not know until
the flood came
and they were all swept away,
so likewise also will be
the arrival of the son of man.
40Then
there will be two men in the field,
one is taken
and one is left;
41two women are
grinding at the mill,
one is taken
and one is left.

28So where the carcass is,
there the eagles
will be gathered.

As often happens, Matthew conflates Mark and Q material, here into a lengthy apocalyptic unit (24:3–25:38). Luke, as previously where there are Markan and Q versions of similar material, keeps them separate (17:20–37 and 21:7–36). The second of the two apocalyptic units in Luke takes its setting and most of its content from Mark, omitting only a few verses from Mark (13:9a, 10, 18, 27, 32, 33) and adding only a small amount of special material (Luke 21:18, 23b–24, 26a, 28, in addition to the conclusion in 21:34–36). Matthew, on the other hand, has added both Q and special material to the Markan framework, omitting some Markan parallel material he used elsewhere (Mark 13:9c-12), inserting some special material (24:10–12), but attaching most of the non-Markan material at the end of the Markan apocalypse. These observations suggest two conclusions: (1) Luke is more likely to have retained the Q apocalypse as a unit, but (2) Matthew may have kept some of the Q material together since he attached it to the end of his discourse.

The integrity of the Q apocalyptic unit may be seen in Matt 24:37–41//Luke 17:26, 27, 30, 34–35.[103] Luke has added special material in 17:[28, 29,] 31, 32, and one verse (17:33) is found elsewhere in Matthew (10:39). A sayings couplet is found in Matt 24:26–27//Luke 17:23–24; in both Matthew and Luke, this couplet precedes the larger cluster. So with considerable confidence we may regard this as an apocalyptic discourse, including at least Q 17:23–24, 26–27, 30, 34–35. It is difficult to know where the Q apocalypse began. Even though only Luke has the sayings in 17:20–21, some scholars have speculated that these sayings, excluding Luke's introduction in 17:20a, were in Q.[104] We shall return to this question shortly.

The ending of the unit in Q is also unclear. The final saying in Luke (17:37) is located earlier in Matthew (24:28); here Matthew is likely to have preserved the Q location best. Luke did not understand the saying; he supposed that it had to do with location, with "where" the day of judgment would occur, and thus placed the saying at the end. However, the saying almost certainly has nothing to do with the issue of the location of the day of judgment. It appears, therefore, that the Q apocalypse concluded at Q 17:35; Luke 17:36 is poorly attested and rightly relegated by most translators to a footnote.[105] Only one verse remains to be located, Q 17:33, which Luke also probably misplaced. Its relocation was occasioned by Luke's addition of special material in 17:31,[106] and thus it does not belong in the Q apocalypse.

The setting for the Markan apocalypse is Jesus' prediction of the destruction of the Temple. This is hardly accidental, for the destruction of the Temple played an important role in Jewish apocalyptic speculation, and appears in the Markan apocalypse too (13:14–18; cf. Luke 21:24). However, the Temple and its destruction play no role at all in the Q apocalypse.

If we set aside for now the question whether Luke 17:20b–21 should be assigned to Q, we are left with what appears to be a three-part composition:

---

103. It is not essential here to decide whether Luke 17:28–29 is Q material omitted by Matthew, material created by Luke, or pre-Lukan material added to Luke's Q. For the options, see Kloppenborg, *Q Parallels*, 192, 194; *Formation*, 156–58. See also Catchpole, "The Law and the Prophets," 102–3.

104. See Kloppenborg, *Q Parallels*, 188.

105. It is attested only by Codex Cantabrigiensis, some miniscules (700, f^{13}), other Old Latin versions, and the Syriac versions.

106. Cf. 21:34 for a similar Lukan moralistic interpretation.

a. Warning about false reports   Q 17:23
  (1) Putative reason for disregarding these reports   17:24
  (2) Aphorism, perhaps intended as a wry comment on 17:23   17:37b
b. Comparison, introduced by "just as" (ὥσπερ)[107] stressing
   the unexpected nature of the "revealing"[108] of the son of
   man   17:26-27, 30
c. Predictive conclusion (a sayings couplet)   17:34-35

Perhaps the closest structural parallel to this is 1 Thess 5:1-3.[109] This is especially striking in part "c" below. Parts "b" and "c" together resemble Luke 17:20b-21:

a. Announcement of topic "concerning times and fateful moments . . ." [περὶ δὲ χρόνων καὶ τῶν καιρῶν])   1 Thess 5:1a
b. Assurance   5:1b
   Reason (invocation of tradition)   5:2
c. Prediction of false reports and unexpected events   5:3a
  (1) Comparison, introduced by "just as" (ὥσπερ)   5:3b
  (2) Predictive conclusion   5:3c

Both Q and 1 Thess 5:1-3 deal with a false sense of security that is shattered—in Q by the revelation of the son of man, in 1 Thessalonians by the "day of the Lord" (5:2). Both cite false reports and both use comparisons introduced by "just as." The image of a thief in the night (1 Thess 5:2) is also found in Q, though in a different context (Q 12:39-40). Perhaps the most striking similarity is that eschatological calculation is excluded in both texts: the day of the Lord and the son of man will both come as a surprise. Nevertheless, there are interesting divergences as well: "son of man" is found in Q but not in 1 Thessalonians, and the latter wishes to provide assurance while Q gives only warning. Further, in Q the focus is on *where* the eschatological event will occur, not, as in 1 Thessalonians, on *when*.

The Q apocalypse must be compared with other apocalyptic discourses. For example, the well-organized discourse in Did 16:3-7 sets forth a clear apocalyptic agenda,[110] of which there is no trace in Q. Correspondingly, the notion of a sudden, unexpected event is not found in Did 16:3-7. By the time 2 Thess 2:1-12 was written, a sudden parousia apparently came to be regarded as an error, because it must be preceded by the "man of lawlessness" (2:3); however, the discourse is quite confused in comparison with Did 16:3-7.

107. Matthew's reading is to be preferred here; Schulz, *Q*, 279.
108. Matthew speaks of the "arrival" (παρουσία) of the son of man. He is the only evangelist to use this word, and he uses it four times. There is no reason why Luke would have introduced "revealing" ("reveal" occurs elsewhere in Q [10:21, 22; 12:2]), so Luke's wording is to be preferred.
109. Schulz (*Q*, 286) cites 1 Thess 5:2-3, but regards 1 Thess 4:16-17 as closer to Q. ApocElij 3:1-4 should also be mentioned, though the age of this tradition is uncertain.
110. The three signs of the truth in Did 16:6, the same as the signs in 1 Thess 4:16, correspond to three signs of falsehood in Did 16:3-4a; 16:4b; 16:5.

The Markan apocalypse evidences inconsistencies which suggest that it is a pastiche. For example, Mark 13:21-22 picks up an idea abandoned since 13:5b-6, and 13:24-27 seems to be the continuation of 13:19-20. The opening question in 13:4 does not seem to find a response until 13:7-8. The notion of a sudden parousia in 13:32-37 is found side by side with apocalyptic timetables (e.g., 13:24-27, 28-29). As in other apocalyptic discourses, admonitions abound. Q, on the other hand, is remarkable for its lack of timetables and admonitions.[111]

Q is consistent in its rejection of apocalyptic timetables. As in the Q apocalypse, so too in Q 12:39-40 the coming of the son of man is sudden and unexpected, like the invasion of a thief. Likewise, in Q 11:29-32 "no sign" is given to "this generation" except the "sign of Jonah," which was earlier interpreted as the prophetic preaching of repentance (11:29-30).[112] It is rather signs of the times to which people are directed (Q 12:54-56), not the signs of the end. Indeed, the apocalyptic notion of "divisions" among people[113] is used in Q not of some future apocalyptic travail but of the present (12:51, 53; cf. 14:26).

The corollary to this rejection of apocalyptic timetables is the emphasis upon what is already present but ignored. And this is consistent with much of what we find elsewhere in Q. Thus in a saying formally similar to Q 17:23 it is stated that a greater than Solomon is here (11:31) and that a greater than Jonah is here (11:32). The kingdom can be experienced now in exorcisms (11:20; cf. Q[?] 10:9). The reason why the present is decisive is spelled out in Q 10:16. Those who "see" and "hear" see and hear now something which was long awaited (10:23-24). The parables of the mustard seed and leaven (Q 13:19-21) also stress what is going on in the present.

Given this evidence, it in necessary to reopen the question whether Luke 17:20b-21 was in Q. Here too apocalyptic speculation is rejected precisely because the kingdom is already present. Though it remains uncertain whether these sayings appeared in Q, they would certainly have fit well there. Moreover, that these sayings are not simply Lukan redaction is shown by their probably independent attestation in GThom 113 (cf. GThom 3).[114] If the notion of the presence of the kingdom in Luke 17:20b-21 can be assigned to Q, we must nevertheless observe that this idea plays no explicit role in the rest of the Q apocalypse. Indeed, aside from the consistent emphasis on "no signs" throughout the Q apocalypse noted earlier, the apocalypse is a rather puzzling unit, with significant internal tensions.

---

111. On timetables, see Schulz, *Q*, 286; on the lack of admonitions, see Piper, *Wisdom*, 142.

112. See also the comment of Catchpole: "Both [Q 11:29-30 and 17:23-30] confront critically ideas associated with the movements of the charismatic-eschatological leaders, and both do so by recourse to the coming of the Son of Man" ("The Law and the Prophets," 105).

113. See Mic 7:2, 5-6; 2ApocBar 70:2-10; 4 Ezra 6:24; Jub 23:16-17; 1 Enoch 99:5; 100:2.

114. See Robinson, "Study of the Historical Jesus," 50-53.

Philipp Vielhauer has argued that Q 17:23 and 17:24 cannot have originally belonged together and are in tension with each other.[115] Q 17:23 has to do with eschatological expectations which appear to be messianic.[116] Matthew's wording of Q 17:23 (=Matt 24:26) is to be preferred except for the last words, "do not believe it."[117] Q 17:24, on the other hand, has to do with the "son of man."[118] These are quite different ideas. The usual interpretation of Q 17:23–24 is that "when the son of man appears on his day, there will be no mistaking the fact any more than one can mistake the occurrence of lightning which is universally visible."[119] But this interpretation is impossible, because it requires that Q 17:23 has to do with false "son of man" claimants. The notion of pretenders to the title "son of man" is an idea that flies in the face of everything we know—such as it is—about the "son of man." Further, the metaphor of lightning[120] in Q 17:24 should be interpreted in relation to 17:26–27, 30, which continues the "son of man" theme, rather than in connection with 17:23. The problematical relationship of 17:23 to 17:24 argues for the same realignment. In that context, 17:24 may have theophanic overtones, but judgment is clearly the basic idea.[121] If this is the case, then the tension between Q 17:23 and 17:24 becomes even more obvious.

115. Vielhauer, "Gottesreich und Menschensohn," 667–68; "Jesus und der Menschensohn," 148–50.

116. Q itself attests people going out to the wilderness because of some sort of eschatological hope in Q 7:24–26. Note also the wilderness sojourn of Jesus in the context of an apparent rejection of messianic hopes (Q 4:1–13).

117. Luke's briefer "Behold, there! Behold, here!" is similar to Q 11:31, 32. However, Matthew's wording is still to be preferred: (1) Luke's wording can be accounted for as assimilation to Mark 13:21; (2) the reference to seeking in the wilderness also occurs in Q 7:27; for "chamber" (ταμεῖον) see Q 12:3. No preference can be established for Luke's form of "go out" (ἀπέρχεσθαι) over Matthew's (ἐξέρχεσθαι). However, the former occurs only twice in Q, the latter eight times, and so is to be preferred. Matthew's "do not believe" is from Mark 13:21; Luke's "pursue" (διώκειν) occurs only here in Luke-Acts with this meaning, so it is not suspect.

118. It is widely agreed that Matthew's "parousia" is redactional (cf. 24:3, 37, 39—the only instances in all four gospels). "Reveal" (ἀποκαλύπτειν) occurs elsewhere in Q (10:21, 22; 12:2). Luke's "in his day" may be from Q, though it is texually uncertain. Since the Q wording for 17:30 is also unclear (except that "parousia" was not in Q), we cannot be sure whether Q referred to the "day of the son of man." If it did, it would be unique, because nowhere else is "day" linked to "son of man."

119. So Marshall, Luke, 660, typical of many commentators.

120. For the metaphor in general see Speyer, "Gewitter." There are stable traditions of metaphoric usage related to lightning. For example, Yahweh's sword that flashes like lightning (Deut 32:41; Hab 3:11; Ezek 21:14–15, 20, 33 [English: 21:9–10, 15, 28]); arrows and lightning rout the enemy (2 Sam 22:15; Ps 17:15 [English: 18:14]; 144:6]). With similar metaphoric stability, the "day of Yahweh" is a day of darkness and gloom (Amos 5:18, 20; Isa 13:9–10; Ezek 30:3; Joel 2:1–2, 10–11; Zeph 1:15–16); i.e., lightning was not part of the "day of Yahweh" imagery. Such stereotyped metaphoric expressions are rare in later Jewish and then in Christian sources, and lightning can be associated with either theophany or judgment. Which is primary, therefore, cannot be established for Q 17:23 simply by reference to metaphoric traditions. For an attempt to determine the kind of lightning envisioned, see Rüstow, "ENTOC YMΩN ECTIN," 203–4; Rüstow concludes that sheet lightning is meant.

121. Speyer ("Gewitter," 1151) emphasizes this, but wants to see Jesus as son of man taking the place here of Yahweh as world judge, something that cannot be deduced from Q.

Q 17:23 also stands in the sharpest possible tension with Q 17:26–27, 30. Q 17:23 assumes such a fevered pitch of eschatological excitement that mere rumors could ignite a popular movement. Q 17:26–27, 30, on the other hand, assumes no such eschatological excitement.

Only one other saying in the Q apocalypse is an appropriate continuation of Q 17:23, and that is Q 17:37b. This latter saying is typically dubbed "enigmatic" or "puzzling" even after an interpretation is suggested, so uncertain does the suggestion seem even to the interpreter. It will be recalled that our reconstruction of the Q apocalypse followed Matthew at this point, placing Q 17:37b (=Matt 24:28) directly after Q 17:23–24 (=Matt 24:26–27). The Matthean reading of the saying is widely and rightly preferred.[122]

There is a perfectly logical interpretation of Q 17:37b, but so transfixed have interpreters been by the notion of the parousia of the son of man that other possibilities have rarely been considered. The saying, I suggest, is a sardonic comment on the suppression of Jewish freedom movements by the Romans. The "eagles" are the Romans.[123] While "eagle" was a polyvalent symbol, it was well known as a symbol of Rome and, in particular, of the Roman legions.[124] Indeed, it was possible to speak by metonymy of the Roman legions or soldiers simply as "eagles,"[125] or to speak of the legionary standard simply as an

Catchpole ("The Law and the Prophets," 105) correctly emphasizes that the lightning represents judgment; but he fails to see the problem this creates for explaining the relationship between 17:23 and 17:24. Thus, when he does explain their connection, he abandons the 'lightning as judgment' explanation and stresses instead the "universal scope" of the lightning as response to the mistaken particularity reflected in Q 17:23; cf. Malmede (*Lichtsymbolik*, 153 n. 38), who sees no connection to judgment.

122. Luke's "body" (σῶμα) is widely recognized as a delicate substitute for Matthew's (and Q's) "carcass" (πτῶμα).

123. This was suggested long ago by Wettstein (*Novum Testamentum Graecum* 1. 502): "Per aquilas, aquilae sive signa militaria Romanorum intelliguntur" (By eagles are to be understood 'eagles' or Roman military standards); see also Brown, "The Matthaean Apocalypse," 12.

124. See esp. Josephus *War* 3.123; the eagle was kept in a special shrine (see, e.g., Cicero *In Catilinam* 1.24). Heroic tales are told of standard-bearers risking life and limb to protect the eagle.

In the Hebrew Bible a distinction is made between the eagle (נשר) and the vulture (פרס); cf. Lev 11:13; Deut 14:12. But sometimes נשר seems to mean "vulture" (Lam 4:19; cf. Hos 8:1). The LXX, which translates נשר as ἀετός, introduces a clarification at Job 39:26–30. Given this general tendency to maintain the distinction, it is probable that "eagle" was intended here, not "vulture" (γύψ). All the more significance thus attaches to the use here of "eagle" rather than "vulture."

In the Hebrew Bible eagles are frequent symbols of foreign conquerors: Ezekiel 17 (Nebuchadrezzar and his army); Hos 8:1 (Assyrians); Lam 4:19 (Babylonians); cf. Jer 48:40; 49:22; Deut 28:49. The Qumran Habakkuk Commentary (1 QpHab 3.8–13) identifies the נשר of Hab 1:8 as the Kittim (=Romans, probably); so too the "eagle vision" in 4 Ezra 11–12; cf. 1 Enoch 90. The presence of an eagle on the Temple is said by Josephus to have triggered a revolt, but it may be doubted whether that eagle was Roman (Josephus *War* 1.648–55; *Ant.* 17.149–57; and see Goodenough, *Jewish Symbols*, 8. 123–25). See also Josephus *Ant.* 18.121–22; *War* 2.169–74; Philo *Leg.* 299–306.

125. Lucan *Civil War* 238; Tacitus *Annales* 15.17; Pliny *Historia Naturalis* 13.23; Caesar *Belli Hispaniensis* 30. Cf. *b. Sanh.* 12a, where two scholars are "captured by an eagle"; the context indicates that Roman soldiers or tax officers are intended.

"eagle."[126] The "body" (*RSV*) or, more properly, "carrion," which causes the "eagles" or vultures to gather would on this interpretation be the typically abortive Jewish popular uprising. The Greek word used here ($\pi\tau\hat{\omega}\mu\alpha$) typically means "corpse" in the New Testament, but more generally it denotes something fallen, collapsed, overthrown, a disaster, destruction. In fact, the word usually has these meanings in the Septuagint. So there may have been a double meaning: corpse as well as tragic failure. The point therefore is that wherever Jewish groups make efforts to resist Roman oppression, the Roman army will invariably be there to devour them.[127]

If this is what Q 17:37b means, then it is apparent why it is so appropriate after 17:23, where such eschatologically motivated activity is implied. Q 17:23 seems to reflect an early stage in the life of the Q group. The group was apparently vulnerable to any eschatological excitement in the Jewish community at large. The initiative came from outside the Q group ("*they* say . . ."), but the Q group shared at this point in the life and hopes of the wider Jewish community. Its own boundaries were not clear. The saying, in fact, sought to establish such boundaries. The warning not to heed these false alarms was clinched by the warning proverb, "Where the carrion is, there the eagles are gathered together."[128]

Implicit in the analysis above is the conclusion that the apocalyptic sayings dealing with the son of man were added later. These sayings are consistent with Q 17:23, 37b in that they also reject apocalyptic watching and waiting. Indeed, these sayings are paradoxical in a way that Q 17:23, 37b are not, since they use apocalyptic language against apocalypticism! And although nothing is said explicitly of the kingdom which is present, that seems to be implied in Q 17:26-27, 30. The comparison of the days of Noah with the days of the son of man makes sense only if it is assumed that a decision could be made now: enter the ark! Strictly speaking, the comparison does violence to the flood story, since Noah issued no invitation to enter his ark, nor does the story imply that Noah's generation should have clamored to get in. Despite this, however, the Q saying implies a present opportunity which the current generation is heedlessly neglecting, just as the guests ignored the invitation to the great banquet.

---

126. Plutarch *Caius Marius* 23.5 and *Cicero* 38.5; Cicero *Philippicae* 14.27; Ovid *Epistulae ex Ponto* 2.8.69–70; Josephus *War* 3.123. Note the term "eagle-bearer" (i.e., the legionary standard-bearer; Greek $\dot{\alpha}\epsilon\tau o\phi\acute{o}\rho o s$; Latin *aquilifer*): see Caesar *Bellum Civile* 3.64; and *Bellum Gallicum* 5.37; Suetonius *Divus Augustus* 10.4.

127. Piper (*Wisdom*, 138–42) rightly notes the inevitability implicit in the "where . . . there, . . ." formulation, but wrongly, in my view, interprets the saying in relation to Q 17:24.

128. The parallel usually cited is Job 39:30. Ehrhardt ("Greek Proverbs," 53–58) calls attention to Job 15:23 LXX (the Masoretic Text differs), and seeks to trace the Septuagintal reading to "a Hellenistic proverb" he finds attested in Cornutus and in parallels cited by Wettstein from Seneca, Martial, Lucan, Lucian and Aelian. But his evidence is unconvincing. What he shows is only that the image of vultures circling above carrion was, as one would expect, a fairly common metaphor. I also do not agree with Guenther's claim ("When 'Eagles' Draw Together," 146) that "the saying's origin is easy to find," namely Hab 1:8 and Job 39:27, 30.

Thus the point of Q 17:26-27, 30—as probably of 17:34-35 as well—is to excoriate the Q people's contemporaries. It is certainly not to promulgate a new idea, the "son of man."[129] What is new in Q 17:26-27, 30 over against 17:23, 37b, is precisely the intention to denounce and threaten. Q 17:26-27, 30 reflects the pain of being ignored, reflected also in the parable of the great banquet and other sayings in Q, a pain arising not out of being personally slighted but out of the sense of being endowed with a message of utterly critical importance which is simply being disregarded. The "son of man" sayings which are added have to do only with judgment.

The reference to the "*day* of the son of man"[130] is unique to Q. It is, apparently, a blending of the "day of the Lord," i.e., the day of judgment, a commonplace in Israelite prophecy,[131] with the figure of the "son of man." However, despite the connection commonly made between Q 17:24, 26-27, 30, and Dan 7:13-14 or other "son of man" texts, the fact is that this connection is so tenuous as to be unconvincing. Nothing specific, such as the comparison with a lightning flash in Q 17:24, connects the Q passage to these Jewish apocalyptic sources.[132] And Q differs from them in one decisive way: the "son of man" in the Q apocalypse is not a redeemer figure, only a judgment figure. Nothing is said of an exaltation of the son of man, or how the son of man will rescue the righteous and destroy their enemies. A "revealing" of the son of man is mentioned in Q 17:30, but this is associated only with the destruction of the heedless, as is clear from the parallelism of this revealing with the flood which destroyed Noah's contemporaries.

There is nothing in Q 17:34-35 to indicate whether the son of man has anything to do with the rapture presumed in this text, or whether the rapture is for salvation or judgment. In any case, such a rapture is not associated in other Jewish apocalyptic texts with the son of man, so again the use of some common apocalyptic son of man imagery appears dubious.[133] The imagery in Q 17:34-35 is certainly surprising when it speaks of a separation of the righteous from the wicked. If such a separation is being anticipated, "wicked" or "righteous" are being redefined, because these verses imply that no difference is discernible between them until the very end.

Finally, it is possible that the son of man in the Q apocalypse is not an

129. Tödt notes the "extreme scantiness of details" about the son of man in these verses (*Son of Man*, 52; see also p. 48), a sharp contrast to the verbal efflorescence in some other Jewish apocalyptic texts.

130. Luke's wording here is to be preferred, as most scholars recognize. Only Matthew of the four canonical gospels uses the word "parousia," and he uses it three other times (24:3, 37, 39). The plural "days" is probably due to Lukan redaction, because he returns to the singular in 17:30. The reference to "day" in Q 17:24 (Luke only) is, however, very suspect textually. Lindars (*Jesus*, 95) argues that the "confusing references to 'days' and 'day'" were in Luke's source, namely Q, and led to his formulation in 7:22.

131. The earliest references to it are in Amos 5:18, 20; the most lurid descriptions are in Zephaniah. The "day" occurs in Q 10:12, [14]; 17:26; cf. 3:17.

132. Only the luminous "son of man" figure in Rev 1:12-16 is at all similar, though see ApocZeph 6:11; Dan 10:6.

133. Mahlon Smith ("To Judge the Son of Man") rightly denies any connection between Dan 7:13 and the sayings of Jesus, except in secondary sayings in Mark and Matthew.

individual but a symbol of the faithful people of God, among whom the Q group numbers itself.[134] Implicit in such an interpretation would, of course, be a judgment by a group of people. If Q[?] 22:28–30 envisions a corporate judge, then we would have attestation of precisely that idea elsewhere in Q. In fact, Q 11:31–32 also seems to attest this kind of judgment rendered not by an individual but by a group. It seems to me that only Q 7:34 and 9:58 will not admit of a corporate interpretation of "son of man," and these two sayings do not stand within the apocalyptic tradition; they are nothing more than circumlocutions for "I" or "that man." A corporate interpretation of the son of man for Q, then, seems at least as plausible as an individual, christological interpretation.

It is not necessary to enter more fully into a discussion of the son of man. However, efforts to solve this enigma need to begin with the texts at hand, not with Daniel 7, 1 Enoch, or 4 Ezra. This does not mean that no apocalyptic traditions stand behind the Q texts. But it does mean that we should seek to explain the Q son of man sayings more on the basis of Q itself than by reference to alleged "sources" of this "title."

It is difficult to assess the significance of the addition of the son of man sayings. However, we can exclude a desire to provide a new reason to ignore the waves of messianic enthusiasm that washed across the community (Q 17:23), since the problem presumed in the son of man sayings is not enthusiasm but its absence. Neither can we say that there has been a shift in eschatological outlook. The rejection of signs, of apocalyptic watching, that we find in Q 17:23, 37b, and elsewhere in Q is only made clearer in the son of man additions. Thus no apocalypticizing of the tradition seems to have occurred, even though new (son of man) language is used. We can observe a shift in context: the level of messianic excitement has subsided, even disappeared. Such waxing and waning of messianic enthusiasm is not an improbable scenario, even within short periods of time.

Two things seem to be new about the son of man sayings. First, they reflect a deep frustration with contemporaries who seem immune to warning, who move through the daily round indifferent to the gravity of the moment. We have seen this frustration again and again in Q. It is a leitmotiv in Q. Second, if a corporate interpretation of the son of man is correct, then we have an indication of a new sense of identity, a sharpening of group boundaries. Earlier, we noted an apparent lack of group self-definition in Q 17:23. The emergence of a more developed group self-definition may have occasioned the use of the son of man title, or the reverse may have occurred. But it was probably not an apocalypticizing tendency that led to this sharpening of group boundaries. Thus we seem to have here two layers: first Q 17:23, 37b, then Q 17:24, 26–27, 30, + 34–35 (?). This means too that a Q "apocalypse" emerged only at a relatively late date. However, determining the age of either stratum is difficult.

134. Moule ("Neglected Features") has argued for a corporate interpretation of the son of man as "true Israel." However, his argument is based on the premise that Jesus or Q had Dan 7:13 in mind.

Parable of the Rapacious Capitalist (Luke 19:12–27//Matt 25:14–30)

Luke 19:12–27

[12]He said therefore,
"A certain nobleman
went into a distant region
to receive for himself a kingdom
and to return.
[13]And summoning ten of his slaves

he gave them ten minas.

And he said to them,
'Do business until I come (back).'
[14]But his subjects hated him,
and they sent an embassy after him
saying, 'We do not want this one
to rule over us.'

[15]And upon his return,
having received the kingdom,
he also ordered to have summoned to him
those slaves to whom he had given
the money in order that he might know
what each had earned doing business.
[16]And the first came forward

saying,
'Master, your mina has earned ten more.'

[17]And he said to him,
'Well done, good slave!
Because you have been trustworthy
in very little,
you are to have authority over ten cities.'

[18]And the second came,

Matt 25:14–30

[14]"For in the same way
a man
going on a journey,

summoned his own slaves and
entrusted to them his possessions.
[15]And to one he gave five talents,
and to another two, and to another one,
to each according to his ability.

and he left on a journey.
Immediately, [16]having departed,
the one receiving five talents
worked with them and gained five more.
[17]Similarly, the one with two [talents]
gained two more.
[18]But the one receiving one [talent],
having departed, dug the ground
and hid his master's money.
[19]After much time,
the master of those slaves came
and settled accounts with them.

[20]And having come forward,
the one receiving five talents
presented five more talents, saying,
'Master, you entrusted five talents to me;
I have gained five more talents!'
[21]His master said to him,
'Well done good and trustworthy slave!
You were trustworthy
over little;
I will appoint you over much.
Enter into the joy of your master.'
[22]And having come forward,

saying,
'Your mina, master, has made
has made five minas!'
¹⁹He said to this one,

'And you,
be over five cities!'

²⁰And the other came saying,

'Master,
behold your mina which I kept
stored away in a napkin.
²¹For I feared you
because you are a severe man,
taking up what you did not put down,
and harvesting what you did not sow.'

²²He said to him,
'I condemn you out of your mouth,
worthless slave!
You knew that I,
I am a severe man,
taking up what I did not put down,
and harvesting where I did not sow?
²³So why did you not
put my money in the bank?
And upon returning
I would have collected it
with interest.'
²⁴And to those present he said,
'Take the mina from him and give
to the one having ten minas.'
²⁵And they said to him,
'Master, he has ten minas!'
²⁶'I say to you that to everyone
who has it will be given,

but from him who has not,
even what he has
he has will be taken away.
²⁷But concerning these enemies of mine,
who did not want me to rule over them,
bring them here and slaughter
them in my presence.'"

the one with two talents also said,
'Master, you entrusted two talents to me.
See, I have gained two more talents!'
²³His master said to him,
'Well done, good and trustworty slave!
You were trustworthy over little;
I appoint you over much.
Enter into the joy of your master.'
²⁴And also having come forward,
the one who received one talent said,
'Master,

I know you,
that you are a cruel man,
harvesting where you did not sow
and gathering whence you did not scatter.
²⁵And being afraid, when I left, I
I hid your talent in the ground.
Behold, take what is yours!'
²⁶And answering,
his master said to him.

'Worthless and indolent slave!
You knew that

I harvest where I did not sow
and I gather whence I did not scatter?
²⁷Therefore what you should have done
was invest the money with bankers,
and upon returning
I would have recovered what was mine
with interest.
²⁸So,
take away the talent and give it
to the one having ten talents.

²⁹For to everyone
who has it will be given,
and he will be extremely rich;
but from him who has not,
even what he has
will be taken from him.
³⁰And [you(pl.)] cast the useless slave
in the outer darkness!
In that place there will be weeping
and gnashing of teeth.'"

Whether this parable belongs in Q is a matter of dispute. That a traditional parable lies behind Luke 19:12-27//Matt 25:14-30 seems clear, and yet the differences between them are so pronounced that many scholars have wondered whether they can be accounted for by attributing them to redaction by the evangelists. Luke, as is widely recognized, offers a secondary version of the parable.[135] The theme of the throne claimant has been artificially imposed upon the parable (19:12, 14, 15, 17, 19, 27). But Matthew's version is not free of redaction either, most clearly in 25:30 (cf. 8:12; 13:42, 50; 22:13; 24:51).

The parable seems to have had an even more extensive history of development, however, for it has three conclusions in both Matthew and Luke: (1) Luke 19:24//Matt 25:28: the rendering of the master's judgment that the money of the cautious slave be given to the most successful slave; (2) Luke 19:26//Matt 25:29: a saying which circulated independently of the parable (cf. Mark 4:25; GThom 41) and which says, "To everyone who has, it will be given; but from the one who does not have, even what he has will be taken from him"[136]; and (3) Luke 19:27 and Matt 25:30: a final act of revenge upon the king's enemies (Luke) or upon the cautious slave (Matthew). The third conclusion in Matthew is particularly ill-fitting, whereas Luke's third conclusion at least does not clash with his second conclusion. It may be merely fortuitous that Matthew and Luke have the same sequence of three conclusions; Matt 25:30 may be the final conclusion simply because its placement before 25:29 would have made the latter anticlimactic, and Luke 19:27 cannot be imagined anywhere else. Therefore inferences concerning a Q origin of the parable probably should not be drawn on the basis of this coincidence.

One of the conclusions, Matt 25:30, suddenly shifts the reader out of the mundane world of ancient finance and master/slave relationships into a final judgment scene, and thus casts the whole parable into an eschatological mold. Otherwise, there is nothing overtly eschatological in the parable, except for Matthean additions such as in 25:21: "enter into the joy of your master." How Luke 19:26//Matt 25:29 relates to the parable will be examined shortly.

However, still another saying inserted into the parable is potentially its main point, hence competing with the other conclusions. Luke 19:17//Matt 25:21 provides a reason for praising the most successful slave (namely, "you were faithful in little, you will be set over much") and a statement of reward, which elaborates this saying. The parable would have worked quite well if the master had said simply, "Well done, good and faithful servant."[137] As it is, the addition of the saying adds a new element—the idea of being faithful in the small things, and a motive—upward mobility. One could well see this as the main

135. See, e.g., Scott, *Hear Then the Parable*, 221-23; Jeremias, *Parables*, 58-60.

136. The relative construction in Mark 4:25 and GThom 41 may be more primitive, if the participial construction in Luke 19:26//Matt 25:29 represents an improvement in the Greek. See Dodd, *Parables*, 116 n. 2, and Crossan, *In Fragments*, 197.

137. Matthew's "good and faithful" may be original, since Luke uses "faithful" later; see Q 12:42.

point of the parable. The saying does not actually fit very well, since what is at issue is not a matter of simply being faithful (the cautious slave was faithful too!), but of being successful in multiplying the master's capital. The "faithful in little/set over much" saying also has the effect of transforming the parable into a test concocted by the master to determine who among the slaves should be elevated to some presumably vacant position(s) of authority over the household.

Many interpreters see this parable as an allegory, and elements peculiar to one or the other evangelist (e.g., "a long time" in Matt 25:19a; 25:21b and 23, noted earlier; 25:30; and Luke 19:27) can be so construed. But there is nothing allegorical in either version of the parable, taken by itself and apart from the redactional activity of the evangelists. Neither, as noted before, is there anything overtly eschatological about the parable.

Although the parable has a number of internal tensions, as just observed, it is quite possible to understand it simply as a master/slave parable. The parable depicts a relatively wealthy and clearly rapacious (Luke 19:21, 22//Matt 25:24, 26) man—no doubt the owner of a large estate—who has slaves who serve as his financial agents.[138] This is a situation we also meet in Matt 18:23-35.[139] The money entrusted to the slaves is neither a gift,[140] since a reckoning is demanded, nor a loan, since the interest as well as the principal belong to the master. Rather, the man has cash on hand which he does not wish to let sit idle while he is away on a journey. Several slaves, therefore, are given various amounts of money.[141] The expectation is that the slaves will multiply their

138. So Goodman, *State and Society in Ancient Galilee*, 38.

139. A slave would not incur such a large debt, so it must be money entrusted to him for investment. This slave has other slaves under him. What is described is a kind of royal team of investors charged with increasing the king's capital. The slave even has the authority to imprison debtors (Matt 18:30). The slave does not wish to be sold (18:25), in part because it will mean loss of status.

The slave in Luke 16:1-7 is not a financial agent but a "steward" ($o\dot{\iota}\kappa o\nu\acute{o}\mu o\varsigma$), holder of an administrative position (see 1 Cor 9:17, 19; Josephus *Ant.* 2.89) which demanded trustworthiness (1 Cor 4:2; cf. Tit 1:7; 1 Pet 4:10). On management as a function of slaves, see Finley, *Ancient Economy*, 75-76. A steward might have other slaves under him (see IgnEph 6:1). It was a comparatively privileged position (Luke 16:3). It should not be assumed that the steward in Luke 16:1-7 merely reduces his profit, since all profit earned by a steward belonged to the master; see Jeremias, *Parables*, 181-82; Crossan, *In Parables*, 109-10; and esp. Kloppenborg, "The Dishonoured Master."

140. Therefore it is incorrect to speak of the "graciousness" of the master, as does Fitzmyer (*Luke*, 1232-33).

141. It is not clear whether Matthew's "talents" or Luke's "mina" is original. Talent and mina are both measures of weight and not coins. The value of each is more uncertain than one would surmise from standard charts, such as that in the *Oxford Annotated Bible* (p. 1547), where a talent is given as 60 minas or 75.558 pounds (presumably of the predominant hellenistic currency, silver, which is the metal mentioned in the parable—Luke 19:15, 23; Matt 25:18, 27). Matthew appears to have the much larger amount, but he may well have had no real idea of the value of a "talent." In 18:25, Matthew implies that the sale of a slave, his wife, and children, plus whatever they owned, would yield enough to pay a 10,000 talent debt! The 10,000 talent number is itself totally improbable, but it appears that we do not have merely exaggeration for effect. Note too that for Matthew five talents (25:16) could be described as "a little" (25:21). So the real difference between Matthew's talents and Luke's

master's capital, hence the anger with the third, cautious slave who did not want to risk loss of the entrusted funds. Only if making more money is the expectation does the treatment of the third slave make sense.

The two successful slaves are highly successful. Luke's three slaves get equal amounts, one mina each; the first slave reports a 1000% increase on his mina, the second a 500% increase. Matthew's slaves get unequal amounts (five talents and two talents), but report equal increases of 100%. Since the master was away on a journey, we may assume that the slaves made short-term loans.[142] Only usurious, not to say extortionary, loans would yield such fantastic results.[143] The two slaves prove to be as rapacious as their master![144] Accordingly, the third slave cannot appear as anything but a useless wimp, and so his funds are transferred to a proven winner. The parable, then, is a peek into the inclement world of ancient finance.[145] No doubt an element of drama was present, since one could never tell how slaves might behave while their master was gone. Many horror stories were told about this (e.g., Mark 12:1-8; Q 12:45). One could draw the inference that this capitalist's success with his slaves was due precisely to his uncompromising refusal to put up with slaves who would not perform to his expectations. Ruthlessness paid dividends.

Given the unsavory nature of the characters in this parable, it is hardly surprising that interpretations were incorporated into the parable itself. The notion that faithfulness in a little can be the basis for a greater responsibility

minas is impossible to determine; one cannot simply use 'standard' values for comparison. Ordinary people never dealt in talents or probably even minas; so, for example, when these are mentioned in the Hebrew Bible, the context is almost always the palace or the Temple.

142. On short-term investments, see Finley, *Ancient Economy*, 53-57, 115-18. On ways of making money in general, see MacMullen, *Roman Social Relations*, 48-52; on the bourgeoisie, Rostovtzeff, *Social and Economic History of the Roman Empire*, 1115-26.

143. MacMullen (*Roman Social Relations*, 52) mentions mortgage as an ordinary form of loan, and calculates that at the typical six to eight percent interest one's money would double in a dozen years. But interest much higher than this is known and rates must have varied widely depending, in part, on the vulnerability of the lendee. Since peasant debt was a serious problem in Palestine (see Oakman, *Jesus and the Economic Questions of His Day*, 72-77, and esp. "Jesus and Agrarian Palestine: The Factor of Debt"; also Appelbaum, "Josephus and the Economic Causes of the Jewish War"), attempts were made to limit usury (see, e.g., Levy, *Economic Life*, 55-56, 95; Levy cites interest rates in hellenistic Egypt of "24 per cent per annum for money loans, 50% for seed; and payments due in six months," and speaks of these rates as "very high"; p. 41). See further, Kloppenborg, "The Dishonoured Master," 482-86.

144. See POxy 3208 (in Horsley, *New Documents*, 1. 53), where a freed man advises a slave friend, who is a financial agent, to be stern with a subordinate slave who has apparently made a large amount of money from a small amount and is unwilling to give the total to the master. On masters and slaves in general, see Finley, *Ancient Economy*, 62-94, esp. 75-76.

145. Note the number of financial technical terms that occur: "money" (ἀργύριον, Luke 19:15, 23; Matt 25:18, 27); "do business" (πραγματεύεσθαι, Luke 19:13; cf. 19:15); "earn more" (προεργάζεσθαι, Luke 19:16); "settle accounts" (συναίρειν λόγον, Matt 25:19); "interest" (τόκος, Luke 19:23; Matt 25:27); "bank" (τράπεζα, Luke 19:23) or "banker" (τραπεζίτης, Matt 25:27); and "collect" (πράσσειν, Luke 19:13). The common usage of most of these terms is attested in Moulton and Milligan, *Vocabulary of the Greek Testament*, s.vv. Further, Luke 19:21b seems to reflect a common saying about banking ("You take up what you did not lay down [i.e., on the money-changer's bench or 'bank']"); see Scott, *Hear Then the Parable*, 229; Fitzmyer, *Luke*, 1237.

(Matt 25:21, 23//Luke 19:17) could be understood as a "Q" theme; cf. Q 12:42–44, where continuing faithfulness during a master's absence results in being set over all the master's possessions. However, the other interpretation, in Matt 25:29//Luke 19:26, seems rather to fly in the face of most of what we find in Q. It asserts that the "haves" get more and the "have nots" lose everything, which is the opposite of what we find in Q; cf. Q 6:20–22, 38; 10:21; 11:9–10; 12:22–31.

It is certainly possible to imagine Matt 25:29//Luke 19:26 as an interpretive addition earlier than Matt 25:21, 23//Luke 19:17. The former corresponds much more to the tenor of the parable. It is hardly a "moral"; it is rather a resigned admission of how things stand: the rich get richer and the poor get poorer.[146] The moral evaluation of the slaves ("good" in Matt 25:21a, 23a// Luke 19:17a; "evil" in Matt 25:26//Luke 19:22) is probably a later addition, along with the saying in Matt 25:21b, 23b//Luke 19:17b.[147] If this moral discrimination on the basis of faithfulness is a later addition, then some basis for assigning the parable to Q might be discerned since, as noted, it resembles Q 12:42–44. Indeed, one might even imagine the parable as having come in Q right after 12:42–46, but neither Matthew nor Luke puts it there.

It is hard to find anything in this parable, except the thematic resonance with Q 12:42–44, which would encourage assigning it to Q. Further, the parable is odd coming, as one would have to suppose, after the Q apocalypse and just before the presumed ending of Q, namely Q 22:28–30. The length of the parable is also against its inclusion in Q. My conclusion is that the parable of the rapacious capitalist was probably not in Q.

Judging the Twelve Tribes (Q 22:28–30)

Luke 22:28–30	Matt 19:28
[28]And you are the ones who have continued with me in my trials. [29]Just as my father conferred on me a kingdom, I in turn confer [a kingdom] on you [30]that you may eat and drink at my table in my kingdom,	[28]Amen, I say to you—you, the ones who have followed me—
	in the renewal when the son of man is seated on his throne of glory,
and you will sit on thrones judging the twelve tribes of Israel.	you also will sit on twelve thrones judging the twelve tribes of Israel.

This is a difficult text to analyze because it occurs in a Markan context both in Matthew and in Luke, and because of significant differences in wording. If

---

146. However, there are possible parallels to this saying, cited in Strack-Billerbeck, *Kommentar*, 1. 661–62, to which may be added several rabbinic sayings in Montefiore, *Rabbinic Anthology*, 223 (selections 594–96).

147. This too may have been a current proverb; see *Ahiqar* 13.192–93; *Genesis Rabbah* 20,5.

the text was in Q, its context can only be conjectured. Crossan has argued that Q ended with (a) the Q apocalypse, (b) the double parable of the Pounds/ Throne Claimant, and (c) the twelve thrones saying.[148] His main argument for this is that the twelve thrones saying "links verbally and thematically, directly and immediately" with the double parable by means of the repeated "kingdom" (Luke 19:12, 15, 27; 22:29, 30).[149] The problem with this proposal is that it requires us to hold that the Lukan reading for both texts represents Q, and that Luke 22:29 was in Q, though it is not attested in Matthew. I do not believe either claim is tenable.

Ernst Bammel has argued that Q 22:28-30 formed the end of Q.[150] However, his argument requires a series of claims which, except for the first, are highly dubious: (a) that Luke's order is in general that of Q; (b) that 22:28, 30a was originally independent of 22:29, 30b; (c) that Luke 9:57–13:30 and 14:15–22:30 were originally independent sequences of sayings; (d) that 22:28, 30a originally followed Luke 13:30; and (e) when the two longer sections were joined Luke 22:28, 30a was moved to the end and amalgamated with 22:29, 30b.[151] No evidence is offered for (b), and (c) is neither demonstrated nor, it would seem, demonstrable.[152] Further, Bammel's argument requires that Luke 22:29, 30a, which have no parallel in Matthew, be assigned to Q.[153]

If the location of this pericope cannot be determined, we can nevertheless consider the text as an interesting, if non-locatable, text in Q. However, here we come upon the problem of determining its wording in Q. The one part of the saying where there is general agreement is at the end: "and you will sit on [twelve] thrones judging the twelve tribes of Israel." I shall consider only some of the more important differences.

1. The Opening of the Saying

The clumsy opening in Matthew's version might be due to the fact that, as in Luke's version, Q began with direct address to "you" followed by some qualifier, such as Matthew's "who have followed me." Luke's "in my trials" is highly suspect both because of the larger context, in which Luke draws a sharp contrast between Judas and others (see 22:3–6, 31–34, 40), and because of his frequent use of the word "trial" ($\pi\epsilon\iota\rho\alpha\sigma\mu\acute{o}s$).[154] On the other hand, Matthew's "follow" is suspect because of its occurrence in 19:27. However, it is not

148. Crossan, *In Fragments*, 203–4; similarly, Lührmann, *Redaktion*, 75.
149. Crossan, *In Fragments*, 203.
150. Bammel, "Das Ende von Q."
151. Bammel, "Das Ende von Q," 45–46.
152. See, e.g., Talbert (*Reading Luke*, 111–12), who finds a chiastic structure extending from 9:51 to 19:44.
153. It is Bammel's thesis that the location of Q 22:28–30 at the end of Q casts the entire work into the testamentary genre, and helps explain why Q has no passion narrative. However, this virtually requires the judgment that the verb "to confer" ($\delta\iota\alpha\tau\iota\theta\acute{\epsilon}\nu\alpha\iota$) was in Q, which is unlikely since it is not attested in Matthew. Moreover, the verb may well not refer to a testamentary disposition; see Behm, "$\delta\iota\alpha\tau\acute{\iota}\theta\eta\mu\iota$," 105.
154. It occurs six times in Luke, once in Acts (20:19), only once in Mark, and twice in Matthew.

unreasonable to suppose that "follow" in 19:27 was what triggered the insertion of 19:28 by Matthew at this point. In any case, "follow" is attested elsewhere in Q (7:9; 9:57, 59). So it seems likely that the Q saying opened with a direct address ("you") followed by a qualifier such as "who have followed me," and that this was a complete phrase, as in Luke; its wording, however, can no longer be determined.[155]

2. "Renewal" versus "kingdom"

Matthew uses the rare word "renewal" or "rebirth" ($\pi\alpha\lambda\iota\gamma\gamma\epsilon\nu\epsilon\sigma\acute{\iota}\alpha$) to designate the time or era when the sitting on thrones will occur.[156] Luke, on the other hand, says this will happen "in my kingdom." Although "kingdom" might seem to be the word one would prefer, since it is attested elsewhere in Q, it is not so obvious as it might seem. "Kingdom" could easily be explained by Luke's apparent addition of "you may eat and drink at my table . . ."; the kingdom would be the logical place for such a meal (cf. Q 13:28–29). In fact, Luke uses "table" twice in the preceding verse (22:27) and in his institution of the Lord's Supper—the immediately preceding text—where reference is made to eating and drinking in the kingdom (22:15–20).[157] Moreover, Luke has recently discussed how "lordship" is to be exercised (22:25–26), so "kingdom" would be easily understandable as a Lukan correction. On the other hand, it is hard to see any reason why Matthew would have substituted "renewal" for "kingdom." The weight of probability, therefore, seems to be on the side of "renewal" as the word used by Q.

3. "Son of man"

In the present passage this title occurs only in Matthew. It is suspect because of the very similar language about the son of man on his glorious throne in

155. If the saying opened with an address to those "who have followed me," this would imply that sitting on thrones and judging are rewards for being followers. This, in fact, is a theme found in sayings which parallel the present saying; see, e.g., Wis 3:8; 5:16; Sir 4:15; 1 Enoch 108:12; Matt 25:34; Mark 10:37; 2 Tim 2:12; Rev 3:21; 5:10; 20:4, 6; 22:5.

156. The use of $\pi\alpha\lambda\iota\gamma\gamma\epsilon\nu\epsilon\sigma\acute{\iota}\alpha$ to refer to a renewal of the world as opposed to the rebirth or reincarnation of the individual seems to be rooted in Stoic usage; see Büchsel, "$\pi\alpha\lambda\iota\gamma\gamma\epsilon\nu\epsilon\sigma\acute{\iota}\alpha$," 686–88. Philo's refutation of this Stoic doctrine gives some idea of its nature (see De aeternitate mundi 45–51 and 76–116). The cosmos in Stoic doctrine is subject to periodic conflagrations and rebirths. What $\pi\alpha\lambda\iota\gamma\gamma\epsilon\nu\epsilon\sigma\acute{\iota}\alpha$ in Matt 19:28 has in common with Stoic usage is primarily its supra-individual reference. It need not—and probably does not—refer to a cosmic regeneration but rather to a regeneration of the nation of Israel with its twelve tribes. This meaning has its closest parallel in Josephus Ant. 11.66, where Josephus speaks of the exiles' return from Babylon as a $\pi\alpha\lambda\iota\gamma\gamma\epsilon\nu\epsilon\sigma\acute{\iota}\alpha\nu$ $\tau\hat{\eta}\varsigma$ $\pi\alpha\tau\rho\acute{\iota}\delta o\varsigma$ (rebirth of the fatherland); cf. Philo Vita Mosis 2.65; 1 Clem 9:4. A similar idea may be reflected in 1 QS 4:25.

157. Marshall (Luke, 817–18) notes that v. 30a is in the subjunctive mood whereas v. 30b is indicative, and sees this as an indication that "two sources have been joined." (For a different explanation see Colpe, "$\acute{o}$ $\upsilon\acute{\iota}o\varsigma$ $\tau o\hat{\upsilon}$ $\grave{\alpha}\nu\theta\rho\acute{\omega}\pi o\upsilon$," 448.) The fact that the agreement in wording between Matthew and Luke is minimal in v. 30a and nearly complete in v. 30b points in the same direction. That is, eating and drinking in the kingdom was not linked in Q to judging the twelve tribes.

Matt 25:31.[158] On the other hand, the Matthean context for the saying contains no clues as to why he would have introduced "son of man" here. The Lukan reading, if that of Q, would have worked at least as well for Matthew, if not better. In fact, since Matthew understood 19:28 as referring to the disciples' reward (see 19:27), the Lukan version would have been much better. What kind of reward is it to judge the twelve tribes of Israel? Nor would the word "throne" necessarily cause Matthew to think of the son of man, as we can see in Matt 5:34 and 23:22. So in this case, the presumption must be in favor of Matthew's "son of man."

4. "Twelve" (thrones)

Matthew, but not Luke, specifies "twelve thrones." This is important because "twelve thrones" may imply the notion of the "Twelve" (disciples or apostles). But Luke's version, "on thrones judging . . ." does not specify how many thrones there are, and thus need not entail the idea of the "Twelve."[159] Here Matthew is probably secondary. It is possible that Luke eliminated the first "twelve" because it will have implied the inclusion of Judas, who figures prominently in this context. But this seems unlikely, because Luke knew that Judas' place among the Twelve was not unalterable; he tells us about Judas' replacement (Acts 1:15–26). It is more likely that Matthew added "twelve" (he refers to the disciples in his context) than that Luke omitted it.[160]

If the idea of the Twelve (disciples) is not presupposed in this saying, however, the idea of the reconstitution of the twelve tribes of Israel probably is. Josephus reflects speculation about the location and number of the missing ten tribes (*Ant.* 11.133; cf. 2 Esdr 13:39–50; 2 ApocBar 78–86; TestMoses 4:9), and the gathering of the twelve tribes was expected by some (TestBen 9:2; probably at Qumran, to judge by numerous allusions in the Temple Scroll, the Community Rule [1 QS 8:1–4], and elsewhere; TestAbr 13:6; Jas 1:1; Luke 24:21; Acts 1:6; 26:7; Rom 11:26; Rev 7:4–8; 21:12 [cf. Ezek 48:30–34; 4 Q 164]).

5. "Judge"

Since the one secure bit of wording in this saying is the prediction that "you will sit on thrones judging the twelve tribes of Israel," we need to consider what this could mean, and which interpretation of "judge" ($\kappa\rho\iota\nu\epsilon\iota\nu$) would be most appropriate. "Judge" may mean "judging" in the sense of distinguishing between the righteous and the wicked and, perhaps, deciding their fate, or it may mean, or at least include the meaning, "govern," as it often does in the Hebrew Bible when judges such as Deborah are mentioned (e.g., Judg 3:10, 30; 4:4; 10:2, 3; 12:7, 8, 9, 11, 13; see also Ps 2:10 LXX; Wis 3:8; PssSol 19:26,

---

158. See 1 Enoch 62:2, 5; 69:29; cf. 45:3; 61:8.
159. Cf. 1 Enoch 108:12, where all of the righteous sit on separate thrones.
160. On the concept "twelve" in Q, see Guenther, *Footprints of Jesus' Twelve*, 23–25.

29). Matthew, it appears, understood "judging" both in the sense of administering justice (see Matt 25:31) and in the sense of "governing." The latter is implicit in Matthew's insertion of 19:28 into a Markan context (cf. Mark 10:17–31), where it must refer to a reward for leaving everything and following Jesus (note 19:27). This reward is probably not administering justice to the twelve tribes of Israel but governing them. Luke, on the other hand, almost certainly took the saying to refer to "governing," as we can see both from the reference to "kingdom" (22:29) and from the context in which he places the saying (22:25–27).

The closest parallels to Q 22:29–30 entail a reward for those who are faithful; this can be seen in Rev 3:21; cf. Dan 7:13–14, 18, 22; 1 Enoch 62:1, 14; Mark 10:37; Rev 2:26–28; 20:4. In these instances, the focus is on a ruling function rather than the administration of justice. This lends support to the view above that κρίνειν means "govern" in Q 22:29–30.[161]

The ideas that emerge in Q 22:28, 30b are not easy to connect with others in Q. Only occasionally do we find hints of some kind of restoration of Israel, perhaps in the "great banquet" parable (14:16–23) and the "gathering" saying (11:23b). The idea of the "Twelve," whether twelve disciples or the twelve tribes of Israel, is not found elsewhere in Q. The apparent promise of a future reward contrasts with other Q passages such as 9:58–60a; 14:26–27 and 17:33, where no reward is promised. If we could be sure that Q 22:28, 30b was in Q, and if we could know its location, it might shed much light on the theology of Q. Unfortunately, there are too many uncertainties to make any such inferences.

The Last Part of Q: A Summary

The following material has been assigned to the last part of Q. Asterisks indicate material which either could not be located in Q or whose presence in

---

161. Boring interprets κρίνειν to mean "judge" rather than "govern" (*Sayings of the Risen Jesus*, 178). He gives two reasons for this. First, "κρίνω does not mean 'govern', except in semitizing Greek," but he does not explain why a text from Q cannot be "semitizing Greek." Second, he argues that Q 22:28–30 reflects "the familiar apocalyptic picture of the saints participating in the judgment of the world (1 Enoch 108:12; 61:8; 62:2; 69:27; 45:3; 1 Cor 6:2; cf. Rev 20:4,11)," and this suggests that "judgment in the critical, condemnatory sense is intended" (p. 178). But only occasionally is it clear that in the relevant parallels a condemnatory judgment is really meant (e.g., 1 Enoch 61:8; 1 QpHab 5:4–5; TestAbr 13:6; 1 Cor 6:2; Jude 14–15//1 Enoch 1:9). More often the parallels deal with governing (Dan 7:13–14, 18, 22; Wis 3:8; 1 Enoch 108:12–13; Jub 32:19; 2 Tim 2:12; Rev 2:26–28; 3:21; 5:10; 20:6; and probably Matt 25:31–34 and Mark 10:37). In any case, Q 22:28–30 may have less to do with an apocalyptic scene of judgment than with a reconstitution of the twelve tribes, in which case "govern" would be more appropriate. Comparable may be *Pss. Sol.* 17:26, where the Davidic messiah gathers and restores the tribes and "judges" (κρίνειν) them in the sense of governing them. The development of courts of twelve is worked out in Baumgarten, "The Duodecimal Courts of Qumran, Revelation, and the Sanhedrin." See also 5 Ezra 1:38–40, and Bergren, "The 'People Coming from the East' in 5 Ezra 1:38."

Q was judged doubtful. Material judged to belong to the deuteronomistic/compositional layer is so indicated.

1. Q 11:52; 12:2, 3   (transitional between third and fourth sections)
2. Q 12:4–12
3. Q 12:22b–31
4. Q 12:33–34
5. Q 12:35–38
6. Q 12:39–40, 42–46
7. Q 12:49–53   (deuteronomistic/compositional layer)
8. Q 12:54–56   (deuteronomistic/compositional layer)
9. Q 12:58–59
10. Q 13:18–19, 20–21   (deuteronomistic/compositional layer)
11. Q 13:24–30
12. Q 13:34–35   (deuteronomistic/compositional layer)
13. Q 14:5
14. Q 14:16–24   (deuteronomistic/compositional layer)
15. Q 14:26–27; 17:33; 14:34–35   (deuteronomistic/compositional layer)
16. Q 15:4–7
17. Q 15:8–10*
18. Q 16:13, 17, 18; 17:3b, 4, 6*
19. Q 17:(20b–21), 23, 37b, 24, 26–27, 30, 34–35
20. Luke 19:12–27//Matt 25:14–30*
21. Q 22:28–30*

As I stated at the beginning of this chapter, it is difficult to discern in this material enough internal coherence to justify calling it a "section" of Q. However, I would call attention to a large central cluster of sayings assigned to the deuteronomistic/compositional stratum of Q. Further, I have noted the large number of parables or parabolic sayings which occur from Q 12:2 to the end of Q. It is curious that few of these are from the deuteronomistic stratum, and some which are (e.g., Q 13:18–19, 20–21) receive their deuteronomistic flavor only from their context. The major example of a parable in the deuteronomistic layer is Q 14:16–24; but this parable may have gained its deuteronomistic character from editing, although no layers within it can be identified.

The analysis has raised the question, whether Luke 19:12–27//Matt 25:14–30 should be assigned to Q, and the location of Q 22:28–30 was judged to be indeterminate. If these decisions are correct, this means that Q ended with an "apocalypse," though an admittedly odd one, because common apocalyptic "watching" is rejected. The "delay of the parousia" seems to be a post-deuteronomistic phenomenon (Q 12:40, 42–46).

Although in many cases strata could be identified in sayings compositions, it was difficult to assess these strata because a deuteronomistic layer could not be separately identified. An exception to this was Q 12:33–36, 49–53, 58–59 (not, to be sure, a single sayings composition but a sequence of Q material), where

12:49–53, 54–56 was assigned to the deuteronomistic layer. One stratum in this sequence was not present but was presupposed: a stratum in which "peace" was central. The next oldest stratum here was Q 12:33–34, 39, 58–59; then, somewhat later, 12:35–38. After the deuteronomistic layer was a later one: Q 12:40 + 42–46. Nevertheless, it was difficult to discern continuities between these pre- and post-deuteronomistic layers and other layers in Q. In some cases, evidence of association with the deuteronomistic stratum was noted (e.g., Q 17:26–27, 30), but the evidence for this was slender. In other cases, strata were distinguished which need not represent any significant elapse of time (e.g., Q 12:22b-23, 25; 12:24, 26b-28; 12:29–31).

In short, aside from the impressively large sequence of deuteronomistic material, no clear picture emerges of the compositional history of the rest of Q. But, as was the case in the third section of Q, the extensive sequence of deuteronomistic material would seem to provide added justification for designating that stratum the compositional level of Q.

Retrospect
Conclusion **and Prospect**

In recent years the Q group or community has awakened a good deal of scholarly interest. It must have been a very early group. Determining its character will probably shed enormous light on the history of the Jesus movement and thus on the origins of Christianity itself. The absence from Q of a passion and resurrection kerygma, which in various ways shaped most of the "apostolic" writings, suggests at the outset that the group which produced and used this document was different from other early Christian groups. The lack of a passion and resurrection kerygma can no longer be dismissed with the explanation that Q presupposed this kerygma and merely provides ethical instructions to supplement it. As we have seen, Q had its own quite different understanding of Jesus' death. Then, too, the absence in Q of named disciples, and probably even of the concept of Twelve disciples, suggests that the picture of the Jesus movement that we get from the canonical gospels is a picture which reflects structures of authority which were erected only later.

Questions about the origins of Christianity, therefore, already urge themselves upon us even before we know the literary history of Q. But that history cannot be written until we have made further progress in determining the stratigraphy of Q. An archaeologist cannot begin to sketch the history of a culture on the basis of a jumbled collection of artifacts; only when a stratigraphy has been established can such a history be written. We are in the same situation with respect to Q.

The Archaeology of Q

"Stratigraphy," a term increasingly used to refer to the literary strata in Q, is coming to be seen as perhaps the central task in Q research. It is this task to which most of this book has been devoted. Assessments of the genre of Q and of its *Sitz im Leben*—the group or community which produced and used Q, and its social and religious situation—cannot be determined with confidence until the history of the composition of Q has been sketched. Genre as well as *Sitz im Leben* may change with a document's development, and any single

251

description of either may be valid only for a particular stage in the composition of Q. But at least it now seems clear that it is legitimate to speak of a history of composition.

The process of establishing the stratigraphy of Q is a difficult and intricate one. It entails writing a history of the composition of Q, and this in turn entails making some basic judgments, which may or may not be justified, about how literary documents developed. This methodology understands literary breaks and tensions or contradictions in the material as evidence of a new literary stratum. It perhaps assumes more consistency on the part of the author(s) than is justified. And detecting shifts in perspective, tensions internal to the text, is often quite a subtle matter. Whether such assumptions and conclusions are justified cannot be established *a priori*; proposals for the separation of strata in Q and their organization into a compositional history will gain credibility only if others also find them convincing. Furthermore, any proposed compositional history must prove illuminating from a historical point of view.

A number of stratigraphic proposals have already been made; these have been reviewed earlier in this book. It is premature to judge any of these adequate or inadequate, including the one proposed in this book. Precisely because the process of determining the stratigraphy of Q is such a delicate process, based upon subtle judgments and, no doubt, biases, it is to be expected that only years of testing and re-examination will determine how much of any proposal can be accepted. Deeply entrenched assumptions, such as the notion that things evolve from the simple to the complex, can be useful heuristically, but they can also be misleading. Taste can play a role too—for example, a widespread modern distaste for apocalypticism. This is true for the study of any document; it is especially true for a document which is not even extant and must be reconstructed! Too ready acceptance of any proposal is cause for suspicion.

In this book a particular method and compositional history have been proposed, not in the belief that these will be the final words on the subject but because it is necessary to set forth a specific proposal so that other voices may enter into the discussion. That, as I see it, is the purpose of an introduction to Q. The term "stratigraphy," however, is a useful addition to the discussion because it helps us to visualize a methodology. At certain points in Q one can detect sayings compositions even where it is not possible to identify specific strata. It is often unclear, however, how one is to characterize any of the strata. One may be able to say with some confidence that one or two or more sayings seem to have been the original core of a particular composition. Likewise, one may say that another saying or two were added "later," and perhaps that other sayings were added still "later." But none of these strata may have such clearly distinguishing characteristics that they may confidently be associated with a stratum found elsewhere in Q. Moreover, "later" is a relative term; a saying could have been added the next day, or it could reflect changes in the self-understanding of a group over a longer period of time. This means that strata identified in one sayings composition cannot always be coordinated with strata in another sayings composition.

The key to stratigraphy is the identification of something which permits the comparison of strata. In geology and paleontology this is the "index fossil," usually a marine animal widely distributed and thus having an evolution which can be known because it occurs in identifiable sequences of geological strata. In archaeology, the key is usually pottery, since it too is common, widely disseminated, and its stylistic evolution can be determined. In the stratigraphy of Q, there is nothing comparable to these. However, there is one layer which, I have argued, is quite distinctive and must be the basis for any relative chronology of Q's literary strata: the deuteronomistic layer. Its themes and tendencies represent a relatively coherent complex. Any attempt to establish the stratigraphy of Q must proceed from that layer as the basis for comparison. The next step, obviously, is to see whether pre-deuteronomistic strata and post-deuteronomistic strata can be coordinated so as to establish stages of redaction.

It is hazardous to seek to establish a stratigraphy of Q based exclusively on genre, e.g., by separating out the sayings material and declaring that to be early. However, genre can provide a control or at least a means of confirming the credibility of one's analysis. But a stratigraphic analysis needs to make sense from a literary point of view. By this I mean that one must seek so far as possible to establish the sequence of the Q material and then demonstrate how a stratigraphic analysis can be shown to make sense in terms of the literary growth of the material. Obviously there is a significant element of circularity in such a procedure, since the analysis is the source of the stratigraphy in the first place. Nevertheless, a stratigraphic analysis which does not make sense in terms of the compositional analysis of the text can hardly be regarded as adequate.

It should be noted that not all of the Q material lends itself to stratigraphic analysis; for example, an isolated saying cannot be assigned to a stratum unless its content clearly requires its association with a particular stratum. Thus a stratigraphic analysis that does not include all the material in Q is not necessarily inferior to one that does.

We turn now to several test cases—instances in which several compositional strata can be detected. Because the deuteronomistic constellation of themes seems to provide the benchmark for a stratigraphy of Q, all cases below are compositions in which a deuteronomistic layer is identifiable. This is not meant as an exhaustive analysis, but it will perhaps illustrate both the usefulness and the difficulties of the method. In each case, stratum 1 is presumed to be the oldest layer. Further, in each case several features are listed which may or may not turn out to be useful in linking that stratum to other similar strata in other sayings compositions. The deuteronomistic strata are in italics.

Stratum	Q Content	Features
A.	6:20b-23	
A1	6:20–21	beatitude form, concern/hope for the poor and oppressed, "kingdom of God"
A2	6:22–23a, b	altered beatitude form, experience of opposition, response to opposition: sufferer rewarded
A3	*6:23c*	*prophetic self-consciousness, opposition inevitable*
B.	7:18–35 (+ 16:16)	
B1	7:24–27, (29?)	John as independent prophet and "more" than a prophet; "Behold, I send you" formula; radical lifestyle (John)
B2	*7:31–35; 16:16*	*John and Jesus on the same level; rejection of Jesus (and John); "this generation" epithet; personified Sophia; non-apocalyptic "son of man" (=Jesus); opposition to kingdom (=community)*
B3	7:18–23, 28	"coming one"=Jesus; miracles attest Jesus; subordination of John to Jesus; concern/hope for poor/oppressed; kingdom of God=community
C.	9:57b-60a	
C1	9:59–60a	radical lifestyle; separation from family; voluntary homelessness
C2	*9:57b-58*	*non-apocalyptic son of man (=Jesus); opposition, rejection inevitable; involuntary homelessness*
D.	10:2–12, 13–15, 16	
D1	10:4–11	radical lifestyle; voluntary homelessness; "peace" message; kingdom of God; rejection possible; response to rejection: abandonment
D2	10:3, 16	"Behold, I send you" formula; opposition, rejection inevitable
D3	*10:2, 12, 13, 15*	*experience of rejection; response to rejection: condemnation; use of gentile examples to shame Israel; woe form; exalted/humbled motif; miracles evoke repentance*
E.	13:24–30, 34–35	
E1	13:24–27	parable form as warning; boundary issue: who is in, who is out
E2	*13:28–29, 34–35*	*feast in kingdom; prophets; Wisdom as sender of prophets (implicit); violent fate of prophets: rejection inevitable; "gathering" task*
F.	12:33–46, 49–53, 54–56, 58–59	
F1	12:33–34, 39, 58–59	admonition form: watchfulness; possibly radical lifestyle
F2	12:35–38	beatitude form; watchfulness; parable to warn
F3	*12:49–53, 54–56*	*explicit affirmation of inevitable dissension; rebuke for failure to understand present; admonition/rhetorical question; beatitude/parable forms*
F4	12:40, 42–46	apocalyptic son of man; delay of the parousia; rhetorical question/beatitude/parable forms

Note that in the test cases above the deuteronomistic layer is sometimes the latest, sometimes an earlier layer. In short, it would appear that the deuteronomistic redaction was not the latest. Note too that there are clearly *over-lapping* features. This is to be expected: there will be elements of continuity through the various layers. Therefore some features may be more useful than others in distinguishing compositional layers.

A radical lifestyle, ranging from John's rejection of urban society and its trappings to the homelessness and voluntary poverty demanded by Jesus, is reflected in several of the pre-deuteronomistic strata: B1, C1, D1, and F1. Rejection or opposition is also reflected in some of these strata, but it is not set forth as inevitable (A2, D1). And a positive message is emphasized in two strata (A1, D1). All of these features contrast with the deuteronomistic stratum, where rejection appears inevitable and the message is primarily one of warning or condemnation. Further, the response to rejection is mild in pre-deuteronomistic strata: in A2, the sufferer is rewarded with a heavenly reward; in D1, the response is the abandonment of the rejectors. This corresponds, perhaps, to the positive message that appears in some of these strata. On the other hand, other features that appear in the pre-deuteronomistic strata are not so easy to coordinate. For example, E1 and F1 and F2 are harder to link to other strata, though a relationship may exist between E1 and F2.

In these test cases, there are only two instances of post-deuteronomistic strata, namely B3 and F4, and it is hard to see any connection between them.

It should be noted that while major strata may be detected in Q—the deuteronomistic/compositional level being the clearest example—we may not conclude that every layer identifiable within each sayings composition or sequence of Q material can be coordinated with other strata. Put differently, one may not reckon only with major redactions of Q. The process of literary growth may have been more complicated than that. Accordingly, I am now more reticent to speak of a "final redaction" of Q. It does seem to me likely that Q 4:1–13 was the last addition to Q, and that it was preceded by an enthusiastic stage represented by Q 10:21–22; 11:2–4, 9–13, and perhaps sayings such as Q 17:6. Nevertheless, I do not imagine that after the compositional stage of Q there were only two redactional stages. Moreover, as the analysis of the strata continues, the definition of what constitutes a "stage" becomes more difficult. A "stage" is more than simply an occasional added saying; I have used the term to refer to strata identifiable in several pericopes and sharing some striking characteristics.

The Call to Israel

At the compositional level of Q the deuteronomistic tradition was used to interpret the meaning for Israel of John, Jesus, and the Q community itself. John and Jesus are placed in the context of a series of prophets whom God sent to call Israel to repentance and renewal but whom Israel rejected. The persecution suffered by the Q community was interpreted as the continued resistance of Israel, now directed against the "prophets" of the Q group.

Q is preoccupied with the mystery of Israel. It sees God's ancient controversy with Israel as having reached its critical juncture, and finds itself drawn into that controversy as the means by which God is bringing about its resolution. Like the sectarians at Qumran, the Q group must have been a movement of reform within Israel. But with John and Jesus the time for Israel has run out. In the brief time before the judgment the Q group still calls Israel to repent. But some passages in Q indicate that the mission has failed and has been virtually abandoned. Q 10:2–16 (the "Mission Discourse") is no longer a mission but an errand of judgment, in which "laborers" who went out to Israel were the instruments of judgment: the reception given them indicated whether the persons were "worthy."

It was the failure of the mission—the experience of consistent rejection—which led to a reconceptualization of the community's situation. This was made possible by the use of deuteronomistic language. But what triggered this reconceptualization was probably not only the experience of failure but also another, very surprising development: gentiles were responding to the message of Jesus. It seems unlikely to me that the Q group was engaged in any mission to the gentiles. They probably looked for the turning of the gentiles toward the God of Israel, but not as a result of missionary activity. However, gentiles did respond to the message of Jesus, and this was a very early development, as we know from Paul. The response of the Q group to this seems to have been an intensification of their call to Israel. For an understanding of this development, too, the deuteronomistic perspective proved useful.

The call to Israel was not first of all a call to believe in Jesus. It was a call to holiness, to the righteousness described in Jesus' preaching. John's call to righteousness was taken seriously as well, and was not relegated to being merely preliminary to Jesus and his preaching. The prominence given John is, in fact, one of the most remarkable features of Q; its presence is, however, comprehensible from the point of view of the deuteronomistic/wisdom tradition that we find in Q.

The rejection of God's appeal to Israel is reflected not only in passages which directly express the deuteronomistic/wisdom perspective but also in the composition of other material and in the addition of new material. We observed, for example, the deuteronomistic/wisdom redaction of the Sermon, the "Mission Charge," the woes, and a section on "who is in and who is out" (i.e., Q 13:24–30, 34–35). In other places, the polemic against Israel was intensified, probably as a result of the deuteronomistic redaction.

"Wisdom Christology" in Q

The wisdom tradition played a critical and insufficiently recognized role in early Christian doctrine, especially in the development of christological and trinitarian dogma. At a number of points, we have had occasion to note features of Q which find their closest analogy in the wisdom tradition. But several caveats regarding the wisdom character of Q are to be in order.

First, it is inaccurate to speak of Q as a wisdom collection, because it clearly contains much that both formally and materially is derivative of the prophetic or other traditions. Second, it is misleading to speak of the wisdom tradition as though it were a unified movement, just as we now recognize that neither Judaism nor Christianity was a monolithic entity. So the fact that some aspects of wisdom (or prophecy or apocalyptic) are discernible in Q does not mean that Q is to be assigned to that tradition. It is even more misleading to speak of "wisdom influence," since such language invokes an entity which did not exist.

Third, even though in Q the role of Jesus is articulated by means of the language and imagery of the wisdom tradition, motifs prominent elsewhere in early Christianity, such as Wisdom's role as creatrix and revealer, are absent from Q. Even the more mundane role of teacher of wisdom does not seem to be very significant for an understanding of the role of Jesus or John in Q, although there are "wisdom" sayings in Q. Wisdom, that is, the personified female figure familiar from Jewish tradition, plays a role in Q only in sayings reflecting a deuteronomistic perspective, where Wisdom is a sender of prophets. This is a role attested occasionally in Jewish sources (see Q 11:49–51; 13:34–35; 7:35 [?]; and cf. Prov 1:20–21; 8:2–3; Wis 7:27; Sir 24:33; 11 Q Ps[a] 1–4; GosThom 52; Heb 1:1–3). Other speculative Wisdom motifs are absent from Q. It would therefore be misleading to place Q on a trajectory leading, say, to the Wisdom christology reflected in the Johannine Prologue or in certain places in Paul.

The question, why we have this distinctive combination of Wisdom with the deuteronomistic tradition, is not easily answered. No doubt some traditions lie behind it. The wisdom tradition, as noted earlier, is sometimes found in conjunction with the deuteronomistic tradition, so there is a precedent for what we find in Q. The two traditions have in common a concern to warn hearers of the fateful consequences of rejecting a message. This was a central preoccupation of the deuteronomistic tradition; Prov 1:20–33 illustrates the same concern with regard to Wisdom. The deuteronomistic perspective seems not to have been part of the Q tradition from the outset; one may speculate that the occasion for its emergence was the failure of the community to gain a hearing for its message. With regard to the figure of Wisdom, one may further speculate that it was a useful concept for a group which found itself, or placed itself, at odds with the majority of Jews. Wisdom provides direct access to the divine, quite apart from the institutionalized means of access to God. Because of this, a group bearing a distinctive message could claim legitimation by an authority superior to that of its detractors. At the same time, the Q group could claim continuity with the past, in that Wisdom had earlier sent prophets who were also rejected.

That Wisdom sends prophets is not, however, the only way of speaking of the prophets or messengers sent to Israel. Thus in Q 11:19–20 we meet the idea that the kingdom of God comes to expression not only in Jesus but in the Jewish exorcists. Likewise, Q 11:29–32 speaks both of the kerygma of Jonah and the sophia of Solomon. Both of these are manifestations of God's reaching out to God's people through envoys of various kinds. We are dealing with the same basic idea in Q 12:10, where it is said that blasphemy against the "son of man" is forgivable but not blasphemy against the spirit. In each case, the messenger is one thing, that which comes to expression through him or her another. One might speak of an envoy philosophy as the theological substratum of Q, and Wisdom as the sender of prophets as one way of expressing this concept. That envoys are "sent" is frequently asserted (Q 11:49; 13:34; 10:3; 7:27; cf. 10:16).

In contrast to Q 12:10, however, rejection of the envoy usually entails the rejection of the one who sent the envoy. This view is most clearly expressed in Q 10:16, but it is implicit elsewhere (Q 7:31–35; 11:19–20, 29–32, 49–51; 13:34–35; 14:16–24; cf. 9:58). In the "Mission Discourse" we meet envoys called "laborers." The rejection of their eschatologically decisive message brings divine judgment. This is stated in Q 10:16, which thus provides the theological underpinning of the whole "Mission Discourse." Of course the idea that the messenger is as the one who sends the messenger is an idea which is not peculiar to the wisdom tradition. The influence here of the deutero-nomistic tradition is especially evident in the negative formulation of Q 10:16: he who *rejects* the messenger rejects the one who sends the messenger. This is what distinguishes Q 10:16 from otherwise similar passages in Mark 9:37b; John 13:20; 12:44–45.

Thus there is a tendency, observable in much of Q, to think in terms of envoys who in one way or another mediate divine reality. The wisdom tradition is not always used to express this idea. What is distinctive of Q, however, is that this envoy concept is integrated, by means of the wisdom and deutero-nomistic traditions, into a larger scheme for speaking of God's approach to Israel and God's controversy with Israel. It is from this perspective that Jewish exorcists, John the Baptist, Jesus, and the "laborers" can be drawn together into a coherent perspective.

The role of Wisdom described above leaves ambiguous the status of Jesus. At times it is clear that Jesus is one of many prophets sent by Wisdom, a status he shares with John. At the same time Jesus occupies a special status. The rejection of Jesus (and of John) brings with it an eschatological condemnation. This is due in part, apparently, to who Jesus is, but to put it this way is misleading. When, for example, Jesus is implicitly identified as one "greater" than Solomon or Jonah, what is meant is probably that Jesus is more significant than either Solomon or Jonah. But why? It is probable that Jesus' significance has to do with the nature of the moment, the "present time," the eschatologically decisive moment (cf. Q 10:23–24). Jesus is "greater" because he is the final messenger of God; this is God's final appeal. It should not be forgotten that Q is not about Jesus but about the call to Israel.

Q in Early Christianity

The deuteronomistic tradition which plays so important a role in Q crops up elsewhere in early Christianity. A highly christianized form of this tradition is found in Ignatius (Magnesians 8:2; cf. Acts 7:51–53; GThom 52) where all the prophets are claimed as Christians or heralds of Christ. Israel's resistance to the prophets is thus the struggle between Christianity and Judaism retrojected into the history of Israel.

A more primitive form of the deuteronomistic tradition presents the prophets of the Hebrew Bible not speaking of Christ but calling Israel to repentance. This more primitive form is found in 5 Ezra 1–2; 1 Thess 2:14–16 (cf. Rom 11:3), and Barn 5:11. A later variation inserts the idea of the son as heir into the deuteronomistic view of history (Mark 12:1–9; GThom 65; cf. Gal 4:21–31). A fragment of the deuteronomistic framework—the wrath incurred by the Jews for killing Jesus—occurs in Matt 27:25 (cf. GPet 7.25). Thus we do find evidence of the deuteronomistic tradition in other early Christian writings. What we find, however, are only occasional instances of an older layer of material protruding through the surface. The tradition itself is no longer very important theologically; it is already part of the past. More precisely, in so far as it is used, it has been christianized and used as anti-Jewish polemic, as in Mark 12:1–9. An earlier form of this tradition, however, may, as argued above, be found in 5 Ezra. What is distinctive of Q, however, is the way in which the deuteronomistic tradition has been united with the tradition of personified Wisdom as sender of prophets.

The use of the deuteronomistic tradition in early Christianity was very early, as its appearance in Q and 5 Ezra demonstrate. If 1 Thess 2:14–16 is not a later insertion, as has been argued,[1] then the tradition may be dated at least to about 50 C.E.[2] Even if 1 Thess 2:14–16 is an insertion, it remains evidence for the history of the use of the deuteronomistic tradition in early Christianity. There does not seem to be a direct connection with Q, however, because the "assemblies of God" (ἐκκλησίαι τοῦ θεοῦ) of which 1 Thess 2:14 speaks are in Judea, and their opponents are "Judeans,"[3] while the Q group, we have argued, was in Galilee. Further, these Judean "Christians," if they may be called that, were engaged in a mission to the gentiles and, again unlike Q, they apparently used

1. See Pearson, "1 Thessalonians 2:13–16"; for a somewhat different argument see Steck, *Israel*, 274–79.
2. Pearson ("1 Thessalonians 2:13–16," 81–83) argues that the insertion must have been made after the destruction of the Temple in 70 C.E. because this destruction is presupposed in 1 Thess 2:16c.
3. This is preferable to the usual translation, "Jews," because of the context (Judea, v. 14) and because of the parallel between the Thessalonians and their compatriots and the "assemblies" in Judea and their compatriots, i.e., Judeans.

the title "Christ." Perhaps a connection is to be seen between 1 Thess 2:14–16 and the "Hellenists" associated in Acts 6–7 with Stephen, who, according to the sermon Luke composed for him in Acts 7:2–52, made use of the deuteronomistic tradition. If, however, 1 Thess 2:14–16 is Pauline, it is still not a tradition important to Paul; the use of the deuteronomistic tradition is attested elsewhere only in Rom 11:3. This tradition was not very important for Paul's own theology or self-understanding because, as Steck rightly observes, it seems to have played no role in Paul's interpretation of his own sufferings and troubles as an apostle.[4]

The above evidence suggests that the Q group may not have been the only group to have made use of the deuteronomistic tradition. Yet the Q group was distinct from other groups in that it did not engage in a mission to gentiles, and in that it continued to observe the Law.

The picture of the tradents of Q that emerges from the Q material seems to require, as many now recognize, a relatively *isolated* community. It was not a community which corresponds very well with any group that we know of in early Christianity. There is no redemptive understanding of Jesus' death, no explicit reference to the resurrection,[5] no hint of any sacramental language, and little evidence, except at a late stage, of any advanced christology. As noted earlier, the group seems not to have engaged in a mission to gentiles, and it continued to observe the Law. Since the developments leading to the emergence of early Christianity, such as non-observance of the Torah, occurred so rapidly, it is hard to imagine a community remaining for so long immune to these developments unless it was both early and isolated. To be sure, the Q document itself was later known to the authors of Matthew and Luke, but they may both have been in the area of Antioch and thus not far distant from the Q group.

Q and Cynicism

One recent trend in Q research is the investigation of parallels between the Q material and Greco-Roman Cynic writings.[6] Occasional reference has already been made to some of these parallels. This investigation is only at an early stage. Cynicism was not a philosophical school so much as a way of life characterized by voluntary poverty, the pursuit of simplicity and virtue, and contempt and ridicule for social convention, especially of the wealthy and powerful. Cynics were individualists who declared their independence from the world and its powers and principalities, who lived instead according to nature. Often they were to be found haranguing the masses in the marketplace. They were recognizable because they adopted a doubled coarse cloak, a

4. Steck, *Israel*, 278 n. 2.
5. See now Kloppenborg, "'Easter Faith' and the Sayings Gospel Q."
6. A precursor of this trend is Georgi, "The Records of Jesus" (1972), though Georgi sketches a background broader than the Cynic one.

traveling bag and a staff, often resorted to begging, and slept wherever they could find a place to lie down.

The primary locus in Q for such Cynic-like behavior is the "Mission Discourse" in Q 10:2-16, though the instructions there may also be seen as designed to differentiate the Q "laborers" from Cynics. More recently the study of synoptic pronouncement stories and chreiai—common among the Cynics, but not exclusive to them—has also prompted comparison with Cynicism. Thirdly, comparison has been made between the Cynics' acerbic social criticism, together with their general philosophy, and the sayings of Jesus. Finally, the suggestion by Kloppenborg that Q at one point belonged to the genre chreia collection likewise entails reflection upon analogies between Q and Cynic chreiai.[7]

One of the first to suggest comparison of the Jesus movement with the Cynics was Theissen, who was able to adduce only the wandering Cynic philosophers as analogies to the "wandering charismatics" who followed Jesus.[8] Among those recently arguing for a 'Cynic Jesus' are especially F. Gerald Downing[9] and Burton L. Mack.[10] A 1986 Claremont dissertation by Leif Vaage explored Cynic parallels to the mission discourse.[11] Recently, Ron Cameron has argued for a Cynic John the Baptist as well.[12]

As might be expected in the early stages of an investigation, there are important divergences among those who find the Cynic analogy persuasive. For example, Mack, who accepts Kloppenborg's stratigraphy of Q, regards only the early sapiential layer as Cynic-like, whereas Kloppenborg himself argues that only at a later stage did Q enter the Cynic orbit in its use of the genre of chreia collection. Moreover, Kloppenborg sees not only similarities between the Jesus of Q and the Cynic sage but striking differences as well; he observes that "the idiom of Q is controlled not by a philosophic notion of freedom, but by a historical and soteriological schema of God's constant invitation of Israel to repent, and by the expectation of the imminent manifestation of the kingdom."[13]

The Cynic paradigm has not been without its detractors. Richard A. Horsley, for example, has criticized it, though his criticisms are directed mainly at Theissen.[14] A more thorough critique is offered by Christopher M. Tuckett,[15] who raises questions about what is to be regarded as "Cynic," about the dating of the sources, about the presence of Cynicism in Galilee, and about a Cynic

7. Kloppenborg, *Formation of Q*, 306–16, 322–25.

8. Theissen, *Sociology*, 14–15.

9. See "Cynics and Christians," "Ears to Hear," *Jesus and the Threat of Freedom*, "Social Contexts," and "Quite Like Q."

10. See especially Mack, *A Myth of Innocence*, chap. 2 ("Jesus in Galilee").

11. Vaage, "Q: The Ethos and Ethics of an Itinerant Intelligence."

12. Cameron, "'What Have You Come Out to See?'"

13. Kloppenborg, *Formation of Q*, 324.

14. See Horsley, *Sociology and the Jesus Movement*, 46–47, 116–18. See also Stegemann, "Vagabond Radicalism."

15. Tuckett, "A Cynic Q?"

genre for Q. Tuckett finds Sato's association of Q with Jewish prophetic traditions to be more persuasive.

Like Cynics, the Q people were intentionally marginal within their societies, and critical of them. Both were "popular" in the sense that they appealed to the populace as a whole, including its marginal elements. At many points, the similarities between them are so striking as to call for continued investigation. To be sure, there may be profound differences between them; but how one assesses these differences depends crucially on one's stratigraphy of Q. If, with Mack, one judges that Kloppenborg's stratigraphy is correct, that this is a Cynic layer, and that the non-Cynic material in it cannot be traced back to Jesus, then one clearly has a Cynic Jesus. The implications of such an analysis are made clear by Mack on the basis of his analysis of the situation in Galilee: "The Cynic analogy repositions the historical Jesus away from a specifically Jewish sectarian milieu and toward the Hellenistic ethos known to have prevailed in Galilee."[16] Jesus becomes less Jewish, or at least his Jewishness is greatly diluted. In fact, the specifically religious content of Jesus' message and life largely disappears in Mack's analysis, though Mack concedes that "a religious piety of some kind must. . .be assumed for Jesus," that is, a piety informed by Jewish ethical and theocratic ideals.[17] Jesus emerges primarily as a social critic, on the margins of society. Moreover, Mack specifically rejects the usual characterization of Jesus as a prophet.[18] The mythic elaboration of Jesus and his message in Q is attributed by Mack to "social formation"[19] —a judgment that is vulnerable to the charge of reductionism. Mack's penetrating and provocative analysis raises many questions, but the decisive issue remains the identification of the earliest Jesus materials, and thus both the stratigraphy of Q and the question of the authentic sayings of Jesus. As often happens in historical research, however, progress is not simply linear; and the investigation of the Cynic analogy may prove useful as well in the recovery of the stratigraphy of Q.

Prospect

The Q hypothesis is now over 150 years old. But Q has yet to yield many of its secrets. It will do so only as new methodologies are developed that allow us to ask new questions of the material. It was the development of new methodologies that re-awakened interest in Q in the 1960s and continues to sustain a lively interest in this lost document. Even if the community which it represented was small and isolated, it is of unusual importance and interest because it is probably the group which has the strongest claim to representing the

16. Mack, *A Myth of Innocence*, 73.
17. Mack, *A Myth of Innocence*, 74.
18. Mack, *A Myth of Innocence*, 67–69, 87.
19. Mack, *A Myth of Innocence*, 84–87.

earliest Jesus movement. Its gospel, Q, was likely was the first; and the spell of this most ancient and original gospel will continue to haunt its readers for years to come.

Works Consulted

Primary Sources

1. Ancient Near East

Lambert, William G. *Babylonian Wisdom Literature*. Oxford: Clarendon Press, 1960.

Pritchard, James B. *Ancient Near Eastern Texts Relating to the Old Testament*. Princeton: Princeton University Press, 1950.

2. Hebrew Bible and Septuagint

Elliger, K. and W. Rudolf, eds. *Biblia Hebraica Stuttgartensia*. 4th ed. Stuttgart: Deutsche Bibelstiftung, 1967–77.

Rahlfs, Alfred, ed. *Septuaginta id est Vetus Testamentum graece iuxta LXX interpretes*. Stuttgart: Würtembergisches Bibelanstalt, 1935.

Nova Vulgata bibliorum sacrorum editio. Vatican City: Libreria Editrice Vaticana, 1979.

3. Pseudepigrapha

Charlesworth, James H., ed. *The Old Testament Pseudepigrapha*. 2 vols. Garden City, NY: Doubleday & Company, 1983–85.

Bensly, Robert L. *The Fourth Book of Ezra*. Intro. by M. R. James. Texts and Studies III, 2. Cambridge: Cambridge University Press, 1895; repr. Nendeln/Liechtenstein: Kraus, 1967.

Black, Matthew, ed. *The Book of Enoch, or I Enoch: A New English Edition with Commentary and Textual Notes*. SVTP 7. Leiden: E. J. Brill, 1985.

Charlesworth, James H., ed. and trans. *The Odes of Solomon*. SBLTT Pseudepigrapha Series 13/7. Missoula: Scholars Press, 1977.

De Jonge, M. *Testamenta XII Patriarcharum*. PVTG 1. 2d ed. Leiden: E. J. Brill, 1970.

Duling, Dennis C. "Testament of Solomon." Pp. 935–87 in *The Old Testament Pseudepigrapha*. Ed. James L. Charlesworth. Vol. 1. Garden City, NY: Doubleday, 1983.

Kraft, Robert A., trans. *The Testament of Job*. SBLTT Pseudepigrapha Series 5/4. Missoula: Society of Biblical Literature and Scholars Press, 1974.

Torrey, C. C., ed. and trans. *The Lives of the Prophets*. JBLMS 1. Philadelphia: Society of Biblical Literature, 1946.

4. Qumran

Lohse, Eduard, ed. *Die Texte aus Qumran: Hebräisch und Deutsch*. 2d rev. & exp. ed. München: Kösel-Verlag, 1971.

Yadin, Yigael. *The Scroll of the War of the Sons of Light against the Sons of Darkness*. Trans. Batya and Chaim Rabin. London: Oxford University Press, 1962.

Gaster, Theodor H., trans. *The Dead Sea Scriptures*. 3d ed. Garden City, NY: Doubleday/Anchor Press, 1976.

Vermes, Geza. *The Dead Sea Scrolls in English*. 3rd ed. Middlesex, England: Penguin Books, 1987.

5. Rabbinic Texts

Marti, Karl and Georg Beer. *'Abôt (Väter): Text, Übersetzung und Erklärung*. Vol. 4/9 of *Die Mischna*. Ed. G. Beer and O. Holtzmann. Giessen: A. Töpelmann, 1927.

Blackman, Philip. *Mishnayoth*. 2d rev. ed. 7 vols. New York: Judaica Press, 1964.

Braude, William G., trans. *The Midrash on Psalms*. 2 vols. Yale Judaica Series 13. New Haven: Yale University Press, 1959.

Danby, Herbert, ed. and trans. *The Mishna*. London: Oxford University Press, 1933.

Epstein, Isidore, ed. *The Babylonian Talmud Translated into English*. 34 vols. London: Soncino, 1935–48.

Montefiore, C. G. and H. Loewe, eds. *A Rabbinic Anthology*. Meridian Books. Cleveland: World; Philadelphia: Jewish Publication Society of America, 1963.

Neusner, Jacob, ed. and trans. *Sifré to Deuteronomy: An Analytical Translation*. 2 vols. Brown Judaic Studies 101. Atlanta: Scholars Press, 1987.

Rabbinowitz, J., trans. *Midrash Rabbah: Deuteronomy*. London: Soncino Press, 1939.

6. New Testament

Nestle, Eberhard and Kurt Aland, eds. *Novum Testamentum Graece*. 26th ed. Stuttgart: Deutsche Bibelgesellschaft, 1979.

Aland, Kurt; Matthew Black; Carlo M. Martini; Bruce Metzger; and Allen Wikgren, eds. *The Greek New Testament*. 3d ed. Stuttgart: Würtemberg Bible Society, 1986.

Aland, Kurt, ed. *Synopsis Quattuor Evangeliorum*. 6th ed. Stuttgart: Würtembergische Bibelanstalt, 1969.

Huck, A. and Heinrich Greeven, eds. *Synopse der drei ersten Evangelien mit Beigabe der johanneischen Parallelstellen—Synopsis of the First Three Gospels with the Addition of the Johannine Parallels*. 13th ed. Tübingen: J. C. B. Mohr [Paul Siebeck], 1981.

American and British Committees of the International Greek New Testament Project, ed. *The Gospel According to St. Luke*. 2 vols. Oxford: Clarendon Press, 1984–87.

Kloppenborg, John S. *Q Parallels: Synopsis, Critical Notes and Concordance*. Sonoma: Polebridge Press, 1988.

———, Marvin W. Meyer, Stephen J. Patterson, and Michael G. Steinhauser. *Q-Thomas Reader*. Sonoma: Polebridge Press, 1990.

Wettstein, J. J. *Novum Testamentum Graecum*, vol. 1. Amsterdam: Dommerian, 1752; repr. Graz, Austria: Akademischen Druck- und Verlagsanstalt, 1962.

7. New Testament Apocrypha

Hennecke, Edgar. *New Testament Apocrypha*. Ed. Wilhelm Schneemelcher. Trans. ed. R. McL. Wilson. 2 vols. Philadelphia: Westminster Press, 1963–64.

James, Montague Rhodes, ed.. *The Apocryphal New Testament*. Oxford: Clarendon Press, 1924.

Cameron, Ron, ed. *The Other Gospels: Non-Canonical Gospel Texts*. Philadelphia: Westminster Press, 1982.

8. Nag Hammadi

Robinson, James M. and Richard Smith, eds. *The Nag Hammadi Library*. 3d rev. ed. New York: Harper & Row, 1988.

Layton, Bentley. *The Gnostic Scriptures: A New Translation*. Garden City, NY: Doubleday & Company, 1987.

Layton, Bentley and Thomas Lambdin. "The Gospel According to Thomas. Critical Edition and Translation." Pp. 50–93 in *Nag Hammadi Codex II,2–7*. Ed. Bentley Layton. Vol. 1. The Coptic Gnostic Library; Nag Hammadi Studies 20. Leiden: E. J. Brill, 1989.

9. Apostolic Fathers

Lake, Kirsopp. *The Apostolic Fathers*. Loeb Classical Library. 2 vols. London: William Heinemann, 1912.

Bihlmeyer, Karl. *Die apostolischen Väter*. 2d ed. Sammlung ausgewählter kirchen- und dogmengeschichtlicher Quellenschriften. 2d Series, vol. 1. Tübingen: J. C. B. Mohr [Paul Siebeck], 1956.

Grant, Robert, ed. *The Apostolic Fathers*. 6 vols. New York: Thomas Nelson & Sons, 1964–68.

Kraft, Robert A., ed. *Barnabas and the Didache*. Vol. 3 of *The Apostolic Fathers*. Ed. Robert Grant. New York: Thomas Nelson & Sons, 1965.

10. Other Greco-Roman Sources

Betz, Hans Dieter, ed. *The Greek Magical Papyri in Translation, including the Demotic Spells*. Chicago: The University of Chicago Press, 1986-.

Colson, F. H. and G. H. Whitaker, trans. *Philo*. 10 vols. and 2 supplements. Loeb Classical Library. London: William Heinemann; New York: G. P. Putnam's Sons, 1929–62.

Duff, J. D., trans. *Lucan: The Civil War, Books I–X*. Loeb Classical Library. London: William Heinemann; New York: G. P. Putnam's Sons, 1928.

Edwards, H. J., trans. *Caesar: The Gallic War*. 2 vols. Loeb Classical Library. Cambridge: Harvard University Press; London: William Heinemann, 1946.

Hock, Ronald F. and Edward N. O'Neil. *The Chreia in Ancient Rhetoric*. Vol. I. *The Progymnasmata*. SBLTT 27. Atlanta: Scholars Press, 1986.

Horsley, G. H. R. *New Documents Illustrating Early Christianity: A Review of the Greek*

Inscriptions and Papyri. North Ryde, NSW: The Ancient History Documentary Research Center, 1981-.

Jackson, John, trans. *Tacitus: The Histories and the Annals.* 4 vols. Loeb Classical Library. Cambridge: Harvard University Press; London: William Heinemann, 1937.

Ker, Walter C. A., trans. *Cicero: Phillippics.* Loeb Classical Library London: William Heinemann; New York: G. P. Putnam's Sons, 1926.

Lord, Louise E., trans. *Cicero: The Speeches.* Loeb Classical Library. Cambridge: Harvard University Press; London: William Heinemann, 1937.

Malherbe, Abraham J., trans. and ed. *The Cynic Epistles: A Study Edition.* SBLSBS 12. Missoula: Scholars Press, 1977.

O'Neil, Edward N., trans. *Teles (The Cynic Teacher).* SBLTT 11. Missoula: Scholars Press, 1977.

Perrin, Bernadotte, trans. *Plutarch's Lives.* 11 vols. Loeb Classical Library. London: William Heinemann; New York: G. P. Putnam's Sons, 1914–26.

Peskett, A. G., trans. *Caesar: The Civil Wars.* Loeb Classical Library. London: William Heinemann; New York: The Macmillan Co., 1914.

Rackham, H., trans. *Pliny: Natural History.* Vol. 4 (Books 12–16). Loeb Classical Library. Cambridge: Harvard University Press; London: William Heinemann, 1945.

Rolfe, J. C., trans. *Suetonius.* 2 vols. Loeb Classical Library. Cambridge: Harvard University Press; London: William Heinemann, 1913.

Stählin, Otto, ed. *Clemens Alexandrinus.* 4 vols. GCS. Leipzig: J. C. Hinrichs, 1936–39.

Thackeray, H. St. J., Ralph Marcus, Allen Wikgren, and Louis Feldman, trans. *Josephus.* 9 vols. Loeb Classical Library. London: William Heinemann; New York: G. P. Putnam's Sons, 1926–65.

Way, A. G., trans. *Caesar: Alexandrian, African and Spanish Wars.* Loeb Classical Library. London: William Heinemann; Cambridge: Harvard University Press, 1955.

Wheeler, Arthur Leslie, trans. *Ovid: Tristia; Ex Ponto.* Loeb Classical Library. London: William Heinemann; New York: G. P. Putnam's Sons, 1924.

Secondary Sources

Andrews, Mary E. "*Peirasmos*: A Study in Form Criticism." *Anglican Theological Review* 24 (1942): 229–44.

Appelbaum, S. "Josephus and the Economic Causes of the Jewish War." Pp. 237–64 in *Josephus, the Bible, and History.* Ed. Louis H. Feldman and Gohei Hata. Detroit: Wayne State University Press, 1989.

Arens, Eduardo. *The HΛΘON-Sayings in the Synoptic Tradition: A Historico-Critical Investigation.* OBO 10. Freiburg: Universitätsverlag; Göttingen: Vandenhoeck & Ruprecht, 1976.

Argyle, A.W. "The Accounts of the Temptation of Jesus in Relation to the Q Hypothesis." *Expository Times* 64 (1952–53): 382.

Aune, David E. *The New Testament and Its Literary Environment.* Library of Early Christianity 8. Philadelphia: Westminster Press, 1987.

_____. *Prophecy in Early Christianity and the Ancient Mediterranean World.* Grand Rapids: Wm. B. Eerdmans, 1983.

Bacon, Benjamin W. "A Turning Point in Synoptic Criticism." *Harvard Theological Review* 1 (1908): 48–69.

_____. *The Beginnings of Gospel Story.* New Haven: Yale University Press, 1909.

_____. "The Plaint of Wisdom in Matthew XXIII 34–39," *The Expositor* 8/10 (1915): 493–511.

_____. "The 'Son' as Organ of Revelation." *Harvard Theological Review* 9 (1916): 382–415.

_____. "Logia" and "Wisdom." Vol. 2, pp. 45–49, 825–29, in *A Dictionary of Christ and the Gospels.* Ed. James Hastings. New York: Charles Scribner's Sons and Edinburgh: T. & T. Clark, 1921.

_____. "The Nature and Design of Q, the Second Synoptic Source." *Hibbert Journal* 22 (1924): 674–88.

_____. "The Q Section on John the Baptist and the *Shemoneh Esreh.*" *Journal of Biblical Literature* 45 (1926): 23–56

_____. "The Redaction of Matthew 12." *Journal of Biblical Literature* 46 (1927): 20–49.

Bailey, Kenneth E. *Through Peasant Eyes: More Lucan Parables, Their Culture and Style.* Grand Rapids: Wm. B. Eerdmans, 1980.

Ballard, Paul H. "Reasons for Refusing the Great Supper." *Journal of Theological Studies* 23 (1972): 341–50.

Bammel, Ernst. "Das Ende von Q." Pp. 39–50 in *Verborum Veritas. Festschrift für Gustav Stählin zum 70. Geburtstag.* Ed. Otto Böcher and Klaus Haacker. Wüppertal: Rolf Brockhaus, 1970

Barth, Gerhard. "Matthew's Understanding of the Law." Pp. 58–164 in *Tradition and Interpretation in Matthew* by Günther Bornkamm, Gerhard Barth and Heinz Joachim Held. Trans. Percy Scott. Philadelphia: Westminster Press, 1963.

Bartsch, Hans-Werner. "Feldrede und Bergpredigt. Redaktionsarbeit in Luk. 6." *Theologische Zeitschrift* 16 (1960): 5–18.

Baumgarten, Joseph M. "The Duodecimal Courts of Qumran, Revelation, and the Sanhedrin." *Journal of Biblical Literature* 95 (1976): 59–78.

Beardslee, William A. "Saving One's Life by Losing It." *Journal of the American Academy of Religion* 47 (1979): 57–72.

Beare, Francis W. "The Parable of the Guests at the Banquet: A Sketch of the History of Its Interpretation." Pp. 1–14 in *Joy of Study.* Ed. Sherman E. Johnson. New York: Macmillan, 1951.

_____. *The Earliest Records of Jesus.* Oxford: Basil Blackwell, 1962.

_____. "The Mission of the Disciples and the Mission Charge: Matthew 10 and Parallels." *Journal of Biblical Literature* 89 (1970): 1–13.

Behm, Johannes and Gottfried Quell. "διατίθημι, διαθήκη." *Theological Dictionary of the New Testament* 2 (1964): 104–34.

Berger, Klaus. "Materialien zu Form und Überlieferungsgeschichte neutestamentlicher Gleichnisse." *Novum Testamentum* 15 (1973): 1–37.

_____. "Hellenistischen Gattungen im Neuen Testament." ANRW 2.25.2. (1984): 1034–432.

_____. and Carsten Colpe. *Religionsgeschichtliches Textbuch zum Neuen Testament.* Texte zum Neuen Testament 1. Göttingen: Vandenhoeck & Ruprecht, 1987.

Bergren, Theodore A. "The 'People Coming from the East' in 5 Ezra 1:38." *Journal of Biblical Literature* 108 (1989): 675–83.

Bertram, Georg and Friedrich Hauck. "μακάριος, μακαρίζω, μακαρισμός." *Theological Dictionary of the New Testament* 4 (1967): 362–70.

Betz, Hans Dieter. *Lukian von Samosata und das Neue Testament: Religionsgeschichtliche und Paränetische Parallelen.* TU 76. Berlin: Akademie-Verlag, 1961.

_____. "The Logion of the Easy Yoke and of Rest (Matt 11:28–30)." *Journal of Biblical Literature* 86 (1967): 10–24.

_____. *Nachfolge und Nachahmung Jesu Christi im Neuen Testament.* BHT 37. Tübingen: J. C. B. Mohr [Paul Siebeck], 1967.

_____. "Jesus as Divine Man." Pp. 114–33 in *Jesus and the Historian.* Ed. Thomas Trotter. Philadelphia: Westminster Press, 1968.

_____. "A Jewish-Christian Cultic *Didache* in Matt. 6:1–18: Reflections and Questions on the Problem of the Historical Jesus." Pp. 55–69 in *Essays on the Sermon on the Mount.* Trans. L. L. Welborn. Philadelphia: Fortress Press, 1985.

_____. "Matt. 6:22–23 and Ancient Greek Theories of Vision." Pp. 71–87 in *Essays on the Sermon on the Mount.*

Black, Matthew. *An Aramaic Approach to the Gospels and Acts.* 3d ed. Oxford: Clarendon Press, 1967.

_____. "Scribe." *Interpreter's Dictionary of the Bible* 4 (1962): 246–48.

Blank, Josef. "Zur Christologie augewählter Wunderberichte." Pp. 104–28 in *Schriftauslegung in Theorie und Praxis.* Biblische Handbibliothek 5. München: Kösel Verlag, 1969.

Blass, F. and A. Debrunner. *A Greek Grammar of the New Testament and Other Early Christian Literature.* Trans. and rev. Robert W. Funk. Chicago: The University of Chicago Press, 1961.

Boring, M. Eugene. *Sayings of the Risen Jesus: Christian Prophecy in the Synoptic Tradition.* SNTSMS 46. Cambridge: Cambridge University Press, 1983.

Bornkamm, Günther. "The Stilling of the Storm." Pp. 52–57 in Günther Bornkamm, Gerhard Barth, and Heinz Joachim Held, *Tradition and Interpretation in Matthew.* Trans. Percy Scott. Philadelphia: Westminster Press, 1963. Originally published in *Wort und Dienst: Jahrbuch der theologischen Schule Bethel* 1 (1948): 49–54.

_____. "Bergpredigt. I. Biblisch." *Religion in Geschichte und Gegenwart.* 3d ed. cols. 1047–50.

_____. *Jesus of Nazareth.* Trans. Irene Fraser McLuskey. New York: Harper & Brothers, 1960.

_____. "λύκος." *Theological Dictionary of the New Testament* 4 (1967): 308–11.

_____. "End-Expectation and Church." Pp. 15–51 in Günther Bornkamm, Gerhard Barth, and Heinz Joachim Held, *Tradition and Interpretation in Matthew.* Trans. Percy Scott Philadelphia: Westminster Press, 1963.

_____. "The Risen Lord and the Earthly Jesus: Matthew 28.16–20." Pp. 203–29 in *The Future of Our Religious Past: Essays in Honour of Rudolf Bultmann.* Ed. James M. Robinson. New York: Harper & Row, 1971.

Bousset, Wilhelm. *Kyrios Christos.* Trans. John Steely. Nashville: Abingdon Press, 1970.

Braun, Herbert. "Qumran und das Neue Testament." *Theologische Rundschau* 28 (1962): 97–234; 29 (1963): 142–76, 189–260; 30 (1964): 1–38, 89–137.

Breech, James. *The Silence of Jesus: The Authentic Voice of the Historical Man.* Philadelphia: Fortress Press, 1983.

Bretscher, Paul. "'Whose Sandals'? (Matt 3:11)." *Journal of Biblical Literature* 88 (1967): 81–87.

Brown, Schuyler. "The Matthaean Apocalypse." *Journal for the Study of the New Testament* 4 (1979): 2–27.

Brox, Norbert. "Suchen und Finden. Zur Nachgeschichte von Mt 7,7b/Lk 11,9b." Pp. 17–36 in *Orientierung an Jesus. Zur Theologie der Synoptiker.* Ed. P. Hoffmann. Freiburg: Herder, 1973.

Brueggemann, Walter. "The Kerygma of the Deuteronomistic Historian." *Interpretation* 22 (1968): 387–402.

Buchanan, George W. "Has the Griesbach Hypothesis Been Falsified?" *Journal of Biblical Literature* 93 (1974): 550–72.

Büchsel, Friedrich. "παλιγγενεσία." *Theological Dictionary of New Testament* 1 (1964): 686–89.

Bultmann, Rudolf. *The History of the Synoptic Tradition.* Trans. John Marsh. Rev. ed. New York: Harper & Row, 1963.

Butts, James R. "The Chreia in the Synoptic Gospels." *Biblical Theology Bulletin* 16 (1986): 132–38.

Cadoux, A. T. *The Parables of Jesus: Their Art and Use.* London: James Clark, 1931.

Cameron, Ron. *Sayings Traditions in the Apocryphon of James.* HTS 34. Philadelphia: Fortress Press, 1984.

———. "'What Did You Come Out To See?' Characterizations of John and Jesus in the Gospels." *Semeia* 49 (1990): 35–69.

Carlston, Charles E. *The Parables of the Triple Tradition.* Philadelphia: Fortress Press, 1975.

Catchpole, David R. "The Law and the Prophets in Q." Pp. 95–109 in *Tradition and Interpretation in the New Testament: Essays in Honor of E. Earle Ellis for His 60th Birthday.* Ed. G. F. Hawthorne. Grand Rapids: Eerdmans; Tübingen: J. C. B. Mohr [Paul Siebeck], 1987.

Chadwick, Henry. *Lessing's Theological Writings.* A Library of Modern Religious Thought. Stanford: Stanford University Press, 1957.

Childs, Brevard S. *The New Testament as Canon: An Introduction.* Philadelphia: Fortress Press, 1984.

Christ, Felix. *Jesus Sophia: Die Sophia-Christologie bei den Synoptikern.* AThANT 57. Zürich: Zwingli Verlag, 1970.

Collins, Raymond. *Introduction to the New Testament.* Garden City, NY: Doubleday & Co., 1983.

Colpe, Carsten. "ὁ υἱὸς τοῦ ἀνθρώπου." *Theological Dictionary of the New Testament* 8 (1972): 400–477.

Conzelmann, Hans. *The Theology of St. Luke.* Trans. Geoffrey Buswell. New York: Harper & Row, 1961.

———. *Jesus.* Trans. J. Raymond Lord. Philadelphia: Fortress Press, 1973.

———, and Andreas Lindemann. *Arbeitsbuch zum Neuen Testament.* UniTaschenbücher 52. Tübingen: J. C. B. Mohr [Paul Siebeck], 1975.

Creed, John Martin. *The Gospel According to St. Luke.* London: Macmillan and Co., 1953.

Crossan, John Dominic. *In Parables: The Challenge of the Historical Jesus*. New York: Harper & Row, 1973.

———. *In Fragments: The Aphorisms of Jesus*. San Francisco: Harper & Row, 1983.

———. "The Hermeneutical Jesus." *Michigan Quarterly Review* 22 (1983): 237–49 (special Issue: *The Bible Its Traditions*. Ed. M. P. O'Connor and David Noel Freedman).

———. "Tradition in the Formation of Q." Unpublished paper for the Annual Meeting of the Society of Biblical Literature (Q Seminar), Boston, December, 1987.

Cullmann, Oscar. *The Christology of the New Testament*. Trans. Shirley C. Guthrie and Charles A. M. Hall. Philadelphia: Westminster Press, 1959

Dahl, Nils Alstup. "The Parables of Growth." *Studia Theologica* 5 (1951): 132–66.

Daniélou, J. "Le Ve Esdras et le Judéo-christianisme Latin au Second Siècle." Pp. 162–71 in *Ex Orbe Religionum: Studia Geo Widengren*. Studies in the History of Religion [*Numen Supp*] 21. Leiden: E. J. Brill, 1972.

Danker, Frederick W. "Luke 16:16—An Opposition Logion." *Journal of Biblical Literature* 77 (1958): 231–43.

Daube, David. "The Last Beatitude." Pp. 196–201 in *The New Testament and Rabbinic Judaism*. London: The Athlone Press of the University of London, 1956.

Davies, W. D. *The Setting of the Sermon on the Mount*. Cambridge: Cambridge University Press, 1963.

Derrett, J. Duncan M. "'You Build the Tombs of the Prophets' (Lk. 11,47–51, Mt. 23,29–31)." Pp. 187–93 in *Studia Evangelica* IV (TU 102). Berlin: Akademie-Verlag, 1968.

Devisch, M. "Le document Q, source de Matthieu. Problématique actuelle." Pp. 71–97 in *L'Évangile selon Matthieu: Rédaction et Theologie*. Ed. M. Didier. BETL 29. Gembloux: J. Duculot, 1972.

———. "La relation entre l'évangile de Marc et le document Q." Pp. 59–91 in *L'Évangile selon Marc: Tradition et rédaction*. Ed. M. Sabbe. BETL 34. Gembloux: J. Duculot, 1974.

Dewey, Arthur. "Quibbling Over Serifs: Observations on Matt 5:18/Luke 16:17." *Forum* 5/2 (1989): 109–20.

Dibelius, Martin. *Die urchristliche Überlieferung von Johannes dem Täufer*. FRLANT 15. Göttingen: Vandenhoeck & Ruprecht, 1911.

———. *From Tradition to Gospel*. Trans. Bertram Lee Woolf. New York: Charles Scribner's Sons, 1935.

———. *James: A Commentary on the Epistle of James*. Rev. Heinrich Greeven. Trans. Michael A. Williams. Ed. Helmut Koester. Hermeneia. Philadelphia: Fortress Press, 1976.

Dihle, Albrecht. *Die Goldene Regel: Eine Einführung in die Geschichte der antiken und frühchristlichen Vulgärethik*. Studienhefte zur Altertumswissenschaft 7. Göttingen: Vandenhoeck & Ruprecht, 1962.

Dodd, C. H. *The Parables of the Kingdom*. New York: Scribner's Sons, 1936.

Donahue, John R. *Are You the Christ? The Trial Narrative in the Gospel of Mark*. SBLDS 10. Missoula: Scholars Press, 1973.

Downing, F. Gerald. "Cynics and Christians." *New Testament Studies* 30 (1983–44): 584–93.

———. "Ears to Hear." Pp. 97–120 in *Alternative Approaches to New Testament Study*. Ed. A. E. Harvey. London: SPCK, 1985.

_____. *Jesus and the Threat of Freedom*. London: SCM Press, 1987.

_____. "The Social Contexts of Jesus the Teacher: Construction or Reconstruction." *New Testament Studies* 33 (1986–87): 439–51.

_____. "Compositional Conventions and the Synoptic Problem." *Journal of Biblical Literature* 107 (1988): 69–85.

_____. "Quite Like Q. A Genre for 'Q': The 'Lives' of Cynic Philosophers." *Biblica* 69 (1988): 196–224.

Duling, Dennis C. "Solomon, Exorcism, and the Son of David." *Harvard Theological Review* 68 (1975): 235–49.

Dungan, David. "Mark—the Abridgement of Matthew and Luke." Pp. 51–97 in *Jesus and Man's Hope*. Ed. David G. Buttrick. Pittsburgh: Pittsburgh Theological Seminary, 1970.

Dupont, Jacques. *Les Béatitudes*. Vol. I: *Le problème littéraire—Les deux versions du Sermon sur la montagne et des Béatitudes*. Bruges: Abbaye de Saint-Andre; Louvain: E. Nauwelaerts, 1958.

_____. "L'origine du récit des tentations de Jésus au désert." *Revue Biblique* 73 (1966): 30–76.

Easton, Burton Scott. "The Beelzebul Sections." *Journal of Biblical Literature* 32 (1913): 57–73.

_____. *The Gospel According to St. Luke: A Critical and Exegetical Commentary*. New York: Charles Scribner's Sons, 1926.

Edwards, Richard A. "The Eschatological Correlative as a *Gattung* in the New Testament." *Zeitschrift für die neutestamentliche Wissenschaft* 60 (1969): 9–20.

_____. "An Approach to the Theology of Q." *Journal of Religion* 51 (1971): 247–69.

_____. *The Sign of Jonah in the Theology of the Evangelists and Q*. SBT 2/18. Naperville: Alec R. Allenson, 1971.

_____. *A Theology of Q: Eschatology, Prophecy, and Wisdom*. Philadelphia: Fortress Press, 1976.

Ehrhardt, Arnold. "Greek Proverbs in the Gospel." Pp. 44–63 in *The Framework of the New Testament Stories*. Cambridge: Harvard University Press, 1964.

Eichhorn, Johann Gottfried. "Über die drey ersten Evangelien. Einige Beyträge zu ihrer künftigen kritischen Behandlung." Pp. 761–996 in vol. 5 of *Allgemeine Bibliothek der biblischen Literatur*. Leipzig: Weidmann, 1794.

Eitrem, Samson. *Die Versuchung Christi*. NorTT Supp 25. Oslo: Grøndahl & søns boktrykkeri, 1924.

Farmer, William R. "A 'Skeleton in the Closet' of Gospel Research." *Biblical Research* 6 (1961): 18–42.

_____. *The Synoptic Problem: A Critical Analysis*. New York: Macmillan; London: Collier-Macmillan, 1964.

_____. "The Two-Document Hypothesis as a Methodological Criterion in Synoptic Research." *Anglican Theological Review* 48 (1966): 380–96.

_____. "A Fresh Approach to Q." Pp. 39–50 in *Christianity, Judaism and Other Greco-Roman Cults. Studies for Morton Smith at Sixty*. Ed. Jacob Neusner. SJLA 12. Part One: New Testament. Leiden: E. J. Brill, 1975.

_____. "Modern Developments of the Griesbach Hypothesis." *New Testament Studies* 23 (1977): 275–95.

Fiebig, Paul. *Jüdische Wundergeschichten des neutestamentlichen Zeitalters unter besonderer Berücksichtung ihres Verhältnisses zum Neuen Testament bearbeitet*. Tübingen: J. C. B. Mohr [Paul Siebeck], 1911.

Finegan, Jack. *The Archeology of the New Testament. The Life of Jesus and the Beginning of the Early Church.* Princeton: Princeton University Press, 1969.

Finkelstein, Louis. "Introductory Study to *Pirke Abot.*" *Journal of Biblical Literature* 57 (1938): 13–50.

Finley, Moses I. *The Ancient Economy.* Berkeley: University of California Press, 1973.

Fitzmyer, Joseph A. "The Priority of Mark and the 'Q' Source in Luke." *Perspective* 2/1–2 (1970): 131–70 (Special issue: *Jesus and Man's Hope.* Ed. David A. Buttrick).

———. *The Gospel According to Luke.* AB 28/28a. New York: Doubleday & Co., 1981–85.

Fleddermann, Harry. "The Householder and the Servant Left in Charge." Pp. 17–26 in *Society of Biblical Literature 1986 Seminar Papers.* Ed. Kent Harold Richards. SBLSPS 25. Atlanta: Scholars Press, 1986.

Foerster, Werner and Gerhard von Rad. "διάβολος." *Theological Dictionary of the New Testament* 2 (1964): 71–81.

———, and Gottfried Quell. "κύριος." *Theological Dictionary of the New Testament* 3 (1965): 1039–98.

Frankemölle, Hubert. *1. Petrusbrief, 2. Petrusbrief, Judasbrief.* Die neue Echter Bibel 18/20. Würzburg: Echter-Verlag, 1987.

Fridrichsen, Anton. "The Conflict of Jesus with the Unclean Spirits." *Theology* 22 (1931): 122–35.

———. *The Problem of Miracle in Primitive Christianity.* Trans. Roy Harrisville and John S. Hanson. Minneapolis: Augsburg Press, 1972.

Friedrich, Gerhard. "κῆρυξ, κηρύσσω." *Theological Dictionary of the New Testament* 3 (1965): 683–718.

———; Helmut Krämer; Rolf Rendtorff; and Rudolf Meyer. "προφήτης." *Theological Dictionary of the New Testament* 6 (1968): 781–861.

Fuller, Reginald H. *The Foundations of New Testament Christology.* New York: Charles Scribner's Sons, 1965.

———. "Das Doppelgebot der Liebe." Pp. 317–29 in *Jesus Christus in Historie und Theologie. Neutestamentliche Festschrift für Hans Conzelmann zum 60. Geburtstag.* Ed. Georg Strecker. Tübingen: J. C. B. Mohr [Paul Siebeck], 1975.

Funk, Robert. *Language, Hermeneutic and the Word of God. The Problem of Language in the New Testament and Contemporary Theology.* New York: Harper & Row, 1966.

———. "The Parables: A Fragmentary Agenda." *Perspective* 2/1–2 (1970): 287–303.

Garland, David E. *The Intention of Matthew 23.* NovT Sup 52. Leiden: E. J. Brill, 1979.

George, Augustin. "La 'forme' des béatitudes jusqu'à Jésus." Pp. 398–403 in *Mélanges Bibliques rédigrés en l'honneur de André Robert.* Travaux de l'institut catholique de Paris 4. Paris: Bloud & Gay, 1955.

Georgi, Dieter. "The Records of Jesus in the Light of Ancient Accounts of Revered Men." Pp. 527–42 in *Society of Biblical Literature 1972 Proceedings,* vol. 2. Ed. Lane C. McGaughy. Missoula: Society of Biblical Literature, 1972. Reprinted (with responses) Berkeley: Center for Hermeneutical Studies, 1973.

———. *The Opponents of Paul in Second Corinthians.* Philadelphia: Fortress Press, 1986.

Gerhardsson, Birger. *Memory and Manuscript: Oral Tradition and Written Transmission in Rabbinic Judaism and Early Christianity.* ASNU 22. 2d ed. Lund: C. W. K. Gleerup; Copenhagen: Munksgaard, 1964.

————. *The Testing of God's Son (Matt 4:1–11 & Par). An Analysis of an Early Christian Midrash*. ConB, N.T. Series 2/1. Lund: C. W. K. Gleerup, 1966.

————. *The Gospel Tradition*. ConB, N.T. Series 15. Lund: Gleerup, 1986.

Gerstenberger, Erhard. "The Woe-Oracles of the Prophets." *Journal of Biblical Literature* 81 (1962): 249–63.

Gnilka, Joachim. *Die Verstockung Israels: Isaias 6,9–10 in der Theologie der Synoptiker*. SANT 3. München: Kösel Verlag, 1961.

————. "Das Christusbild der Spruchquelle." Pp. 110–26 in *Jesus Christus nach frühen Zeugnissen des Glaubens*. Biblische Handbibliothek 8. München: Kösel-Verlag, 1970.

Goldberg, Arnold M. *Untersuchungen über die Vorstellung von der Schekhinah in der frühen rabbinischen Literatur*. Studia Judaica 5. Berlin: Walter de Gruyter, 1969.

Goodenough, Erwin R. *Jewish Symbols in the Greco-Roman Period*. 9 vols. New York: Pantheon, 1953–68.

Goodman, Martin. *State and Society in Roman Galilee, A.D. 132–212*. Totowa, NJ: Rowman and Allanheld, 1983.

Gould, E. P. "Matt. xii.43–45." *Journal of Biblical Literature* 2 (1883): 62.

Grant, Frederick C. "The Mission of the Disciples. Mt. 9:35–11:1 and Parallels." *Journal of Biblical Literature* 35 (1916): 293–314.

Grässer, Erich. "Jesus in Nazareth (Mark VI.1–6a): Notes on the Redaction and Theology of St. Mark." *New Testament Studies* 16 (1969–70): 1–23.

Griesbach, Johann Jakob. *Commentatio qua Marci evangelium totum e Matthaei et Lucae commentariis decerptum esse monstratur, I–II*. Jena: 1789–90; Latin [rev., 1794 version] with English translation by Bernard Orchard: pp. 74–102, 103–35 in *J. J. Griesbach: Synoptic and Critical Studies 1776–1976*. Ed. B. B. Orchard and Thomas Longstaff. SNTSMS 34. London: Cambridge University Press, 1979.

Grobel, Kendrick. "How Gnostic is the Gospel of Thomas?" *New Testament Studies* 8 (1962): 367–73.

Grundmann, Walter. "Die Bergpredigt nach der Lukasfassung." Pp. 180–89 in *Studia Evangelica I* (TU 73). Berlin: Akademie-Verlag, 1959.

————. *Das Evangelium nach Matthäus*. THKNT 1. 2d ed. Berlin: Evangelische Verlagsanstalt, 1971.

————. *Das Evangelium nach Lukas*. THKNT 3. 6th ed. Berlin: Evangelische Verlagsanstalt, 1971.

————. "Weisheit im Horizont des Reiches Gottes. Eine Studie zur Verkündigung Jesu nach der Spruchüberlieferung Q." Pp. 175–99 in *Die Kirche des Anfangs. Festschrift für Heinz Schürmann zum 65. Geburtstag*. Ed. R. Schackenburg, J. Ernst and J. Wanke. Leipzig: St. Benno, 1977.

Guenther, Heinz. *The Footprints of Jesus' Twelve in Early Christian Traditions*. American University Studies 7/7. New York, Berne, Frankfort am Main: Peter Lang, 1985.

————. "When 'Eagles' Draw Together." *Forum* 5/2 (1989): 140–50.

Güttgemanns, Erhardt. *Candid Questions Concerning Gospel Form Criticism: A Methodological Sketch of the Fundamental Problematics of Form and Redaction Criticism*. PTMS 26. Trans. William O. Doty. Pittsburgh: Pickwick, 1979.

Hadot, Pierre. "Forms of Life and Forms of Discourse in Ancient Philosophy." *Critical Inquiry* 16 (1990): 483–505.

Haenchen, Ernst. "Matthäus 23." *Zeitschrift für Theologie und Kirche* 48 *(1951):* 38–63=pp. 29–54 *in Gott und Mensch: Gesammelte Aufsätze von Ernst Haenchen.* Tübingen: J. C. B. Mohr [Paul Siebeck], 1965.

_____. "Gnosis. II. Gnosis und NT." *Die Religion in Geschichte und Gegenwart*[3] 2, cols. 1652–56.

_____. *Der Weg Jesu. Eine Erklärung des Markus-Evangeliums und der kanonischen Parallelen.* De Gruyter Lehrbuch (Sammlung Töpelmann). 2d ed. Berlin: Walter de Gruyer, 1968.

_____. *The Acts of the Apostles: A Commentary.* Trans. Bernard Noble and Gerald Shinn with Hugh Anderson; rev. trans. R. McL. Wilson. Philadelphia: Westminster Press, 1971

Hahn, Ferdinand. *Mission in the New Testament.* SBT 47. Trans. Frank Clarke. London: SCM Press, 1965.

_____. *The Titles of Jesus in Christology: Their History in Early Christianity.* Trans. Harold Knight and George Ogg. London: Lutterworth, 1969.

_____. "Die Worte vom Licht Lk 11,33–36." Pp. 107–38 in *Zur Theologie der Synoptiker. Für Josef Schmid.* Ed. Paul Hoffmann with N. Brox and W. Pesch. Freiburg: Herder, 1973.

Hammer, Paul L. "Devil." *Interpreter's Dictionary of the Bible* 1 (1962): 838.

Hare, Douglas R. A. *The Theme of Jewish Persecution of Christians in the Gospel According to St. Matthew.* SNTSMS 6. Cambridge: Cambridge University Press, 1967.

Harnack, Adoph von. *New Testament Studies II: The Sayings of Jesus. The Second Source of St. Matthew and St. Luke.* Trans. J. R. Wilkinson. New York: G. P. Putnam's Sons; London: Williams & Norgate, 1908.

Hasler, Viktor. "Das Herzstück der Bergpredigt. Zum Verständnis der Antithesen in Mt 5:21–48." *Theologische Zeitschrift* 15 (1959): 90–106.

Havener, Ivan. *Q: The Sayings of Jesus.* GNS 19. Wilmington: Michael Glazier, 1987.

Hawkins, John Caesar. *Horae Synopticae. Contributions to the Synoptic Problem.* 2d rev. ed. Oxford: Clarendon Press, 1909; reprinted Grand Rapids: Baker Book House, 1968.

Held, Heinz Joachim. "Matthew as Interpreter of the Miracle Stories." Pp. 165–299 in *Tradition and Interpretation in Matthew* by Günther Bornkamm, Gerhard Barth and Heinz Joachim Held. Trans. Percy Scott. Philadelphia: Westminster Press, 1963.

Hengel, Martin. *The Charismatic Leader and His Followers.* Trans. James Greig. New York: Crossroad, 1981.

Hoffmann, Paul. "'Πάντες ἐργάται ἀδικίας.' Redaktion und Tradition in Lk 13,22–30." *Zeitschrift für die neutestamentliche Wissenschaft* 58 (1967): 188–214.

_____. "Die Anfänge der Theologie in der Logienquelle." Pp. 134–52 in *Gestalt und Anspruch des Neuen Testament.* Ed. J. Schreiner and G. Dautzenberg. Würzburg: Echter-Verlag, 1969.

_____. "Die Versuchungsgeschichte in der Logienquelle." *Biblische Zeitschrift* 13 (1969): 207–23.

_____. "Auslegung der Bergpredigt." Parts 1–5. *Bibel und Leben* 10 (1969): 57–65, 111–22, 175–89, 264–75; 11 (1970): 89–104.

_____. "Jesusverkündigung in der Logienquelle." Pp. 50–70 in *Jesus in den Evan-*

gelien. Ed. H. Haag, R. Kilian and W. Pesch. SBS 45. Stuttgart: Katholisches Bibelwerk, 1970.

―――. "Die Offenbarung des Sohnes. Die apokalyptischen Voraussetzungen und ihre Verarbeitung im Q-Logion Mt 11,27 par Lk 10,22." *Kairos* 4 (1970): 269–88.

―――. "Lk 10,5–11 in der Instruktionsrede der Logienquelle." Pp. 37–53 in *Evangelisch-Katholischer Kommentar zum Neuen Testament,* Preliminary Study 3. Zürich: Benziger Verlag; Neukirchen: Neukirchener Verlag, 1971.

―――. *Studien zur Theologie der Logienquelle.* NTAbh 8. Münster: Aschendorff, 1972.

―――. Review of Siegfried Schulz, *Q: Die Spruchquelle der Evangelisten. Biblische Zeitschrift* 19 (1975): 104–15.

―――. "Der Q-Text der Sprüche vom Sorgen Mt 6,25–33/Lk 12,22–31: Ein Rekonstruktionsversuch." Pp. 128–55 in *Studien zum Matthäusevangelium: Festschrift für Wilhelm Pesch.* Ed. L. Schenke. Stuttgart: Katholisches Bibelwerk, 1988.

Holtzmann, Heinrich Julius. *Die synoptischen Evangelien; Ihr Ursprung und geschichtlicher Charakter.* Leipzig: Wilhelm Engelmann, 1863.

Horsley, Richard A. *Jesus and the Spiral of Violence: Popular Resistance in Roman Palestine.* San Francisco: Harper & Row, 1987.

―――. "Questions about Redactional Strata and the Social Relations Reflected in Q." Pp. 186–203 in *Society of Biblical Literature 1989 Seminar Papers.* Ed. David J. Lull. SBLSPS 28. Atlanta: Scholars Press, 1989.

―――. *Sociology and the Jesus Movement.* New York: Crossroad, 1989.

Hultgren, Arland J. *Jesus and His Adversaries: The Form and Function of the Conflict Stories in the Synoptic Tradition.* Minneapolis: Augsburg Press, 1979.

Institute for Antiquity and Christianity. *Pap. Q.* Claremont: Institute for Antiquity and Christianity, 1985.

Jacobson, Arland D. "Wisdom Christology in Q." Ph. D. diss., Claremont Graduate School, 1978.

―――. "The Literary Unity of Q." *Journal of Biblical Literature* 101 (1982): 365–89.

―――. "The History of the Composition of the Synoptic Sayings Source, Q." Pp. 285–94 in *Society of Biblical Literature 1987 Seminar Papers.* Ed. Kent Harold Richards. SBLSPS 26. Atlanta: Scholars Press, 1987.

Jeremias, Joachim. *Heiligengräber in Jesu Umwelt (Mt. 23,29; Lk 11,47). Eine Untersuchung zur Volksreligion der Zeit Jesu.* Göttingen: Vandenhoeck & Ruprecht, 1958.

―――. *The Parables of Jesus.* Trans. S. H. Hooke. Rev. ed.. New York: Charles Scribner's Sons, 1963.

―――. *Unknown Sayings of Jesus.* Trans. Reginald Fuller. 2d ed. London: SPCK, 1964.

―――. *The Prayers of Jesus.* Trans. John Bowden, C. Burchard, J. Reumann. SBT 2/6. Naperville, IL: Alec R. Allenson, 1967.

―――. *Jerusalem in the Time of Jesus. An Investigation into Economic and Social Conditions during the New Testament Period.* Trans. F. H. and C. H. Cave. Philadelphia: Fortress Press, 1969.

―――. *New Testament Theology,* vol. 1: *The Proclamation of Jesus.* Trans. John Bowden. New York: Charles Scribner's Sons, 1971.

Jervell, Jacob. *Luke and the People of God. A New Look at Luke-Acts.* Minneapolis: Augsburg Press, 1972.

Jeske, Richard. "Wisdom and the Future in the Teaching of Jesus." *Dialog* 11 (1972): 108–17.

Johnson, Marshall D. "Reflections on a Wisdom Approach to Matthew's Christology." *Catholic Biblical Quarterly* 36 (1974): 44–64.

Johnson, Sherman E. "The Biblical Quotations in Matthew." *Harvard Theological Review* 36 (1943): 135–53.

Jonas, Hans. *Gnostic Religion: The Message of the Alien God and the Beginnings of Christianity*. 2d ed., rev. Boston: Beacon, 1963.

Jülicher, Adolf. *Die Gleichnisreden Jesu*, vol. 2: *Auslegung der Gleichnisreden der drei ersten Evangelien*. Freiburg, Leipzig, Tübingen: J. C. B. Mohr [Paul Siebeck], 1899.

Jüngel, Eberhard. *Paulus und Jesus: Eine Untersuchung zur Präzisierung der Frage nach dem Ursprung der Christologie*. HUT 2. Tübingen: J. C. B. Mohr [Paul Siebeck], 1962.

Käsemann, Ernst. "The Beginnings of Christian Theology." Pp. 82–107 in *New Testament Questions of Today*. Trans. W. J. Montague. Philadelphia: Fortress Press, 1969.

———. "Lukas 11,14–28." Pp. 242–48 in vol. 1 of *Exegetische Versuche und Besinnungen*. 2d ed. Göttingen: Vandenhoeck & Ruprecht, 1960.

———. "The Problem of the Historical Jesus." Pp. 15–47 of *Essays in New Testament Themes*. SBT 41. London: SCM Press, 1964.

———. "On the Topic of Primitive Christian Apocalyptic." *Journal for Theology and Church* 6 (1969): 99–133.

Keck, Leander E. "Oral Traditional Literature and the Gospels: The Seminar." Pp. 103–22 in *The Relationships Among the Gospels: An Interdisciplinary Dialogue*. Ed. William O. Walker. Trinity University Monographs in Religion 5. San Antonio: Trinity University Press, 1978.

Kee, Howard Clark. *Jesus in History: An Approach to the Study of the Gospels*. 2d ed. New York: Harcourt, Brace, Jovanovich, 1977.

Kelber, Werner. *The Oral and Written Gospel. The Hermeneutics of Speaking and Writing in the Synoptic Tradition, Mark, Paul, and Q*. Philadelphia: Fortress Press, 1983.

Kennedy, George A. "Classical and Christian Source Criticism." Pp. 125–55 in *The Relationships Among the Gospels: An Interdisciplinary Dialogue*. Trinity University Monographs in Religion 5. San Antonio: Trinity University Press, 1978.

———. *New Testament Interpretation through Rhetorical Criticism*. Studies in Religion. Chapel Hill, NC: University of North Carolina, 1984.

Kieffer, R. "Wisdom and Blessing in the Beatitudes of St. Matthew and St. Luke." Pp. 291–95 in *Studia Evangelica VI* (TU 112). Berlin: Akademie-Verlag, 1973.

Kloppenborg, John S. "Wisdom Christology in Q." *Laval Théologique et Philosophique* 34 (1978): 129–47.

———. "Tradition and Redaction in the Synoptic Sayings Source." *Catholic Biblical Quarterly* 46 (1984): 34–62.

———. "The Formation of Q and Antique Instructional Genres." *Journal of Biblical Literature* 105 (1986): 443–62.

———. *The Formation of Q: Trajectories in Ancient Wisdom Collections*. Studies in Antiquity and Christianity. Philadelphia: Fortress Press, 1987.

——. "Formative and Redactional Layers in Q." An unpublished paper for the SBL Q Seminar, December, 1987.

——. "Symbolic Eschatology and the Apocalypticism of Q." *Harvard Theological Review* 80 (1987): 287–306.

——. "The Dishonoured Master (Luke 16,1–8a)." *Biblica* 70 (1989): 474–95.

——. *"The Formation of Q* Revisited: A Response to Richard Horsley." Pp. 204–15 in *Society of Biblical Literature* 1989 Seminar Papers. Ed. David J. Lull. SBLSPS 28. Atlanta: Scholars Press, 1989.

——. "'Easter Faith' and the Sayings Gospel Q." *Semeia* 49 (1990): 71–99.

Klostermann, Erich. *Das Matthäusevangelium.* HNT 4. 2d ed. Tübingen: J. C. B. Mohr [Paul Siebeck], 1927.

Knigge, Heinz-Dieter. "The Meaning of Mark. The Exegesis of the Second Gospel." *Interpretation* 22 (1968): 53–70.

Knox, Wilfred L. *The Sources of the Synoptic Gospels,* vol. 2: *St. Luke and St. Matthew.* Ed. H. Chadwick. Cambridge: Cambridge University Press, 1957.

Koch, Klaus. *The Growth of the Biblical Tradition.* Trans. S. M. Cupitt. London: Adam & Charles Black, 1969.

Koenig, John. *New Testament Hospitality: Partnership with Strangers as Promise and Mission.* OBT 17. Philadelphia: Fortress Press, 1985.

Koester, Helmut. *Synoptische Überlieferung bei den apostolischen Vätern.* TU 65. Berlin: Akademie-Verlag, 1957.

——. "GNOMAI DIAPHOROI: The Origin and Nature of Diversification in the History of Early Christianity." Pp. 114–57 in H. Koester and J. M. Robinson, *Trajectories Through Early Christianity.* Philadelphia: Fortress Press 1971.

——. "One Jesus and Four Primitive Gospels." Pp. 158–204 in *Trajectories Through Early Christianity.*

——. "Apocryphal and Canonical Gospels." *Harvard Theological Review* 73 (1980): 105–30.

——. "Überlieferung und Geschichte der frühchristlichen Evangelienliteratur." *ANRW* 2.25.2 (1984): 1463–1542.

——. "Q—At the Conclusion of Five Years of the Seminar." Unpublished paper for the Annual Meeting of the Society of Biblical Literature (Q Seminar), Boston, December, 1987.

Kraft, Robert A. "'Ezra' Materials in Judaism and Christianity." *ANRW* 2.19.1. (1979): 119–36.

——. "Towards Assessing the Latin Text of '5 Ezra': The 'Christian' Connection." Pp. 158–69 in *Christians Among Jews and Gentiles: Essays in Honor of Krister Stendahl on His Sixty-fifth Birthday.* Ed. George W. E. Nickelsburg with G. W. MacRae. Philadelphia: Fortress Press, 1986.

Krämer, Michael. "Ihr seid das Salz der Erde...Ihr seid das Licht der Welt. Die vielgestaltige Wirkkraft des Gotteswortes des Heiligen Schrift für das Leben der Kirche aufgezeigt am Beispiel Mt 5,13–16." *Münchener theologische Zeitschrift* 28 (1977): 133–57.

Küchler, Max. *Frühjüdische Weisheitstraditionen: Zum Fortgang weisheitlichen Denkens im Bereich des frühjüdischen Jahweglaubens.* OBO 26. Freiburg: Universitätsverlag; Göttingen: Vandenhoeck & Ruprecht, 1979.

Kuhn, H.-W. *Enderwartung und gegenwärtiges Heil. Untersuchung zu den Gemeindeliedern von Qumran mit einem Anhang über Eschatologie und Gegenwart in der Verkündigung Jesu.* Göttingen: Vandenhoeck & Ruprecht, 1966.

Kuhn, Karl Georg; G. von Rad and Walter Gutbrod. "'Ισραήλ." *Theological Dictionary of the New Testament* 3 (1965): 356–91.

Kümmel, Werner G. "Die Weherufe über die Schriftgelehrten und Pharisäer (Mt 23,13–36)." Pp. 135–47 in *Antijudaismus im Neuen Testament: Exegetische und systematische Beiträge*. Ed. W. Eckert, N. P. Levinson and M. Stohr. Abhandlungen zum christlich-jüdischen Dialog 2. München: Chr. Kaiser, 1967.

_____. *Promise and Fulfilment: The Eschatological Message of Jesus*. Trans. Dorothea M. Barton. SBT 23. 2d ed. London: SCM Press, 1969.

_____. *The New Testament: The History of the Investigation of its Problems*. Trans. S. McLean Gilmour and Howard C. Kee. Nashville: Abingdon Press, 1972.

_____. *Jesu Antwort an Johannes den Täufer. Ein Beispiel zum Methodenproblem in der Jesusforschung*. Sitzungsberichte der Wissenschaftlichen Gesellschaft an der Johann Wolfgang Goethe-Universität Frankfurt/Main 11,4. Weisbaden: Franz Steiner, 1974.

_____. *Introduction to the New Testament*. Trans. Howard C. Kee. Rev. ed. Nashville: Abingdon Press, 1975.

Lachmann, Karl. "De ordine narrationum in evangeliis synopticis." *Theologische Studien und Kritiken* 8 (1835): 570–90=(partial trans.) in N. H. Palmer, "Lachmann's Argument." *New Testament Studies* 13 (1966–67): 368–78.

Laufen, Rudolf. *Die Doppelüberlieferungen der Logienquelle und des Markusevangeliums*. BBB 54. Bonn: Peter Hanstein, 1980.

Leivestad, Ragnar. "An Interpretation of Matt 11:19." *Journal of Biblical Literature* 71 (1952): 179–81.

Levy, Jean Philippe. *The Economic Life of the Ancient World*. Trans. John G. Biran. Chicago: The University of Chicago Press, 1967.

Lindars, Barnabas. *Jesus Son of Man: A Fresh Examination of the Son of Man Sayings in the Gospels in the Light of Recent Research*. London: SPCK, 1983.

Lindemann, Andreas. "Literaturbericht zu den synoptischen Evangelien 1978–1983." *Theologische Rundschau* 49 (1984): 223–76, 311–71.

Linnemann, Eta. *Jesus of the Parables: Introduction and Exposition*. Trans. John Sturdy. New York: Harper & Row, 1966.

_____. "Jesus und der Täufer." Pp. 219–36 in *Festschrift für Ernst Fuchs*. Ed. Gerhard Ebeling, Eberhard Jüngel, and Gerd Schunack. Tübingen: J. C. B. Mohr [Paul Siebeck], 1973.

_____. "Zeitansage und Zeitvorstellung in der Verkündigung Jesu." Pp. 237–63 in *Jesus Christus in Historie und Theologie: Neutestamentliche Festschrift für Hans Conzelmann zum 60*. Ed. Georg Strecker. Tübingen: J. C. B. Mohr [Paul Siebeck], 1975.

Linton, Olof. "The Q-Problem Reconsidered." Pp. 43–59 in *Studies in New Testament and Early Christian Literature: Essays in Honor of Allen P. Wikgren*. Ed. David E. Aune. NovTSup 33. Leiden: E. J. Brill, 1972.

_____. "The Parable of the Children's Game. Baptist and Son of Man (Matt. XI.16–19=Luke VII.31–5): A Synoptic Text-critical, Structural and Exegetical Investigation." *New Testament Studies* 22 (1975–76): 159–79.

Lohmeyer, Ernst. "Die Versuchung Christi." *Zeitschrift für systematische Theologie* 14 (1937): 619–50=pp. 81–122 in *Urchristliche Mystik: Neutestamentliche Studien*. Darmstadt: Hermann Gentner Verlag, 1956.

_____, and Werner Schmauch. *Das Evangelium des Matthäus*. MeyerK, Sonderband. Göttingen: Vandenhoeck & Ruprecht, 1956.

Lohr, Charles. "Oral Techniques in the Gospel of Matthew." *Catholic Biblical Quarterly* 23 (1961): 403–35.

Lord, Albert B. "The Gospels as Oral Traditional Literature." Pp. 33–91 in *The Relationships Among the Gospels: An Interdisciplinary Dialogue*. Ed. William O. Walker. Trinity University Monographs in Religion 5. San Antonio: Trinity University Press, 1978.

Lorenzmeier, Theodor. "Zum Logion Mt 12,28; Lk 11,20." Pp. 289–304 in *Neues Testament und christliche Existenz: Festschrift für Herbert Braun zum 70. Geburtstag*. Ed. H. D. Betz and Luise Schottroff. Tübingen: J. C. B. Mohr [Paul Siebeck], 1973.

Lüdemann, Gerd. *Early Christianity According to the Traditions in Acts*. Trans. John Bowden. Minneapolis: Fortress Press, 1989.

Lührmann, Dieter. *Die Redaktion der Logienquelle*. WMANT 33. Neukirchen-Vluyn: Neukirchener Verlag, 1969.

––––––. "Liebet eure Feinde (Lk 6,27–36/Mt 5,39–48)." *Zeitschrift für Theologie und Kirche* 69 (1972): 412–38.

––––––. "The Gospel of Mark and the Sayings Collection Q." *Journal of Biblical Literature* 108 (1989): 51–71.

Luz, Ulrich. "Die wiederentdeckte Logienquelle." *Evangelische Theologie* 33 (1973): 527–33.

––––––. "Das Jesusbild der vormarkinischen Tradition." Pp. 347–74 in *Jesus Christus in Historie und Theologie: Neutestamentliche Festschrift für Hans Conzelmann zum 60*. Ed. Georg Strecker. Tübingen: J. C. B. Mohr [Paul Siebeck], 1975.

Mack, Burton L. *Anecdotes and Arguments: The Chreia in Antiquity and Early Christianity*. Occasional Papers 10. Claremont: Institute for Antiquity and Christianity, 1987.

––––––. "The Kingdom That Didn't Come: A Social History of the Q Tradents." Pp. 608–35 in *Society of Biblical Literature 1988 Seminar Papers*. Ed. David J. Lull. SBLSPS 27. Atlanta: Scholars Press, 1988.

––––––. *A Myth of Innocence: Mark and Christian Origins*. Philadelphia: Fortress Press, 1988.

––––––. *Rhetoric and the New Testament*. Minneapolis: Fortress Press, 1990.

––––––, and Vernon Robbins. *Patterns of Persuasion in the Gospels*. Foundations and Facets/Literary Facets. Sonoma: Polebridge Press, 1989.

MacMullen, Ramsay. *Roman Social Relations: 50 B.C. to A.D. 284*. New Haven: Yale University Press, 1974.

McNeile, Alan Hugh. *The Gospel According to St. Matthew*. London: Macmillan & Co.; New York: St. Martin's Press, 1961.

Malherbe, Abraham J. "Cynics." Pp. 201–3 in *Interpreter's Dictionary of the Bible, Supplement*. Nashville: Abingdon Press, 1976.

––––––. "Self-Definition Among Epicureans and Cynics." Pp. 46–59 in vol. 3 of *Jewish and Christian Self-Definition*. Ed. Ben Meyer and E. P. Sanders. Philadelphia: Fortress Press, 1982.

Malmede, Hans H. *Die Lichtsymbolik im Neuen Testament*. Studies in Oriental Religions 15. Wiesbaden: Otto Harrassowitz, 1986.

Manson, T. W. *The Sayings of Jesus*. London: SCM Press, 1949.

––––––. "The Lord's Prayer." *Bulletin of the John Rylands Library* 38 (1955–56): 99–113, 436–48.

March, W. Eugene. "Prophecy." Pp. 141–77 in *Old Testament Form Criticism*. Ed. John H. Hayes. San Antonio: Trinity University Press, 1974.

Marshall, I. Howard. *The Gospel of Luke*. NIGTC. Grand Rapids: Wm. B. Eerdmans, 1978.

Marxsen, Willi. *Introduction to the New Testament: An Approach to its Problems*. Trans. Geoffrey Buswell. Philadelphia: Fortress Press, 1968.

_____. *Mark the Evangelist: Studies in the Redaction History of the Gospel*. Trans. James Boyce, Don Juel, William Poehlmann with Roy Harrisville. Nashville: Abingdon, 1969.

Meeks, Wayne A. *The Moral World of the First Christians*. Library of Early Christianity 6. Philadelphia: Westminster Press, 1986.

Meinertz, Max. "'Dieses Geschlecht' im Neuen Testament." *Biblische Zeitschrift* 1 (1957): 283–89.

Metzger, Bruce. *A Textual Commentary on the Greek New Testament: A Companion Volume to the United Bible Societies' Greek New Testament (3rd ed.)*. London and New York: United Bible Societies, 1971.

Meyer, Paul D. "The Community of Q." Ph.D. diss., University of Iowa, 1967.

_____. "The Gentile Mission in Q." *Journal of Biblical Literature* 89 (1970): 405–17.

Meyer, Rudolf. *Der Prophet aus Galiläa: Studie zum Jesusbild der drei ersten Evangelien*. Darmstadt: Wissenschaftliche Buchgesellschaft, 1940.

Miller, Robert J. "The Rejection of Prophets in Q." *Journal of Biblical Literature* 107 (1988): 225–40.

Minear, Paul. *Commands of Christ: Authority and Implications*. Nashville: Abingdon Press, 1972.

Mitton, C. Leslie. "New Wine in Old Wine Skins: IV. Leaven." *Expository Times* 84 (1972–73): 339–43.

Montefiore, Hugh. "A Comparison of the Parables of the Gospel according to Thomas and of the Synoptic Gospels." Pp. 40–78 in Hugh Montefiore and H. E. W. Turner, *Thomas and the Evangelists*. SBT 35. Naperville: Alec R. Allenson, 1962.

Moore, George Foot. *Judaism in the First Centuries of the Christian Era*. 3 vols. Cambridge: Harvard University Press, 1927–30.

Moule, C. F. D. *An Idiom Book of New Testament Greek*. 2d ed. Cambridge: Cambridge University Press, 1960.

_____. "Neglected Features in the Problem of 'The Son of Man.'" Pp. 413–28 in *Neues Testament und Kirche: Für Rudolf Schnackenburg*. Ed. J. Gnilka. Freiburg: Herder, 1974.

Moulton, James Hope and George Milligan. *The Vocabulary of the Greek Testament Illustrated from the Papyri and Other Non-Literary Sources*. London: Hodder and Stoughton, 1914–29; reprinted Grand Rapids: Wm. B. Eerdmans, 1980.

Müller, Ulrich B. *Prophetie und Predigt im Neuen Testament: Formgeschichtliche Untersuchungen zur urchristlichen Prophetie*. SNT 10. Gütersloh: Gerd Mohn, 1975.

Mussner, Franz. "Der nicht erkannte Kairos (Mt 11,16–19=Lk 7,31–35)". *Biblica* 40 (1959): 599–612.

Neirynck, Frans. *The Minor Agreements of Matthew and Luke against Mark with a Cumulative List*. BETL 37. Louvain: Leuven University Press, 1974.

_____. "Jesus and the Sabbath. Some Observations on Mk II,27." Pp. 227–70 in *Jésus aux origines de la christologie.* Ed. J. Dupont. BETL 40. Gembloux: J. Duculot; Louvain: Leuven University Press, 1975.

———. "The Symbol Q (=Quelle)." *Ephemerides Theologicae Lovanienses* 54 (1978): 119–25.

———. "Once More: The Symbol Q." *Ephemerides Theologicae Lovanienses* 55 (1979): 382–83.

———. "Recent Developments in the Study of Q." Pp. 29–75 in *LOGIA. Les Paroles de Jésus—The Sayings of Jesus.* Ed. Jöel Delobel. BETL 59. Louvain: Leuven University Press, 1982.

———. "The Sermon on the Mount in the Gospel Synopsis." *Ephemerides Theologicae Lovanienses* 52 (1976): 350–57.

Neusner, Jacob. *Development of a Legend: Studies in the Traditions Concerning Yohanan ben Zakkai.* SPB 16. Leiden: E. J. Brill, 1970.

———. "Comparing Judaisms." *History of Religions* 18 (1978): 177–91.

Noack, Bent. *SATANÁS und SOTERÍA: Untersuchungen zur neutestamentlichen Dämonologie.* Copenhagen: G. E. C. Gads Forlag, 1948.

Norwood, Frederick A. "'Compel them to come in': The History of Luke 14:23." *Religion in Life* 23 (1953–54): 516–27.

Nyberg, H. S. "Zum grammatischen Verständnis zum Matth. 12:44f." *Coniectanea Neotestamentica* 13 (1949): 1–11

Oakman, Douglas. "Jesus and Agrarian Palestine: The Factor of Debt." Pp. 57–73 in *SBL 1985 Seminar Papers.* Ed. Kent H. Richards. Atlanta: Scholars Press, 1985.

———. *Jesus and the Economic Questions of His Day.* Studies in the Bible and Early Christianity 8. Lewiston, NY: The Edwin Mellen Press, 1986.

O'Hagan, Angelo. "'Greet no one on the way' (Lk 10,4b)." *Studii Biblici Franciscani Liber Annus* 16 (1965–66): 69–84.

Ong, Walter J. *Orality and Literacy: The Technologizing of the Word.* New Accents. London; New York: Methuen, 1982.

Orchard, B. B. *Matthew, Luke & Mark.* Manchester: Koinonia, 1976.

———, and Thomas R. W. Longstaff, eds. *J. J. Griesbach: Synoptic and Critical Studies 1776–1976.* SNTSMS 34. London: Cambridge University Press, 1979.

Palmer, N. H. "Lachmann's Argument." *New Testament Studies* 13 (1966–67): 368–78.

Pearson, Birger A. "1 Thessalonians 2:13–16: A Deutero-Pauline Interpolation." *Harvard Theological Review* 64 (1971): 79–94.

Percy, Ernst. *Die Botschaft Jesu. Eine traditionskritische und exegetische Untersuchung.* LUA, n.F. 1/49, Nr. 5. Lund: C. W. K. Gleerup, 1953.

Perrin, Norman. *Rediscovering the Teaching of Jesus.* New York: Harper & Row, 1967.

———. "The Son of Man in the Synoptic Tradition." *Biblical Research* 13 (1968): 3–25.

———. *What is Redaction Criticism?* Guides to Biblical Scholarship. Philadelphia: Fortress Press, 1969.

———, and Dennis C. Duling. *The New Testament: An Introduction.* 2d ed. New York: Harcourt, Brace, Jovanovich, 1982.

Pesch, Wilhelm. "Theologische Aussagen der Redaktion von Matthäus 23." Pp. 286–99 in *Orientierung an Jesus: Zur Theologie der Synoptiker. Für Josef Schmid.* Ed. Paul Hoffmann with N. Brox and W. Pesch. Freiburg: Herder, 1973.

Peterson, Norman. *Literary Criticism for New Testament Critics*. Guides to Biblical Scholarship. Philadelphia: Fortress Press, 1978.

Piper, R. A. *Wisdom in the Q Tradition: The Aphoristic Teaching of Jesus*. SNTSMS 61. Cambridge: Cambridge University Press, 1988.

Pokorný, Petr. "The Temptation Stories and Their Intention." *New Testament Studies* 20 (1973–74): 115–27.

Polag, Athanasius. *Die Christologie der Logienquelle*. WMANT 45. Neukirchen-Vluyn: Neukirchener Verlag, 1977.

———. *Fragmenta Q*. Neukirchen-Vluyn: Neukirchener Verlag, 1979.

———. "Die theologische Mitte der Logienquelle." Pp. 103–11 in *Das Evangelium und die Evangelien: Vorträge vom Tübinger Symposium 1982*. Ed. Peter Stuhlmacher. WUNT 28. Tübingen: J. C. B. Mohr [Paul Siebeck], 1983.

Popper, Karl. *The Logic of Scientific Discovery*. London: Hutchinson, 1959.

Resch, Alfred. *Agrapha: aussercanonische Schriftfragmente*. TU 30. Leipzig: J. C. Hinrichs, 1906.

Robbins, Vernon K. *Jesus the Teacher: A Socio-Rhetorical Interpretation of Mark*. Philadelphia: Fortress Press, 1984.

———. "The Chreia." Pp. 1–23 in *Greco-Roman Literature and the New Testament: Selected Forms and Genres*. Ed. David E. Aune. SBLSBS 21. Atlanta: Scholars Press, 1988.

Robertson, A. T. *The Christ of the Logia*. New York: George H. Doran, 1924.

Robinson, James M. *The Problem of History in Mark*. SBT 21. London: SCM Press, 1957.

———. *A New Quest of the Historical Jesus*. SBT 25. London: SCM Press, 1959.

———. "Basic Shifts in German Theology." *Interpretation* 16 (1962): 76–97.

———. "The Formal Structure of Jesus' Message." Pp. 91–110, 273–84 in *Current Issues in New Testament Interpretation*. Ed. William Klassen and Graydon Snyder. New York: Harper & Row, 1962.

———. "Die Hodajot-Formel in Gebet und Hymnus des Frühchristentums." Pp. 194–235 in *Apophoreta: Festschrift für Ernst Haenchen*. Ed. W. Eltester and K. H. Kettler. BZNW 30. Berlin: Verlag Alfred Töpelmann, 1964.

———. "The New Hermeneutic at Work." *Interpretation* 18 (1964): 346–59.

———. Review of Albrecht Dihle, *Die Goldene Regel*. *Journal of the History of Philosophy* 4 (1966): 84–87.

———. "Kerygma and History in the New Testament." Pp. 20–70 in H. Koester and J. M. Robinson, *Trajectories through Early Christianity*. Philadelphia: Fortress Press 1971.

———. "LOGOI SOPHON: On the Gattung of Q." Pp. 71–113 in *Trajectories through Early Christianity*.

———. "Jesus as Sophos and Sophia: Wisdom Tradition and the Gospels." Pp. 1–16 in *Aspects of Wisdom in Judaism and Early Christianity*. Ed. Robert L. Wilken. University of Notre Dame Center for the Study of Judaism and Christianity in Antiquity 1. Notre Dame: University of Notre Dame Press, 1975.

———. "The Study of the Historical Jesus after Nag Hammadi." *Semeia* 44 (1988): 45–55.

———. "Very Goddess and Very Man: Jesus' Better Self." Pp. 111–22 in *Encountering Jesus: A Debate on Christology*. Ed. Stephen T. Davis. Atlanta: John Knox, 1988.

Robinson, William Childs, Jr. "The Way of the Lord: A Study of History and Eschatology in the Gospel of Luke." Ph.D. diss., University of Basel, 1962.

Rohde, Joachim. *Rediscovering the Teaching of Evangelists*. Trans. Dorothea M. Barton. London: SCM Press, 1968.

Rostovtzeff, Mikhail Ivanovich. *The Social and Economic History of the Roman Empire*. 2 vols. 2d ed. Oxford: Oxford University Press, 1957.

Rüstow, A. "ΕΝΤΟC ΥΜΩΝ ΕCΤΙΝ. Zur Deutung von Lukas 17:20-21." *Zeitschrift für die neutestamentliche Wissenschaft* 51 (1960): 197-224.

Saldarini, Anthony J. *Pharisees, Scribes and Sadducees in Palestinian Society: A Sociological Approach*. Wilmington, DE: Michael Glazier, 1988.

Sanday, William, ed. *Oxford Studies in the Synoptic Problem*. Oxford: Oxford University Press, 1911.

Sanders, E. P. "The Argument from Order and the Relationships between Matthew and Luke." *New Testament Studies* 15 (1968-69): 249-61.

_____. *Jesus and Judaism*. Philadelphia: Fortress Press, 1985.

Sanders, James A. *Canon and Community: A Guide to Canonical Criticism*. Guides to Biblical Scholarship. Philadelphia: Fortress Press, 1984.

Satake, Akira. *Die Gemeindeordnung in der Johannesapokalypse*. WMANT 21. Neukirchen-Vluyn: Neukirchener Verlag, 1966.

_____. "Das Leiden der Jünger 'um meinetwillen'." *Zeitschrift für die neutestamentliche Wissenschaft* 67 (1976): 4-19.

Sato, Migaku. *Q und Prophetie: Studien zur Gattungs- und Traditionsgeschichte der Quelle Q*. WUNT 2/29. Tübingen: J. C. B. Mohr [Paul Siebeck], 1987.

Sawyer, John F. A. "The Ruined House in Ecclesiastes 12: A Reconstruction of the Original Parable." *Journal of Biblical Literature* 94 (1975): 519-31.

Schenk, Wolfgang. *Synopse zur Redenquelle der Evangelien*. Düsseldorf: Patmos Verlag, 1978.

_____. "Der Einfluss der Logienquelle auf das Markusevangelium." *Zeitschrift für die neutestamentliche Wissenschaft* 70 (1979): 141-65.

Schillebeeckx, Edward. *Jesus: An Experiment in Christology*. New York: Seabury, 1979.

Schleiermacher, Friedrich D. E. "Über die Zeugnisse des Papias von unsern beiden ersten Evangelien." *Theologische Studien und Kritiken* 5 (1832): 735-68.

Schmidt, Daryl. "The LXX *Gattung* 'Prophetic Correlative.'" *Journal of Biblical Literature* 96 (1977): 517-22.

Schmithals, Walter. "Evangelien, Synoptische." *Theologische Realenzyklopadie* 10 (1982): 570-626.

_____. *Einleitung in die drei ersten Evangelien*. Berlin: Walter de Gruyter, 1985.

Schnackenburg, Rudolf. "'Ihr seid das Salz der Erde, das Licht der Welt.' Zu Mt 5,13-16." Pp. 177-200 in *Schriften zum Neuen Testament*. München: Kösel-Verlag, 1971.

_____. "Der Sinn der Versuchung Jesu bei den Synoptikern." Pp. 101-28 in *Schriften zum Neuen Testament*.

_____. "Zur Traditionsgeschichte von Joh 4,46-54." *Biblische Zeitschrift* 8 (1964): 58-88.

Schneider, Gerhard. "Das Bildwort von der Lampe. Zur Traditionsgeschichte eines Jesus-Wortes." *Zeitschrift für die neutestamentliche Wissenschaft* 61 (1970): 183-209.

Schnider, Franz. *Jesus der Prophet.* OBO 2. Freiburg: Universitätsverlag; Göttingen: Vandenhoeck & Ruprecht, 1973.

Schniewind, Julius. *Das Evangelium nach Matthäus.* NTD 2. 12th ed. Göttingen: Vandenhoeck & Ruprecht, 1968.

Schottroff, Luise. "Non-Violence and the Love of One's Enemies." Pp. 9–39 in *Essays on the Love Commandment* by Luise Schottroff, Reginald H. Fuller, Christoph Burchard and M. Jack Suggs. Trans. Reginald H. and Ilse Fuller. Philadelphia: Fortress Press, 1978.

————. "Gleichnis vom grossen Gastmahl in der Logienquelle." *Evangelische Theologie* 47 (1987): 192–211.

————, and Wolfgang Stegemann. *Jesus von Nazareth: Hoffnung der Armen.* Stuttgart: W. Kohlhammer, 1978.

Schrage, Wolfgang. *Das Verhältnis des Thomas-Evangeliums zur synoptischen Tradition und zu den koptischen Evangelien-Übersetzungen; zugleich ein Beitrag zur gnostischen Synoptikerdeutung.* Berlin: Alfred Töpelmann, 1964.

Schrenk, Gottlob. "βιάζομαι, βιαστής." *Theological Dictionary of the New Testament* 1 (1964): 609–14.

————, and Gottfried Quell. "δίκη, δίκαιος, δικαιοσύνη, δικαιόω, κτλ." *Theological Dictionary of the New Testament* 2 (1964): 174–225.

Schulz, Siegfried. *Q: Spruchquelle der Evangelisten.* Zürich: Theologischer Verlag, 1972.

Schürmann, Heinz. "Die Warnung des Lukas von der Falschlehre in der 'Predigt am Berge' Lk 6,20–49." *Biblische Zeitschrift* 10 (1966): 57–81.

————. "Mt 10,5b–6 und die Vorgeschichte des synoptischen Aussendungsberichtes." Pp. 137–49 in *Traditionsgeschichtliche Untersuchungen zu den synoptischen Evangelien.* Düsseldorf: Patmos-Verlag, 1968.

————. *Das Lukasevangelium I: Kommentar zu Kap. 1,1–9,50.* THKNT 3. Freiburg: Herder, 1969.

Schweitzer, Albert. *The Mystery of the Kingdom of God.* Trans. Walter Lowrie. New York: Schocken, 1914.

————. *The Quest of the Historical Jesus.* Trans. W. Montgomery. New York: Macmillan, 1964.

Schweizer, Eduard; Hermann Kleinknecht; Friedrich Baumgartel; Werner Bieder and Erik Sjoberg. "πνεῦμα, κτλ." *Theological Dictionary of the New Testament* 6 (1968): 332–455.

————. "Formgeschichtliches zu den Seligpreisungen Jesu." *New Testament Studies* 19 (1972–73): 121–26.

————. *The Good News According to Matthew.* Trans. David E. Green. Atlanta: John Knox, 1975.

Scott, Bernard Brandon. *Hear Then the Parable. A Commentary on the Parables of Jesus.* Minneapolis: Fortress Press, 1989.

Seeley, David. "Was Jesus like a Philosopher? The Evidence of Martyrological and Wisdom Motifs in Q, Pre-Pauline Traditions, and Mark." Pp. 540–49 in *SBL 1989 Seminar Papers.* Ed. David J. Lull. Atlanta: Scholars Press, 1989.

Seitz, O. J. F. "The Commission of Prophets and 'Apostles'. A Re-examination of Matthew 23,34 with Luke 11,49." Pp. 236–40 in *Studia Evangelica IV* (TU 102). Berlin: Akademie-Verlag, 1968.

Sellew, Philip Harl. "Early Collections of Jesus' Words: The Development of Dominical Discourses." Th.D. diss., Harvard University, 1985.

Sieber, John H. "A Redactional Analysis of the Synoptic Gospels with Regard to the Question of the Sources of the Gospel According to Thomas." Ph.D. diss., Claremont Graduate School, 1965.

Smith, Charles W. F. *The Jesus of the Parables.* Rev. ed. Philadelphia: United Church Press, 1975.

Smith, Mahlon. "To Judge the Son of Man: Sifting the Synoptic Sayings with Circumspection." A paper distributed to the Jesus Seminar, Sonoma, 1989.

Smith, Morton. "A Comparison of Early Christian and Early Rabbinic Tradition." *Journal of Biblical Literature* 82 (1963): 169–76.

_____. *Tannaitic Parallels to the Gospels.* SBLMS 6. Philadelphia: Society of Biblical Literature, 1968.

_____. *Jesus the Magician.* San Francisco: Harper & Row, 1978.

Smyth, Herbert Weir. *Greek Grammar.* Rev. Gordon M. Messing. Cambridge: Harvard University Press, 1956.

Speyer, Wolfgang. "Gewitter." *Reallexikon für Antike und Christentum* 10 (1978): 1107–72.

Stanton, Graham N. "On the Christology of Q." Pp. 27–42 in *Christ and Spirit in the New Testament.* Ed. B. Lindars and S. S. Smalley. Cambridge: Cambridge University Press, 1973.

_____. "5 Ezra and Matthean Christianity in the Second Century." *Journal of Theological Studies* 28 (1977): 67–83.

Steck, Odil Hannes. *Israel und das gewaltsame Geschick der Propheten. Untersuchung zur Überlieferung des deuteronomistischen Geschichtsbildes im Alten Testament, Spätjudentum und Urchristentum.* WMANT 23. Neukirchen-Vluyn: Neukirchener Verlag, 1967.

Stegemann, Wolfgang. "Vagabond Radicalism in Early Christianity? A Historical and Theological Discussion of a Thesis Proposed by Gerd Theissen." Pp. 148–68 in *God of the Lowly: Socio-Historical Interpretations of the Bible.* Ed. Willy Schottroff and Wolfgang Stegemann. Trans. M. J. O'Connell. Maryknoll, NY: Orbis Books, 1984.

Steinhauser, Michael G. *Doppelbildworte in den synoptischen Evangelien: Eine form- und traditionskritische Studie.* FB 44. Würzburg: Echter-Verlag, 1981.

Stendahl, Krister. "Matthew." Pp. 769–98 in *Peake's Commentary on the Bible.* London: Thomas Nelson and Sons, 1962.

_____. *The School of St. Matthew and Its Use of the Old Testament.* Philadelphia: Fortress Press, 1968.

Stoldt, Hans-Herbert. *History and Criticism of the Markan Hypothesis.* Trans. and ed. Donald L. Niewyk. Macon, GA: Mercer University Press; Edinburgh: T. & T. Clark, 1980.

Strack, Hermann L. and Paul Billerbeck. *Kommentar zum Neuen Testament aus Talmud und Midrasch, 3: Das Evangelium nach Matthäus.* 5th ed. München: C. H. Beck'sche Verlagsbuchhandlung, 1969.

Strecker, Georg. *Der Weg der Gerechtigkeit: Untersuchung zur Theologie des Matthäus.* FRLANT 82. 3rd rev. ed. Göttingen: Vandenhoeck & Ruprecht, 1971.

Streeter, Burnett Hillman. *The Four Gospels: A Study of Origins.* London: Macmillan, 1924.

Suggs, M. Jack. *Wisdom, Christology, and Law in Matthew's Gospel*. Cambridge: Harvard University Press, 1970.

———. "The Antitheses as Redactional Products." Pp. 433–44 in *Jesus Christus in Historie und Theologie. Neutestamentliche Festschrift für Hans Conzelmann zum 60. Geburtstag*. Ed. Georg Strecker. Tübingen: J. C. B. Mohr [Paul Siebeck], 1975.

Suhl, Alfred. Review of Migaku Sato, *Q und Prophetie*. *Theologische Literaturzeitung* 114 (1989): 669–72.

Talbert, Charles H. and Edgar V. McKnight. "Can the Griesbach Hypothesis be Falsified?" *Journal of Biblical Literature* 91 (1972): 338–68.

Talbert, Charles H. "Oral and Independent or Literary and Interdependent? A Response to Albert B. Lord." Pp. 93–102 in *The Relationships Among the Gospels: An Interdisciplinary Dialogue*. Ed. William O. Walker. Trinity University Monographs in Religion 5. San Antonio: Trinity University Press, 1978.

———. *Reading Luke: A Literary and Theological Commentary on the Third Gospel*. New York: Crossroad, 1988

Tannehill, Robert C. *The Sword of His Mouth*. SBLSS 1. Philadelphia: Fortress Press; Missoula: Scholars Press, 1975.

Taylor, Vincent. "The Original Order of Q." Pp. 95–118 in *New Testament Essays*. Grand Rapids: Wm. B. Eerdmans, 1972.

Theissen, Gerd. "Wanderradikalismus. Literatursoziologische Aspekte der Überlieferung von Worten Jesu im Urchristentum." *Zeitschrift für Theologie und Kirche* 70 (1973): 245–71; ET by Antoinette Wire: "Itinerant Radicalism: The Tradition of Jesus' Sayings from the Perspective of the Sociology of Literature." *Radical Religion* 2 (1975): 84–93.

———. "'Wir haben alles verlassen' (Mark 10:28): Nachfolge und soziale Entwurzelung in der jüdische-palestinischen Gesellschaft des I. Jahrhunderts n. Chr." *Novum Testamentum* 10 (1977): 161–96.

———. *The Sociology of Early Palestinian Christianity*. Trans. John Bowden. Philadelphia: Fortress Press, 1978.

———. "Legitimation and Subsistence: An Essay on the Sociology of Early Christian Missionaries." Pp. 27–67 in *The Social Setting of Pauline Christianity*. Trans. and ed. John H. Schütz. Philadelphia: Fortress Press, 1982.

———. *Biblical Faith: An Evolutionary Approach*. Trans. John Bowden. Philadelphia: Fortress Press, 1985.

Thomas, Kenneth J. "Torah Citations in the Synoptics." *New Testament Studies* 24 (1977–78): 85–96.

Thrall, William Flint and Addison Hibbard. *A Handbook to Literature*. Rev. ed. by C. Hugh Holman. New York: Odyssey, 1962.

Thyen, Hartwig. "ΒΑΠΤΙΣΜΑ ΜΕΤΑΝΟΙΑΣ ΕΙΣ ΑΦΕΣΙΝ ΑΜΑΡΤΙΩΝ." Pp. 131–68 in *The Future of Our Religious Past: Essays in Honour of Rudolf Bultmann*. Ed. James M. Robinson. New York: Harper & Row, 1971.

Tiede, David L. *The Charismatic Figure as Miracle Worker*. SBLDS 1. Missoula: Scholars Press, 1972.

Tigay, Jeffrey H., ed. *Empirical Models for Biblical Criticism*. Philadelphia: University of Pennsylvania Press, 1985.

Tödt, Heinz Eduard. *The Son of Man in the Synoptic Tradition*. Trans. Dorothea M. Barton. Philadelphia: Westminster Press, 1965. Orig. pub. as *Der Menschensohn in der synoptischen Überlieferung*. Gütersloh: Gerd Mohn, 1959.

Trilling, Wolfgang. "Die Täufertradition bei Matthäus." *Biblische Zeitschrift* 3 (1959): 271–89.

Tuckett, Christopher M. "The Griesbach Hypothesis in the 19th Century." *Journal for the Study of the New Testament* 3 (1979): 29–60.

———. *The Revival of the Griesbach Hypothesis. An Analysis and Appraisal.* SNTSMS 44. Cambridge: Cambridge University Press, 1982.

———. "A Cynic Q?" Biblica 70 (1989): 349–76.

Turner, Nigel. *Grammatical Insights into the New Testament.* Edinburgh: T. & T. Clark, 1965.

Tyson, Joseph B. "Sequential Parallelism in the Synoptic Gospels." *New Testament Studies* 22 (1975–76): 276–308.

Urbach, E. E. "Sages." *Encyclopaedia Judaica* 14 (1971): cols. 636–55.

———. *The Sages—Their Concepts and Beliefs.* Trans. Israel Abrahams. 2 vols. Jerusalem: The Hebrew University/Magnes Press, 1975.

Uro, Risto. *Sheep Among the Wolves: A Study on the Mission Instructions of Q.* Annales Academiae Scientiarum Fennicae, Dissertationes Humanarum Litterarum 47. Helsinki: Suomalainen Tiedeakatemia, 1987.

Vaage, Leif Eric. "Q: The Ethos and Ethics of an Itinerant Intelligence." Ph. D. Diss., Claremont Graduate School, 1987.

Vassiliadis, Petros. "Prolegomena to a Discussion on the Relationship Between Mark and the Q Document." *Deltion Biblikon Meleton* 3 (1975): 31–46.

———. "The Nature and Extent of the Q Document." *Novum Testamentum* 20 (1978): 49–73.

Vielhauer, Philipp. "Gottesreich und Menschensohn in der Verkündigung Jesu." Pp. 51–79 in *Festschrift für Gunther Dehn.* Ed. W. Schneemelcher. Neukirchen: Kreis Moers, 1957.

———. "Jesus und der Menschensohn. Zur Diskussion mit Heinz Eduard Tödt und Eduard Schweizer." *Zeitschrift für Theologie und Kirche* 60 (1963): 133–77.

———. "Jewish-Christian Gospels." Pp. 117–65 in *New Testament Apocrypha.* Ed. Edgar Hennecke. Rev. Wilhelm Schneemelcher. Trans. ed. R. McL. Wilson. Vol. 1. Philadelphia: Westminster Press, 1963.

———. *Geschichte der urchristlichen Literatur.* De Gruyter Lehrbuch. Berlin: Walter de Gruyter, 1975.

Vögtle, Anton. "Wunder und Wort in urchristlicher Glaubenswerbung (Mt 11,2–5/Lk 7,18–23)." Pp. 219–42 in *Das Evangelium und die Evangelien: Beiträge zur Evangelienforschung.* Düsseldorf: Patmos-Verlag, 1971.

———. "Die sogenannte Taufperikope Mk 1,9–11. Zur Problematik der Herkunft und des ursprunglichen Sinns." Pp. 105–39 in *Evangelisch-Katholischer Kommentar zum Neuen Testament.* Preliminary Study 4. Zürich: Benziger Verlag; Neukirchen-Vluyn: Neukirchener Verlag, 1972.

Wanke, Joachim. "'Kommentarworte.' Älteste Kommentierungen von Herrenworten." *Biblische Zeitschrift* 24 (1980): 208–33.

———. *"Bezugs- und Kommentarworte" in den synoptischen Evangelien: Beobachtungen zur Interpretationsgeschichte der Herrenworte in der vorevangelischen Überlieferung.* ETS 44. Leipzig: St. Benno-Verlag, 1981.

Weiser, Alfons. *Die Knechtsgleichnisse der synoptischen Evangelien.* SANT 29. München: Kösel-Verlag, 1971.

Weiss, Johannes. "Die Verteidigung Jesu gegen den Vorwurf des Bündnisses mit Beelzebul." *Theologische Studien und Kritiken* 63 (1890): 555–69.

Weisse, Christian Hermann. *Die evangelische Geschichte kritisch und philosophisch bearbeitet.* 2 vols. Leipzig: Breitkopf und Hartel, 1838.

Wellhausen, Julius. *Einleitung in die drei ersten Evangelien.* Berlin: Georg Reimer, 1905.

Wernle, Paul. *Die synoptische Frage.* Freiburg: J. C. B. Mohr [Paul Siebeck], 1899.

_____. *Die Quellen des Lebens Jesu.* Religionsgeschichtliche Volksbücher 1/1. Halle: Gebauer-Schwetschke, 1904.

Westermann, Claus. *Basic Forms of Prophetic Speech.* Trans. Hugh Clayton White. Philadelphia: Westminster Press, 1967.

Wetter, Gilles P. *"Der Sohn Gottes": Eine Untersuchung über den Charakter und die Tendenz des Johannes-Evangeliums.* FRLANT 9. Göttingen: Vandenhoeck & Ruprecht, 1916.

Wilckens, Ulrich and Georg Fohrer. "σοφία, σοφός, σοφίζω." *Theological Dictionary of the New Testament* 7 (1971): 465–528.

Wilke, Christian Gottlob. *Der Urevangelist; oder exegetisch-kritische Untersuchung über das Verwandtschaftverhältnis der drei ersten Evangelien.* Dresden/Leipzig: G. Fleischer, 1838.

Windisch, Hans. *The Meaning of the Sermon on the Mount.* Trans. S. MacLean Gilmour. Philadelphia: Westminster Press, 1951.

_____. "ἀσπάζομαι, κτλ." *Theological Dictionary of the New Testament* 1 (1964): 496–502.

Wink, Walter. *John the Baptist in the Gospel Tradition.* SNTSMS 7. Cambridge: Cambridge University Press, 1968.

Wolff, Hans Walter. "The Kerygma of the Deuteronomic Historical Work." Pp. 83–100 in Walter Brueggemann and H. W. Wolff, *The Vitality of Old Testament Traditions.* Atlanta: John Knox Press, 1975.

Worden, Ronald. "Redaction Criticism of Q: A Survey." *Journal of Biblical Literature* 94 (1975): 532–46.

Zeller, Dieter. "Der Zusammenhang der Eschatologie in der Logienquelle." Pp. 67–77 in *Gegenwart und kommendes Reich: Schülergabe A. Vögtle zum 65. Geburtstag.* Ed. P. Fiedler and D. Zeller. SBB. Stuttgart: Katholisches Bibelwerk, 1977.

_____. "Die Bildlogik des Gleichnisses Mt 11:16f/Lk 7:31f." *Zeitschrift für die neutestamentliche Wissenschaft* 68 (1977): 252–57.

_____. "Prophetisches Wissen um die Zukunft in synoptischen Jesusworten." *Theologie und Philosophie* 52 (1977): 258–71.

_____. *Die weisheitlichen Mahnsprüche bei den Synoptikern.* FB 17. Würzburg: Echter-Verlag, 1977.

_____. "Weisheitliche Überlieferung in der Predigt Jesu." Pp. 94–111 in *Religiöse Grunderfahrungen.* Ed. W. Strolz. Freiburg: Herder, 1977.

_____. "Redaktionsprozesse und wechselnder 'Sitz im Leben' bein Q-Material." Pp. 395–409 in *LOGIA. Les Paroles de Jésus—The Sayings of Jesus.* Ed. Joël Delobel. BETL 59. Louvain: Leuven University Press, 1982.

_____. *Kommentar zur Logienquelle.* Stuttgarter kleiner Kommentar, N.T. 21. Stuttgart: Verlag Katholisches Bibelwerk, 1984.

Index of Authors

Index of Passages

1. Ancient Near Eastern Writings

2. Hebrew Bible

3. Apocrypha

4. Pseudepigrapha

5. Qumran Writings

6. Mishnah and Talmud

10. Early Christian Literature

11. Nag Hammadi Texts

12. Greco-Roman and Other Literature

Index of Subjects